DB2 for the COBOL programmer

Part 2: An Advanced Course

DB2

for the

COBOL

programmer

Part 2: An Advanced Course

Steve Eckols

Mike Murach & Associates, Inc.

4697 West Jacquelyn Avenue, Fresno, California 93722, (209) 275-3335

Editorial team: Doug Lowe
                           Anne Prince
                           Sheila Lynch

Production/Design: Steve Ehlers

Related books

DB2 for the COBOL Programmer, Part 1: An Introductory Course,
    Steve Eckols
Structured ANS COBOL, Part 1: A Course for Novices,
    Mike Murach & Paul Noll
Structured ANS COBOL, Part 2: An Advanced Course,
    Mike Murach & Paul Noll
VS COBOL II: A Guide for Programmers and Managers, Anne Prince
MVS TSO, Part 1: Concepts and ISPF, Doug Lowe
MVS TSO, Part 2: Commands and Procedures, Doug Lowe
IMS for the COBOL Programmer, Part 1: Data Base Processing,
    Steve Eckols
*IMS for the COBOL Programmer, Part 2: DC and Message Format
    Service*, Steve Eckols
How to Design and Develop Business Systems, Steve Eckols

Thanks to Micro Focus Incorporated and XDB Systems, Inc. for providing the software used to develop the CICS/DB2 programs presented in chapters 7 and 8.

ISBN: 0-911625-64-X

Library of Congress Cataloging-in-Publication Data

Eckols, Steve.
  DB2 for the COBOL programmer.

  Includes indexes.
  Contents: Pt. 1. An introductory course -- pt. 2.
An advanced course.
  1.Data base management. 2. IBM Database 2.
3. COBOL (Computer program language) 4. SQL (Computer
program language). I. Title.
QA76.9.D3E32 1991   005.75'65   91-30359
ISBN 0-911625-59-3 (pbk. : v. 1 : alk. paper)
ISBN 0-911625-64-X (pbk. : v. 2 : alk. paper)

Contents

Preface

If you design and develop application programs, it's likely that you work with a data base management system now, or that you will soon. DB2, developed for IBM's MVS operating system, has become the foremost DBMS in the IBM mainframe world, and it sets the DBMS standard for other computers.

To access DB2 data, you issue statements in SQL, the Structured Query Language. Originally developed by IBM, SQL has become the industry-wide standard for relational data base languages. That means that you can use SQL in programs written in a variety of different languages. And you can use it on computers from PCs to mainframes, developed by many different computer manufacturers. As a result, knowing DB2 is a plus for any application programmer, and it's essential for MVS programmers.

DB2 for the COBOL Programmer is a two-book series that's designed to teach you all you need to know. The first book in the series, *Part 1: An Introductory Course*, covers the basic features and functions you need to know to write COBOL application programs that process DB2 data. This book, *Part 2: An Advanced Course*, expands on the material in *Part 1*. It teaches skills that are beyond the basics, but that should still be in your professional repertoire.

This book has four sections. Section 1 shows you how to use advanced DB2 programming features (scalar functions, alternative error handling, dynamic SQL, distributed processing, and locking). Section 2 describes how to access DB2 data from CICS programs. (CICS is a widely used IBM software product that supports interactive application programs.) Section 3 presents DB2 data base administration subjects programmers should understand. And section 4 shows you how to work with IBM's QMF (Query Management Facility).

Why this book is effective

I've been an application programmer, so I know the challenges you'll face in designing and developing programs that process DB2 data. *DB2 for the COBOL Programmer* is effective because I kept your needs in mind constantly as I planned, illustrated, and wrote it. My overall goal is to help you build on what you already know so you can quickly become an effective, productive, and professional DB2 programmer. As a result, *DB2 for the COBOL Programmer* has the following characteristics that distinguish it from other DB2 books on the market.

Emphasis on the practical rather than the theoretical   Several successful DB2 books have been written by computer scientists who are interested in theoretical topics. For example, you can find pages and pages on topics like how thoroughly DB2 and SQL implement all possible operations from mathematical set theory. If you're a theoretician, these are important issues.

If you're an application programmer, they're not. Although they can help you gain insight into why DB2 works the way it does, more often than not, they get in the way when you try to learn what you *really* need to know. So, I've covered only a few theoretical issues in this book (there are a few you *do* need to know), and I've put them in their proper perspective for an application programmer.

Emphasis on programming rather than data base administration   Many of the other DB2 books on the market have been written by people who have lots of experience as data base administrators (DBAs). And their books reflect that. DBAs have to deal with issues like the detailed internal structure of stored DB2 data and the technical options that optimize system performance. If you're a DBA, these are critical points.

If you're an application programmer, they're not. The whole point of having DBAs is so users like programmers won't have to deal with the technicalities. So, as with theoretical issues, I've put technical DBA topics in their proper perspective. This book *does* include a four-chapter section on data base administration topics, but it emphasizes how those topics are useful for programmers.

Emphasis on COBOL application programs rather than ad hoc processing   One argument in favor of relational data base management systems like DB2 is that they put greater computing power in the hands of end users. Most other DB2 books make this a central point and present SQL as it can be used interactively by an end user to access and process DB2 data on demand. This is called "ad hoc" processing.

However, the fact is that performance considerations cause many shops to restrict the amount of ad hoc work users can do. Moreover, it's not as easy for end users to work with SQL as its planners might have hoped. And finally, letting end users change stored data in an uncontrolled way can quickly lead to corrupted data bases.

So, although DB2 supports on-line, user-directed processing, most DB2 work is still done the old-fashioned way: through application programs. Unfortunately, when other DB2 books address application programming, it's often as an aside or as a topic that appears three quarters of the way through the book. In *DB2 for the COBOL Programmer*, I've assumed from the start that you're a programmer and you want to develop application programs. By far, COBOL is the most commonly used programming language for application development, so that's what I've used in most of my examples.

The COBOL programs you develop will run in complicated production environments and access large sets of data. However, the chances are that your program *testing* environment will be simpler and more isolated, and that your sets of test data will be smaller. Therefore, for some program development work, you *may* be able to use ad hoc processing facilities efficiently.

I introduced one of those facilities, SPUFI, in *Part 1*. SPUFI is IBM's "no frills" interactive interface to DB2. You can use SPUFI to manage test data and experiment with SQL statements before you code them in your programs. In section 4 of this book, I'll present another ad hoc facility, IBM's Query Management Facility (QMF). QMF provides functions that are similar to SPUFI's, but it's easier to use, and its output is easier to format.

Required background

To get the most out of this book, you need to be familiar with the SQL and COBOL programming techniques I presented in *Part 1: An Introductory Course*. If you need a copy of *Part 1*, you'll find ordering information at the end of this book.

I designed both *Part 1* and *Part 2* of *DB2 for the COBOL Programmer* so they work alongside other Mike Murach and Associates books. For example, if you need to improve your COBOL skills, you can learn what you need to know from Mike Murach and Paul Noll's *Structured ANS COBOL, Part 1* and *Part 2*. And, if you need to learn MVS skills, such as how to work with job control language and the TSO editor, you can use Doug Lowe's *MVS JCL* and his *MVS TSO, Part 1: Concepts and ISPF*. You can find ordering information for these titles at the end of this book too.

How to use this series

I arranged the content of *DB2 for the COBOL Programmer* in the most logical sequence for a "typical" programmer with "typical" tasks to do. If you're that typical programmer, I suggest you read the two parts of the *DB2 for the COBOL Programmer* set straight through from start to finish. After you've finished *Part 1*, continue with *Part 2*.

However, you're probably not a typical programmer with typical tasks to do. Therefore, I organized the content of these two books in modular sections so you can tailor your study plan to meet your needs and interests. Figure P-1 lists the eight sections that make up this series and shows you how they're organized. As you can see, after you've learned the prerequisite concepts and skills in sections 1 and 2 of *Part 1*, you can read any of the other sections in either book.

For example, within this book, you can read about QMF (section 4) before you read about advanced DB2 programming techniques, CICS, or data base administration (section 1, 2, or 3). You can even read sections in this book before you read section 3 or 4 in *Part 1*. For instance, if you need to learn about CICS right way, you can read section 2 in this book immediately after you finish section 2 of *Part 1*.

The organization *within* these modular sections varies. In some of the sections, the chapters are sequential; later chapters depend on earlier chapters. That's true of sections 2, 3, and 4 of this book. For example, when you study CICS in section 2, you should read its chapters (6, 7, and 8) in sequence. In contrast, the chapters in section 1 of this book (and in sections 3 and 4 of *Part 1*) are independent; you can read them in any order you like.

After you've developed your DB2 skills, you'll find this series will make a handy reference for you to use on the job. The figures I've included throughout both books are a valuable resource. Also, I've included appendixes with the basic syntax of all the SQL statements I present, SQL error code values you may need to look up, and a summary of the data types DB2 supports. And probably most important, you can use the program examples I've presented as models for programs you develop.

A note on the sample programs

One of the great strengths of the *DB2 for the COBOL Programmer* series is the set of sample programs it includes. Altogether, I've presented 17 complete programs in the two books. This book contains a program that illustrates advanced error-handling facilities, three programs that demonstrate dynamic SQL, and two programs that access DB2 data from the CICS environment.

Basic DB2 concepts and skills

These sections are prerequisite to the other sections in both parts.

Part	Section	Section title	Chapters	Read the chapters in this section in...
1	1	Introduction	1	
	2	A basic subset of embeded SQL	2-4	sequence

Intermediate and advanced topics

After you've read the prerequisite material, you may continue with *any* of these sections.

Part	Section	Section title	Chapters	Read the chapters in this section in...
1	3	Expanding the basic subset	5-9	any order you like
	4	Program development	10-11	any order you like
2	1	Advanced DB2 programming techniques	1-5	any order you like
	2	DB2 in CICS programs	6-8	sequence
	3	Data base administration	9-12	sequence
	4	Query Management Facility	13-15	sequence

Figure P-1   The basic organization of *Part 1* and *Part 2* of *DB2 for the COBOL Programmer*

The programs in this book and in *Part 1* all operate on the same set of realistic DB2 data. As a result, although the programs are independent, they do have some features in common. Those features will make it easier for you to understand the programs themselves and the DB2 concepts and facilities they illustrate.

After you've used the program examples for training, they'll become handy references for you to use on the job every day. In fact, if you use them as models for your own programs, you'll save yourself hours of coding, testing, and debugging time.

I developed and tested the batch programs with DB2 version 2.2, under VS COBOL II, release 2. Although IBM has just released version 2.3 of DB2, most of the changes it introduces involve performance issues that are behind the scenes for programmers. So, the program examples in this book and *Part 1* are unaffected by the new version. These programs will all continue to work and be useful models for you under DB2 version 2.3. (I developed the CICS/DB2 programs in chapters 7 and 8 on an OS/2 workstation using the CICS OS/2 Option for Micro Focus COBOL/2 Workbench version 1.0.8 from Micro Focus, and XDB version 2.41 from XDB Systems.)

Conclusion

I'm enthusiastic about DB2. It's a powerful, comprehensive, and sophisticated program that lets you accomplish complicated tasks with relative ease. But I'm just as enthusiastic about helping you learn DB2 so you can work more productively and more professionally. So, please let me know how this book works for you by sending me any comments you have on it. (Feel free to use the postage-paid comment form at the back of this book.) Good luck!

Steve Eckols
Fresno, California
March, 1992

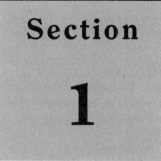

Section

1

Advanced DB2 programming techniques

This section consists of five chapters that present advanced SQL features. These features are not essential to basic DB2 training, but you may need to know them in some programming situations.

Chapter 1 covers data manipulation. In it, you'll learn how to convert data from one type to another, do basic string manipulations, and perform operations with time and date items. Chapter 2 covers some error-handling features you may need to use in your shop. Chapter 3 covers dynamic SQL, an advanced feature that lets programs execute SQL statements they generate as they execute. Chapter 4 introduces distributed processing under DB2 and covers the considerations you need to keep in mind when you develop programs for a distributed environment. Finally, chapter 5 covers locking and concurrency issues.

All of the chapters in this section are independent of one another, so you can read them in any order you like.

Chapter 1

How to use advanced data manipulation features

This chapter presents DB2 features you can use for data manipulation. Because much of the data manipulation you can do with DB2 depends on the data types of the DB2 elements you're working with, you need to understand data types. So topic 1 presents a review of them. You should read this topic before you read the other topics in this chapter.

Topics 2 and 3 present scalar functions. You can use scalar functions to perform tasks like converting data from one format to another, extracting substrings, and determining the absolute age of a date item. Topic 2 describes the DB2 scalar functions you can use to manipulate string and numeric data. It also covers a scalar function that lets you provide a substitute value for nulls. Then, topic 3 covers the DB2 scalar functions you can use with date and time items. Topics 2 and 3 are independent. So after you've read topic 1, you can skip topic 2 and read topic 3, if you want to.

DB2's date and time processing features aren't limited to the scalar functions topic 3 presents. As a result, topic 4 offers a deeper look at how you can manipulate date and time items in expressions. To understand the material in topic 4, you must be familiar with the scalar functions for working with dates and times. So, you should read topic 3 before you read topic 4.

Frankly, these features may be of limited use for you as an application programmer. For example, many of the functions covered in topics 2 and 3 let you convert data from one format to another. In COBOL, you can do that simply by moving a value from one kind of field to another. Even so, you may encounter some situations where these functions will save you some work. You should at least know they're available and what they do, even if you use them only rarely.

Topic 1   A review of DB2 data types

In *Part 1: An Introductory Course*, you learned about most of DB2's data types. This topic reviews what you need to know about those data types to understand the content of topics 2, 3, and 4.

The eleven DB2 data types fall into three broad categories: string, numeric, and date and time. This topic presents all eleven data types by category. In addition, this topic introduces two sample tables that use some of the most common DB2 data types. I'll use those tables in the examples that follow in topics 2, 3, and 4.

String data types

Figure 1-1 presents the four DB2 data types for string data. The first two, CHAR and VARCHAR, are for standard EBCDIC character data. They differ in that the length of the value in a CHAR column is fixed, while the length of the value in a VARCHAR column is variable, up to a maximum length set by the creator of the table.

A DBA can't define a CHAR column with a length greater than 254 bytes. That's also the limit for standard VARCHAR columns. However, if the DBA is willing to sacrifice some processing capabilities, DB2 does support VARCHAR columns up to more than 32,000 bytes long. Because a table row must fit on a single page in the table space where the table is stored, the exact upper limit depends on the page size (either 4K or 32K) and on the space the other table columns use.

COBOL programs process CHAR data through host variables with simple alphanumeric pictures. For example, a 30-byte CHAR column's host variable would be defined with PIC X(30) and DISPLAY usage. Because DISPLAY usage is the default, it's usually omitted from the field definition.

The host variable for a VARCHAR item is more complicated. As you can see in figure 1-1, it has two components. Both of these components are coded as 49-level items subordinate to a group item. The first of the two components is a binary halfword numeric item (PIC S9(4) COMP) that contains the actual length of the column's value. The other component contains the value itself. In your program, you should define this component as alphanumeric, and you should provide enough space for the largest value the column can contain.

The other two kinds of string data, GRAPHIC and VARGRAPHIC are for fixed-length and variable-length columns that contain *double-byte*

DB2 data type	Kind of data	Description
CHAR	Fixed-length character (EBCDIC) data	Up to 254 bytes of alphanumeric data. Defined in COBOL as PIC X(n) where *n* is the number of characters the column contains. A typical example is: `01   CUSTNO           PIC X(6).`

VARCHAR	Variable-length character (EBCDIC) data	A variable amount of alphanumeric data. The number of bytes in the data component is stored in a halfword. A typical COBOL example is:
		
		`01   NOTES.`
		`     49   NOTES-LEN    PIC S9(4) COMP.`
		`     49   NOTES-TEXT   PIC X(254).`
		
		The text component has a maximum length of 254 bytes in a "short" VARCHAR column. In a "long" VARCHAR column, which is subject to some processing restrictions, the text component's length can be over 32,000 bytes. The exact maximum length depends on the table's page size and the sizes of the other columns in the table.

GRAPHIC	Fixed-length DBCS data	Up to 127 characters of Double Byte Character Set (DBCS) data. Defined in COBOL with DISPLAY-1 usage and PIC G(n) where *n* is the number of characters the column contains. A typical example is:
		
		`01   DBCS-NAME         PIC G(20)`
		`                       DISPLAY-1.`

VARGRAPHIC	Variable-length DBCS data	A variable amount of DBCS data. The number of characters in the data component is stored in a halfword. A typical COBOL example is:
		
		`01   EXPL.`
		`     49   EXPL-LEN     PIC S9(4) COMP.`
		`     49   EXPL-TEXT    PIC G(127)`
		`                       DISPLAY-1.`
		
		The text component has a maximum length of 127 characters in a "short" VARGRAPHIC column. As with VARCHAR, a "long" VARGRAPHIC column can be defined so it stores more characters, but it's subject to some processing restrictions. The exact maximum length depends on the table's page size and the sizes of the other columns in the table.

Figure 1-1   String data types

character set (*DBCS*) data. "Double-byte" means that two bytes of storage are required to store one DBCS character. In contrast, only one byte is required to store one character of EBCDIC data. DBCS data is used for special purposes, such as storing text in non-Western languages (like Japanese) or representing chemical structures.

The maximum length of a GRAPHIC column is 127 DBCS characters. That's 254 bytes, the same as the maximum length of a CHAR column value. To code the PICTURE clause for a DBCS item, you use G instead of X. So, the definition for a 40-character DBCS item would be PIC G(40) with DISPLAY-1 usage. The structure of the host variable for a variable-length DBCS item is the same as for VARCHAR: a 49-level binary halfword (PIC S9(4) COMP) for the length field, and another 49-level item for the text component. Again, because this is a DBCS item, you code the PICTURE clause for the text component with G instead of X, and you specify DISPLAY-1 usage.

Numeric data types

The next category of DB2 data types is for numeric data. As you can see in figure 1-2, four data types fall into this category: SMALLINT, INTEGER, DECIMAL, and FLOAT. These are the kinds of DB2 data you can use in arithmetic expressions.

SMALLINT and INTEGER specify columns that contain binary numeric data. COBOL host variables for both SMALLINT and INTEGER columns specify COMP usage, but they have pictures that allow different size values: PIC S9(4) for SMALLINT and PIC S9(9) for INTEGER. Figure 1-2 shows that the values of a SMALLINT item can range from −32,768 to +32,767, and the values of an INTEGER item can range from less than −2 billion to more than +2 billion.

The DECIMAL data type specifies packed decimal data. A host variable for a column with this data type has COMP-3 usage and a picture with an implied decimal point. Unlike the host variables for SMALLINT and INTEGER data, host variables for DECIMAL data can vary in size. The largest possible DECIMAL value has 15 digits (or, under DB2 version 2.3, 31 digits). The number of digits in a DECIMAL item is called its *precision*. The number of digits to the right of the implicit decimal point is called the *scale* of the item. So, a DECIMAL item defined with a precision of 9 and a scale of 2 can contain a value up to 9,999,999.99.

You'll use SMALLINT, INTEGER, and DECIMAL data often in your COBOL programs. In contrast, you'll seldom need to use the fourth type of data: FLOAT. A FLOAT item contains a floating point number that's stored in exponential form. Depending on how a DBA defines a FLOAT column, it

DB2 data type	Kind of data	Description
SMALLINT	Halfword integer data	A halfword integer may contain whole-number values between -32,768 and 32,767. It is always defined in COBOL with COMP usage and PIC S9(4). A typical COBOL definition is: `10   INVCOUNT   PIC S9(4) COMP.`
INTEGER	Fullword integer data	A fullword integer may contain whole-number values between -2,147,483,648 and 2,147,483,647. It is always defined in COBOL with COMP usage and PIC S9(9). A typical COBOL definition is: `10   INVCOUNT   PIC S9(9) COMP.`
DECIMAL(p,s)	Packed decimal data	A decimal value contains an implicit decimal point. The value *p* (which cannot be greater than 15, or, under DB2 version 2.3, 31) specifies how many digits the number can contain, and the value *s* specifies how many of those digits are to the right of the implicit decimal point. The abbreviations p and s stand for precision and scale. A typical COBOL definition is: `10   INVTOTAL   PIC S9(7)V99 COMP-3.` This is an appropriate host variable definition for a column defined with DECIMAL(9,2).

FLOAT(n)	Floating point data	A floating point number, either single-precision (if *n* is less than 22) or double-precision (if *n* is between 22 and 53). COBOL definitions do not include a PIC clause and are simply a field name followed by COMP-1 (for single-precision) or COMP-2 (for double-precision). Examples are:
		
		`10   SINGLE-PRECISION-NUMBER   COMP-1.`
		
		`10   DOUBLE-PRECISION-NUMBER   COMP-2.`

Figure 1-2 Numeric data types

can contain a single-precision number (4 bytes) or a double-precision number (8 bytes). Notice in figure 1-2 that the COBOL host variable definition for a FLOAT column value doesn't include a PICTURE clause. Instead, after the data name, the definition simply includes either USAGE COMP-1 for a single-precision item, or USAGE COMP-2 for a double-precision item.

Date and time data types

The last three basic data types, DATE, TIME, and TIMESTAMP, are shown in figure 1-3. A DB2 DATE item consists of three components: year, month, and day. A TIME item consists of an hour, a minute, and a second. The third kind of item, a TIMESTAMP, has the parts of both a DATE and TIME item, plus an even more precise time element: a microsecond.

As you can see, DB2's DATE, TIME, and TIMESTAMP data types are represented as simple character strings that are 10, 8, and 26 characters long. For each data type, figure 1-3 shows two typical host variable definitions. The first is a simple character item that's large enough to hold the entire date, time, or timestamp string. The second is a group item that defines each component of the string individually. (If your shop has changed DB2's default date and time formats, you'll have to adjust these host variables accordingly. I'll have more to say about other time formats in topic 3.)

Incidentally, DB2 uses a more efficient storage format to actually store DATE, TIME, and TIMESTAMP data in a table. From a practical point of view, however, you can think of these data types as the character strings described in figure 1-3.

The VARCUST and INV tables

In the next three topics, I'll show you lots of examples of DB2 features that manipulate different kinds of data. For those examples, I'll use two tables that I presented in *Part 1: An Introductory Course*. One of these tables, VARCUST, contains information about customers. It uses both fixed-length and variable-length character data, and it allows nulls in some columns. The other table, INV, contains information about invoices issued to customers represented in the VARCUST table. It contains numeric and date data in addition to character data. Figure 1-4 presents the DCLGEN output for the two tables, and figure 1-5 presents their contents. You can refer back to these figures as you study the examples I present in topics 2, 3, and 4.

Terms

double-byte character set
DBCS
precision
scale

DB2 data type	Kind of data	Description

DATE	Date	A 10-byte string. A typical example is:
		
		`01   INVDATE              PIC X(10).`
		
		The internal structure of a date item is yyyy-mm-dd. To identify the parts of a DB2 date, you can move the value to a group item like
		
		`01   EDITED-DATE.`
		`     05   ED-YEAR         PIC X(4).`
		`     05   FILLER          PIC X.`
		`     05   ED-MONTH        PIC XX.`
		`     05   FILLER          PIC X.`
		`     05   ED-DAY          PIC XX.`

TIME	Time	An 8-byte string. A typical example is:
		
		`01   START-TIME           PIC X(8).`
		
		The internal structure of a time item is hh.mm.ss. To identify the parts of a DB2 time, you can move the value to a group item like
		
		`01   EDITED-TIME.`
		`     05   ET-HOUR         PIC XX.`
		`     05   FILLER          PIC X.`
		`     05   ET-MINUTE       PIC XX.`
		`     05   FILLER          PIC X.`
		`     05   ET-SECOND       PIC XX.`

TIMESTAMP	Date and time	A 26-byte string. A typical example is:
		
		`01   START-TIME           PIC X(26).`
		
		The internal structure of a timestamp item is yyyy-mm-dd-hh.mm.ss.mmmmmm. To identify the parts of a DB2 timestamp, you can move the value to a group item like
		
		`01   EDITED-TIMESTAMP.`
		`     05   ETS-YEAR        PIC X(4).`
		`     05   FILLER          PIC X.`
		`     05   ETS-MONTH       PIC XX.`
		`     05   FILLER          PIC X.`
		`     05   ETS-DAY         PIC XX.`
		`     05   FILLER          PIC X.`
		`     05   ETS-HOUR        PIC XX.`
		`     05   FILLER          PIC X.`
		`     05   ETS-MINUTE      PIC XX.`
		`     05   FILLER          PIC X.`
		`     05   ETS-SECOND      PIC XX.`
		`     05   FILLER          PIC X.`
		`     05   ETS-MSECOND     PIC X(6).`

Figure 1-3   Date and time data types

DCLGEN output for the VARCUST table

```
*****************************************************************
*  DCLGEN  TABLE(MMADBV.VARCUST)                                *
*          LIBRARY(MMA002.DCLGENS.COBOL(VARCUST))               *
*          ACTION(REPLACE)                                      *
*          STRUCTURE(CUSTOMER-ROW)                              *
*          APOST                                                *
*  ... IS THE DCLGEN COMMAND THAT MADE THE FOLLOWING STATEMENTS *
*****************************************************************
       EXEC SQL DECLARE MMADBV.VARCUST TABLE
       ( CUSTNO                          CHAR(6) NOT NULL,
         FNAME                           VARCHAR(20) NOT NULL,
         LNAME                           VARCHAR(30) NOT NULL,
         ADDR                            VARCHAR(30) NOT NULL,
         CITY                            VARCHAR(20) NOT NULL,
         STATE                           CHAR(2) NOT NULL,
         ZIPCODE                         CHAR(10) NOT NULL,
         HOMEPH                          CHAR(16),
         WORKPH                          CHAR(16),
         NOTES                           VARCHAR(254)
       ) END-EXEC.
*****************************************************************
* COBOL DECLARATION FOR TABLE MMADBV.VARCUST                   *
*****************************************************************
   01  CUSTOMER-ROW.
       10 CUSTNO              PIC X(6).
       10 FNAME.
          49 FNAME-LEN        PIC S9(4) USAGE COMP.
          49 FNAME-TEXT       PIC X(20).
       10 LNAME.
          49 LNAME-LEN        PIC S9(4) USAGE COMP.
          49 LNAME-TEXT       PIC X(30).
       10 ADDR.
          49 ADDR-LEN         PIC S9(4) USAGE COMP.
          49 ADDR-TEXT        PIC X(30).
       10 CITY.
          49 CITY-LEN         PIC S9(4) USAGE COMP.
          49 CITY-TEXT        PIC X(20).
       10 STATE               PIC X(2).
       10 ZIPCODE             PIC X(10).
       10 HOMEPH              PIC X(16).
       10 WORKPH              PIC X(16).
       10 NOTES.
          49 NOTES-LEN        PIC S9(4) USAGE COMP.
          49 NOTES-TEXT       PIC X(254).
*****************************************************************
* THE NUMBER OF COLUMNS DESCRIBED BY THIS DECLARATION IS 10    *
*****************************************************************
```

Figure 1-4   DCLGEN output for the VARCUST and INV tables (part 1 of 2)

DCLGEN output for the INV table

```
*************************************************************** *
* DCLGEN TABLE(MMADBV.INV)                                      *
*        LIBRARY(MMA002.DCLGENS.COBOL(INV))                     *
*        ACTION(REPLACE)                                        *
*        STRUCTURE(INVOICE-ROW)                                 *
*        APOST                                                  *
* ... IS THE DCLGEN COMMAND THAT MADE THE FOLLOWING STATEMENTS  *
*************************************************************** *
      EXEC SQL DECLARE MMADBV.INV TABLE
        ( INVCUST                      CHAR(6) NOT NULL,
          INVNO                        CHAR(6) NOT NULL,
          INVDATE                      DATE NOT NULL,
          INVSUBT                      DECIMAL(9, 2) NOT NULL,
          INVSHIP                      DECIMAL(7, 2) NOT NULL,
          INVTAX                       DECIMAL(7, 2) NOT NULL,
          INVTOTAL                     DECIMAL(9, 2) NOT NULL,
          INVPROM                      CHAR(10) NOT NULL
        ) END-EXEC.
*************************************************************** *
* COBOL DECLARATION FOR TABLE MMADBV.INV                        *
*************************************************************** *
  01  INVOICE-ROW.
      10 INVCUST              PIC X(6).
      10 INVNO                PIC X(6).
      10 INVDATE              PIC X(10).
      10 INVSUBT              PIC S9999999V99 USAGE COMP-3.
      10 INVSHIP              PIC S99999V99 USAGE COMP-3.
      10 INVTAX               PIC S99999V99 USAGE COMP-3.
      10 INVTOTAL             PIC S9999999V99 USAGE COMP-3.
      10 INVPROM              PIC X(10).
*************************************************************** *
* THE NUMBER OF COLUMNS DESCRIBED BY THIS DECLARATION IS 8      *
*************************************************************** *
```

Figure 1-4   DCLGEN output for the VARCUST and INV tables (part 2 of 2)

Objectives

1. List the four DB2 data types for string data and code an appropriate COBOL host variable definition for each.

2. List the four DB2 data types for numeric data and code an appropriate COBOL host variable definition for each.

3. List the three DB2 data types for date and time data and code an appropriate COBOL host variable definition for each.

VARCUST table

CUSTNO	FNAME	LNAME	ADDR	CITY	STATE	ZIPCODE	HOMEPH	WORKPH	NOTES
400001	KEITH	MCDONALD	4501 W MOCKINGBIRD	DALLAS	TX	75209	214-555-8029	-------	-----------
400002	ARREN	ANELLI	40 FORD RD	DENVILLE	NJ	07834	-------		-----------
400003	SUSAN	HOWARD	1107 SECOND AVE #312	REDWOOD CITY	CA	94063	415-555-2131	415-555-1468	-----------
400004	CAROL ANN	EVANS	74 SUTTON CT	GREAT LAKES	IL	60088	708-555-4137	-------	-----------
400005	ELAINE	ROBERTS	12914 BRACKNELL	CERRITOS	CA	90701	-------	-------	-----------
400006	PAT	HONG	73 HIGH ST	SAN FRANCISCO	CA	94114	-------	-------	-----------
400007	PHIL	ROACH	25680 ORCHARD	DEARBORN HTS	MI	48125	-------	-------	-----------
400008	TIM	JOHNSON	145 W 27TH ST	SO CHICAGO HTS	IL	60411	-------	-------	-----------
400009	MARIANNE	BUSBEE	3920 BERWYN DR S #199	MOBILE	AL	36608	205-555-2406	205-555-6778X23	-----------
400010	ENRIQUE	OTHON	BOX 26729	RICHMOND	VA	23261	804-555-5583	-------	-----------
400011	WILLIAM C	FERGUSON	BOX 1283	MIAMI	FL	34002-1283	305-555-2098	-------	-----------
400012	S D	HOEHN	PO BOX 27	RIDDLE	OR	97469	503-555-0394	------	-----------
400013	DAVID R	KEITH	BOX 1266	MAGNOLIA	AR	71757-1266	-------	-------	-----------
400014	R	BINDER	3425 WALDEN AVE	DEPEW	NY	14043	716-555-3005	-------	-----------
400015	VIVIAN	GEORGE	229 S 18TH ST	PHILADELPHIA	PA	19103	-------	215-555-3780X548	-----------
400016	J	NOETHLICH	11 KINGSTON CT	MERRIMACK	NH	03054	603-555-9237	-------	-----------

INV table

INVCUST	INVNO	INVDATE	INVSUBT	INVSHIP	INVTAX	INVTOTAL	INVPROM
400012	062308	1990-12-22	200.00	4.45	.00	204.45	PCQ3
400011	062309	1990-12-22	15.00	.00	.00	15.00	PCQ3
400011	602310	1990-02-22	140.00	7.50	.00	147.50	PCQ3
400014	602311	1990-02-22	178.23	3.19	.00	181.42	PCQ3
400002	602312	1991-02-22	162.00	11.07	.00	173.07	PCQ3
400011	602313	1991-03-14	22.00	.50	.00	22.50	RXTY
400003	602314	1991-03-14	140.00	.00	9.80	149.80	RXTY
400004	602315	1991-03-14	178.23	3.19	.00	181.42	RXTY
400010	602316	1991-03-14	140.00	7.50	.00	147.50	RXTY
400011	062317	1991-03-17	289.00	9.00	.00	298.00	RXTY
400012	062318	1991-03-17	199.99	.00	.00	199.99	PCQ3
400015	062319	1991-03-17	178.23	3.19	.00	181.42	RXTY
400015	062320	1991-03-17	3245.00	160.00	.00	3405.00	RXTY
400001	062321	1991-04-03	200.00	5.60	.00	205.60	PCQ4
400014	062322	1991-04-03	15.00	.00	.00	15.00	PCQ4
400011	062323	1991-04-11	925.00	24.00	.00	949.00	PCQ4
400014	062324	1991-04-14	178.23	3.19	.00	181.42	PCQ4
400002	062325	1991-04-17	140.00	7.50	.00	147.50	PCQ3
400011	062326	1991-04-20	178.23	3.19	.00	181.42	PCQ4
400003	062327	1991-04-23	200.00	7.50	14.00	221.50	PCQ4
400004	062328	1991-04-24	178.23	3.19	.00	181.42	PCQ4
400010	062329	1991-04-29	140.00	7.50	.00	147.50	PCQ4
400011	062330	1991-04-30	2295.00	14.00	.00	2309.00	PCQ4
400012	062331	1991-05-07	178.23	.00	.00	178.23	PCQ4
400013	062332	1991-05-09	178.23	.00	.00	178.23	PCQ4
400015	062333	1991-05-17	178.23	.00	.00	178.23	PCQ4

Figure 1-5. Contents of the VARCUST and INV tables

Topic 2   How to use scalar functions with string and numeric data

DB2 provides a set of functions that you can use for tasks like data conversion and string manipulation. In this topic, I'll show you how to code and use these scalar functions in your SQL statements to manipulate string and numeric data types. It's easiest to understand scalar functions if you think about the kinds of data you can manipulate with them. So, that's how I've organized them in this topic. After I present an overview that applies to all scalar functions, I'll describe specific scalar functions for working with string data, numeric data, and nulls. (DB2 also provides several scalar functions that you use specifically with date and time data. I'll cover them in topic 3.)

Overview of scalar functions

In chapter 6 of *Part 1: An Introductory Course*, I showed you how to use column functions. A *column function* operates on the values in a specified column in all of the rows that meet a selection condition, and produces one result. Because the single result a column function produces represents data from multiple rows, column functions are often called *aggregate functions*.

In contrast, the operation of a *scalar function* involves only one row at a time. Instead of processing a number of rows to produce a single aggregate result, a scalar function operates independently for each row selected for the results table. The scalar function produces a different result for each row.

You can use scalar functions more freely than you can column functions. For example, you can code a scalar function as a column specification along with column names in a SELECT that will return a multi-row results table. Also, you can include scalar functions in the WHERE clauses of your SQL statements.

Each scalar function produces a single-value result based on the specifications you supply as one or more *arguments*. Some scalar functions can have multiple arguments, but most require only one. You code the necessary arguments in parentheses right after the *function name*.

Consider SUBSTR, a scalar function that extracts a substring from a character string. For example, to return the first character from the FNAME column in the VARCUST table, you'd code

```
SUBSTR(FNAME,1,1)
```

Here, SUBSTR is the function name, and FNAME, 1, and 1 are the arguments. If you translated this function into English, it would read, "Extract a substring from the FNAME column (the first argument) that starts at character 1 (the second argument) and that's 1 character long (the third argument)."

With its three arguments, SUBSTR is more complicated than most scalar functions. Of DB2's 20 scalar functions, 15 use just one argument. If a function requires more than one argument, you code them all in one set of parentheses following the function name, and you separate them from each other with commas, as in the example I just presented.

Frankly, scalar functions are more likely to be useful in ad hoc processing than in application programs. However, you may encounter some situations where they will be useful. As I present the functions, I'll give some perspective on how you can use them. Often, the result of a scalar function is used entirely within DB2, and your program doesn't need to retrieve its result at all. That's the case when you use a scalar function in a predicate. But if you plan to use a scalar function in a column specification of a SELECT statement, you need to provide a host variable for it.

How to work with character columns

Figure 1-6 presents the syntax of three scalar functions you might use with string data: SUBSTR, LENGTH, and HEX. All of these functions work with both character and graphic data, in both their fixed-length and variable-length forms. Because you're unlikely to need to work with graphic data, I'll use character columns in my examples.

The function I just showed you, SUBSTR, lets you extract a substring from a character expression. It requires two arguments: the source string, and the position in the source string where the substring you want to extract starts. SUBSTR also has an optional third argument that lets you specify the length of the substring.

For example, figure 1-7 shows a SELECT statement that uses the SUBSTR function I presented a moment ago. This function extracts the first letter from the value in the FNAME column.

```
SUBSTR(expression,start[,length])
```

> Returns the characters from the string identified by the first argument, *expression*, beginning at the character identified by the second argument, *start*. The second argument must be a number (a binary integer) between 1 and the maximum length of the string identified by *expression*. The third argument, *length*, specifies how many characters should be returned in the result. It must a number (a binary integer) ranging from 1 to the length of the string identified by *expression*. If *length* isn't specified, all of the characters in the first argument from the *start* position through its end are returned. The result may be null.
>
> If *length* is specified or *expression* is fixed-length, the result of the function is a fixed-length character string, COBOL PIC X(n). Otherwise, the function returns the substring in a variable-length column, and you need to provide the same sort of two-level host variable you use for data from a VARCHAR column.

```
LENGTH(expression)
```

> Returns the length of the value of *expression*.
>
> The result of the function is a fullword integer (COBOL PIC S9(9) COMP). The result may be null.

```
HEX(expression)
```

> Returns the hexadecimal value of *expression*. *Expression* may be anything, as long as it's not longer than 254 EBCDIC characters or 127 DBCS characters.
>
> If *expression* is a character item, the result of the function is a character string that contains two bytes for each byte in *expression*. If *expression* is a graphic data item, the result contains four bytes for each character it contains. The result may be null.

Figure 1-6   Scalar functions for working with string data

If you omit the length argument, DB2 returns every character in the source string from the starting position through its end. So,

```
SUBSTR(FNAME,1)
```

returns the entire value of the column FNAME.

If you supply a length value, or if the source expression is a fixed-length column, DB2 returns the substring in a fixed-length column. If you don't specify a length and the source expression is a variable-length column, the result will be variable-length. Make sure you define your program's host variable appropriately for the data the function will return.

Figure 1-8 presents a more complicated SELECT statement that uses the SUBSTR function. This SELECT statement produces a single-column

SQL statement

```
  .
  .
  .
SELECT LNAME,
       FNAME,
       SUBSTR(FNAME,1,1)
  FROM MMADBV.VARCUST
  WHERE STATE = 'CA'
  .
  .
```

Results table

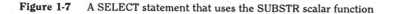

LNAME	FNAME	3
HOWARD	SUSAN	S
ROBERTS	ELAINE	E
HONG	PAT	P

Figure 1-7 A SELECT statement that uses the SUBSTR scalar function

results table that contains the names of customers who live in California. What's complicated about it is the text manipulation it specifies. As you can see in the results table in the figure, the names are formatted so the last name appears first, followed by a comma and a space, then by the first letter of the first name, and, finally, by a period. To perform this formatting, the column specification in the SELECT clause uses concatenation operators (||) to combine a column, two literals, and the result of the SUBSTR function.

The other two scalar functions in figure 1-6 are less useful than SUBSTR. LENGTH returns the number of bytes required to store the value of the expression you specify as its argument. And HEX returns a hexadecimal representation, in character string form, of any expression. Although these functions are of limited value in COBOL programs, they're easy to understand, so I'd like to show them to you here.

Figure 1-9 shows a SELECT statement that illustrates the LENGTH function with one of the variable-length columns from the VARCUST table in figure 1-5. In figure 1-9, I've selected the FNAME and LNAME column values of customers who live in California. Between the column specifications for the FNAME and LNAME columns, I included the LENGTH function to report the number of characters in the LNAME column. You can see its result in column 2 of the results table.

SQL statement

```
.
.
SELECT LNAME,            || ',' ||
       SUBSTR(FNAME1,1)  || '.'
  FROM MMADBV.VARCUST
  WHERE STATE = 'CA'
.
.
```

Results table

1

HOWARD, S.
ROBERTS, E.
HONG, P.

Figure 1-8   A SELECT statement that uses a SUBSTR scalar function in a concatenation operation

SQL statement

```
.
.
SELECT LNAME,
       LENGTH(LNAME),
       FNAME
  FROM MMADBV.VARCUST
  WHERE STATE = 'CA'
.
.
```

Results table

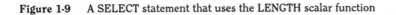

LNAME	2	FNAME
HOWARD	6	SUSAN
ROBERTS	7	ELAINE
HONG	4	PAT

Figure 1-9   A SELECT statement that uses the LENGTH scalar function

SQL statement

```
.
.
.
SELECT FNAME,
       SUBSTR(FNAME,1,3),
       HEX(SUBSTR(FNAME,1,3)),
       INVNO,
       HEX(INVNO),
       INVTOTAL,
       HEX(INVTOTAL)
  FROM MMADBV.VARCUST,MMADBV.INV
  WHERE STATE = 'CA' AND INVCUST = CUSTNO
.
.
```

Results table

FNAME	2	3	4	5	6	7
SUSAN	SUS	E2E4E2	062314	F0F6F2F3F1F4	149.80	000014980C
SUSAN	SUS	E2E4E2	062327	F0F6F2F3F2F7	221.50	000022150C

Figure 1-10   A SELECT statement that uses the HEX scalar function

Frankly, the chances are slim that you'll ever need to use this function in a COBOL program. That's because when you retrieve a variable-length column, the length of its contents is returned along with the contents themselves.

Figure 1-10 shows a sample SELECT statement that demonstrates how the HEX function works. It retrieves information from the VARCUST and INV tables for invoices issued to California customers and uses the HEX function to convert it to hexadecimal form. The first column in the results table contains the values from the FNAME column. As you can see, only two rows were retrieved, and the FNAME column in both contains the value SUSAN.

Column 2 contains the result of the function

```
SUBSTR(FNAME,1,3)
```

As you'd expect, the value in both rows is SUS, the first three characters in the FNAME column.

The third column uses the HEX function to convert the result of the SUBSTR function I used for column 2 into hexadecimal form. Besides showing how the HEX function works, this example also illustrates how you can nest one function within another. In this case, I coded the SUBSTR scalar function as the argument for the HEX function. Because the SUBSTR function is evaluated first, DB2 effectively processes

```
HEX('SUS')
```

to produce the hexadecimal value

```
E2E4E2
```

in column 3 for both of the rows.

Columns 4 and 5 of the results table contain the character and hexadecimal representations of the contents of the INVNO column from the selected rows. (If you look back to the DCLGEN output for the INV table in figure 1-4, you'll see that the INVNO column has the CHAR data type.) Columns 6 and 7 contain the numeric and hexadecimal representations of the contents of the INVTOTAL column from the selected rows. Unlike INVNO, the INVTOTAL column has a numeric data type (DECIMAL). If you examine the hexadecimal representation of the INVTOTAL column values, you'll see they're consistent with what you'd expect for packed-decimal data.

You can use the HEX function to display some interesting information, but it's not useful in most cases. Although you may come across situations that require you to use HEX, I don't think you will often.

How to convert numeric data from one type to another

Figure 1-11 shows the syntax of four of DB2's scalar functions, INTEGER, DIGITS, FLOAT, and DECIMAL, that are used to convert numeric data. In COBOL programming situations, you're probably not going to need these functions often. They're more appropriate for ad hoc processing tasks and for on-line maintenance of tables. However, they're easy to understand.

INTEGER requires a single numeric argument, and it returns a binary fullword whose value is the whole-number part of the argument. This function truncates any fractional part of the argument's value, and it doesn't round. So, if you code INTEGER(1.999), the result of the function is 1. If you want to process the value INTEGER returns in a COBOL program, you have to code your own host variable with PIC S9(9) COMP.

DIGITS also processes a numeric argument, but returns a character string. The result is a character column that contains the digits that make up the absolute value of the argument. In COBOL, you can obtain the same results by retrieving a numeric column directly, then moving it into a

`INTEGER(expression)`

> Returns only the whole-number part of *expression*. *Expression* must be a number.
>
> The result of the function is a binary fullword, COBOL PIC S9(9) COMP. The result may be null.

`DIGITS(expression)`

> Returns a character string of the digits that make up the absolute value of *expression*. The result doesn't include a decimal point or a sign. *Expression* must evaluate to a binary or decimal number.
>
> The result of the function is a fixed-length character value, COBOL PIC X(n). The length, n, depends on the data type of *expression*. If the data type of *expression* is SMALLINT, n is 5; if it's INTEGER, n is 10; if it's DECIMAL, n is the precision of the decimal value. The result may be null.

`FLOAT(expression)`

> Returns the double-precision floating point equivalent of *expression*. *Expression* must be a number.
>
> To use the result of the function in a COBOL program, code a host variable with COMP-2 usage. The result may be null.

`DECIMAL(expression[,precision[,scale]])`

> Returns a decimal representation of *expression*, the first argument. The second argument is the precision of the result and must be an integer value between 1 and 15. The third argument is the scale of the result and must be an integer value between 0 and *precision*.
>
> To use the result of the function in a COBOL program, code a host variable with COMP-3 usage and with a PIC clause that accurately reflects the precision and scale of the number: PIC S9(precision − scale)V9(scale). The result may be null if *expression* is null.

Figure 1-11   Scalar functions for working with numeric data

numeric field that's redefined with an alphanumeric picture. So you probably won't use the DIGITS function often.

If you do need to use the DIGITS function in a program, you have to code your own alphanumeric host variable to contain the character string it returns. The size of that host variable depends on the kind of numeric data the function will process. Valid data types are SMALLINT, INTEGER, and DECIMAL. If the data type of the function's argument is SMALLINT, your COBOL host variable should have PIC X(5); if the argument's data type is INTEGER, the variable should have PIC X(10). If the argument has the

DECIMAL data type, the host variable's size should match the number's precision.

FLOAT converts the number you identify in its argument into a double-precision floating point number. To work with its result in COBOL, code a host variable definition with COMP-2 usage.

Figure 1-12 presents a SELECT statement that illustrates the operation of the INTEGER, DIGITS, and FLOAT functions. This statement accesses the INV table I presented in figures 1-4 and 1-5. The first column in the results table, INVNO, contains the unique invoice number that identifies each row in the table. Because the data type of this column is CHAR, I can't manipulate it with the numeric scalar functions, even though its name sounds numeric and its contents look numeric. The second column, INVTOTAL, contains the total amount billed on an invoice. It was defined with DECIMAL(9,2).

The other column specifications in the SELECT statement in figure 1-12 use the INTEGER, DIGITS, and FLOAT functions. As you can see, the argument for each function is simply the column name INVTOTAL. To process this statement, DB2 retrieves the INVNO and INVTOTAL values from each row of the base table that meets the selection condition. Then, it applies the functions to the INVTOTAL value in each row to produce the contents of columns 3, 4, and 5.

The third column produced by the SELECT statement in figure 1-12 contains the result of the INTEGER function. As you can see, INTEGER removed the fractional part from the numbers it processed. For example, in the first row in the results table, the INVTOTAL value 22.50 was reduced to 22 by the INTEGER function.

The fourth column in the results table was produced by the DIGITS function. Because the INVTOTAL column was defined as DECIMAL(9,2), the length of the character string DIGITS produced was 9 bytes. Notice that although the INVTOTAL column's value includes an implicit decimal point before the last two digits, the value produced by the DIGITS function doesn't include it.

The fifth column in the table shows the result of the FLOAT function. As you can see, it is simply the value in the INVTOTAL column, converted into double-precision floating point form. Although this form may be useful in some situations, you're not likely to need it in typical applications.

The last of the functions in figure 1-11, DECIMAL, converts a numeric value to decimal format. It has a more complicated syntax than INTEGER, DIGITS, or FLOAT. That's because you specify not just an expression that's the source of the value it manipulates, but also the precision and scale of the decimal number it will produce. Precision, the second argument of the DECIMAL function, is the total number of digits for the decimal value.

SQL statement

```
      .
      .
SELECT INVNO,
       INVTOTAL,
       INTEGER(INVTOTAL),
       DIGITS(INVTOTAL),
       FLOAT(INVTOTAL)
   FROM MMADBV.INV
   WHERE INVCUST = '400011'
   ORDER BY INVNO
      .
      .
```

Results table

INVNO	INVTOTAL	3	4	5
062313	22.50	22	000002250	+0.2250000000000E+02
062317	298.00	298	000029800	+0.2980000000000E+03
062323	949.00	949	000094900	+0.9490000000000E+03
062326	181.42	181	000018142	+0.1814200000000E+03
062330	2309.00	2309	000230900	+0.2309000000000E+04

Figure 1-12   A SELECT statement that uses the INTEGER, DIGITS, and FLOAT scalar functions with simple column names as their arguments

Scale, the third argument of the DECIMAL function, is the number of those digits that are to the right of the implicit decimal point.

By the way, although the precision and scale arguments are optional on the DECIMAL scalar functions, you should always code them. If you omit the precision argument, the default depends on the data type of the expression you specify as the first argument. If the data type is FLOAT, the default is 15; if it's INTEGER, the default is 11; and if it's SMALLINT, the default is 5. The default for the scale argument is zero, regardless of the data type.

When you code a COBOL host variable for the result of the DECIMAL function, you use COMP-3 (packed-decimal) usage. Be sure the picture for the variable contains the correct number of digits on both sides of the assumed decimal point. For example, if you code a DECIMAL function like

```
DECIMAL(INVTOTAL,11,4)
```

you need to code PIC S9(7)V9(4) for the associated host variable. The total number of digits represented in the COBOL PIC (here, 7+ 4) must equal the precision you specify on the function.

If you specify a precision on the DECIMAL function that's too small for the derived value, you'll get an error. For example,

```
DECIMAL(INVTOTAL,5,2)
```

will yield an error because the precision of the INVTOTAL column is 9, and I specified a precision of only 5 for the result. A statement that produces this kind of error will fail with SQLCODE −406.

Figure 1-13 illustrates the operation of the DECIMAL function. This is the same SELECT statement I showed you in figure 1-12, except I replaced the functions in that example with two DECIMAL functions. Remember, the definition of the INVTOTAL column is DECIMAL(9,2). The first DECIMAL function in figure 1-13 specifies just that, and its result is the same as the contents of the second column, whose specification was simply the INVTOTAL column itself.

The second DECIMAL function in figure 1-13 represents the values stored in the INVTOTAL column with more digits for both precision and scale. As you can see, DB2 added the necessary trailing zeros to the values it returned to make them conform to the specification of the function. In both columns 3 and 4, you can see that DB2 doesn't show leading zeros. However, they're there.

As I mentioned earlier, the DECIMAL function is more useful in ad hoc work than in application programs. After all, to convert a number to decimal format in a program, all you have to do is move it to a COMP-3 field. However, you might find it useful within DB2 operations if you need to use integer data in computations that could yield non-integer results. For example, if you used the AVG function to get the average of a column containing integer data, the result would be an integer, which probably isn't what you want. But if you used the DECIMAL function to convert the integer data to decimal data before you calculated the average, the result would be a decimal.

How to provide substitute values for nulls

The VALUE scalar function lets you code your SELECT statements so that null won't be returned as the value of a column. Thus, if you use the VALUE function in a column specification, you may not have to provide an indicator variable for the host variable for that column. You can use VALUE with any column whose value can be null.

Figure 1-14 presents the syntax of the VALUE function. Unlike other DB2 functions, the VALUE function has a variable number of arguments. The operation of the VALUE function is simple: DB2 scans the list of argu-

SQL statement

```
.
.
.
SELECT INVNO,
       INVTOTAL,
       DECIMAL(INVTOTAL,9,2),
       DECIMAL(INVTOTAL,15,7),
   FROM MMADBV.INV
   WHERE INVCUST = '400011'
   ORDER BY INVNO
.
.
.
```

Results table

INVNO	INVTOTAL	3	4
062313	22.50	22.50	22.5000000
062317	298.00	298.00	298.0000000
062323	949.00	949.00	949.0000000
062326	181.42	181.42	181.4200000
062330	2309.00	2309.00	2309.0000000

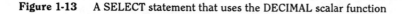

Figure 1-13   A SELECT statement that uses the DECIMAL scalar function

ments from left to right and returns the first argument whose value is not null.

In the simplest case, the VALUE function has two arguments, such as the name of a column whose value can be null and a literal value. If the value of the column you specified for the first argument is null, DB2 returns the literal (the second argument).

You can also list more than two arguments in a VALUE function. For example, suppose you want to produce a results table from the VARCUST table that includes a way to contact each customer. The preferred method is through a home phone number. If that isn't available, the second-best method is through a work phone number. And if that isn't available, the results table should show the literal "NO PHONE NUMBER."

The SELECT statement in figure 1-15 produces this results table. Its VALUE function,

```
VALUE ('(H): ' || HOMEPH,
       '(W): ' || WORKPH,
       'NO PHONE NUMBER')
```

looks complicated, but it's straightforward. The first substitution value is a concatenation of the literal string "(H): " and the contents of the HOMEPH

```
VALUE(expression,expression[,expression...])
```

Returns the first expression in the list that does not evaluate to null.

Figure 1-14   The scalar function for providing substitute values for nulls

column. If the HOMEPH column is null, this entire expression evaluates to null. In that case, the second argument (the work phone identified with the literal "(W): ") is used, if it isn't null. Finally, if both phone number columns are null, the function provides the literal "NO PHONE NUMBER."

Notice that the last argument in the VALUE function in figure 1-15 is a literal. If you want to insure that the VALUE function returns a non-null value, you should specify a literal value or a column that doesn't allow nulls as the last argument. That way, even if all the other arguments in the VALUE function are null, the last argument will always cause the VALUE function to return a non-null value. If you don't specify a literal or non-nullable column as the last argument, the VALUE function might return a null value. In that case, you'll have to provide an indicator variable for it. (Incidentally, there's no point in placing a literal value or a column that doesn't allow nulls anywhere in the list of arguments other than at the end because DB2 will always ignore the remaining arguments once it finds the non-null value.)

You may also want to use the VALUE function if you work with tables that contain numeric columns whose values may be null. Remember, if you code an arithmetic expression that refers to an item whose value is null, the result of the expression will be null. In that case, you may want to use the VALUE function to substitute zero for null.

Terms

column function
aggregate function
scalar function
argument
function name

Objectives

1. Describe the difference between a scalar function and a column function.

SQL statement

```
        .
        .
SELECT CUSTNO,
       FNAME,
       LNAME,
       VALUE('(H): ' || HOMEPH,
             '(W): ' || WORKPH,
             'NO PHONE NUMBER')
    FROM MMADBV.VARCUST
    ORDER BY 1
        .
        .
```

Results table

CUSTNO	FNAME	LNAME	4
400001	KEITH	MCDONALD	(H): 214-555-8029
400002	ARREN	ANELLI	NO PHONE NUMBER
400003	SUSAN	HOWARD	(H): 415-555-2131
400004	CAROL ANN	EVANS	(H): 708-555-4137
400005	ELAINE	ROBERTS	NO PHONE NUMBER
400006	PAT	HONG	NO PHONE NUMBER
400007	PHIL	ROACH	NO PHONE NUMBER
400008	TIM	JOHNSON	NO PHONE NUMBER
400009	MARIANNE	BUSBEE	(H): 205-555-2406
400010	ENRIQUE	OTHON	(H): 804-555-5583
400011	WILLIAM C	FERGUSON	(H): 305-555-2098
400012	S D	HOEHN	(H): 503-555-0394
400013	DAVID R	KEITH	NO PHONE NUMBER
400014	R	BINDER	(H): 716-555-3005
400015	VIVIAN	GEORGE	(W): 215-555-3780X548
400016	J	NOETHLICH	(H): 603-555-9237

Figure 1-15   A SELECT statement that uses the VALUE scalar function

2. Code a SELECT that uses the SUBSTR scalar function to extract a sub-string from a character string.

3. Code a SELECT that uses the INTEGER, DIGITS, FLOAT, and DECIMAL scalar functions to convert numeric data from one type to another.

4. Code a SELECT that uses the VALUE scalar function to provide substitute values for null.

Topic 3 How to use scalar functions with date and time data

This topic presents twelve scalar functions that let you perform operations on DB2 date and time data. You can do four kinds of operations with these functions. First, you can change the format of a date or time character string with the CHAR function. Second, you can determine an absolute date from a DB2 date with the DAYS function. (You can use an absolute date to calculate age differences.) Third, you can extract the components of a date as numbers and then do basic arithmetic on them with the YEAR, MONTH, DAY, HOUR, MINUTE, SECOND, and MICROSECOND functions. And fourth, you can create an item with a date or time data type from a compatible source with the DATE, TIME, or TIMESTAMP function.

Many of the examples I'll present in this topic use the DB2 *special registers* CURRENT DATE, CURRENT TIME, and CURRENT TIMESTAMP. These are keywords you can code in an expression where date or time data is called for. When the expression is processed, the current value is substituted for the keyword. Then, the statement is processed with that value. Of course, you can also operate on columns that contain date and time data with these scalar functions. I'll present examples that use that data too.

I'll start this topic by giving you a general overview of scalar functions. If you've already read topic 2, this material will be familiar to you. If that's the case, you can skip forward to the heading "How to format and use dates and times as character strings."

Overview of scalar functions

In chapter 6 of *Part 1: An Introductory Course*, I showed you how to use column functions. A *column function* operates on the values in a specified column in all of the rows that meet a selection condition and produces one result. Because the single result a column function produces represents data from multiple rows, column functions are often called *aggregate functions.*

In contrast, the operation of a *scalar function* involves only one row at a time. Instead of processing a number of rows to produce a single aggregate result, a scalar function operates independently for each row selected for the results table. The scalar function produces a different result for each row.

You can use scalar functions more freely than you can column functions. For example, you can code a scalar function as a column specification along with column names in a SELECT that will return a multi-row results table. Also, you can include scalar functions in the WHERE clauses of your SQL statements.

Each scalar function produces a single-value result based on the specifications you supply as one or more *arguments*. Some scalar functions can have multiple arguments, but most require only one. You code the necessary arguments in parentheses right after the *function name*.

Consider CHAR, a scalar function that lets you change the way the parts of a date or time item are represented in a character string. For example, to return a character string that contains the content of the INV table column INVDATE in ISO format, you could use the function

```
CHAR(INVDATE,ISO)
```

(I'll describe ISO and other date formats in a moment.) Here, CHAR is the function name, and the function has two arguments: INVDATE and ISO. If you translated this function into English, it would read, "Reformat the character string representation of the column INVDATE so it's in ISO format."

With its two arguments, CHAR is more complicated than most scalar functions. Of DB2's 20 scalar functions, 15 use just one argument. If a function requires more than one argument, you code them all in one set of parentheses following the function name, and you separate them from each other with commas, as in the example I just presented.

Frankly, scalar functions are more likely to be useful in ad hoc processing than in application programs. However, you may encounter some situations where they will be useful. As I present the functions, I'll give some perspective on how you can use them. Often, the result of a scalar function is used entirely within DB2, and your program doesn't need to retrieve its result at all. That's the case when you use a scalar function in a predicate. But if you plan to use a scalar function in a column specification of a SELECT statement, you need to provide a host variable for it.

How to format and use dates and times as character strings

When a program retrieves DB2 date or time data, it receives a single character string that has an internal structure. For example, the default structure for a date character string is

```
yyyy-mm-dd
```

The first four characters represent the year, the sixth and seventh represent the month, and the ninth and tenth represent the day. Your program can process these components as separate text strings as long as it can identify them properly.

With the CHAR scalar function, you can direct DB2 to return time and date character strings to your programs in formats different from the default. (This default can be either DB2's general default or your shop's site-specific default). Figure 1-16 presents the syntax of the CHAR function. As you can see, you can code two arguments on it. The first argument names the date or time item you want to process, and the second argument specifies the format DB2 should use when it constructs the character string for that item.

The output the function produces depends on the data type of the first argument. If it's a date item, the function produces a character string that represents a date. And, if it's a time item, the function produces a character string that represents a time.

You can specify one of five values for the format argument. Each directs DB2 to put the components of a date or time value together in a different way. As you can see in figure 1-16, the ISO, USA, EUR, and JIS formats each return a date string that uses ten characters or a time string that uses eight characters. But they differ in the sequence DB2 uses for the components and in the characters it uses to separate them.

If you don't code a format argument on the CHAR function, DB2 defaults to ISO (unless your DBA has set the system default to something else). Of course, because the reason for using the CHAR function is to guarantee that the date or time will follow a specific format, I recommend that you always specify its *format* argument. That way, if the system default changes, the function will still operate the way you want it to.

Figures 1-17 and 1-18 illustrate the results CHAR produces. Each figure shows a part of a SELECT statement that creates a simple results table containing different formats for the current date or time. The elements in the SELECT in figure 1-17 specify columns that will contain data drawn from the special register CURRENT DATE. The elements in the example in figure 1-18 specify columns that will contain data drawn from the special register CURRENT TIME. As you can see, the values the different versions of the CHAR function returned correspond to the string layouts in figure 1-16.

Notice that the date and time items that were specified directly in the first column in these examples have the same formats as the character representations for the date and time items in ISO format in column 2. That's because ISO is the standard format for date and time items on my system. DB2 defaults to ISO as the format for date and time data when no other

```
CHAR(expression[,format])
```

Returns a character string representation of the date or time value of *expression* in the format indicated by *format*. *Format* may be one of the following. Each produces date or time values as shown.

Format argument	Standard	Date format	Time format
ISO	International Standards Organization	$yyyy-mm-dd$	$hh.mm.ss$
USA	IBM American Standard	$mm/dd/yyyy$	$hh:mm \begin{Bmatrix} AM \\ PM \end{Bmatrix}$
EUR	IBM European Standard	$dd.mm.yyyy$	$hh.mm.ss$
JIS	Japanese Industrial Standard Christian Era	$yyyy-mm-dd$	$hh:mm:ss$
LOCAL		Site-specific	Site-specific

Figure 1-16 The scalar function for changing the format of date and time character strings

SQL statement

```
.
.
SELECT CURRENT DATE,
       CHAR(CURRENT DATE,ISO),
       CHAR(CURRENT DATE,USA),
       CHAR(CURRENT DATE,EUR),
       CHAR(CURRENT DATE,JIS)
.
.
```

Results table

1	2	3	4	5
1991-07-16	1991-07-16	07/16/1991	16.07.1991	1991-07-16

Figure 1-17 Using the CHAR scalar function to change the display format of a date value

SQL statement

```
.
.
SELECT  CURRENT TIME,
        CHAR(CURRENT TIME,ISO),
        CHAR(CURRENT TIME,USA),
        CHAR(CURRENT TIME,EUR),
        CHAR(CURRENT TIME,JIS)
.
.
```

Results table

1	2	3	4	5
15.49.37	15.49.37	03:49 PM	15.49.37	15:49:37

Figure 1-18   Using the CHAR scalar function to change the display format of a time value

option is specified, either as a precompiler option or as an installation option. On your system, the default may be different.

Figures 1-17 and 1-18 don't illustrate LOCAL, the last format option of the CHAR function. If your shop has installed a local date and time formatting routine, this is how you can specify that it should be used. You should realize that a local routine can return strings with more or fewer characters than the ones produced by the DB2-defined versions. For example, if your shop uses a routine that includes the name of the month in a date instead of its number, you might get a string like

```
SEPTEMBER 15, 1991
```

in response to

```
CHAR('1991-09-15',LOCAL)
```

To be able to use the LOCAL option, an exit routine must have been installed for date and time on your system.

If your program retrieves data from a time or date item processed by CHAR, you need to code the receiving host variable so it agrees with the layout of the character string. If you don't need to manipulate the individual components, you can simply code a PIC X(n) field for a date or a time item, where n is the number of characters in the string. However, if you want to access the components of these strings separately, you need to provide

CHAR format	Appropriate COBOL group item for date data			Appropriate COBOL group item for time data		
ISO and JIS	01	EDITED-DATE.		01	EDITED-TIME.	
	05	ED-YEAR	PIC X(4).	05	ET-HOUR	PIC XX.
	05	FILLER	PIC X.	05	FILLER	PIC X.
	05	ED-MONTH	PIC XX.	05	ET-MINUTE	PIC XX.
	05	FILLER	PIC X.	05	FILLER	PIC X.
	05	ED-DAY	PIC XX.	05	ET-SECOND	PIC XX.
USA	01	EDITED-DATE.		01	EDITED-TIME.	
	05	ED-MONTH	PIC XX.	05	ET-HOUR	PIC XX.
	05	FILLER	PIC X.	05	FILLER	PIC X.
	05	ED-DAY	PIC XX.	05	ET-MINUTE	PIC XX.
	05	FILLER	PIC X.	05	FILLER	PIC X.
	05	ED-YEAR	PIC X(4).	05	ET-AM-PM	PIC XX.
EUR	01	EDITED-DATE.		01	EDITED-TIME.	
	05	ED-DAY	PIC XX.	05	ET-HOUR	PIC XX.
	05	FILLER	PIC X.	05	FILLER	PIC X.
	05	ED-MONTH	PIC XX.	05	ET-MINUTE	PIC XX.
	05	FILLER	PIC X.	05	FILLER	PIC X.
	05	ED-YEAR	PIC X(4).	05	ET-SECOND	PIC XX.

Figure 1-19   COBOL group item descriptions for date and time character strings produced by the CHAR function

more detailed host variable structures. Figure 1-19 presents group items you can use for date and time character strings in ISO, USA, EUR, and JIS formats. I haven't listed any guidelines for the LOCAL format because it varies from one site to another.

How to determine and use the number of elapsed days represented by a date

The ways DB2 lets you manipulate date and time string formats may be useful to you in some situations. However, the strengths of DB2's date and time features are more apparent when you use them with arithmetic expressions. In the next topic, I'll cover these issues in more detail. Now, though, I'd like to introduce a scalar function that you can use in basic operations with date data: DAYS. Figure 1-20 presents its syntax.

DAYS returns the number of days that have elapsed between December 31, 0000 and the date you specify as its argument. For example

```
DAYS('1991-07-16')
```

```
DAYS(expression)
```

> Returns a binary integer (PIC S9(9) COMP) that contains the number of days that have elapsed between December 31, 0000 and *expression*. *Expression* may be a date value, a timestamp, or a string that DB2 can interpret as a date. The result may be null.

Figure 1-20   The scalar function for determining the absolute age of a date item

returns the value

```
727029
```

Frankly, there aren't many applications that call for you to find out that almost three quarters of a million days have passed over the last two millennia. However, there may be applications that require you to determine the *difference* between two dates. The easiest way to do that is to get the elapsed number of days for each date and subtract one from the other.

Figure 1-21 shows a SELECT statement that produces a results table containing the invoice number, customer number, and date for each invoice in the INV table. In addition, it includes a fourth column that contains the age of each invoice. This column specification determines the age:

```
DAYS(CURRENT DATE) - DAYS(INVDATE)
```

Because the DAYS function returns a numeric value, you can use it in an expression like this one.

The results table in the figure was generated when the current date was 1991-07-18. So, for the first row in the table, you can imagine that the expression in the SELECT statement is interpreted as

```
DAYS('1991-07-18') - DAYS('1990-12-22')
```

Then, the DAYS functions cause the absolute elapsed days for the two dates to be substituted in the expression:

```
727031 - 726823
```

Finally, the elapsed date for INVDATE is subtracted from the one for the current date to give the final result: 208.

If you want to retrieve the result of a DAYS function into your program, you need to code an appropriate host variable. The result of the DAYS function is a binary fullword, PIC S9(9) COMP.

SQL statement

```
.
.
SELECT INVNO,
       INVCUST,
       INVDATE,
       DAYS(CURRENT DATE) - DAYS(INVDATE),
       ' DAYS OLD'
    FROM MMADBV.INV
    ORDER BY 4 DESC
.
.
```

Results table

INVNO	INVCUST	INVDATE	4	5
062309	400011	1990-12-22	208	DAYS OLD
062308	400012	1990-12-22	208	DAYS OLD
062311	400014	1991-02-22	146	DAYS OLD
062310	400011	1991-02-22	146	DAYS OLD
062312	400002	1991-02-22	146	DAYS OLD
062314	400003	1991-03-14	126	DAYS OLD
062313	400011	1991-03-14	126	DAYS OLD
062316	400010	1991-03-14	126	DAYS OLD
062315	400004	1991-03-14	126	DAYS OLD
062317	400011	1991-03-17	123	DAYS OLD
062320	400015	1991-03-17	123	DAYS OLD
062319	400015	1991-03-17	123	DAYS OLD
062318	400012	1991-03-17	123	DAYS OLD
062321	400001	1991-04-03	106	DAYS OLD
062322	400014	1991-04-03	106	DAYS OLD
062323	400011	1991-04-11	98	DAYS OLD
062324	400014	1991-04-14	95	DAYS OLD
062325	400002	1991-04-17	92	DAYS OLD
062326	400011	1991-04-20	89	DAYS OLD
062327	400003	1991-04-23	86	DAYS OLD
062328	400004	1991-04-24	85	DAYS OLD
062329	400010	1991-04-29	80	DAYS OLD
062330	400011	1991-04-30	79	DAYS OLD
062331	400012	1991-05-07	72	DAYS OLD
062332	400013	1991-05-09	70	DAYS OLD
062333	400015	1991-05-17	62	DAYS OLD

Figure 1-21   Using the DAYS scalar function to determine elapsed time

How to use the components of date and time items as numbers

If you need to work with the components of a date or time in a numeric expression, you can use one of the scalar functions listed in figure 1-22. These functions let you extract any part of a date, time, or timestamp value as a binary number. You can use the result of any of these functions directly in an arithmetic expression.

`YEAR(expression)`

> Returns the year component of the date, timestamp, or date duration *expression*. The result of the function is a binary fullword, COBOL PIC S9(9) COMP. The result may be null.

`MONTH(expression)`

> Returns the month component of the date, timestamp, or date duration *expression*. The result of the function is a binary fullword, COBOL PIC S9(9) COMP. The result may be null.

`DAY(expression)`

> Returns the day component of the date, timestamp, or date duration *expression*. The result of the function is a binary fullword, COBOL PIC S9(9) COMP. The result may be null.

`HOUR(expression)`

> Returns the hour component of the time, timestamp, or time duration *expression*. The result of the function is a binary fullword, COBOL PIC S9(9) COMP. The result may be null.

`MINUTE(expression)`

> Returns the minute component of the time, timestamp, or time duration *expression*. The result of the function is a binary fullword, COBOL PIC S9(9) COMP. The result may be null.

`SECOND(expression)`

> Returns the second component of the time, timestamp, or time duration *expression*. The result of the function is a binary fullword, COBOL PIC S9(9) COMP. The result may be null.

`MICROSECOND(timestamp)`

> Returns the microsecond component of *timestamp*. (You may not specify a time or time duration.) The result of the function is a binary fullword, COBOL PIC S9(9) COMP. The result may be null.

Figure 1-22   Scalar functions for extracting the numeric components of date, time, and timestamp items

To extract one of the parts of a date as a numeric value, you can use the YEAR, MONTH, or DAY function. HOUR, MINUTE, and SECOND let you extract parts of a time value. The SELECT statement in figure 1-23 illustrates how to code these functions and the result each produces. For

SQL statement

```
   .
   .
SELECT CURRENT DATE,
       MONTH(CURRENT DATE),
       DAY(CURRENT DATE),
       YEAR(CURRENT DATE),
       CURRENT TIME,
       HOUR(CURRENT TIME),
       MINUTE(CURRENT TIME),
       SECOND(CURRENT TIME)
   .
   .
```

Results table

1	2	3	4	5	6	7	8
1991-07-16	7	16	1991	15.49.37	15	49	37

Figure 1-23   Using the MONTH, DAY, YEAR, HOUR, MINUTE, and SECOND scalar functions to extract numeric values from date and time items

example, when the value of CURRENT DATE is 1991-07-16, applying the MONTH, DAY, and YEAR functions to it yields 7, 16, and 1991, all as separate numeric values.

You can use any of the functions in figure 1-22 with timestamp items. You can also use another function in this category, MICROSECOND, to extract the microsecond component of a timestamp. Figure 1-24 illustrates each of these scalar functions with a timestamp as its argument.

As with the DAYS function, these functions are most likely to be useful within SQL operations. It's unlikely that you'll need to retrieve the results of these functions in a program, but if you do, you have to code your own host variable. Each function's result is a binary fullword (PIC S9(9) COMP).

To understand how you might use these functions, look at figure 1-25. This SELECT statement uses the MONTH and YEAR functions in its WHERE clause to retrieve INV table rows that have an INVDATE value with the current month in the *previous* year. The WHERE clause specifies a compound condition with two predicates. The first,

```
MONTH(INVDATE) = MONTH(CURRENT DATE)
```

SQL statement

```
     .
     .
     .
SELECT CURRENT TIMESTAMP,
       MONTH(CURRENT TIMESTAMP),
       DAY(CURRENT TIMESTAMP),
       YEAR(CURRENT TIMESTAMP),
       HOUR(CURRENT TIMESTAMP),
       MINUTE(CURRENT TIMESTAMP),
       SECOND(CURRENT TIMESTAMP)
       MICROSECOND(CURRENT TIMESTAMP)
     .
     .
```

Results table

1	2	3	4	5	6	7	8
1991-07-16-15.49.37.816232	7	16	1991	15	49	37	816232

Figure 1-24   Using the MONTH, DAY, YEAR, HOUR, MINUTE, SECOND, and MICROSECOND scalar functions to extract numeric values from a timestamp item

```
     .
     .
     .
SELECT *
   FROM MMADBV.INV
   WHERE MONTH(INVDATE) = MONTH(CURRENT DATE) AND
         YEAR(INVDATE) =  YEAR(CURRENT DATE) - 1
     .
     .
```

Figure 1-25   A SELECT statement that uses the MONTH and YEAR scalar functions to retrieve rows from the INV table from the current month in the previous year

specifies that the month component of the INVDATE column in a row must match the MONTH component of the current date for a row to be selected. The second condition,

```
     YEAR(INVDATE) =  YEAR(CURRENT DATE) - 1
```

specifies that the year component of INVDATE must be one less than the year component of the current date for the row to be selected. Because the

YEAR function (like all the functions in figure 1-22) returns a numeric value, you can use that value in an arithmetic expression.

The functions in figure 1-22 also let you extract component information from DB2 durations. Durations are central to arithmetic operations that are performed directly on DB2 date and time data. In the next topic, I'll describe durations in detail.

How to create a date, time, or timestamp item

Three date and time scalar functions let you create a date, time, or timestamp item. Not surprisingly, those functions are DATE, TIME, and TIMESTAMP. Figure 1-26 presents the syntax for these functions. I'm covering them last because their usefulness is limited, especially in application programs. The features they provide are likely to be easier to accomplish in other ways.

One use for the DATE function might be to return a date value after performing arithmetic on a date that's been converted to absolute format by the DAYS function. For example, suppose you want to return the due date of an invoice. Assuming all invoices are due 30 days after the invoice date, you could use the DATE function like this:

```
DATE(DAYS(INVDATE) + 30)
```

Here, the DAYS function first converts the invoice date to absolute format. Then, 30 is added to calculate the absolute due date. Finally, the DATE function is used to convert this value back into DATE format. (In the next topic, you'll see a more straightforward way to do the same thing using durations.)

You might also find these functions useful if you have to work extensively with data stored in timestamp format. Then, you can use the DATE and TIME functions to extract the corresponding components, as figure 1-27 illustrates.

You can also create a timestamp item by combining a date item and a time item with the TIMESTAMP function. When you use this function, the microsecond component of the timestamp is set to zero, as figure 1-28 shows.

Terms

special register
column function
aggregate function
scalar function

argument
function name

DATE(expression)

Returns a date item in default format. The result may be null. *Expression* can be:

- a date.

- a timestamp.

- a positive integer representing the number of elapsed days since December 31, 0000.

- a 10-character string representation of a date (yyyy-mm-dd) where yyyy represents the year, mm represents the month, and dd represents the day.

- a 7-character string representation of a date (yyyyddd) where yyyy represents the year and ddd represents the day of the year (between 1 and 366).

TIME(expression)

Returns a time item in default format. The result may be null. *Expression* can be:

- a time.

- a timestamp.

- an 8-character string representation of a time (hh.mm.ss) where hh represents the hour, mm represents the minute, and ss represents the second.

TIMESTAMP(expression1[,expression2])

Returns a timestamp item. The result may be null. The TIMESTAMP function operates differently depending on whether you specify one argument or two.

If you specify only *expression1*, it can be:

- a timestamp.

- an 26-character string representation of a timestamp (yyyy-mm-dd-hh.mm.ss.mmmmmm).

- a 14-character string representation of a timestamp (yyyymmddhhmmss); with this form, the timestamp the function produces contains zero for its microsecond component.

If you specify both *expression1* and *expression2*:

- *Expression1* must be a date or a string representation of a date, and *expression2* must be a time or a string representation of a time; with this form, the timestamp the function produces contains zero for its microsecond component.

Figure 1-26   Scalar functions for creating a date, time, or timestamp item

SQL statement

```
    .
    .
SELECT CURRENT TIMESTAMP,
       DATE(CURRENT TIMESTAMP),
       TIME(CURRENT TIMESTAMP)
    .
    .
```

Results table

1	2	3
1991-07-16-15.51.29.484811	1991-07-16	15.51.29

Figure 1-27   A SELECT statement that uses the DATE and TIME functions to process a timestamp

SQL statement

```
    .
    .
SELECT CURRENT TIMESTAMP,
       CURRENT DATE,
       CURRENT TIME,
       TIMESTAMP(CURRENT DATE,CURRENT TIME)
    .
    .
```

Results table

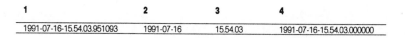

1	2	3	4
1991-07-16-15.54.03.951093	1991-07-16	15.54.03	1991-07-16-15.54.03.000000

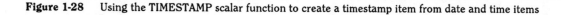

Figure 1-28   Using the TIMESTAMP scalar function to create a timestamp item from date and time items

Objectives

1. Code an expression in a SELECT that uses CURRENT DATE, CURRENT TIME, or CURRENT TIMESTAMP.

2. Code an expression in a SELECT that uses the CHAR scalar function to convert the character representation of a date or time item to another format.

3. Code an expression in a SELECT that uses the DAYS scalar function to determine the absolute age of a date item.

4. Code an expression in a SELECT that uses the YEAR, MONTH, DAY, HOUR, MINUTE, SECOND, or MICROSECOND function to extract a numeric component from a date, time, or timestamp item.

5. Code an expression in a SELECT that uses the DATE, TIME, or TIMESTAMP function to convert appropriate data to a format compatible with a date, time, or timestamp item.

Topic 4   How to use date and time data in expressions

In addition to manipulating dates and times with the scalar functions I presented in topic 3, you can also use dates and times directly in some arithmetic operations. In this topic, I'll show you how. I assume that you're already familiar with the date and time scalar functions. So if you haven't read topic 3 yet, you should read it before you start this topic.

Valid operations using dates and times

Figure 1-29 shows the ways you can use dates and times in arithmetic operations. I want you to notice two things here. First, you can use dates and times only in addition and subtraction operations. It doesn't make sense to use a date or time in a multiplication or division operation, and DB2 won't let you.

Second, all of the valid arithmetic operations with dates and times involve a *duration*. A duration is simply an elapsed period, or interval, of time. The duration is either one of the components of the operation or the result of it.

As you can see in figure 1-29, the only expressions where you can specify two date or time items are subtraction operations, and their results are durations. If you think about that, it makes sense. The difference between two dates (or times) is the amount of elapsed time, or the duration, between them.

In all of the other valid operations, a duration is part of the expression, and the result is a date or time item. That makes sense too. For example, if you add an elapsed period of time to a date or time, you get another date or time.

Obviously, durations are central to expressions that involve dates and times. You must understand durations thoroughly to use dates and times in arithmetic operations. So, I'd like to take a closer look at them.

Labeled and decimal durations

DB2 can work with two different kinds of durations. One kind is a *labeled duration*. The other kind, a *decimal duration*, has two subtypes: *date duration* and *time duration*. When DB2 produces a duration as the result of an expression, it produces a decimal duration. When you specify a duration in

Addition operations	Result format
date + duration	date
time + duration	time
timestamp + duration	timestamp

Subtraction operations	Result format
date − duration	date
time − duration	time
timestamp − duration	timestamp
date − date	duration
time − time	duration

Figure 1-29   Acceptable arithmetic operations involving date and time data

an expression, it can be either a labeled duration or one of the decimal durations.

Labeled durations use numbers combined with special keywords that represent units of time measurement. Figure 1-30 shows these keywords. They're valid only in expressions with date or time items. For example, you can code an expression like

```
INVDATE + 3 MONTHS
```

Here, "3 MONTHS" is a labeled duration. As figure 1-29 indicates, the result of this expression will be a date item. (By the way, the keywords for labeled durations have nothing to do with the YEAR, MONTH, DAY, HOUR, MINUTE, SECOND, and MICROSECOND scalar functions I introduced in figure 1-22 in topic 3.)

As I mentioned earlier, an expression that produces a duration (by subtracting either a date from a date or a time from a time), produces one of the decimal duration types. If the values in the expression are dates, the result is a date duration. If the values are times, the result is a time duration.

DB2 uses formats compatible with its DECIMAL data type for time and date durations. In fact, if you need to store a duration in a table, you use a DECIMAL column. If you use a DECIMAL item in the context of a duration, DB2 interprets it as a duration. If you need to retrieve a duration into a COBOL program, you do it through a packed-decimal host variable (usage

n YEAR	or	*n* YEARS
n MONTH	or	*n* MONTHS
n DAY	or	*n* DAYS
n HOUR	or	*n* HOURS
n MINUTE	or	*n* MINUTES
n SECOND	or	*n* SECONDS
n MICROSECOND	or	*n* MICROSECONDS

Figure 1-30   How to code durations as labeled values

COMP-3). Figure 1-31 shows how you can define COBOL and DB2 data items for date and time durations, presents their formats, and offers examples of each.

As you can see in figure 1-31, a decimal representation of a date duration is not a single value, but really three different values all represented in one item. The first four positions in a date duration contain the number of years, the next two contain the number of months, and the last two contain the number of days.

Figure 1-31 presents several examples of date durations. For instance, if a date duration's decimal value is 00000115, DB2 interprets it as no years (0000 in the first through fourth positions), 1 month (01 in the fifth and sixth positions), and 15 days (15 in the last two positions). Don't make the mistake of interpreting this duration as 115 days.

DB2 handles time durations through a DECIMAL data element that has six decimal positions. The first two positions represent the number of hours in the time duration, the next two represent the number of minutes, and the last two represent the number of seconds. Note that a DB2 time duration doesn't have a microsecond component. If you use a time duration in an expression that affects a timestamp, the number of microseconds in the duration is considered to be zero.

Even though date and time durations have decimal formats, you probably shouldn't use them in standard arithmetic. If you do, you may destroy the relationship among the three values each contains. For example, if a date duration contains the value 00010628 (1 year, 6 months, and 28 days) and you add 7 to it to increase the duration by one week, the result is 00010635 (1 year, 6 months, and 35 days). But this doesn't make sense because 35 days is more than one month.

Because durations have a structure that lets DB2 identify their components, you can specify them as the operands of some of the functions I presented in topic 3. In figure 1-22 in that topic, I introduced the YEAR,

Date duration

DB2 column definition	DEC(8,0)
COBOL host variable	PIC S9(8) COMP-3
Form	yyyymmdd
Examples	00000000 = 0 years, 0 months, 0 days
	00000100 = 0 years, 1 month, 0 days
	00000115 = 0 years, 1 month, 15 days
	00000600 = 0 years, 6 months, 0 days
	00010000 = 1 year, 0 months, 0 days
	00020600 = 2 years, 6 months, 0 days

Time duration

DB2 column definition	DEC(6,0)
COBOL host variable	PIC S9(6) COMP-3
Form	hhmmss
Examples	000000 = 0 hours, 0 minutes, 0 seconds
	000130 = 0 hours, 1 minute, 30 seconds
	120000 = 12 hours, 0 minutes, 0 seconds

Figure 1-31   Durations represented as decimal values

MONTH, DAY, HOUR, MINUTE, and SECOND functions. Each lets you specify a duration as its argument and returns the component you specify as a binary fullword. You can specify a date duration as the argument for the MONTH, DAY or YEAR function. And you can specify a time duration as the argument for the HOUR, MINUTE, or SECOND function.

How to use expressions that operate on dates and times in column specifications

You can use an arithmetic expression that operates on a date or time item in a column specification in a SELECT statement. Figure 1-32, for example, shows a SELECT that produces a list of invoices with the age of each invoice (in weeks) shown in the fourth column of its results table. This column was produced by a complicated column specification that's based on the expression

CURRENT DATE - INVDATE

SQL statement

```
.
.
SELECT INVNO,
       INVCUST,
       INVDATE,
       INTEGER ((   DAY(CURRENT DATE - INVDATE)) / 7      ) +
              ((MONTH(CURRENT DATE - INVDATE)) * 52/12) +
              (( YEAR(CURRENT DATE - INVDATE)) * 52      ),
       ' WEEKS OLD'
       FROM MMADBV.INV
       ORDER BY 4 DESC
.
.
```

Results table

INVNO	INVCUST	INVDATE	4	5
062309	400011	1990-12-22	29	WEEKS OLD
062308	400012	1990-12-22	29	WEEKS OLD
062311	400014	1991-02-22	20	WEEKS OLD
062310	400011	1991-02-22	20	WEEKS OLD
062312	400002	1991-02-22	20	WEEKS OLD
062314	400003	1991-03-14	17	WEEKS OLD
062313	400011	1991-03-14	17	WEEKS OLD
062316	400010	1991-03-14	17	WEEKS OLD
062315	400004	1991-03-14	17	WEEKS OLD
062317	400011	1991-03-17	17	WEEKS OLD
062320	400015	1991-03-17	17	WEEKS OLD
062319	400015	1991-03-17	17	WEEKS OLD
062318	400012	1991-03-17	17	WEEKS OLD
062321	400001	1991-04-03	15	WEEKS OLD
062322	400014	1991-04-03	15	WEEKS OLD
062323	400011	1991-04-11	14	WEEKS OLD
062324	400014	1991-04-14	13	WEEKS OLD
062325	400002	1991-04-17	13	WEEKS OLD
062326	400011	1991-04-20	12	WEEKS OLD
062327	400003	1991-04-23	11	WEEKS OLD
062328	400004	1991-04-24	11	WEEKS OLD
062329	400010	1991-04-29	10	WEEKS OLD
062330	400011	1991-04-30	10	WEEKS OLD
062331	400012	1991-05-07	9	WEEKS OLD
062332	400013	1991-05-09	9	WEEKS OLD
062333	400015	1991-05-17	8	WEEKS OLD

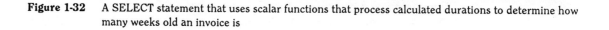

Figure 1-32   A SELECT statement that uses scalar functions that process calculated durations to determine how many weeks old an invoice is

This expression appears three times in the SELECT, each time as the argument of one of the scalar functions DAY, MONTH, and YEAR. These functions extract the elements of the duration that was calculated by the expression and return them as integers that can be used in arithmetic

```
     .
     .
     .
SELECT INVNO,
       INVCUST,
       INVDATE,
       INTEGER ((DAYS(CURRENT DATE) - DAYS(INVDATE)) / 7),
       ' WEEKS OLD'
    FROM MMADBV.INV
     .
     .
     .
```

Figure 1-33   A SELECT statement that uses the DAYS function in an expression to determine how many weeks old an invoice is

operations. The results of the DAY, MONTH, and YEAR functions are used in simple expressions that calculate the number of weeks represented by the days, months, and years components of the duration. Finally, those values are added, and the INTEGER function truncates any decimal part of the sum.

The statement in figure 1-32 illustrates how you can use dates in expressions. In addition, it shows how you can use durations as well as dates and times as the arguments of some of the scalar functions I showed you in topic 3. However, the statement is cumbersome.

Figure 1-33 shows a simpler SELECT statement that produces a results table similar to the one in figure 1-32. Here, I applied the DAYS function to the CURRENT DATE and INVDATE values to determine the number of absolute elapsed days each represents. Then, I subtracted one of the DAYS values from the other to determine how many days separate the two. Last, to determine the number of elapsed weeks between the two dates, I divided that difference by seven.

How to use expressions that operate on dates and times in selection conditions

You can also code predicates containing expressions that manipulate date and time items. For example, figure 1-34 presents a SELECT statement that uses labeled durations in its WHERE clause to retrieve rows from the INV table that are between a year and a year and a month old.

This is like the statement I presented in figure 1-25 in topic 3 that uses the MONTH and YEAR scalar functions to retrieve rows from the current month in the previous year. However, that's a little different from retrieving rows that are between one year and one year and one month old. Imagine

```
   .
   .
   .
SELECT *
   FROM MMADBV.INV
   WHERE INVDATE BETWEEN (CURRENT DATE - 1 YEAR - 1 MONTH)
                     AND (CURRENT DATE - 1 YEAR)
   .
   .
```

Figure 1-34   A SELECT statement that uses labeled durations in expressions in the WHERE clause to retrieve rows from the INV table that are between one year and one year and one month old

that the statements in figures 1-25 and 1-35 were executed on July 15, 1991. The SELECT in figure 1-25 would return invoices with dates between 1990-07-01 and 1990-07-31. In contrast, the one in figure 1-34 would return invoices with dates between 1990-06-15 and 1990-07-15.

Also, notice that you can use more than one labeled duration in an expression. In the first expression in this statement's WHERE clause, I coded one labeled duration with the YEAR keyword and a second with the MONTH keyword.

Figure 1-35 presents another example of a statement that uses expressions that operate on dates in predicates. This example is a complex SQL statement that uses UNIONs to combine the results tables generated by four SELECTs. Each SELECT uses one or two arithmetic expressions involving dates in its WHERE clause. This example illustrates how you might select data for an accounting report called an aged trial balance. In an aged-trial-balance report, outstanding accounts receivable items are grouped and listed by age.

In an application program, you probably would adopt a different approach to this problem. You might code a simpler SELECT that retrieves all the invoices ordered by date, then handle control breaks related to age through COBOL rather than SQL. However this example illustrates how extensively you can use expressions involving dates and times in your SQL statements. And if you're working in an ad hoc environment, such as through QMF, the approach figure 1-35 illustrates would be appropriate.

Exceptional situations in date and time arithmetic operations

Date and time arithmetic works smoothly except when you're dealing with a few exceptional situations. For date operations, those situations involve months that have different numbers of days. For example, suppose the

SQL statement

```
.
.
     SELECT 'OVER 90 DAYS ',INVNO,INVDATE,INVTOTAL,INVCUST
        FROM MMADBV.INV
        WHERE INVDATE < CURRENT DATE - 90 DAYS
UNION ALL
     SELECT '75 - 90 DAYS ',INVNO,INVDATE,INVTOTAL,INVCUST
        FROM MMADBV.INV
        WHERE (INVDATE >= CURRENT DATE - 90 DAYS) AND
              (INVDATE <   CURRENT DATE - 75 DAYS)
UNION ALL
     SELECT '60 - 75 DAYS ',INVNO,INVDATE,INVTOTAL,INVCUST
        FROM MMADBV.INV
        WHERE (INVDATE >= CURRENT DATE - 75 DAYS) AND
              (INVDATE <   CURRENT DATE - 60 DAYS)
UNION ALL
     SELECT '30 - 60 DAYS ',INVNO,INVDATE,INVTOTAL,INVCUST
        FROM MMADBV.INV
        WHERE (INVDATE >= CURRENT DATE - 60 DAYS) AND
              (INVDATE <   CURRENT DATE - 30 DAYS)
ORDER BY 3
.
.
```

Results table

1	INVNO	INVDATE	INVTOTAL	INVCUST
OVER 90 DAYS	062308	1990-12-22	204.45	400012
OVER 90 DAYS	062309	1990-12-22	15.00	400011
OVER 90 DAYS	062310	1991-02-22	147.50	400011
OVER 90 DAYS	062311	1991-02-22	193.89	400014
OVER 90 DAYS	062312	1991-02-22	173.07	400002
OVER 90 DAYS	062313	1991-03-14	22.50	400011
OVER 90 DAYS	062314	1991-03-14	149.80	400003
OVER 90 DAYS	062315	1991-03-14	181.42	400004
OVER 90 DAYS	062316	1991-03-14	147.50	400010
OVER 90 DAYS	062317	1991-03-17	298.00	400011
OVER 90 DAYS	062318	1991-03-17	199.99	400012
OVER 90 DAYS	062319	1991-03-17	181.42	400015
OVER 90 DAYS	062320	1991-03-17	3405.00	400015
OVER 90 DAYS	062321	1991-04-03	219.60	400001
OVER 90 DAYS	062322	1991-04-03	16.05	400014
OVER 90 DAYS	062323	1991-04-11	949.00	400011
OVER 90 DAYS	062324	1991-04-14	193.89	400014
OVER 90 DAYS	062325	1991-04-17	147.50	400002
75 - 90 DAYS	062326	1991-04-20	181.42	400011
75 - 90 DAYS	062327	1991-04-23	221.50	400003
75 - 90 DAYS	062328	1991-04-24	181.42	400004
75 - 90 DAYS	062329	1991-04-29	147.50	400010
75 - 90 DAYS	062330	1991-04-30	2309.00	400011
60 - 75 DAYS	062331	1991-05-07	178.23	400012
60 - 75 DAYS	062332	1991-05-09	178.23	400013
60 - 75 DAYS	062333	1991-05-17	178.23	400015

Figure 1-35   A complex statement that uses expressions with labeled durations in its selection conditions

CURRENT DATE is 1991-07-31. Then you might expect the result of the expression

```
CURRENT DATE - 1 MONTH
```

to be 1991-06-31. But that date is invalid, because June has only 30 days. So, this expression is evaluated to 1991-06-30. If an arithmetic operation with a date would evaluate to a date that doesn't exist, DB2 uses the last day of the corresponding month in the result.

The same consideration applies in leap years too. For example, the expression

```
'1995-01-31' + 1 MONTH
```

evaluates to 1995-02-28, the last day of the next month. However, the expression

```
'1996-01-31' + 1 MONTH
```

evaluates to 1996-02-29, because 1996 is a leap year, and the 29th is the last day of February in a leap year.

Whenever an expression yields a date result that has been modified because of differing numbers of days in different months, DB2 sets the value of the communication area field SQLWARN6 to W. In the next chapter, I'll describe this and other SQLCA fields.

The only exceptional situation you need to be aware of when you're using time arithmetic has to do with adding 24 hours to a time item. In most cases, you can add 24 HOURS to an item and the result is the same time. The only exception is if you're adding 24 to 00.00.00. Then, the result is 24.00.00. In most situations, this won't present a problem.

Terms

duration
labeled duration
decimal duration
date duration
time duration

Objectives

1. List the arithmetic operations that are valid for date and time data.

2. Describe the difference between a date or time duration and a labeled duration.

3. Describe the structures of date and time durations.

4. Explain why you probably shouldn't use date and time durations in standard arithmetic expressions.

5. Code a SELECT that uses an expression that does date or time arithmetic in a column specification.

6. Code a SELECT that uses an expression that does date or time arithmetic in a selection condition.

Chapter 2

How to use advanced error-handling features

To work with DB2 effectively, your programs need to monitor the success of the SQL statements they issue and respond appropriately to unusual conditions. In *Part 1: An Introductory Course*, I described how you can do that by checking the return code DB2 stores in the SQLCODE field of its communication area after it executes each statement. As you may recall, DB2 sets the value of SQLCODE to zero to report that a statement executed successfully. If a statement isn't successful, DB2 sets the value of SQLCODE to a non-zero value, and that value is usually negative. The specific action your program should take to handle a non-zero return code depends on your application and the error code value. For most DB2 COBOL programs, this approach to error handling is sufficient. If it's sufficient for you, you may be able to skip this chapter. However, some applications, and some shops' standards, call for more.

In this chapter, I'll present additional error-handling features and techniques you may need to know. First, I'll describe the fields in the SQL communication area that contain useful information you may need to check. Then, I'll show you how to use DSNTIAR, a routine your programs can call to produce formatted error messages with more detail than the SQLCODE field provides by itself. Next, I'll show you how to use the SQL WHENEVER statement to control error processing. And finally, I'll present a sample program that uses these techniques.

How to use data in the fields in the SQL communication area

Figure 2-1 shows the COBOL code for the SQL communication area, the SQLCA. The precompiler supplies this code in response to the statement

```
INCLUDE SQLCA
```

Although I showed you the SQLCA in *Part 1: An Introductory Course*, I discussed only one part of it in any detail: SQLCODE. In addition to SQLCODE, you may need to evaluate the contents of a few other SQLCA fields. I've shaded the ones I think you may find important.

Even if you don't need to use all of the SQLCA fields, you may still be curious about what they are. As a result, I've listed all of them in figure 2-2 along with a brief description of their contents and an indication of their value in a COBOL program. Here again, I've shaded the ones you're most likely to need.

In addition to SQLCODE, the SQLCA fields you should know about are SQLERRD(3) and the SQLWARN fields. DB2 uses these fields to report a handful of unusual conditions, none of which it considers an error. So, depending on your application, you may need to check these fields in addition to SQLCODE.

DB2's primary use of SQLERRD is to pass technical diagnostic information to a program. SQLERRD is an array of six fullword items. Each has the same COBOL description as SQLCODE: PIC S9(9) USAGE COMP-4. (COBOL COMP-4 usage is the same as COMP.) Only one of these fullwords, the third of the six, contains information you may find useful. After an INSERT, DELETE, or UPDATE statement, SQLERRD(3) contains the number of rows the statement affected. You can then use that value to verify the operation of the statement.

The other communication area fields you might use are the warning fields. These warning fields are all subordinate to the group item SQLWARN. DB2 sets the values of these indicator fields to W to report certain kinds of unusual conditions. You can check SQLWARN0 to find out if DB2 set any of the *other* warning fields to signal an error. If the value of SQLWARN0 isn't W, neither is the value of any of the other SQLWARN fields, and there's no need to examine them individually. However, if the

```
01  SQLCA.
    05 SQLCAID    PIC X(8).
    05 SQLCABC    PIC S9(9) COMP-4.
    05 SQLCODE    PIC S9(9) COMP-4.
    05 SQLERRM.
       49 SQLERRML PIC S9(4) COMP-4.
       49 SQLERRMC PIC X(70).
    05 SQLERRP    PIC X(8).
    05 SQLERRD    OCCURS 6 TIMES
                  PIC S9(9) COMP-4.
    05 SQLWARN.
       10 SQLWARN0 PIC X.
       10 SQLWARN1 PIC X.
       10 SQLWARN2 PIC X.
       10 SQLWARN3 PIC X.
       10 SQLWARN4 PIC X.
       10 SQLWARN5 PIC X.
       10 SQLWARN6 PIC X.
       10 SQLWARN7 PIC X.
    05 SQLEXT     PIC X(8).
```

Figure 2-1   COBOL code for the SQL communication area

value of SQLWARN0 is W, so is the value of one of the other SQLWARN fields. In that case, your program may need to check them.

SQLWARN1 contains W if a column's contents had to be truncated when DB2 moved them into a host variable. If you use current DCLGEN definitions for host variables, you shouldn't encounter this error because the host variables DCLGEN defines are always the right size. Even if this error does occur, it may not be a real problem, depending on your application requirements.

SQLWARN2 contains W if some of the rows weren't considered by a column function because the column being processed contained null values. This is likely to be significant only for the AVG column function. You can refer back to *Part 1: An Introductory Course* for more information about column functions (chapter 6) and nulls (chapter 9).

DB2 sets SQLWARN3's value to W if the number of host variables a statement names and the number of columns the statement processes differ. This can happen when you code statements that don't explicitly name all of the columns they process, such as SELECT * or INSERT without a list of column names. If you avoid these constructs, this probably isn't something you have to worry about.

SQLWARN4 applies only to UPDATE or DELETE statements that are processed dynamically. (In chapter 3, I'll describe dynamic SQL.) SQLWARN4's value is set to W if a dynamically processed UPDATE or

SQLCA field	Data type	Description	Value in COBOL
SQLCAID	8-byte string	Text string that identifies the SQLCA	None
SQLCABC	Binary fullword	Length of the entire SQLCA	None
SQLCODE	Binary fullword	SQL return code	Essential
SQLERRM	Variable-length string	Data items that are substituted in error messages	None
SQLERRML	Binary halfword	Length of data in SQLERRM	None
SQLERRMC	70-byte string	Text component for SQLERRM	None
SQLERRP	8-byte string	DB2 diagnostic information	None
SQLERRD(1)	Binary fullword	Error code from DB2's Relational Data System	None
SQLERRD(2)	Binary fullword	Error code from DB2's Data Manager	None
SQLERRD(3)	Binary fullword	Number of rows affected by an INSERT, DELETE, or UPDATE statement	May be important
SQLERRD(4)	Binary fullword	Estimate of resources required for a prepared SQL statement	Almost none
SQLERRD(5)	Binary fullword	Location of an SQL error in a statement processed dynamically	Almost none
SQLERRD(6)	Binary fullword	Error code from DB2's Buffer Manager	None
SQLWARN0	1-byte string	Contains W if any other WARN field contains W	May be important
SQLWARN1	1-byte string	Contains W if a string was truncated when stored in a host variable	May be important
SQLWARN2	1-byte string	Contains W if null values were excluded during the processing of a column function	May be important
SQLWARN3	1-byte string	Contains W if the number of columns and host variables don't match	May be important
SQLWARN4	1-byte string	Contains W if an UPDATE or DELETE statement to be issued dynamically doesn't have a WHERE clause	May be important
SQLWARN5	1-byte string	Contains W if the SQL statement is appropriate only for SQL/DS	Almost none
SQLWARN6	1-byte string	Contains W if an arithmetic operation produces an unusual date or timestamp	May be important
SQLWARN7	1-byte string	Not in use (reserved)	None
SQLEXT	8-byte string	Not in use (reserved)	None

Figure 2-2   SQLCA fields

Procedure Division

```
CALL "DSNTIAR" USING SQLCA
                     ERROR-MESSAGE
                     ERROR-LINE-LENGTH.
```

Working-Storage Section

```
*
 01  ERROR-MESSAGE.
*
     05  ERROR-MESSAGE-LENGTH          PIC S9(4)  COMP
                                                  VALUE +640.
     05  ERROR-MESSAGE-LINE            PIC X(80)
                                       OCCURS 8 TIMES
                                       INDEXED BY EML-INDEX.
*
 01  ERROR-LINE-LENGTH                 PIC S9(9)  COMP
                                                  VALUE +80.
*
```

Figure 2-3   Elements you can include in a COBOL program to use DB2's DSNTIAR routine

DELETE doesn't include a WHERE clause. Unless you're using dynamic SQL and you need to test for this condition, you won't want to evaluate SQLWARN4.

Finally, SQLWARN6 is set to W if an arithmetic expression produces a date or timestamp item whose value had to be adjusted as a result of differing numbers of days in different months. If your SQL statements don't do date arithmetic, you don't need to worry about this problem. For more information about date arithmetic, refer to topic 4 in chapter 1.

How to use the DSNTIAR error-reporting routine

To deal with error conditions, you may be expected to use *DSNTIAR*, a standard error-reporting routine IBM supplies as a part of DB2. DSNTIAR takes data from the communication area, adds explanatory text, and structures it in a more readable form. Figure 2-3 shows an example of the Procedure Division and Working-Storage Section code that you can include in your programs to use DSNTIAR.

The top section of the figure shows a CALL statement that invokes DSNTIAR. It requires three arguments. The first argument is the name of the SQL communication area itself, SQLCA. The second argument

(ERROR-MESSAGE in figure 2-3) identifies the data area where you want DSNTIAR to return the formatted error message it creates. The third argument (ERROR-LINE-LENGTH in figure 2-3) is a numeric item that contains the length of the individual text lines the routine should return.

DSNTIAR divides all of the text for a message (which can vary in length) into as many as eight lines. The length of each of these lines is the value you supply for the third argument. In the example in figure 2-3, I specified 80 as the line-length value on the third argument, so the maximum length of an eight-line message DSNTIAR can return to my program is 640 characters.

The third argument must be a binary fullword (PIC S9(9) COMP), and the value you specify for it must be between 72 and 240. A line length of 79 or 80 is appropriate for display at a terminal. If you intend to print the message, a line length of 120 or 132 may be more appropriate. And if you intend to save the message on DASD, the maximum length of 240 may be your best choice. If your shop expects you to use DSNTIAR, it probably has a standard for the line-length value you should use.

The size of the data area you need to provide for DSNTIAR depends on the line length you select. Because the routine can return up to eight lines, you need to provide a data area that's eight times the size of a single line.

DSNTIAR uses a variable-length field as its data area. So, your definition of the data area must have two parts: a length component and a data component. The length component is first. It's a binary halfword item (PIC S9(4) COMP), and its value is the length of the data component. In figure 2-3, I called the length component ERROR-MESSAGE-LENGTH and assigned a value of +640 to it.

Depending on your program or shop requirements, you may be able to code the description of the data component of this variable-length field as a single, long alphanumeric field with the same number of characters you specified for the length component (640 in this example). That will probably be appropriate if you want to store the information DSNTIAR returns in a log data set. However, if you want to print or display the message, you need to be able to identify the formatted lines it contains. In figure 2-3, I used an eight-element table in the definition of the data area. Each element represents one of the eight 80-character lines of the formatted message.

Figure 2-4 shows two examples of the formatted output DSNTIAR produces. As you can see, the output includes more than just the value of SQLCODE and its text meaning. It also contains the values of the SQLERRD fields. But frankly, you don't need most of the information in DSNTIAR's output. When a statement isn't successful for any but obvious reasons, it's a problem for your DBA to resolve.

DSNTIAR output after a successful SELECT statement

```
DSNT400I SQLCODE = 000,  SUCCESSFUL EXECUTION
DSNT416I SQLERRD = 110  0  0  1  0  0 SQL DIAGNOSTIC INFORMATION
DSNT416I SQLERRD = X'FFFFFF92'  X'00000000'  X'00000000'  X'FFFFFFFF'
         X'00000000'  X'00000000'
```

DSNTIAR output after an unsuccessful SELECT statement

```
DSNT404I SQLCODE = 100, NOT FOUND:  ROW NOT FOUND FOR FETCH, UPDATE,
         OR DELETE, OR THE RESULT OF A QUERY IS AN EMPTY TABLE
DSNT415I SQLERRP = DSNXRFCH SQL PROCEDURE DETECTING ERROR
DSNT416I SQLERRD = 110  0  0  1  0  0 SQL DIAGNOSTIC INFORMATION
DSNT416I SQLERRD = X'FFFFFF92'  X'00000000'  X'00000000'  X'FFFFFFFF'
         X'00000000'  X'00000000' SQL DIAGNOSTIC INFORMATION
```

Figure 2-4   Formatted error-reporting output from the DSNTIAR routine

How to use the WHENEVER statement to specify global error-processing actions

In *Part 1: An Introductory Course,* I showed you how to use an IF statement after each SQL action statement to evaluate SQLCODE to make sure the statement was successful. And in most cases, that's the best way to check for errors in your programs. But DB2 also provides another method you may find useful from time to time: the WHENEVER statement. This statement lets you specify an action that a program should take when certain DB2 conditions arise. After you've issued the WHENEVER statement, it remains in effect. If any subsequent SQL statement generates a condition for which you've provided a WHENEVER statement, the condition will be handled with the response you specified.

Unfortunately, the WHENEVER statement has some problems that reduce its usefulness. To begin with, if you take a look at the syntax of WHENEVER in figure 2-5, you'll see that your options are limited. You can direct DB2 to trap three different conditions: SQLERROR, SQLWARNING, and NOT FOUND. Each corresponds to different values that can be returned in SQLCODE, as figure 2-5 shows. On first impression, it might seem like the range of options WHENEVER provides would make it easy for you to handle anything that could go wrong when you execute a DB2 statement. And for the simplest of programs, that's true.

However, consider the two options WHENEVER lets you code to specify what should happen when an exceptional condition occurs: CONTINUE and GOTO. CONTINUE causes your program to go on after the specified

The SQL WHENEVER statement

```
EXEC SQL
    WHENEVER  {SQLERROR  } {{GOTO }  paragraph-name}
              {SQLWARNING} {{GO TO}                 }
              {NOT FOUND } { CONTINUE              }
END-EXEC.
```

Explanation

SQLERROR   Specifies that the indicated action should be taken if SQLCODE has a negative value.

SQLWARNING   Specifies that the indicated action should be taken if SQLCODE has any positive value other than
                    +100 or if the value of SQLWARN0 is W.

NOT FOUND   Specifies that the indicated action should be taken if SQLCODE's value is +100.

{GOTO }   Specifies that the program should branch to *paragraph-name*.
{GO TO} paragraph-name

CONTINUE   Specifies that program execution should continue uninterrupted.

Figure 2-5   The SQL WHENEVER statement

error occurs as if nothing had happened. The other alternative, GOTO, causes an unconditional branch to a paragraph that deals with the problem. That's a violation of a principle of structured programming.

Even if you're not bothered by that, you'd still find it difficult to resume processing from the point where you were before the WHENEVER statement caused a branch. As a result, the GOTO facility WHENEVER provides is most appropriate for branches to an exit routine that processes the error and then ends the program. If that's unsatisfactory, you have to code your program so it keeps track of where it was and what it was doing before the GOTO was executed so it can resume processing there.

Another problem with WHENEVER is that it doesn't discriminate sufficiently between different conditions. The implications of different SQLCODE values, which to WHENEVER are simply "errors," can vary considerably. For example, the error that occurs when a program tries to add a row to a table with a duplicate key value should probably be handled differently than the error that occurs if the program tries to access a table that's damaged or missing. The first condition is something you can expect. Although it's an error from the point of view of DB2, it's not catastrophic and shouldn't cause a program to end. On the other hand, an error like a missing table is drastic and has different implications. So, handling "normal" errors and "abnormal" errors through the WHENEVER facility is a challenge.

Moreover, the way DB2 implements WHENEVER processing has the potential to lead to programming mistakes. That's because WHENEVER is actually a precompiler directive that has an effect on your program's source code. It's not a statement that DB2 processes at the time you execute your program.

When the precompiler encounters a WHENEVER statement, it changes it to a comment. Then, from that point forward in your source code, the precompiler inserts conditional statements in standard COBOL after each SQL statement it encounters to implement the error checking the WHENEVER statement specifies. The precompiler doesn't back up to insert similar statements for SQL statements that precede it.

As long as you're aware of this, it shouldn't be a problem. For simple programs, just code the WHENEVER statements before any action SQL statements your program uses. For more complicated programs that force you to use multiple WHENEVER statements, make sure that you place them immediately before each action SQL statement and that each WHENEVER statement specifies the proper action for that SQL statement.

If you're a CICS programmer, you should take note of the way WHENEVER works. That's because the CICS command HANDLE CONDITION serves a function similar to WHENEVER, and it has a similar syntax. However, unlike WHENEVER, HANDLE CONDITION *is* processed at execution time. So, don't automatically code DB2 WHENEVER statements the same way you code CICS HANDLE CONDITION commands, or they may not have the effect you expect.

Although WHENEVER may present a few problems, some shops have adopted error-processing standards that require programmers to use it. Probably the most common requirement is to use WHENEVER SQLERROR GOTO to specify a paragraph that logs a problem (such as with DSNTIAR), closes open files, and ends the program. If your shop's management insists you take this approach, of course you should. However, if the decision is yours, I suggest that you use the more explicit approach of coding a COBOL IF statement that evaluates SQLCODE after each SQL statement, instead of using the WHENEVER statement.

A maintenance program that uses alternative error-handling techniques

In chapter 8 of *Part 1: An Introductory Course*, I presented two versions of a maintenance program that moves data for paid invoices from a set of active tables to a set of history tables. Here, I'd like to present a third version of that program to illustrate the error-handling features I introduced in this chapter. If you haven't read chapter 8 in the first book, you may not understand all of the SQL in this program. However, I think the error-handling techniques it presents will still be easy to follow.

The tables and the operation of the maintenance program   The maintenance program processes the seven tables whose CREATE TABLE statements are illustrated in figure 2-6. I organized the tables in this figure in two ways. First, I grouped them by the kind of data they contain. The three tables in the first row (INV, INVHIST, and WORKTABLE) contain invoice data, the two in the second row (LITEM and LIHIST) contain line item data related to invoices, and the two in the third row (FINTRAN and FTHIST) contain financial transaction information about invoices. If you examine the figure, you'll see that the tables in each of the three rows have identical structures. For example, all three of the invoice tables have the same number, type, and sequence of columns.

I also grouped the tables in figure 2-6 into columns by their status. The tables in the left column contain active data, and the ones in the middle column contain inactive, or history, data. The table in the right column is a work table that contains data temporarily.

Each row in the INV table represents one sales transaction. The program in this chapter will use two columns from the INV table: INVNO (a unique key column that contains the invoice number) and INVTOTAL (a column that contains the total dollar amount billed for a sale). Although the invoice table contains several other columns, it doesn't contain data for the specific items sold under the invoice or for financial transactions associated with it, like payments and credits. That information is stored in the two other kinds of tables this program uses.

Line item information is stored in the LITEM table. Each product or service that's sold under a given invoice is represented by a different row in the LITEM table. For example, if a customer buys three different items on one invoice, one row in the INV table represents the overall transaction, and three rows in the LITEM table represent its details. The value in the LIINVNO column contains the invoice number, linking the row to the INV table row that "owns" it.

The financial transactions that take place after an invoice is issued are recorded in the FINTRAN table. A new row is added to this table for each financial transaction. Most invoices will have only one row in this table, the row that contains information for one complete payment. However, some customers may make partial payments and have credits or adjustments applied to an invoice. When that happens, each transaction is stored in a

Active tables

Invoice data

```
CREATE TABLE MMADBV.INV
  (INVCUST   CHAR(6)        NOT NULL,
   INVNO     CHAR(6)        NOT NULL,
   INVDATE   DATE           NOT NULL,
   INVSUBT   DECIMAL(9,2)   NOT NULL,
   INVSHIP   DECIMAL(7,2)   NOT NULL,
   INVTAX    DECIMAL(7,2)   NOT NULL,
   INVTOTAL  DECIMAL(9,2)   NOT NULL,
   INVPROM   CHAR(10)       NOT NULL)
   IN DATABASE MMADB
```

Line item data

```
CREATE TABLE MMADBV.LITEM
  (LINVNO    CHAR(6)        NOT NULL,
   LIPCODE   CHAR(10)       NOT NULL,
   LIQTY     DECIMAL(7)     NOT NULL,
   LIPRICE   DECIMAL(7,2)   NOT NULL,
   LIDISC    DECIMAL(7,2)   NOT NULL)
   IN DATABASE MMADB
```

Financial transaction data

```
CREATE TABLE MMADBV.FINTRAN
  (FTINVNO   CHAR(6)        NOT NULL,
   FTDATE    DATE           NOT NULL,
   FTAMT     DECIMAL(9,2)   NOT NULL,
   FTCHECK   CHAR(20),
   FTCCARD   CHAR(20),
   FTEXP     CHAR(5),
   FTNOTE    VARCHAR(254))
   IN DATABASE MMADB
```

History tables

```
CREATE TABLE MMADBV.INVHIST
  (INVCUST   CHAR(6)        NOT NULL,
   INVNO     CHAR(6)        NOT NULL,
   INVDATE   DATE           NOT NULL,
   INVSUBT   DECIMAL(9,2)   NOT NULL,
   INVSHIP   DECIMAL(7,2)   NOT NULL,
   INVTAX    DECIMAL(7,2)   NOT NULL,
   INVTOTAL  DECIMAL(9,2)   NOT NULL,
   INVPROM   CHAR(10)       NOT NULL)
   IN DATABASE MMADB
```

```
CREATE TABLE MMADBV.LIHIST
  (LINVNO    CHAR(6)        NOT NULL,
   LIPCODE   CHAR(10)       NOT NULL,
   LIQTY     DECIMAL(7)     NOT NULL,
   LIPRICE   DECIMAL(7,2)   NOT NULL,
   LIDISC    DECIMAL(7,2)   NOT NULL)
   IN DATABASE MMADB
```

```
CREATE TABLE MMADBV.FTHIST
  (FTINVNO   CHAR(6)        NOT NULL,
   FTDATE    DATE           NOT NULL,
   FTAMT     DECIMAL(9,2)   NOT NULL,
   FTCHECK   CHAR(20),
   FTCCARD   CHAR(20),
   FTEXP     CHAR(5),
   FTNOTE    VARCHAR(254))
   IN DATABASE MMADB
```

Work table

```
CREATE TABLE MMADBV.WORKTABLE
  (INVCUST   CHAR(6)        NOT NULL,
   INVNO     CHAR(6)        NOT NULL,
   INVDATE   DATE           NOT NULL,
   INVSUBT   DECIMAL(9,2)   NOT NULL,
   INVSHIP   DECIMAL(7,2)   NOT NULL,
   INVTAX    DECIMAL(7,2)   NOT NULL,
   INVTOTAL  DECIMAL(9,2)   NOT NULL,
   INVPROM   CHAR(10)       NOT NULL)
   IN DATABASE MMADB
```

Figure 2-6   The CREATE TABLE statements for the seven tables processed by version 3 of the maintenance program

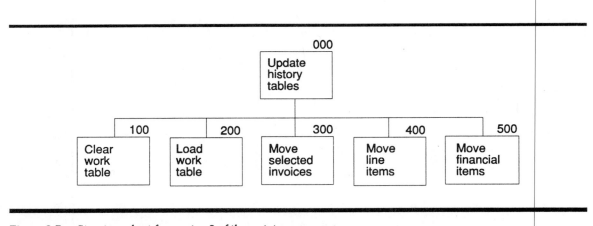

Figure 2-7   Structure chart for version 3 of the maintenance program

separate row. The two columns in this table that the program refers to are
FTINVNO and FTAMT. The FTINVNO column links each transaction row to
a row in the INV table, and the FTAMT column contains the dollar amount
of the transaction.

When the FTAMT column value in every row in the FINTRAN table for
a particular invoice add up to the INVTOTAL column value in that invoice's
INV table row, the invoice has been paid. That's where the maintenance program comes in. It moves the row for each paid invoice from the current
invoice table to the invoice history table, INVHIST. At the same time, it
moves all of the rows in the LITEM and FINTRAN tables associated with
that invoice to their related history tables, LIHIST and FTHIST.

The design and source code for the maintenance program   Figures 2-7
and 2-8 present the program structure chart and COBOL source code for
this version of the maintenance program. The structure chart in figure 2-7
reflects the steps the program goes through as it updates the tables. Each
of the modules subordinate to module 000 issues one or two SQL statements to insert or delete rows from the affected tables.

The program begins by preparing a temporary work table that contains
invoice data for all paid invoices. First, module 100 issues a simple
DELETE statement to clear WORKTABLE. Then, module 200 does a mass
insert to copy rows for paid invoices to it from the INV table. The other
SQL statements in the program will use this table to determine which rows
need to be moved from active tables to history tables.

Modules 300, 400, and 500 each contain a pair of SQL statements to
process invoice, line item, or financial transaction rows. The first statement
in each pair is an INSERT statement that does a mass insert of selected

rows into one of the history tables. The second statement in each pair is a DELETE statement that removes those same rows from the active table. The rows that these statements process are those associated with invoice numbers represented by rows in WORKTABLE.

These SQL statements depend on subqueries that are based on WORKTABLE. If you want to refresh your memory about subqueries and study the first two versions of this program, you can turn back to chapter 8 in *Part 1: An Introductory Course*. Here, though, I'd like to emphasize the error-handling techniques this version of the program illustrates. In the source code in figure 2-8, I've shaded the error-handling elements I especially want you to notice.

First, page through the Procedure Division. Notice that I didn't explicitly code conditions after each SQL statement to check the contents of SQLCODE. That's because I used WHENEVER statements to handle error processing. As you can see, the modules that issue SQL statements are clean and simple. (If you read chapter 8 in the first book, you may recall that much of the code in the first versions of this program was just for error checking.)

As you page through the program, notice that instead of coding conditions after each SQL statement, I coded a DISPLAY statement that uses one of the values in the SQLCA, SQLERRD(3). After each statement, SQL reports the number of rows it changed in that SQLCA field. So, these DISPLAY statements provide a running progress report on the program's actions.

As I mentioned earlier, this program takes care of error handling with WHENEVER statements. I coded them at the start of the program's Procedure Division. As a result, they apply to all of the SQL statements that follow.

The first WHENEVER statement specifies what the program should do when it encounters the NOT FOUND condition for one of the tables it processes. In this program, NOT FOUND means that one of the tables contained no rows. Although that's not likely, it is possible, and it wouldn't necessarily be due to an error. So, on this statement, I coded CONTINUE.

Because a program continues processing after a DB2 error unless there is a statement to tell it to do otherwise, I didn't need to code the first WHENEVER statement in the program in figure 2-8. However, in programs that use multiple WHENEVER statements to deal with the same condition, you may need to use WHENEVER with CONTINUE to deactivate a previous WHENEVER that specifies a GOTO.

The other two WHENEVER statements specify GOTO actions. For both the SQLERROR and SQLWARNING conditions, the program should branch to the paragraph named 000-STOP-RUN. So, any return codes other than

```
000100 IDENTIFICATION DIVISION.
000200*
000300 PROGRAM-ID.           UPDTHST3.
000400*
000500 ENVIRONMENT DIVISION.
000600*
000700 DATA DIVISION.
000800*
000900 WORKING-STORAGE SECTION.
001000*
001100 01  SWITCH.
001200*
001300     05  UPDATE-SUCCESSFUL-SW    PIC X        VALUE "Y".
001400         88  UPDATE-SUCCESSFUL                VALUE "Y".
001500*
001600 01  ERROR-MESSAGE.
001700*
001800     05  ERROR-MESSAGE-LENGTH    PIC S9(4)    COMP
001900                                              VALUE +640.
002000     05  ERROR-MESSAGE-LINE      PIC X(80)
002100                                 OCCURS 8 TIMES
002200                                 INDEXED BY EML-INDEX.
002300*
002400 01  ERROR-LINE-LENGTH           PIC S9(9)    COMP
002500                                              VALUE +80.
002600*
002700     EXEC SQL
002800         INCLUDE SQLCA
002900     END-EXEC.
003000*
003100 PROCEDURE DIVISION.
003200*
003300 000-UPDATE-HISTORY-TABLES.
003400*
003500     EXEC SQL
003500         WHENEVER NOT FOUND CONTINUE
003700     END-EXEC.
003800*
003900     EXEC SQL
004000         WHENEVER SQLERROR GO TO 000-STOP-RUN
004100     END-EXEC.
004200*
004300     EXEC SQL
004400         WHENEVER SQLWARNING GO TO 000-STOP-RUN
004500     END-EXEC.
```

Figure 2-8   COBOL source code for version 3 of the maintenance program (part 1 of 3)

zero and +100 will cause this program to branch to that paragraph. The
paragraph does some error-processing tasks and then ends the program
with a STOP RUN statement. Notice that, although this paragraph immediately follows module 000, it isn't executed unless one of the WHENEVER

```
004600*
004700        PERFORM 100-CLEAR-WORK-TABLE.
004800        PERFORM 200-LOAD-WORK-TABLE.
004900        PERFORM 300-MOVE-SELECTED-INVOICES.
005000        PERFORM 400-MOVE-LINE-ITEMS.
005100        PERFORM 500-MOVE-FINANCIAL-ITEMS.
005200        DISPLAY "UPDATE COMPLETED SUCCESSFULLY.".
005300        STOP RUN.
005400*
005500 000-STOP-RUN.
005600*
005700        DISPLAY "UPDATE COMPLETED UNSUCCESSFULLY.".
005800        CALL "DSNTIAR" USING SQLCA
005900                             ERROR-MESSAGE
006000                             ERROR-LINE-LENGTH.
006100        DISPLAY ERROR-MESSAGE-LINE(1).
006200        DISPLAY ERROR-MESSAGE-LINE(2).
006300        DISPLAY ERROR-MESSAGE-LINE(3).
006400        DISPLAY ERROR-MESSAGE-LINE(4).
006500        DISPLAY ERROR-MESSAGE-LINE(5).
006600        DISPLAY ERROR-MESSAGE-LINE(6).
006700        DISPLAY ERROR-MESSAGE-LINE(7).
006800        DISPLAY ERROR-MESSAGE-LINE(8).
006900        STOP RUN.
007000*
007100 100-CLEAR-WORK-TABLE.
007200*
007300        EXEC SQL
007400           DELETE FROM MMADBV.WORKTABLE
007500        END-EXEC.
007600        DISPLAY SQLERRD(3) " ROWS DELETED FROM WORK TABLE.".
007700*
007800 200-LOAD-WORK-TABLE.
007900*
008000        EXEC SQL
008100           INSERT INTO MMADBV.WORKTABLE
008200               SELECT *
008300                   FROM  MMADBV.INV INVOICE
008400                   WHERE INVTOTAL =
008500                       (SELECT SUM(FTAMT)
008600                           FROM MMADBV.FINTRAN
008700                           WHERE FTINVNO = INVOICE.INVNO)
008800        END-EXEC.
008900        DISPLAY SQLERRD(3) " ROWS INSERTED IN WORK TABLE.".
009000*
```

Figure 2-8   COBOL source code for version 3 of the maintenance program (part 2 of 3)

statements causes control to branch there in response to an error. That's because during a normal run, the main module, 000-UPDATE-HISTORY-TABLES, ends with its own STOP RUN statement, just before the paragraph 000-STOP-RUN.

```
009100 300-MOVE-SELECTED-INVOICES.
009200*
009300        EXEC SQL
009400            INSERT INTO MMADBV.INVHIST
009500                SELECT *
009600                    FROM  MMADBV.WORKTABLE
009700        END-EXEC.
009800        DISPLAY SQLERRD(3) " ROWS INSERTED IN INVHIST TABLE.".
009900        EXEC SQL
010000            DELETE FROM MMADBV.INV
010100                WHERE INVNO IN
010200                    (SELECT INVNO
010300                        FROM MMADBV.WORKTABLE)
010400        END-EXEC.
010500        DISPLAY SQLERRD(3) " ROWS DELETED FROM INV TABLE.".
010600*
010700 400-MOVE-LINE-ITEMS.
010800*
010900        EXEC SQL
011000            INSERT INTO MMADBV.LIHIST
011100                SELECT *
011200                    FROM  MMADBV.LITEM
011300                    WHERE LIINVNO IN
011400                        (SELECT INVNO
011500                            FROM MMADBV.WORKTABLE)
011600        END-EXEC.
011700        DISPLAY SQLERRD(3) " ROWS INSERTED IN LIHIST TABLE.".
011800        EXEC SQL
011900            DELETE FROM MMADBV.LITEM
012000                WHERE LIINVNO IN
012100                    (SELECT INVNO
012200                        FROM MMADBV.WORKTABLE)
012300        END-EXEC.
012400        DISPLAY SQLERRD(3) " ROWS DELETED FROM LITEM TABLE.".
012500*
012600 500-MOVE-FINANCIAL-ITEMS.
012700*
012800        EXEC SQL
012900            INSERT INTO MMADBV.FTHIST
013000                SELECT *
013100                    FROM  MMADBV.FINTRAN
013200                    WHERE FTINVNO IN
013300                        (SELECT INVNO
013400                            FROM MMADBV.WORKTABLE)
013500        END-EXEC.
013600        DISPLAY SQLERRD(3) " ROWS INSERTED IN FTHIST TABLE.".
013700        EXEC SQL
013800            DELETE FROM MMADBV.FINTRAN
013900                WHERE FTINVNO IN
014000                    (SELECT INVNO
014100                        FROM MMADBV.WORKTABLE)
014200        END-EXEC.
014300        DISPLAY SQLERRD(3) " ROWS DELETED FROM FINTRAN TABLE.".
014400*
```

Figure 2-8   COBOL source code for version 3 of the maintenance program (part 3 of 3)

The paragraph 000-STOP-RUN contains a number of DISPLAY statements. First, it displays a message to report that the program was unable to complete the update. Then, it calls the DSNTIAR routine. This CALL and the Working-Storage fields it references are the same as the ones I showed you in figure 2-3. After control returns to the program from the DSNTIAR routine, the program issues eight DISPLAY statements, one for each of the eight lines of output DSNTIAR can return.

Figure 2-9 shows an example of the kind of output this program might generate during an unsuccessful run. As the display messages at the top of the screen indicate, the program executed normally as it processed the invoice and line item tables. However, when it started to process financial transaction data, it encountered a serious error: The FTHIST table couldn't be found. As a result, the program reported that it was unable to complete the update successfully, displayed the message generated by DSNTIAR, and ended.

In a production environment, a program like this might also write the output from the DSNTIAR routine to a data set or table, invoke another routine to process it further, or display specific error messages that describe the problem. Also, a program might issue a ROLLBACK statement to reverse the table changes it had requested during the current unit of work. (You can refer back to chapter 4, topic 2 in *Part 1: An Introductory Course* for more information about the ROLLBACK statement.)

Error handling with ANSI standard SQL

Depending on your shop's practices, you may have to deal with another approach to error handling. With release 2.2, IBM made several additions to SQL syntax, so DB2 follows ANSI standards more closely. A new precompiler option, STDSQL, lets you choose whether your SQL should be interpreted according to the ANSI standards or according to DB2 rules. STDSQL(86) specifies ANSI rules, and STDSQL(NO) specifies DB2 rules. STDSQL(NO) is the default, so in most cases you won't need to worry about the differences with ANSI.

If STDSQL(86) is in effect in your shop instead of the default, you don't code an INCLUDE statement for the SQLCA. If you do, you'll get a precompiler error. That's because the precompiler automatically includes the SQLCA. Its error code field isn't called SQLCODE, but SQLCADE. The precompiler also automatically inserts Procedure Division code that moves the contents of SQLCADE to another field that just happens to be named SQLCODE. Even though the precompiler includes the COBOL to move error codes to SQLCODE, it doesn't add a definition for SQLCODE, so you

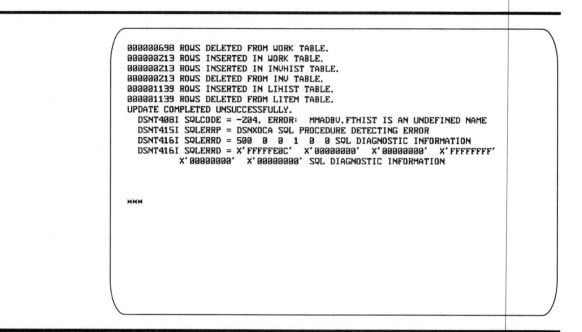

```
000000698 ROWS DELETED FROM WORK TABLE.
000000213 ROWS INSERTED IN WORK TABLE.
000000213 ROWS INSERTED IN INVHIST TABLE.
000000213 ROWS DELETED FROM INV TABLE.
000001139 ROWS INSERTED IN LIHIST TABLE.
000001139 ROWS DELETED FROM LITEM TABLE.
UPDATE COMPLETED UNSUCCESSFULLY.
  DSNT408I SQLCODE = -204, ERROR:   MMADBV.FTHIST IS AN UNDEFINED NAME
  DSNT415I SQLERRP = DSNXOCA SQL PROCEDURE DETECTING ERROR
  DSNT416I SQLERRD = 500  0  0  1  0  0 SQL DIAGNOSTIC INFORMATION
  DSNT416I SQLERRD = X'FFFFFE0C'  X'00000000'  X'00000000'  X'FFFFFFFF'
            X'00000000'  X'00000000' SQL DIAGNOSTIC INFORMATION



***
```

Figure 2-9   Display output from an unsuccessful run of version 3 of the maintenance program

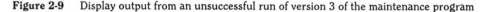

have to do that yourself. It must be a binary fullword, and it can't be a part of a group item. So, you'd code

```
01  SQLCODE    PIC S9(9) COMP.
```

instead of

```
INCLUDE SQLCA
```

if STDSQL(86) was in effect.

STDSQL(86) also requires that you code host variable definitions between two statements I haven't discussed: BEGIN DECLARE SECTION and END DECLARE SECTION. For more information about STDSQL(86), refer to the manual *IBM DATABASE 2 Version 2 Application Programming and SQL Guide Release 2.*

Discussion

Although DB2 provides several error-handling facilities, I want to point out again that most of the work you'll do for handling errors will involve simple checks of the value of SQLCODE after you execute your SQL statements. You can refer to appendix B for a list of the error codes that can occur in application programs. If you need a description of an SQLCODE value that isn't in appendix B, refer to the manual *IBM Database 2 Messages and Codes*.

Term

DSNTIAR

Objectives

1. Extract information from the SQLERRD and SQLWARN fields of the SQL communication area.

2. Code the data definitions and COBOL statement necessary to use the DSNTIAR routine to retrieve formatted information about SQL errors.

3. Code WHENEVER statements to specify appropriate program responses to SQL conditions.

Chapter 3

How to use dynamic SQL

Dynamic SQL is an advanced feature you can use in your programs to create and prepare SQL statements while the programs run. This chapter introduces dynamic SQL and covers four different approaches to using it. Each of the topics in this chapter depends on the ones that precede it, so you should read them in order.

Topic 1 is an overview of dynamic SQL. In that topic, I'll present the four approaches you can use to issue SQL statements dynamically. You use two of these approaches to issue statements other than SELECT, such as INSERT and DELETE. Because those statements are easier to work with than dynamic SELECT statements, I'll cover them first in topics 2 and 3. Topic 2 presents the simplest way to issue a statement dynamically: with the EXECUTE IMMEDIATE statement. Then, topic 3 shows a more sophisticated way, with the PREPARE and EXECUTE statements.

Topic 4 shows you the approach you're most likely to use for working with dynamic SELECT statements. Dynamic SELECTs require that you use DB2's cursor feature. So in topic 4, I'll show you the special features of the DECLARE CURSOR, OPEN, and FETCH statements for working with dynamic SELECTs. Although there's another approach for working with dynamic SELECT statements, you're not likely to need the capabilities it provides. So I won't describe it in detail.

Frankly, you're not likely to need to use dynamic SQL in many COBOL programs. After all, the purpose of application programs is to "prepackage" SQL statements so they work in predictable ways. On top of that, dynamic SQL operations are relatively inefficient. After you've learned the concepts behind dynamic SQL in topic 1, you may decide that you don't need to use it. If so, you can skip topics 2, 3, and 4 and be confident that you aren't missing critical DB2 information. You can always return to them later if you have to develop a program that uses dynamic SQL.

In this topic, I'll describe what dynamic SQL is and how it's different from the SQL you've learned so far. Then, I'll list the SQL statements you can and cannot process dynamically. When you work with dynamic SQL, your programming approach will depend on the kind of statement you want to use and how you want to use it. So, I'll introduce different approaches to using dynamic SQL and the statements you use for each. Finally, I'll show you how to code the data area you use to build a dynamic SQL statement.

As I mentioned in the chapter opener, this topic is prerequisite to the other topics in this chapter. After you've finished it, you may decide that you really don't need to use dynamic SQL. If so, you can skip the other topics in this chapter. You'll have the background you need, and you can come back to this chapter later, if you find yourself facing a programming problem that calls for dynamic SQL.

How dynamic SQL and static SQL are different

All of the program examples in *Part 1: An Introductory Course* and the program example in chapter 2 use *static SQL*. That means that the SQL statements they issue were coded, precompiled, compiled, and bound before execution time. With static SQL, the tables your SQL statements access and the functions they perform are fixed before the program that contains them runs.

Although a static SQL statement performs predetermined functions, that doesn't mean its operations are narrowly constrained. Because you can use host variables in a static SQL statement, its operation can vary. As a result, you can code application programs that issue static SQL statements to meet a wide variety of application requirements. In fact, static SQL lets you accomplish nearly all of the tasks you need to perform in application programs.

In a sense, you can think of a static SQL statement as being like a COBOL statement. For example, a COBOL READ statement that retrieves a record from a customer master file is similar to a static SELECT statement that retrieves a specified results table from a customer table. The READ and the SELECT can retrieve different data each time they run, but their function is always retrieval, and they always access the same collections of data (that is, the same file or table).

In contrast, *dynamic SQL* lets you build and issue statements that can vary completely from one execution to another. Your program constructs a text string that contains the specifications for the statement and stores it in a host variable. Then, when you invoke the statement dynamically at program run time, DB2 interprets the string, translates it into an executable SQL statement, binds it, and runs it.

This is above and beyond using host variables to alter the operation of a statement. This is using a host variable to modify the statement itself. One time, the dynamic SQL statement may be an UPDATE for the active customer table, the next time an UPDATE for the inactive customer table, and then a DELETE for the active customer table.

Figure 3-1 compares the preparation and execution of programs that use only static SQL with programs that use dynamic SQL as well. The simpler flowchart on the left side of the figure shows that after you've coded a program that uses static SQL and prepared it for execution, its execution is straightforward. The static SQL statements it contains are "prepackaged" for execution, and they operate relatively efficiently.

The more complicated flowchart on the right side of figure 3-1 illustrates the preparation and execution process for a program that uses dynamic SQL. The pre-execution steps are the same: Code the program and prepare it for execution. When the program is executed, any static SQL statements it contains are processed as prepackaged units, just as in a program that doesn't use dynamic SQL. However, for the dynamic SQL statements it uses, the program has to do some substantial processing.

First, the program that uses dynamic SQL has to format a text string that contains the SQL statement. The technical term for it is the *statement string*. Usually, formatting the statement string requires capturing some processing specifications from a user.

Second, after the statement string has been formatted, it must be translated so DB2 can run it. This requires the same sort of processing that's done for static SQL statements during the precompile step of the program preparation process. Then, the statement must be bound.

Keep in mind that all of this "dynamic program preparation" happens in the production environment at program run-time. That means the program probably has to compete for resources with many other programs. And statement translation and binding take lots of resources. In contrast, the translate and bind step for static SQL statements takes place in a development environment, where its performance impact is less severe.

Because of these processing costs, dynamic SQL is appropriate only when programs must perform functions that you can't anticipate before execution time. Frankly, the ability to make such radical changes to program

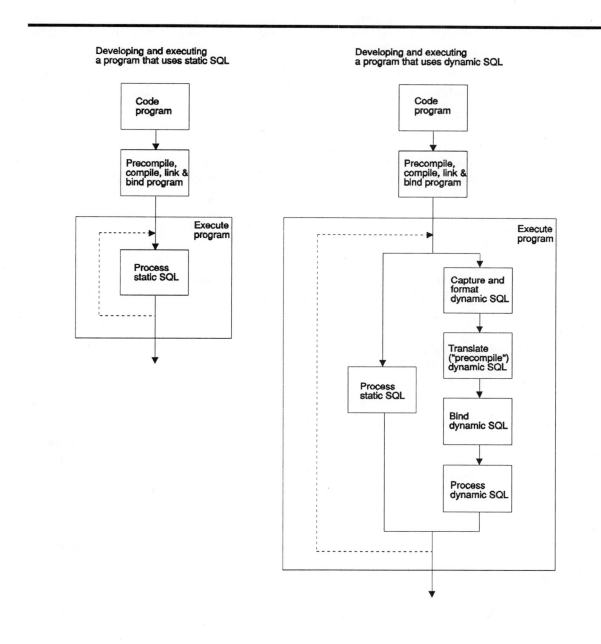

Figure 3-1 Static versus dynamic SQL

functions is unnecessary in most business applications. On top of that, IBM already provides an end-user tool for ad hoc processing: QMF.

Statements you can and can't issue dynamically

You can't process all SQL statements dynamically. Figure 3-2 lists the ones you can and the ones you can't. If you need to develop a program that uses dynamic SQL, it will probably involve the basic SQL data manipulation statements: SELECT, INSERT, UPDATE, and DELETE. You can also issue Data Definition Language (DDL) statements like CREATE and ALTER dynamically. I'll present DDL statements in section 3.

The statements you can't issue dynamically fall into three groups. First, you can't issue cursor-processing statements (OPEN, FETCH and CLOSE) dynamically. (But, as you'll see in a moment, you must use cursor-processing statements to work with data you retrieve through a SELECT you issue dynamically.) Second, you can't issue precompiler directives (INCLUDE, DECLARE, or WHENEVER) dynamically. That's because your program will already have been precompiled and compiled when it processes a statement dynamically. And third, you can't issue any statements for dynamic SQL processing dynamically. Their purpose is to invoke *other* statements dynamically, and they must be embedded in an application program.

Approaches to issuing SQL statements dynamically

Depending on what you need to do with dynamic SQL, the COBOL programming challenges you face can range from trivial to difficult. The kind of statement you want to issue dynamically and how you want to use it affect the programming technique you'll use. Figure 3-3 shows four ways you can use dynamic SQL and the programming approach you need to use for each.

For all dynamic statements except SELECT, your task is relatively straightforward. So, I'll describe the two ways to issue non-SELECT statements first. Then, I'll present the more complicated approaches you have to take when you work with SELECTs dynamically.

Using the EXECUTE IMMEDIATE statement   The first technique is the simplest. It's appropriate when your program needs to issue a statement like INSERT, UPDATE, or DELETE dynamically, and it needs to issue it only once. To do that, you use the SQL EXECUTE IMMEDIATE statement. With EXECUTE IMMEDIATE, DB2 translates your statement string, binds it, executes it, and forgets it. Later in this topic, I'll show you how to provide a data area for a statement string in your COBOL program. And I'll show you how to use EXECUTE IMMEDIATE in topic 2.

Statements that are allowed as dynamic SQL statements

Statements you may be likely to use	Statements you're not likely to use
DELETE	ALTER
INSERT	COMMENT
SELECT	COMMIT
UPDATE	CREATE
	DROP
	EXPLAIN
	GRANT
	LABEL
	LOCK TABLE
	REVOKE
	ROLLBACK

Statements that are *not* allowed as dynamic SQL statements

Cursor processing	Precompiler directives	Dynamic SQL
OPEN	DECLARE	EXECUTE IMMEDIATE
FETCH	INCLUDE	PREPARE
CLOSE	WHENEVER	EXECUTE
		DECLARE

Figure 3-2   Statements that are and are not allowed in dynamic SQL

Using the PREPARE and EXECUTE statements   If you expect that your program will need to execute the same dynamic SQL statement more than once, using EXECUTE IMMEDIATE is inefficient. That's because it translates and binds the statement each time it's issued. So, instead of using the EXECUTE IMMEDIATE statement for non-SELECT statements that are issued more than once, it's more efficient to use the second technique figure 3-3 presents: the PREPARE and EXECUTE statements.

The PREPARE statement translates and binds the statement string. However, unlike EXECUTE IMMEDIATE, PREPARE doesn't execute the statement right away. Instead, it retains it in an executable form called a *prepared statement*. PREPARE also associates a symbolic name that you supply with the prepared statement. DB2 maintains the prepared statement until the current unit of work ends or another PREPARE uses the same symbolic name.

Processing for a dynamic non-SELECT statement executed once	Processing for a dynamic non-SELECT statement executed more than once	Processing for a dynamic SELECT statement that produces a known results table	Processing for a dynamic SELECT statement that produces an unknown results table
Format non-SELECT statement in a variable-length string host variable EXECUTE IMMEDIATE	Format non-SELECT statement in a variable-length string host variable PREPARE EXECUTE	Format SELECT statement in a variable-length string host variable DECLARE CURSOR PREPARE OPEN FETCH CLOSE	Format SELECT statement in a variable-length string host variable DECLARE CURSOR PREPARE DESCRIBE Allocate storage for host variables OPEN FETCH CLOSE

Figure 3-3   Approaches to dynamic SQL

After it has prepared a statement, a program can execute it multiple times. To invoke the prepared statement, your program uses the EXECUTE statement. On it, you specify the symbolic name you supplied on the PREPARE statement. I'll show you how to use PREPARE and EXECUTE in topic 3.

Using the PREPARE statement with cursor-processing statements
The other two programming techniques in figure 3-3 let you issue SELECT statements dynamically. This is more complicated than working with non-SELECT statements. In some programming situations, it's just slightly more complicated, and in others it's dramatically so. The complexity you'll have to face depends on whether you know the type and format of the columns you'll retrieve.

When you issue a SELECT statement dynamically, you must process the results table it creates through a cursor, even if you know the statement will return a single-row results table. So, instead of using the EXECUTE statement to invoke a prepared SELECT statement, you need to use special forms of the DECLARE CURSOR, OPEN, FETCH, and CLOSE statements.

As I mentioned earlier, there are two programming techniques that let you issue dynamic SELECT statements. When you know in advance how many and what kind of columns will be returned as a result of the SELECT, you use the third approach figure 3-3 shows. This is called a *fixed-list SELECT*. In topic 4, I'll show you how to do a fixed-list SELECT.

The last approach to dynamic SQL lets you issue a completely flexible SELECT. You can use this approach when you can't anticipate what kind of data your program will retrieve. This sort of dynamic SELECT, called a *variable-list SELECT*, raises some difficult programming challenges. To process a variable-list SELECT, not only must your program use all of the features for retrieving data from a fixed-list SELECT, but it must also do two more steps.

First, after the program issues a PREPARE statement, it issues a DESCRIBE statement to collect information about the structure of the results table the SELECT will create. The information is returned to the program in a special data area called the *SQL Descriptor Area*, or *SQLDA*.

After your program evaluates the data in the SQLDA to find out what your SELECT statement will return, it has to prepare main storage to provide a place for the retrieved data. To do this, it uses pointer variables to identify the storage it will use. As you can imagine, this is a difficult, cumbersome undertaking, and it's unusual for COBOL programs. In fact, under older VS COBOL, you can't do it at all. It takes advanced features of VS COBOL II to be able to process a variable-list SELECT. And even then, it's not easy.

Fortunately, I don't think you'll ever be expected to write a program that does a variable-list SELECT in COBOL. So, I'm not going to cover this approach in detail. After all, other facilities, like QMF, let you do such work. If you need to write this kind of a program, refer to the *IBM Database 2 Version 2 Application Programming and SQL Guide* after you've read the rest of this chapter. (This chapter provides the background you need to put the information in that manual to use.)

How to construct a statement string

To issue an SQL statement dynamically through any of the four approaches I just described, a program must first construct a proper statement string. The statement string is a text string representation of the SQL statement that you pass to DB2 through a program host variable.

The amount of work a program must do to construct a statement string depends on the application's requirements. In the simplest case, a program may let a user key in an entire SQL statement, then use it directly in a PREPARE or an EXECUTE IMMEDIATE statement. However, it's more likely that a program will prompt a user for one or more specific elements (like a table name or a selection condition), then use COBOL's string-handling features to combine that data with literals to build a complete statement string. You'll see examples of this approach in the sample programs in topics 2, 3, and 4.

Regardless, to be able to provide a proper statement string, you need to know three things as you write your program. First, you need to know how to code the program host variable for the statement string. Second, you need to know what elements you can't include in a statement string. And third, you need to know how to use a special feature called a parameter marker.

Data area for a statement string   The data area that you use to construct a statement string for dynamic processing must be compatible with DB2's VARCHAR data type. That means that it needs to be a group item that starts with a binary halfword (PIC S9(4) COMP). The value of this field specifies how many characters are in the variable-length string. As with a host variable for a VARCHAR column, the text component follows the length component. Here's a sample item:

```
01   SQL-STATEMENT.
*
     49   SQL-STATEMENT-LEN     PIC S9(4) COMP VALUE +320.
     49   SQL-STATEMENT-TEXT    PIC X(320).
```

When you use this kind of structure for a dynamic SQL statement string, you can set the value of the length field to the maximum size of the TEXT component.

The size I selected for the length of the text component, 320, is arbitrary. I selected 320 because it's the amount of data that fits into four 80-character lines. That's enough for most dynamic SQL statements I'd issue. However, the upper limit for the length of an SQL statement is over 32K. You can code as large a text component as you need, as long as you don't exceed the upper limit. And you're almost certain not even to approach the limit. But whatever size you use, just specify it as the value of the length component, as I did in this example.

What you can't include in a statement string   Unlike the embedded SQL statements you code along with your COBOL, the text string you construct for a dynamic SQL statement should not be bracketed between EXEC SQL and END-EXEC. They're necessary only for SQL statements that are processed by the precompiler, and dynamic SQL statements aren't.

Also, when you construct a statement string for a dynamic SQL statement, you can't include any host variables in it. Actually, the entire statement string that contains the SQL statement is one large host variable.

Parameter markers   Although you can't include host variables in a statement string, you can use a feature that lets you achieve a similar result: parameter markers. A *parameter marker* is simply a question mark you include in a statement string. When a prepared statement is executed, you need to supply a value for each parameter marker that was in its original statement string. Then, DB2 substitutes those values for the parameter markers before it executes the SQL statement.

Parameter markers are valid only in prepared statements; you can't use them in statements you issue with EXECUTE IMMEDIATE. When I introduce the PREPARE statement in topic 3, I'll list the rules you have to follow when you use parameter markers. And you'll see examples of parameter markers in the sample programs in topics 3 and 4.

Discussion

Experts differ on the performance implications of dynamic SQL. Some argue that because dynamic binds occurs on an ad hoc basis, they can't be tuned to optimize overall system performance. On the other hand, others argue that because a dynamic bind occurs at the last minute, it lets the DB2 optimizer choose the best way to process tables based on current information.

Both sides agree, however, that dynamic SQL can use an unpredictable amount of system resources. To help limit the resources dynamic SQL can use, release 2.1 of DB2 introduced a *governor* feature, called the *Resource Limit Facility (RLF)*. This facility can interrupt the execution of a dynamic SQL statement if it uses system resources that exceed a threshold value. When the RLF cancels a dynamic SQL statement, DB2 returns an SQL-CODE value of −905. Even if the governor interrupts the processing of one dynamic statement, the program that issued it continues to run and can issue other statements.

Terms

static SQL
dynamic SQL
statement string
prepared statement
fixed-list SELECT
variable-list SELECT

SQL Descriptor Area
SQLDA
parameter marker
governor
Resource Limit Facility
RLF

Objectives

1. Describe the difference between static and dynamic SQL.

2. Explain why dynamic SQL can present performance problems.

3. List the SQL statements you can and cannot use dynamically.

4. Describe when it's appropriate to use EXECUTE IMMEDIATE to issue an SQL statement dynamically.

5. Describe when it's appropriate to use the PREPARE and EXECUTE statements to issue an SQL statement dynamically.

6. Code the data area for a statement string.

How to use EXECUTE IMMEDIATE to issue
non-SELECT statements dynamically

The easiest way to work with dynamic SQL is to use the EXECUTE
IMMEDIATE statement. You can use EXECUTE IMMEDIATE to run any of
the dynamic-eligible statements I listed in figure 3-2 in topic 1 except
SELECT. But you should use it only for the statements you intend to execute only once. In this topic, I'll show you the syntax of EXECUTE
IMMEDIATE and describe how you can use it. Then, I'll show you an
application program that puts EXECUTE IMMEDIATE to work.

The syntax and operation of the EXECUTE IMMEDIATE statement

Figure 3-4 presents the syntax of the EXECUTE IMMEDIATE statement. All
you code on it is the name of a host variable that contains the statement
string you want to execute. This host variable must be compatible with
DB2's VARCHAR data type. When DB2 processes EXECUTE IMMEDIATE,
it translates, binds, and executes the statement contained in the host variable. After the statement has finished executing, DB2 disposes of it.

The statement string must not be bracketed by EXEC SQL and
END-EXEC, and it may not contain host variable names. In addition, the
statement string you use in an EXECUTE IMMEDIATE statement can't
include any parameter markers.

If there's a problem with a statement you try to issue with EXECUTE
IMMEDIATE, DB2 reports it through the SQLCODE field. An error can be
one of two types. First, a statement may be invalid because it contains a
syntax error. Second, a statement may fail for an operational reason, such
as not being able to access the data it requests. The same kinds of problems
can occur with static SQL statements. The difference is that syntax errors in
static SQL are reported during program preparation, while in dynamic SQL,
they are reported during program execution.

Using EXECUTE IMMEDIATE in a program

A program can use a single EXECUTE IMMEDIATE statement to issue different kinds of SQL statements dynamically. All the program has to do is
change the contents of the statement string so it contains the text for the

The SQL EXECUTE IMMEDIATE statement

```
EXEC SQL
    EXECUTE IMMEDIATE :host-var
END-EXEC.
```

Explanation

host-var   The name of the COBOL host variable that contains the statement string to be translated, bound, and
                      executed. Must contain data compatible with the DB2 VARCHAR data type.

Figure 3-4   The SQL EXECUTE IMMEDIATE statement

statement to be executed. For example, the EXECUTE IMMEDIATE statement may issue an INSERT statement, then a DELETE statement, then an UPDATE statement, then another INSERT.

The program example I'll show you here uses EXECUTE IMMEDIATE just to issue DELETE statements. Although the function of the statement doesn't vary from one statement to the next, the table it processes does. This program can process tables that have a structure like the CUST table I used throughout *Part 1: An Introductory Course*. Figure 3-5 shows the DCLGEN output for that table.

The program here is based on a hypothetical application that uses the CUST table as a master table, the source of data for a number of temporary work tables. All of the temporary tables have the same structure as the CUST table. In other words, they contain the same number of columns with the same lengths, data types, and names. The temporary tables are extracted from the CUST table so users can manipulate them without worrying about damaging the CUST table or causing processing bottlenecks. The purpose of the program I'll show you here is to let users delete specified rows from any of the temporary work tables.

The operation of the DYNAM1 program   Figure 3-6 shows a screen from a sample session with this program, called DYNAM1. Like the program examples from *Part 1: An Introductory Course*, this program operates under TSO and doesn't use alternative screen formatting techniques. It uses COBOL DISPLAY and ACCEPT statements to do screen output and input. For a production program, you may be likely to use CICS to provide a more elegant user interface. However, the simple approach this program

```
*****************************************************************
* DCLGEN TABLE(MMADBV.CUST)                                     *
*         LIBRARY(MMA002.DCLGENS.COBOL(CUST))                   *
*         ACTION(REPLACE)                                       *
*         STRUCTURE(CUSTOMER-ROW)                               *
*         APOST                                                 *
* ... IS THE DCLGEN COMMAND THAT MADE THE FOLLOWING STATEMENTS  *
*****************************************************************
      EXEC SQL DECLARE MMADBV.CUST TABLE
      ( CUSTNO                        CHAR(6) NOT NULL,
        FNAME                         CHAR(20) NOT NULL,
        LNAME                         CHAR(30) NOT NULL,
        ADDR                          CHAR(30) NOT NULL,
        CITY                          CHAR(20) NOT NULL,
        STATE                         CHAR(2) NOT NULL,
        ZIPCODE                       CHAR(10) NOT NULL
      ) END-EXEC.
*****************************************************************
* COBOL DECLARATION FOR TABLE MMADBV.CUST                       *
*****************************************************************
  01   CUSTOMER-ROW.
       10 CUSTNO           PIC X(6).
       10 FNAME            PIC X(20).
       10 LNAME            PIC X(30).
       10 ADDR             PIC X(30).
       10 CITY             PIC X(20).
       10 STATE            PIC X(2).
       10 ZIPCODE          PIC X(10).
*****************************************************************
* THE NUMBER OF COLUMNS DESCRIBED BY THIS DECLARATION IS 7      *
*****************************************************************
```

Figure 3-5   DCLGEN output for the CUST table

takes to screen input and output will let you focus on what it's intended to illustrate: dynamic SQL.

Each time it performs its main processing loop, the program prompts the user for the name of the table to be accessed and the customer number for the row to be deleted from that table. In the example in figure 3-6, you can see three iterations of this process. For each, the user wants to delete the row for customer 400002 from one of the temporary work tables. You can imagine that these temporary work tables were generated on three different days. The dates the tables were generated are reflected in their names. So, CUST0727, CUST0728, and CUST0729 were generated on July 27, 28, and 29.

The user specified table CUST0727 in the first iteration. In that instance, a row wasn't deleted. The SQLCODE the program displayed for the attempted DELETE operation, +100, indicates that a row couldn't be found in that table with that customer number. The program doesn't

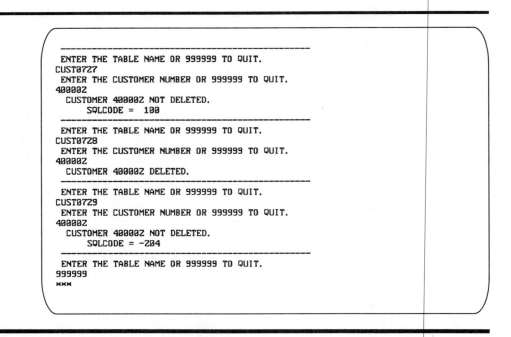

```
 ------------------------------------------------
  ENTER THE TABLE NAME OR 999999 TO QUIT.
 CUST0727
  ENTER THE CUSTOMER NUMBER OR 999999 TO QUIT.
 400002
   CUSTOMER 400002 NOT DELETED.
      SQLCODE =  100
 ------------------------------------------------
  ENTER THE TABLE NAME OR 999999 TO QUIT.
 CUST0728
  ENTER THE CUSTOMER NUMBER OR 999999 TO QUIT.
 400002
   CUSTOMER 400002 DELETED.
 ------------------------------------------------
  ENTER THE TABLE NAME OR 999999 TO QUIT.
 CUST0729
  ENTER THE CUSTOMER NUMBER OR 999999 TO QUIT.
 400002
   CUSTOMER 400002 NOT DELETED.
      SQLCODE = -204
 ------------------------------------------------
  ENTER THE TABLE NAME OR 999999 TO QUIT.
 999999
 ***
```

Figure 3-6   Operation of the DYNAM1 program

display a specific error message that explains what +100 means, but it
would be easy to add.

In the second iteration, the user specified the table CUST0728. This
time, the DELETE operation was successful. Because the statement was
processed successfully, the program doesn't display the SQLCODE value.

In the third iteration, a different kind of error occurred. This time, the
user specified the table name CUST0729, and the SQLCODE that resulted
was −204. That means that the table named in the statement doesn't exist.
After the third iteration of the program, the user keyed in 999999 for the
table name. The program interpreted that as a signal to end, and it did.

This program may receive non-zero return code values other than +100
and −204. For example, if the user names a table that exists but that
doesn't contain a column named CUSTNO, SQL will return −206 as the
SQLCODE value. Regardless of the cause of a non-zero return code, the
program handles it in the same way: It reports that the statement was
unsuccessful, displays the SQLCODE value, and prompts the user to
enter another table name.

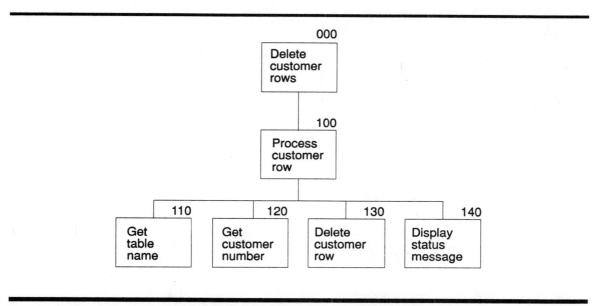

Figure 3-7   Structure chart for the DYNAM1 program

The design of the DYNAM1 program   Now, consider the structure chart for the DYNAM1 program in figure 3-7. This program repeatedly executes module 100-PROCESS-CUSTOMER-ROW until the user signals that the program should end by entering 999999 in response to the prompt for either the table name or the customer number.

Each time module 100 runs, it invokes 110-GET-TABLE-NAME to prompt the user for the name of the table to be processed. If the user keys in a value other than 999999, module 100 continues with 120-GET-CUSTOMER-NUMBER. If the user keys in a value other than 999999 for the customer number, module 100 first performs module 130 to format and issue the dynamic DELETE statement, and then it performs module 140 to report its success to the user.

The source code for the DYNAM1 program   Figure 3-8 presents the COBOL source code for the DYNAM1 program. In the Working-Storage Section, I've shaded the field definitions I want you to notice. The first two, TABLE-NAME and CUSTOMER-NUMBER, are text fields that contain the values the user enters in response to the inquiries modules 110 and 120 make. Module 110 includes the statement

```
ACCEPT TABLE-NAME.
```

```
000100   IDENTIFICATION DIVISION.
000200 *
000300   PROGRAM-ID.             DYNAM1.
000400 *
000500   ENVIRONMENT DIVISION.
000600 *
000700   INPUT-OUTPUT SECTION.
000800 *
000900   FILE-CONTROL.
001000 *
001100   DATA DIVISION.
001200 *
001300   FILE SECTION.
001400 *
001500   WORKING-STORAGE SECTION.
001600 *
001700   01  SWITCH.
001800 *
001900       05  END-OF-DELETES-SW        PIC X     VALUE "N".
002000           88  END-OF-DELETES                 VALUE "Y".
002100 *
002200   01  WORK-FIELDS.
002300 *
002400       05  TABLE-NAME               PIC X(15).
002500       05  CUSTOMER-NUMBER          PIC X(6).
002600       05  DELETE-STATEMENT.
002700           49  DELETE-STATEMENT-LEN     PIC S9(4)
002800                                        COMP VALUE +320.
002900           49  DELETE-STATEMENT-TEXT    PIC X(320).
003000       05  EDITED-SQLCODE           PIC -(4).
003100 *
003200       EXEC SQL
003300           INCLUDE SQLCA
003400       END-EXEC.
003500 *
003600   PROCEDURE DIVISION.
003700 *
003800   000-DELETE-CUSTOMER-ROWS.
003900 *
004000       PERFORM 100-PROCESS-CUSTOMER-ROW
004100           UNTIL END-OF-DELETES.
004200       STOP RUN.
004300 *
004400   100-PROCESS-CUSTOMER-ROW.
004500 *
004600       PERFORM 110-GET-TABLE-NAME.
004700       IF NOT END-OF-DELETES
004800           PERFORM 120-GET-CUSTOMER-NUMBER.
004900       IF NOT END-OF-DELETES
005000           PERFORM 130-DELETE-CUSTOMER-ROW
005100           PERFORM 140-DISPLAY-STATUS-MESSAGE.
005200 *
```

Figure 3-8   COBOL source code for the DYNAM1 program (part 1 of 2)

```
005300  110-GET-TABLE-NAME.
005400  *
005500      DISPLAY "--------------------------------------------------".
005600      DISPLAY "ENTER THE TABLE NAME OR 999999 TO QUIT."
005700      ACCEPT TABLE-NAME.
005800      IF TABLE-NAME = "999999"
005900          MOVE "Y" TO END-OF-DELETES-SW.
006000  *
006100  120-GET-CUSTOMER-NUMBER.
006200  *
006300      DISPLAY "ENTER THE CUSTOMER NUMBER OR 999999 TO QUIT."
006400      ACCEPT CUSTOMER-NUMBER.
006500      IF CUSTOMER-NUMBER = "999999"
006600          MOVE "Y" TO END-OF-DELETES-SW.
006700  *
006800  130-DELETE-CUSTOMER-ROW.
006900  *
007000      MOVE SPACE TO DELETE-STATEMENT-TEXT.
007100      STRING "DELETE FROM MMADBV." TABLE-NAME
007200          " WHERE CUSTNO = '"    CUSTOMER-NUMBER  "'"
007300          DELIMITED BY SIZE
007400          INTO DELETE-STATEMENT-TEXT.
007500  *
007600      EXEC SQL
007700          EXECUTE IMMEDIATE :DELETE-STATEMENT
007800      END-EXEC.
007900  *
008000  140-DISPLAY-STATUS-MESSAGE.
008100  *
008200      IF SQLCODE = 0
008300          DISPLAY " CUSTOMER " CUSTOMER-NUMBER " DELETED."
008400      ELSE
008500          DISPLAY " CUSTOMER " CUSTOMER-NUMBER " NOT DELETED."
008600          MOVE SQLCODE TO EDITED-SQLCODE
008700          DISPLAY "    SQLCODE = " EDITED-SQLCODE.
```

Figure 3-8   COBOL source code for the DYNAM1 program (part 2 of 2)

and module 120 includes the statement

```
ACCEPT CUSTOMER-NUMBER.
```

So, when module 130 executes, these fields already contain the right values for the dynamic DELETE statement.

The next item in the shaded block, DELETE-STATEMENT, is the data area that will contain the statement string the EXECUTE IMMEDIATE statement will process. Finally, the field EDITED-SQLCODE is simply a numeric-edited field that the program uses if it needs to display a non-zero SQLCODE value. (The PIC clause for EDITED-SQLCODE may look strange to you, but it simply specifies that the value moved into the field should be displayed with a leading minus sign, if it's negative. I used only four minus signs because no SQLCODE value has more than three digits.)

Now, look at the Procedure Division code in module 130. It constructs and executes the statement string for the dynamic DELETE. First, the module moves space to DELETE-STATEMENT-TEXT, the text component of the variable-length item DELETE-STATEMENT. Then, it uses a COBOL STRING statement to combine the values the user entered for the table name and customer number variables with literals to construct the statement string. So, when the program processes the statement

```
STRING "DELETE FROM MMADBV." TABLE-NAME
       " WHERE CUSTNO = '"   CUSTOMER-NUMBER   "'"
       DELIMITED BY SIZE
       INTO DELETE-STATEMENT-TEXT.
```

after the user entered CUST0727 for the table name and 400002 for the customer number, it stores

```
DELETE FROM MMADBV.CUST0727 WHERE CUSTNO = '400002'
```

in DELETE-STATEMENT-TEXT.

Notice that the statement string doesn't include EXEC SQL and END-EXEC as delimiters for the statement. Also, notice that I supplied the customer number value for this statement as a literal in the text string, not through a host variable. That's because you can't use a host variable in a dynamic SQL statement.

The next lines in module 130,

```
EXEC SQL
    EXECUTE IMMEDIATE :DELETE-STATEMENT
END-EXEC.
```

are the EXECUTE IMMEDIATE statement that processes the statement string. This statement simply names the program host variable that contains the statement string that is to be executed dynamically. Here, the EXECUTE IMMEDIATE statement is bracketed by EXEC SQL and END-EXEC and contains a host variable. That's not a violation of the coding rules for dynamic statements because EXECUTE IMMEDIATE *isn't* the dynamic statement; it *invokes* the dynamic statement.

Discussion

At this point, you're probably not overwhelmed by the complexity of using EXECUTE IMMEDIATE. In fact, you may think it's trivial. I wouldn't disagree. However, my reason for presenting it in its own topic is to introduce dynamic SQL with a simple example that provides a foundation for the more complicated examples in the next two topics.

Remember that if you plan to issue the same SQL statement more than once during the execution of a program, using the EXECUTE IMMEDIATE statement isn't the best approach. It's more efficient to use two other SQL statements: PREPARE and EXECUTE. The next topic shows you how to use them.

Objective

Given application and table specifications, code a program that uses the EXECUTE IMMEDIATE statement to issue a non-SELECT statement dynamically.

Topic 3 How to use PREPARE and EXECUTE to issue non-SELECT statements dynamically

The two statements I'll present in this topic, PREPARE and EXECUTE, separate the functions of EXECUTE IMMEDIATE. PREPARE causes a statement string to be translated and bound, and it produces a prepared statement. EXECUTE invokes that prepared statement. DB2 retains the prepared statement during the current unit of work, so your program can invoke it again and again. However, if you issue a COMMIT statement or your program ends, the prepared statement is dropped.

The syntax and operation of the PREPARE statement

Figure 3-9 presents the syntax of the PREPARE statement. You can use PREPARE for both SELECT and non-SELECT statements. However, in this topic, I'll discuss how to use it only with non-SELECT statements.

Two items are required when you code the PREPARE statement. The first, *prepared-statement-name*, is a symbolic name that identifies the prepared statement. You can use any name you want, but it must be no more than 18 EBCDIC characters long. Later, you'll specify this name on the EXECUTE statements that invoke the prepared statement. You should realize that if the statement name you specify is already in use, the newly prepared statement will replace the old one. In some cases, that may be what you want to happen, and in others it may not be.

The second required item for the PREPARE statement is the FROM clause. On it, you specify the name of the program host variable that contains the statement string you want to process. As with EXECUTE IMMEDIATE, this host variable must be defined so it's compatible with DB2's VARCHAR data type.

The optional clause of the PREPARE statement, INTO, lets you specify a storage area that will receive information about the prepared statement. Although receiving this kind of information is necessary when you work with variable-list SELECTs, it's not important for non-SELECTs. And because this topic covers non-SELECTs only, I won't cover the INTO clause here.

If the statement string you process with a PREPARE statement contains an error, DB2 reports the error through the SQLCA. So, after you

The SQL PREPARE statement

```
EXEC SQL
    PREPARE prepared-statement-name
        [INTO sqlda-name]
            FROM :host-var
END-EXEC.
```

Explanation

prepared-statement-name	A symbolic name, 18 or fewer characters long, you create to identify the prepared statement. It should not refer to a prepared statement currently associated with an open cursor.
sqlda-name	The name of an SQL Descriptor Area where information about the prepared statement will be stored.
host-var	The name of the COBOL host variable that contains the statement string to be translated, bound, and associated with *prepared-statement-name*.

Figure 3-9   The SQL PREPARE statement

issue a PREPARE statement, your program should evaluate SQLCODE before it attempts to use the prepared statement.

As I pointed out in topic 2 when I described EXECUTE IMMEDIATE, you can't use host variables in a statement string. However, you can use parameter markers. If you need to use PREPARE and EXECUTE, you're almost certain to need to use parameter markers as well. After all, it's unlikely that you'd want to execute a prepared statement more than once if it did exactly the same thing each time.

To include a parameter marker in a statement string, just code a question mark (?). Then, when you invoke the prepared statement, you supply the value DB2 will substitute for each parameter marker on the EXECUTE statement. You'll see examples of parameter markers in the sample programs in this topic and in topic 4.

DB2 imposes some restrictions on how you can use parameter markers. These restrictions are listed in figure 3-10. First, you can't use a parameter marker where you can't use a host variable in static SQL. So, although you can use a parameter marker in a WHERE clause, you can't use one in a FROM clause in place of a table name. Also, you can't use a parameter marker on both sides of an operator, either in an arithmetic expression or in a comparison.

Parameter markers may not be used:

- where a host variable would not be allowed in a static statement
  (as in FROM ?)

- as column specifications
  (as in SELECT ?, ?, ?)

- as both elements in a comparison
  (as in WHERE ? = ?)

- as both elements of an arithmetic operation
  (as in WHERE INVTOTAL = ? + ?)

Figure 3-10   Restrictions for using parameter markers

The syntax and operation of the EXECUTE statement

After you've prepared a non-SELECT statement, you use the EXECUTE
statement to invoke it. Figure 3-11 presents the syntax of EXECUTE. As
you can see, there are two items you can code on the EXECUTE statement.
The first item is simply the symbolic name you assigned to the dynamic
SQL statement on the PREPARE statement.

You code the second item, the USING clause, when you issue an
EXECUTE statement for a prepared statement that uses parameter markers.
On the USING clause, you name the host variables that contain the values
DB2 should substitute for the parameter markers. The number of parameter markers in the prepared statement and the number of items you list
on the USING clause must be the same. The first argument of USING will
replace the first parameter marker, the second argument will replace the
second parameter marker, and so on.

Another way to provide values for parameter markers is through an
SQL Descriptor Area. The SQLDA is an advanced feature that you probably
won't use with EXECUTE, so I won't present the details of using it here.

Using PREPARE and EXECUTE in a program

Here, I'll present a modified version of the DYNAM1 program I used in
topic 2 when I described the EXECUTE IMMEDIATE statement. Like
DYNAM1, this program, DYNAM2, lets a user specify a table and a
customer number to delete a row from a temporary customer table. However, I designed and coded DYNAM2 so its processing is less wasteful of
system resources than DYNAM1's.

The SQL EXECUTE statement

```
EXEC SQL
    EXECUTE prepared-statement-name
        [USING {:host-var[,:host-var...]}  ]
               {DESCRIPTOR sqlda-name     }
END-EXEC.
```

Explanation

prepared-statement-name	The symbolic name specified on the PREPARE statement that processed the prepared statement you want to execute. The prepared statement may not be a SELECT statement.
host-var	The name of a COBOL host variable whose name will be substituted for a parameter marker in the prepared SQL statement.
sqlda-name	The name of an SQL Descriptor Area that contains descriptions of the host variables whose values are to be substituted for parameter markers in the prepared statement.

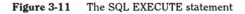

Figure 3-11   The SQL EXECUTE statement

The operation of the DYNAM2 program   Figure 3-12 presents a short session with the DYNAM2 program. First, the program asks for the name of the table to be processed. In the example in figure 3-12, the user entered CUST0730.

Although it's not obvious in figure 3-12, the program prepares the executable statement right after it accepts the table name from the user. It uses a parameter marker for the customer number in the statement's WHERE clause instead of including the customer number as a literal in the statement string, as DYNAM1 did. Then, the program can execute the prepared statement multiple times to delete rows from the specified table, and it won't be necessary to prepare the statement each time.

If you continue to examine the screen in figure 3-12, you'll see that the program prompted the user for customer numbers without asking for the table name again until the user entered 999999 to signal that there were no more transactions for the current table. Then, the program prompted the user again for a new table name. The user entered CUST0731. This time, the statement couldn't be prepared successfully. The PREPARE statement failed with SQLCODE −204, because that table doesn't exist.

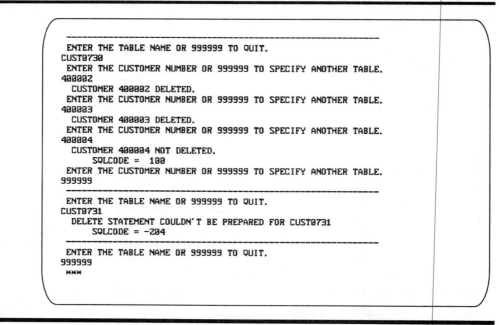

```
-----------------------------------------------------------------
  ENTER THE TABLE NAME OR 999999 TO QUIT.
CUST0730
  ENTER THE CUSTOMER NUMBER OR 999999 TO SPECIFY ANOTHER TABLE.
400002
   CUSTOMER 400002 DELETED.
  ENTER THE CUSTOMER NUMBER OR 999999 TO SPECIFY ANOTHER TABLE.
400003
   CUSTOMER 400003 DELETED.
  ENTER THE CUSTOMER NUMBER OR 999999 TO SPECIFY ANOTHER TABLE.
400004
   CUSTOMER 400004 NOT DELETED.
       SQLCODE =  100
  ENTER THE CUSTOMER NUMBER OR 999999 TO SPECIFY ANOTHER TABLE.
999999
-----------------------------------------------------------------
  ENTER THE TABLE NAME OR 999999 TO QUIT.
CUST0731
   DELETE STATEMENT COULDN'T BE PREPARED FOR CUST0731
       SQLCODE = -204
-----------------------------------------------------------------
  ENTER THE TABLE NAME OR 999999 TO QUIT.
999999
  ***
```

Figure 3-12   Operation of the DYNAM2 program

The design of the DYNAM2 program   Figure 3-13 shows the structure
chart for DYNAM2. Module 100 first performs module 110 to get the name
of the table to be processed. Next, it invokes module 120 to prepare the
statement that will delete rows from the table. After it has prepared the
dynamic DELETE statement, the program can repeatedly perform module
130 to delete rows from the specified table, as you saw in the example in
figure 3-12.

Module 130 has three subordinates. The first, 140-GET-CUSTOMER-
NUMBER, prompts the user for the customer number for the row to be
deleted. Module 150 issues an EXECUTE statement to run the dynamic
DELETE statement module 120 prepared. Finally, module 160 reports the
success or failure of the prepared statement.

The source code for the DYNAM2 program   Now, look at the source
code for the program in figure 3-14. The Working-Storage Section is almost
the same as in the DYNAM1 program. In fact, the only difference is that I
added another switch with a condition name to let the program control two
levels of repetitive processing (customer within table) instead of just one.

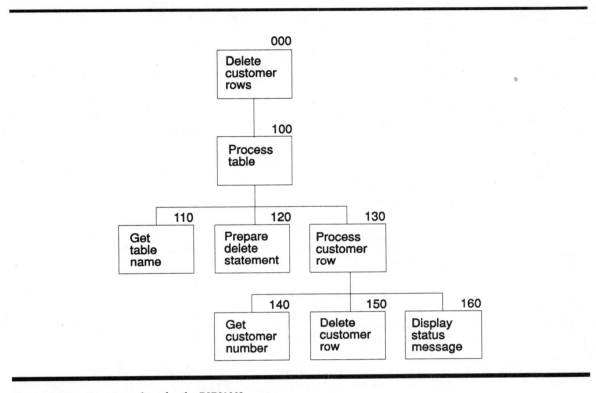

Figure 3-13   Structure chart for the DYNAM2 program

In the Procedure Division, I want you to notice the code I shaded in module 120. It formats the statement string for the dynamic DELETE statement and then prepares it. As in DYNAM1, this program uses the COBOL STRING statement to combine the literal text for the statement with data entered by the user. The STRING statement in DYNAM1 combined literals with two variables: TABLE-NAME and CUSTOMER-NUMBER. In this program, the STRING statement is different:

```
STRING "DELETE FROM MMADBV." TABLE-NAME " WHERE CUSTNO = ?"
       DELIMITED BY SIZE
       INTO DELETE-STATEMENT-TEXT.
```

As you can see, this statement does use the value of TABLE-NAME, but it doesn't use CUSTOMER-NUMBER. It includes a parameter marker, ?, instead. As you'll see in a moment, this parameter marker will be replaced with a value supplied by the user when the prepared statement is executed.

```
000100   IDENTIFICATION DIVISION.
000200 *
000300   PROGRAM-ID.         DYNAM2.
000400 *
000500   ENVIRONMENT DIVISION.
000600 *
000700   INPUT-OUTPUT SECTION.
000800 *
000900   FILE-CONTROL.
001000 *
001100   DATA DIVISION.
001200 *
001300   FILE SECTION.
001400 *
001500   WORKING-STORAGE SECTION.
001600 *
001700   01   SWITCHES.
001800 *
001900        05   END-OF-DELETES-SW       PIC X     VALUE "N".
002000             88   END-OF-DELETES                VALUE "Y".
002100        05   END-OF-CUSTOMERS-SW     PIC X     VALUE "N".
002200             88   END-OF-CUSTOMERS              VALUE "Y".
002300 *
002400   01   WORK-FIELDS.
002500 *
002600        05   TABLE-NAME                   PIC X(15).
002700        05   CUSTOMER-NUMBER              PIC X(6).
002800        05   DELETE-STATEMENT.
002900             49   DELETE-STATEMENT-LEN    PIC S9(4)
003000                                          COMP VALUE +320.
003100             49   DELETE-STATEMENT-TEXT   PIC X(320).
003200        05   EDITED-SQLCODE               PIC -(4).
003300 *
003400        EXEC SQL
003500            INCLUDE SQLCA
003600        END-EXEC.
003700 *
003800   PROCEDURE DIVISION.
003900 *
004000   000-DELETE-CUSTOMER-ROWS.
004100 *
004200        PERFORM 100-PROCESS-TABLE
004300            UNTIL END-OF-DELETES.
004400        STOP RUN.
004500 *
004600   100-PROCESS-TABLE.
004700 *
004800        PERFORM 110-GET-TABLE-NAME.
004900        IF NOT END-OF-DELETES
005000            MOVE "N" TO END-OF-CUSTOMERS-SW
005100            PERFORM 120-PREPARE-DELETE-STATEMENT
005200            PERFORM 130-PROCESS-CUSTOMER-ROW
005300                UNTIL END-OF-CUSTOMERS.
005400 *
```

Figure 3-14   COBOL source code for the DYNAM2 program (part 1 of 2)

```
005500  110-GET-TABLE-NAME.
005600  *
005700      DISPLAY "-------------------------------------------------"
005800          "------------".
005900      DISPLAY "ENTER THE TABLE NAME OR 999999 TO QUIT.".
006000      ACCEPT TABLE-NAME.
006100      IF TABLE-NAME = "999999"
006200          MOVE "Y" TO END-OF-DELETES-SW.
006300  *
006400  120-PREPARE-DELETE-STATEMENT.
006500  *
006600      MOVE SPACE TO DELETE-STATEMENT-TEXT.
006700      STRING "DELETE FROM MMADBV." TABLE-NAME " WHERE CUSTNO = ?"
006800          DELIMITED BY SIZE
006900          INTO DELETE-STATEMENT-TEXT.
007000      EXEC SQL
007100          PREPARE DELSTMT FROM :DELETE-STATEMENT
007200      END-EXEC.
007300      IF SQLCODE NOT = 0
007400          MOVE "Y" TO END-OF-CUSTOMERS-SW
007500          DISPLAY " DELETE STATEMENT COULDN'T BE PREPARED FOR "
007600              TABLE-NAME
007700          MOVE SQLCODE TO EDITED-SQLCODE
007800          DISPLAY "      SQLCODE = " EDITED-SQLCODE.
007900  *
008000  130-PROCESS-CUSTOMER-ROW.
008100  *
008200      PERFORM 140-GET-CUSTOMER-NUMBER.
008300      IF NOT END-OF-CUSTOMERS
008400          PERFORM 150-DELETE-CUSTOMER-ROW
008500          PERFORM 160-DISPLAY-STATUS-MESSAGE.
008600  *
008700  140-GET-CUSTOMER-NUMBER.
008800  *
008900      DISPLAY "ENTER THE CUSTOMER NUMBER OR 999999 "
009000          "TO SPECIFY ANOTHER TABLE.".
009100      ACCEPT CUSTOMER-NUMBER.
009200      IF CUSTOMER-NUMBER = "999999"
009300          MOVE "Y" TO END-OF-CUSTOMERS-SW.
009400  *
009500  150-DELETE-CUSTOMER-ROW.
009600  *
009700      EXEC SQL
009800          EXECUTE DELSTMT USING :CUSTOMER-NUMBER
009900      END-EXEC.
010000  *
010100  160-DISPLAY-STATUS-MESSAGE.
010200  *
010300      IF SQLCODE = 0
010400          DISPLAY " CUSTOMER " CUSTOMER-NUMBER " DELETED."
010500      ELSE
010600          DISPLAY " CUSTOMER " CUSTOMER-NUMBER " NOT DELETED."
010700          MOVE SQLCODE TO EDITED-SQLCODE
010800          DISPLAY "      SQLCODE = " EDITED-SQLCODE.
```

Figure 3-14   COBOL source code for the DYNAM2 program (part 2 of 2)

After the program has formatted the statement string with the STRING statement, it issues the PREPARE statement:

```
EXEC SQL
    PREPARE DELSTMT FROM :DELETE-STATEMENT
END-EXEC.
```

I supplied two values on this statement. The first, DELSTMT, is a symbolic name I made up to identify the prepared statement. I'll use this name in the EXECUTE statement that invokes the prepared statement. The second value I supplied, DELETE-STATEMENT, is the name of the variable-length data area where I constructed the statement string.

Finally, I included error-checking code in module 120 to verify the success of the PREPARE statement. If the PREPARE statement results in a non-zero SQLCODE value, some error occurred and the statement wasn't prepared. If the PREPARE statement fails, module 120 sets END-OF-CUSTOMERS-SW to Y, and displays the value of SQLCODE. As you can see in the session example in figure 3-12, the second time the program tried to issue a PREPARE statement, it was unsuccessful because the table the user requested didn't exist. Although I could have omitted this error-checking code, it's less wasteful of system resources to use the information as a result of the PREPARE statement to report the failure and not to proceed.

After module 120 ends, module 100 continues. If the PREPARE statement in module 120 was successful, END-OF-CUSTOMERS-SW is N, and the statement

```
PERFORM 130-PROCESS-CUSTOMER-ROW
    UNTIL END-OF-CUSTOMERS.
```

causes module 130 to be executed. (If module 120 sets END-OF-CUSTOMERS-SW to Y, module 130 isn't invoked at all.) Module 130 invokes module 140 to prompt the user for the number of a customer to be deleted. The user's entry is accepted into the program variable CUSTOMER-NUMBER. If the user doesn't signal that there are no more rows to be deleted from the current table by entering 999999, module 130 continues.

To delete the specified row from the current table, module 130 invokes module 150. Module 150 contains nothing but an SQL EXECUTE statement that names the prepared statement created in module 120:

```
EXEC SQL
    EXECUTE DELSTMT USING :CUSTOMER-NUMBER
END-EXEC.
```

Notice that the EXECUTE statement uses DELSTMT, the symbolic name I assigned to the prepared statement. Also, the EXECUTE statement names the program host variable whose value will be substituted for the parameter marker in the prepared statement. Because the prepared statement DELSTMT uses only one parameter marker, this EXECUTE statement's USING clause names only one host variable: CUSTOMER-NUMBER. If a prepared statement uses more than one parameter marker, the EXECUTE statement needs to supply substitution values for each of them.

Discussion

In DYNAM2, you can see that parameter markers let you use a dynamic SQL statement much like a static SQL statement. But, by implementing this program with dynamic SQL, I was able to let the user work with one program to access many different tables, and I didn't have to code DELETE statements that explicitly name each.

However, if the tables the user needs to work with are known in advance, it is more efficient to do a separate static DELETE statement for each table. The real utility of this program is in situations where there is no way to know in advance which tables are available to the user.

Objectives

1. Given application and table specifications, code a program that uses the PREPARE and EXECUTE statements to issue a non-SELECT statement dynamically.

2. List situations where it's not acceptable to use parameter markers in a prepared SQL statement.

How to use PREPARE and the cursor-processing statements to issue SELECT statements dynamically

To use SELECT statements dynamically, you have to take a different approach than you do with all other statements. If you are going to use a *fixed-list SELECT* (that is, if you know what the structure of the results table will be when you code your program), dynamic SELECTs are fairly straightforward. You simply use the PREPARE statement and the cursor-processing statements DECLARE CURSOR, OPEN, FETCH, and CLOSE.

On the other hand, if you need to issue a *variable-list SELECT* (in other words, if you can't anticipate the structure of the results table the statement will return), the task is more complex. In that case, after you prepare the SELECT statement, you have to use the SQL DESCRIBE statement to determine the structure of the results table the SELECT will generate. Then, you have to prepare the storage areas for the results table's columns. That's a complicated programming task, and because it's beyond what you'll probably ever need to do in COBOL, I won't cover it in this book. So, if you have to write a program that does a variable-list SELECT, you'll need to refer to the DB2 manuals for more information. The place to start is the *IBM Database 2 Version 2 Application Programming and SQL Guide*.

In this topic, I'll show you how to do a fixed-list dynamic SELECT. First, I'll present the forms of the DECLARE CURSOR, OPEN, FETCH, and CLOSE statements you have to use when you process a SELECT statement dynamically. Then, I'll show you a program that contains a fixed-list SELECT.

The syntax and operation of the DECLARE CURSOR, OPEN, FETCH, and CLOSE statements for use with a dynamic SELECT

Figure 3-15 illustrates the operation of the statements you use to process a fixed-list dynamic SELECT and compares them with the operation of the PREPARE and EXECUTE statements that you learned in topic 3. To process a fixed-list dynamic SELECT, a program uses five different SQL

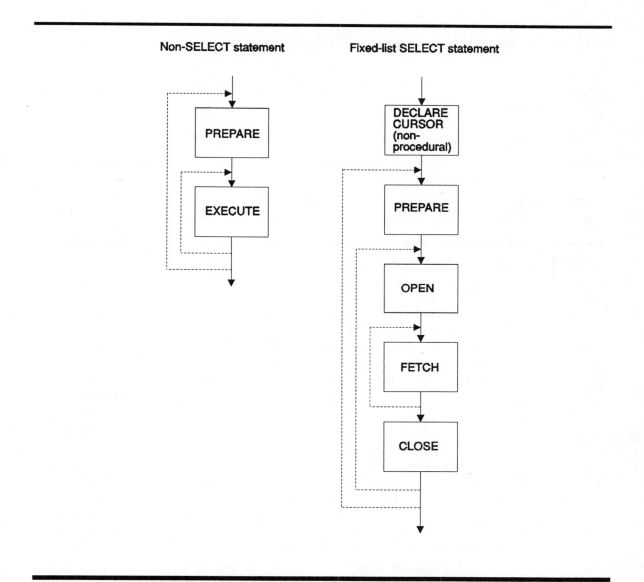

Non-SELECT statement   Fixed-list SELECT statement

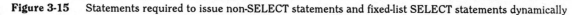

Figure 3-15 Statements required to issue non-SELECT statements and fixed-list SELECT statements dynamically

statements instead of just the two used with any non-SELECT statement that may be executed more than once.

First, the program must include a DECLARE CURSOR statement. Then, it must issue a PREPARE statement to create a prepared SELECT. After the program has prepared the SELECT, it can OPEN the cursor to

The SQL DECLARE CURSOR statement for working with a dynamic SELECT

```
EXEC SQL
    DECLARE cursor-name CURSOR FOR prepared-select-name
END-EXEC.
```

Explanation

cursor-name   The name to be used for the cursor for processing a results table generated by a dynamic SELECT
                           statement.

prepared-select-name   The name of a prepared SELECT statement (specified on a PREPARE statement) that will be
                           processed when this cursor is opened.

Figure 3-16   The SQL DECLARE CURSOR statement for working with a dynamic SELECT

generate the results table, FETCH rows from the results table, then CLOSE
the cursor. Although working with a fixed-list dynamic SELECT requires
more statements than a non-SELECT dynamic statement, it's easy to understand. Just keep in mind that the OPEN, FETCH, and CLOSE statements
together take the place of the EXECUTE statement.

Figure 3-16 shows the syntax of the DECLARE CURSOR statement for
dynamic SQL. It's simpler than the version of the statement for static SQL
because it doesn't include a SELECT statement. Instead, it simply specifies
the name of a prepared SELECT.

Remember, DECLARE CURSOR is a declarative statement, not a proce-
dural statement. As a result, you can code a DECLARE CURSOR statement
for a dynamic SELECT before the PREPARE statement that creates the
prepared statement. But because the OPEN statement generates the cursor-
controlled results table from the prepared SELECT, you *do* need to issue a
PREPARE statement for the SELECT before you issue the OPEN statement.

The syntax of the OPEN statement for dynamic processing, presented
in figure 3-17, is much like the version for static SQL. However, this version
includes a USING clause that specifies the host variables that contain substitute values for the parameter markers in the prepared SELECT. These are
like the values you code on the USING clause of the EXECUTE statement
when you work with dynamic statements other than SELECT. The OPEN
statement's USING clause also lets you specify an SQL Descriptor Area for
the prepared SELECT; this option is for variable-list SELECTs, not fixed-list
SELECTs, so I won't illustrate it here.

The SQL OPEN statement for working with a dynamic SELECT

```
EXEC SQL
    OPEN cursor-name USING {:host-var[,:host-var...]}
                           {DESCRIPTOR sqlda-name    }
END-EXEC.
```

Explanation

cursor-name	The name of a cursor that has been specified in a DECLARE CURSOR statement for a prepared SELECT statement.
host-var	The COBOL name of the host variable whose value DB2 will substitute for the corresponding parameter marker in the prepared SELECT. Be sure to precede each COBOL host variable name with a colon.
sqlda-name	The name of an SQLDA that describes the host variables whose values will be substituted for parameter markers in the prepared SELECT. Useful only with a variable-list SELECT.

Figure 3-17   The SQL OPEN statement for working with a dynamic SELECT

For fixed-list dynamic SELECTs, the FETCH statement that retrieves data from the cursor-controlled results table is just like it is in static SQL. On it, you name the host variables where DB2 will return the contents of the rows you FETCH. As you can see in the syntax of the FETCH statement in figure 3-18, you can also specify an SQL Descriptor Area on the USING clause. But as with the OPEN statement, this isn't important for fixed-list SELECTs; it's relevant only for variable-list SELECTs.

As in static SQL, you need to issue a CLOSE statement to release a cursor-controlled results table when you've finished working with it. You must close a cursor if you want to prepare another SELECT statement for it; a PREPARE statement that specifies a statement name associated with an open cursor will fail.

There aren't any syntax differences between static and dynamic SQL for CLOSE. Just specify the cursor name after the statement name. I've included the syntax of the CLOSE statement in figure 3-19 just so all of the statements for cursor processing in dynamic SQL appear here.

Using a fixed-list dynamic SELECT in a program

Now, I'd like to show you a sample program that uses a fixed-list SELECT. This program, DYNAM3, operates with the same customer tables as the

The SQL FETCH statement for working with a dynamic SELECT

```
EXEC SQL
    FETCH cursor-name
            INTO {:host-var[,:host-var...]}
                 {:host-structure        }
          [USING DESCRIPTOR sqlda-name]
END-EXEC.
```

Explanation

cursor-name	The name of an open cursor.
host-var	The COBOL name of the host variable where DB2 will place the data it fetches from the corresponding column in the results table produced by the prepared SELECT. Be sure to precede each COBOL host variable name with a colon.
host-structure	The COBOL name of the group item where DB2 will place the data it fetches from the results table. Be sure to precede the COBOL host structure name with a colon.
sqlda-name	The name of an SQLDA that describes the host variables to be used to receive the results of the prepared SELECT. Useful only with a variable-list SELECT.

Figure 3-18   The SQL FETCH statement for working with a dynamic SELECT

DYNAM1 and DYNAM2 programs I presented in topics 2 and 3. But instead of deleting rows, this program lets the user display data from a range of rows in the current table. To do that, it generates a SELECT statement whose WHERE clause uses the BETWEEN keyword. The WHERE clause contains two parameter markers, one for each of the options of BETWEEN.

As with the program examples in topics 2 and 3, I'll first show you an example of this program's screen interactions with a user. Then, I'll present and describe its structure chart and source code.

The operation of the DYNAM3 program   The screens in figure 3-20 illustrate a session with the DYNAM3 program. At the start of the session, in part 1 of the figure, the program prompted the user for the name of the table to be accessed. The user entered CUST0803. Then, the program generated the prepared SELECT to retrieve rows from that table. After the SELECT statement has been prepared, the program can use it over and over to retrieve ranges of customer rows from the specified table.

Next, the program prompted the user for the starting and ending values for the range. In this example, the user entered customer number 400006

The SQL CLOSE statement for working with a dynamic SELECT

```
EXEC SQL
    CLOSE cursor-name
END-EXEC.
```

Explanation

cursor-name   The name of an open cursor that you want to release.

Figure 3-19   The SQL CLOSE statement for working with a dynamic SELECT

as the starting value and 400008 as the ending value. After it captured these values, the program issued an OPEN statement to generate the cursor-controlled results table. When it did, these values were substituted for the parameter markers in the prepared SELECT. The result was that the three rows that met the selection condition were retrieved. You can see the data these rows contain in part 1 of figure 3-20. After it displayed the last row from the results table, the program displayed a message to indicate it had reached the end of the cursor-controlled results table. At this point, the program closed the cursor.

Then, the program prompted the user to enter the starting and ending values for another range in the same table. The user entered 400015 and 400020. Because the SELECT statement that names the current table had already been prepared, the program was able simply to issue another OPEN statement for the cursor with these new values for the parameter markers. This time, only two rows met the condition, because rows with customer numbers 400017 through 400020 weren't in the CUST0803 table.

The user didn't want to do another browse of the CUST0803 table, so he entered 999999 in response to the starting value prompt, as you can see in the screen in part 2 of figure 3-20. Then, the program asked for the name of another table or 999999 to end the session. Because the user was interested in looking at data from another of the temporary customer tables, he entered CUST0804. Then, DYNAM3 rebuilt the statement string for the SELECT, and it issued the PREPARE statement again to create a new prepared statement that will access the table CUST0804 instead of CUST0803.

To view data from the second table, the user entered the same range values that he used for the first browse of the CUST0803 table: 400006 through 400008. This time, the table contained two rows. After the user

Part 1

The user did two
dynamic queries for data
in the CUST0803 table.

```
    ---------------------------------------------------------------
    ENTER THE TABLE NAME TO BROWSE OR 999999 TO QUIT.
    CUST0803
    ---------------------------------------------------------------
    ENTER THE STARTING CUSTOMER NUMBER OR 999999
    TO QUIT OR BROWSE A DIFFERENT TABLE.
    400006
    ENTER THE ENDING CUSTOMER NUMBER.
    400008
        400006 P. HONG                       SAN FRANCISCO      CA
        400007 P. ROACH                      DEARBORN HEIGHTS   MI
        400008 T. JOHNSON                    SO CHICAGO HTS     IL
    THAT'S THE LAST ROW.
    ---------------------------------------------------------------
    ENTER THE STARTING CUSTOMER NUMBER OR 999999
    TO QUIT OR BROWSE A DIFFERENT TABLE.
    400015
    ENTER THE ENDING CUSTOMER NUMBER.
    400020
        400015 V. GEORGE                     PHILADELPHIA       PA
        400016 J. NOETHLICH                  MERRIMACK          NH
    THAT'S THE LAST ROW.
    ---------------------------------------------------------------
    ***
```

Part 2

The user changed the
current table to
CUST0804, then did one
more query.

```
    ENTER THE STARTING CUSTOMER NUMBER OR 999999
    TO QUIT OR BROWSE A DIFFERENT TABLE.
    999999
    ---------------------------------------------------------------
    ENTER THE TABLE NAME TO BROWSE OR 999999 TO QUIT.
    CUST0804
    ---------------------------------------------------------------
    ENTER THE STARTING CUSTOMER NUMBER OR 999999
    TO QUIT OR BROWSE A DIFFERENT TABLE.
    400006
    ENTER THE ENDING CUSTOMER NUMBER.
    400008
        400006 P. HONG                       SAN FRANCISCO      CA
        400008 T. JOHNSON                    SO CHICAGO HTS     IL
    THAT'S THE LAST ROW.
    ---------------------------------------------------------------
    ENTER THE STARTING CUSTOMER NUMBER OR 999999
    TO QUIT OR BROWSE A DIFFERENT TABLE.
    999999
    ---------------------------------------------------------------
    ENTER THE TABLE NAME TO BROWSE OR 999999 TO QUIT.
    999999
    ***
```

Figure 3-20   Operation of the DYNAM3 program

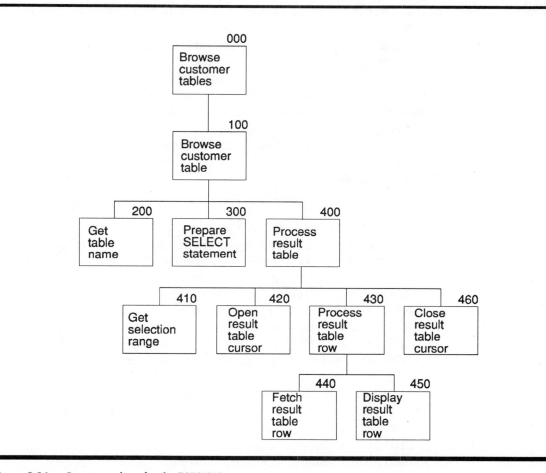

Figure 3-21   Structure chart for the DYNAM3 program

examined the data in those rows, he entered 999999 to end processing of the CUST0804 table, and 999999 again to end the program.

The design of the DYNAM3 program   The structure chart for the DYNAM3 program is in figure 3-21. The program performs module 100 for each table the user specifies. First, module 100 invokes module 200 to accept the name of the table to be processed. If the user doesn't enter 999999 to signal the end of the program, module 100 invokes module 300 to prepare the SELECT statement for the table the user specified in module 200. Then, module 100 performs module 400 for as many separate browses

of the current table as the user wants. For each browse, module 400 uses
the statement prepared in module 300.

Each time it runs, module 400 accepts the range limits for the browse
by performing module 410. If the user doesn't enter 999999 to indicate that
no more browses should be done for the current table, module 400 pro-
ceeds by opening the cursor-controlled results table in module 420. Then,
module 400 repeatedly executes module 430, once for each row in the
cursor-controlled results table. Module 430, in turn, invokes subordinate
modules to issue a FETCH statement to get the next row and to display its
contents. Finally, after it has displayed the last row or the user has entered
999999 to end the browse, module 400 performs module 460 to close and
release the cursor-controlled results table.

The source code for the DYNAM3 program   Now that you have the
operation of the program in mind, you should find it easy to follow its
source code in figure 3-22. You'll recognize that it's a modification of the
DYNAM1 and DYNAM2 programs from topics 2 and 3.

The program's Working-Storage Section is like that in DYNAM1 and
DYNAM2, except I included a couple more fields. First, I added another
switch field to let the program manage its more complicated processing.
Then, I added two text fields, HIGH-CUSTOMER-NUMBER and LOW-
CUSTOMER-NUMBER. The program uses these fields to store the range
limit values it accepts from the user. And, as you'll see in a moment, it uses
them as substitution values for the parameter markers it includes in its prepared SELECT. I also included a work field called FNAME-STRING that the
program uses to format data for display.

Also in the Working-Storage Section, I coded this DECLARE CURSOR
statement for the dynamic SELECT:

```
EXEC SQL
    DECLARE SELCURS CURSOR FOR DYNAMSELECT
END-EXEC.
```

SELCURS is the name I chose for the cursor, and DYNAMSELECT is the
name I will assign to the prepared SELECT statement in the PREPARE
statement.

Notice that this DECLARE CURSOR statement doesn't contain a
SELECT component. Instead, the SELECT component is provided indi-
rectly by the prepared SELECT that is created by the PREPARE statement

```
000100    IDENTIFICATION DIVISION.
000200  *
000300    PROGRAM-ID.        DYNAM3.
000400  *
000500    ENVIRONMENT DIVISION.
000600  *
000700    INPUT-OUTPUT SECTION.
000800  *
000900    FILE-CONTROL.
001000  *
001100    DATA DIVISION.
001200  *
001300    FILE SECTION.
001400  *
001500    WORKING-STORAGE SECTION.
001600  *
001700    01   SWITCHES.
001800  *
001900         05   END-OF-SELECTS-SW        PIC X      VALUE "N".
002000              88   END-OF-SELECTS                  VALUE "Y".
002100         05   END-OF-BROWSES-SW        PIC X      VALUE "N".
002200              88   END-OF-BROWSES                  VALUE "Y".
002300         05   END-OF-CUSTOMERS-SW      PIC X      VALUE "N".
002400              88   END-OF-CUSTOMERS                VALUE "Y".
002500  *
002600    01   WORK-FIELDS.
002700  *
002800         05   TABLE-NAME                          PIC X(15).
002900         05   HIGH-CUSTOMER-NUMBER                PIC X(6).
003000         05   LOW-CUSTOMER-NUMBER                 PIC X(6).
003100         05   SELECT-STATEMENT.
003200              49   SELECT-STATEMENT-LEN      PIC S9(4)
003300                                             COMP VALUE +320.
003400              49   SELECT-STATEMENT-TEXT     PIC X(320).
003500         05   EDITED-SQLCODE                      PIC -(4).
003600         05   FNAME-STRING.
003700              10   FNAME-INITIAL            PIC X.
003800              10   FILLER                   PIC X(19).
003900  *
004000         EXEC SQL
004100              INCLUDE CUST
004200         END-EXEC.
004300  *
004400         EXEC SQL
004500              INCLUDE SQLCA
004600         END-EXEC.
004700  *
004800         EXEC SQL
004900              DECLARE SELCURS CURSOR FOR DYNAMSELECT
005000         END-EXEC.
005100  *
005200    PROCEDURE DIVISION.
005300  *
005400    000-BROWSE-CUSTOMER-TABLES.
005500  *
005600         PERFORM 100-BROWSE-CUSTOMER-TABLE
005700              UNTIL END-OF-SELECTS.
005800         STOP RUN.
005900  *
```

Figure 3-22   COBOL source code for the DYNAM3 program (part 1 of 3)

```
006000   100-BROWSE-CUSTOMER-TABLE.
006100 *
006200       PERFORM 200-GET-TABLE-NAME.
006300       IF NOT END-OF-SELECTS
006400           MOVE "N" TO END-OF-BROWSES-SW
006500           PERFORM 300-PREPARE-SELECT-STATEMENT
006600           PERFORM 400-PROCESS-RESULT-TABLE
006700               UNTIL END-OF-BROWSES.
006800 *
006900   200-GET-TABLE-NAME.
007000 *
007100       DISPLAY "----------------------------------------------".
007200       DISPLAY "ENTER THE TABLE NAME TO BROWSE OR 999999 TO QUIT.".
007300       ACCEPT TABLE-NAME.
007400       IF TABLE-NAME = "999999"
007500           MOVE "Y" TO END-OF-SELECTS-SW.
007600 *
007700   300-PREPARE-SELECT-STATEMENT.
007800 *
007900       MOVE SPACE TO SELECT-STATEMENT-TEXT.
008000       STRING "SELECT * FROM MMADBV."
008100           TABLE-NAME
008200           " WHERE CUSTNO BETWEEN ? AND ?"
008300           DELIMITED BY SIZE
008400           INTO SELECT-STATEMENT-TEXT.
008500 *
008600       EXEC SQL
008700           PREPARE DYNAMSELECT FROM :SELECT-STATEMENT
008800       END-EXEC.
008900 *
009000   400-PROCESS-RESULT-TABLE.
009100 *
009200       PERFORM 410-GET-SELECTION-RANGE.
009300       IF NOT END-OF-BROWSES
009400           MOVE "N" TO END-OF-CUSTOMERS-SW
009500           PERFORM 420-OPEN-RESULT-TABLE-CURSOR
009600           PERFORM 430-PROCESS-RESULT-TABLE-ROW
009700               UNTIL END-OF-CUSTOMERS
009800           PERFORM 460-CLOSE-RESULT-TABLE-CURSOR.
009900 *
010000   410-GET-SELECTION-RANGE.
010100 *
010200       DISPLAY "----------------------------------------------".
010300       DISPLAY "ENTER THE STARTING CUSTOMER NUMBER OR 999999".
010400       DISPLAY "TO QUIT OR BROWSE A DIFFERENT TABLE."
010500       ACCEPT LOW-CUSTOMER-NUMBER.
010600       IF LOW-CUSTOMER-NUMBER = "999999"
010700           MOVE "Y" TO END-OF-BROWSES-SW
010800       ELSE
010900           DISPLAY "ENTER THE ENDING CUSTOMER NUMBER."
011000           ACCEPT HIGH-CUSTOMER-NUMBER.
011100 *
```

Figure 3-22   COBOL source code for the DYNAM3 program (part 2 of 3)

```
011200    420-OPEN-RESULT-TABLE-CURSOR.
011300 *
011400        EXEC SQL
011500            OPEN SELCURS USING :LOW-CUSTOMER-NUMBER,
011600                               :HIGH-CUSTOMER-NUMBER
011700        END-EXEC.
011800        IF SQLCODE NOT = 0
011900            MOVE "Y"      TO END-OF-CUSTOMERS-SW
012000            MOVE SQLCODE TO EDITED-SQLCODE
012100            DISPLAY " PROCESSING ERROR  - SQLCODE " EDITED-SQLCODE.
012200 *
012300    430-PROCESS-RESULT-TABLE-ROW.
012400 *
012500        PERFORM 440-FETCH-RESULT-TABLE-ROW.
012600        IF NOT END-OF-CUSTOMERS
012700            PERFORM 450-DISPLAY-RESULT-TABLE-ROW.
012800 *
012900    440-FETCH-RESULT-TABLE-ROW.
013000 *
013100        EXEC SQL
013200            FETCH SELCURS INTO :CUSTOMER-ROW
013300        END-EXEC.
013400        IF SQLCODE = 100
013500            MOVE "Y" TO END-OF-CUSTOMERS-SW
013600            DISPLAY "THAT'S THE LAST ROW."
013700        ELSE
013800            IF SQLCODE NOT = 0
013900                MOVE "Y"      TO END-OF-CUSTOMERS-SW
014000                MOVE SQLCODE TO EDITED-SQLCODE
014100                DISPLAY " PROCESSING ERROR  - SQLCODE "
014200                        EDITED-SQLCODE.
014300 *
014400    450-DISPLAY-RESULT-TABLE-ROW.
014500 *
014600        MOVE FNAME TO FNAME-STRING.
014700        DISPLAY "    " CUSTNO " " FNAME-INITIAL ". " LNAME
014800                " " CITY " " STATE.
014900 *
015000    460-CLOSE-RESULT-TABLE-CURSOR.
015100 *
015200        EXEC SQL
015300            CLOSE SELCURS
015400        END-EXEC.
015500 *
```

Figure 3-22   COBOL source code for the DYNAM3 program (part 3 of 3)

in module 300. Before the PREPARE statement is issued, module 300 executes this COBOL STRING statement:

```
STRING "SELECT * FROM MMADBV."
       TABLE-NAME
       " WHERE CUSTNO BETWEEN ? AND ?"
       DELIMITED BY SIZE
       INTO SELECT-STATEMENT-TEXT.
```

to format the statement string for the SELECT.

For example, after the user entered the table name CUST0803, which the ACCEPT statement in module 200 stored in the field TABLE-NAME, this string statement caused the value

```
SELECT * FROM MMADBV.CUST0803 WHERE CUSTNO BETWEEN ? AND ?
```

to be stored in the field SELECT-STATEMENT-TEXT. This is a properly formatted statement string for a dynamic SELECT. It doesn't include EXEC SQL or END-EXEC, and it doesn't include any host variables. However, it does use two parameter markers.

After it has formatted the statement string, module 300 issues

```
EXEC SQL
    PREPARE DYNAMSELECT FROM :SELECT-STATEMENT
END-EXEC.
```

to create the prepared SELECT statement. Note that the statement name I specified, DYNAMSELECT, is the same one I used in the DECLARE CURSOR statement. The operand of the FROM clause, SELECT-STATEMENT, is a Working-Storage group item that's compatible with DB2's VARCHAR data type. Its text component is SELECT-STATEMENT-TEXT, the field where the COBOL STRING statement stored the statement string.

After the program has prepared this SELECT statement, it can be used repeatedly by opening the SELCURS cursor. The OPEN statement has to supply proper substitution values for the parameter markers that are in the statement string. Module 410 uses COBOL ACCEPT statements to capture those values and store them in the LOW-CUSTOMER-NUMBER and HIGH-CUSTOMER-NUMBER fields.

Then, module 420 issues the OPEN statement:

```
EXEC SQL
    OPEN SELCURS USING :LOW-CUSTOMER-NUMBER,
                       :HIGH-CUSTOMER-NUMBER
END-EXEC.
```

Because I associated the prepared statement name DYNAMSELECT with the cursor name SELCURS in the DECLARE CURSOR statement, this OPEN statement will cause the DYNAMSELECT prepared statement to be executed.

Just before the prepared statement is executed, the current values of the program variables I specified on the OPEN statement's USING clause (LOW-CUSTOMER-NUMBER and HIGH-CUSTOMER-NUMBER) are substituted for its parameter markers. The first item you specify on the USING clause of the OPEN statement is substituted for the first parameter marker in the prepared statement, the second item is substituted for the second parameter marker, and so on. So, when the value of LOW-CUSTOMER-NUMBER is 400006 and the value of HIGH-CUSTOMER-NUMBER is 400008, DB2 uses

```
SELECT * FROM MMADBV.CUST0803
       WHERE CUSTNO BETWEEN 400006 AND 400008
```

as the final form for the prepared SELECT.

After the program has generated the cursor-controlled results table, it uses a FETCH statement (in module 440) to retrieve each of its rows. There's nothing unusual about this FETCH statement. It's just like one you might code in a static SQL program.

The program monitors the SQLCODE value in module 440 after each FETCH statement. When the value DB2 returns is 100, the program has already retrieved the last row in the results table, so the browse ends. Then, the program issues a CLOSE statement for the cursor (in module 460). As with the FETCH statement, there's nothing unusual about the CLOSE statement.

Because the program prepared the SELECT with parameter markers, another cursor-controlled results table can be generated by it. It's not necessary to prepare the statement again to access a different set of rows from the same table. All the program has to do is accept the new range limits for the parameter markers and re-open the cursor. This program provides this capability by performing module 400-PROCESS-RESULT-TABLE repeatedly within 100-BROWSE-CUSTOMER-TABLE. However, if the user wants to access a different table, it is necessary to reformat the statement string and issue the PREPARE statement again. The program does this by performing 100-BROWSE-CUSTOMER-TABLE repeatedly within 000-BROWSE-CUSTOMER-TABLES.

Terms

fixed-list SELECT
variable-list SELECT

Objectives

1. Given application and table specifications, code a program that uses a fixed-list SELECT statement.

2. Describe the difference between a fixed-list SELECT and a variable-list SELECT.

Chapter 4

How to work
with distributed DB2 data

With release 2.2 of DB2, IBM added support for *distributed data* management. In the most obvious case, that means a program running on one machine can process DB2 data stored on another machine. In this chapter, I'll give you a brief overview of the concepts and terms you need to know to work with distributed data. Then, I'll present the SQL considerations you need to keep in mind when you develop programs that process distributed data. Finally, I'll offer some perspective on how support for distributed data will change with DB2 Version 2 Release 3.

Concepts for DB2 distributed data processing

Like just about everything else in the MVS world, the facilities that support DB2 distributed data are complicated. However, most of the complexity is behind the scenes, at least as far as an application programmer is concerned. To develop application programs that access and change distributed data, you need to understand DB2 subsystems and the components required for DB2 to do distributed processing. Here, I'll present them.

Subsystems   DB2 operates as an MVS *subsystem*. A subsystem is a software product that operates in its own MVS address space. DB2 isn't the only software product that runs as a subsystem. So do CICS, TSO, IMS, and many others.

Typically, a subsystem supports other programs. The subsystem may do that by providing storage for, and directly managing, the execution of the programs, like CICS does. Or, a subsystem may be available on demand to provide services for programs in other address spaces. That's how the data base management systems IMS and DB2 work.

Figure 4-1 shows that an application program accesses DB2 data through a DB2 subsystem. The program issues a request to the DB2 subsystem with SQL, and the subsystem performs the specified table operation. Then, the subsystem responds by returning status information to the program through its SQLCA. If the statement is a SELECT or a FETCH, the DB2 subsystem can also return data to the program.

Figure 4-1 shows how all DB2 data access is done in shops that run only one copy of DB2. However, a shop can run more than one DB2 subsystem. Perhaps, for example, the shop's managers want to support different applications in different environments. Or, they want to provide separate production and program-development environments. Regardless of the reason for using multiple subsystems, each one operates independently of the others. So, the objects that one DB2 subsystem "owns" are managed, accessed, and updated by that subsystem, not by others. (An *object* is simply anything that can be created or manipulated with SQL, such as a table or an index.)

Before version 2.2, a program accessing DB2 through one subsystem could not process data managed by another subsystem, even if the other subsystem ran on the same machine. But now, if the proper set-up work has been done, it's possible for users on one subsystem to process data "owned" by another subsystem.

The subsystem through which you access DB2 data directly is called your *local subsystem*. The adjective "local" describes the resources you can access through it. For example, a *local table* is one that resides in the table space your local subsystem owns.

In contrast, other subsystems you can access are *remote subsystems*. As you'd expect, the adjective "remote" is used to describe resources you can access through a remote subsystem. A table you can process through a remote subsystem is called a *remote table*.

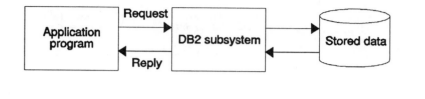

Figure 4-1   DB2 operates as a subsystem

Figure 4-2 illustrates how DB2 version 2.2 supports distributed processing between two subsystems. Your application program interacts with DB2
through your local subsystem, just as if you weren't going to do any distributed processing. However, if your program issues an SQL statement that
identifies a remote object rather than a local one, DB2 routes your statement to the remote subsystem. As the figure shows, your request is processed by the DB2 subsystem that owns the data you want to access. When
that processing is complete, the remote subsystem sends a reply back to
your local subsystem, which in turn passes it to your program. At the least,
the reply consists of information in the SQLCA that reports the success or
failure of the statement. Also, if the statement involved data retrieval (that
is, if the statement was a SELECT or a FETCH), the remote subsystem
sends that data to your local subsystem too.

A remote subsystem *can* be one that really *is* remote: One that runs on
a computer system that is not located at your local site, but that's attached
to your site with telecommunication links. However, it doesn't have to be. A
remote subsystem can also operate in the same machine as your local subsystem. The only thing that makes a remote subsystem remote is that it's
not the one where you initiated contact with DB2. In other words, any subsystem that isn't your local subsystem is remote.

Figure 4-3 shows a distributed processing situation with two remote
subsystems. One runs on the "home" computer system, the one where the
local subsystem runs. The other remote subsystem runs on a different
machine. The other machine might be in the same room as the "home"
machine, or it might be thousands of miles away.

Components required to do distributed processing   For two DB2 subsystems to be able to interact the way figures 4-2 and 4-3 illustrate, three
components need to be in place. All three are more the responsibilities of

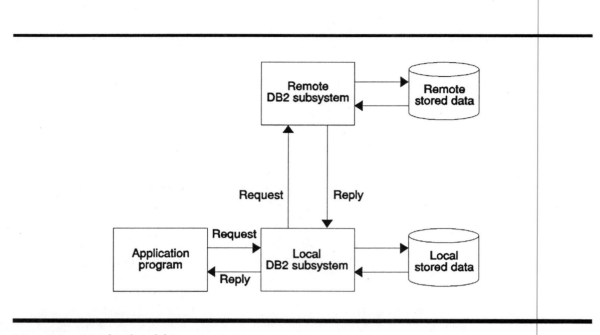

Figure 4-2   DB2 distributed data processing

data base administrators, systems programmers, and system operators than of application programmers. So, in strictly practical terms, you may not even need to know they exist. Still, I think you'll develop a better appreciation of DB2's complicated distributed processing if you know what these three components are: DB2's Distributed Data Facility, the Communication Data Base, and VTAM.

First, for two subsystems to participate in distributed data processing, a DB2 component called the *Distributed Data Facility*, or *DDF*, must be active for both. The DDF coordinates the communication of the subsystems. Installing and operating the DDF are the responsibilities of your shop's DBA and system operations staffs.

Second, the DDF needs to have a special collection of system tables called the *Communication Data Base*, or *CDB*. The CDB contains information about the subsystems that participate with one another in the distributed processing scheme. Its contents can be technical, such as detailed descriptions of the protocols that are used during communication between two subsystems. As with installing and operating the DDF, creating and maintaining the CDB isn't the responsibility of application programmers.

And third, both subsystems need to use the facilities of *VTAM*, the *Virtual Telecommunications Access Method*. VTAM enables the DB2

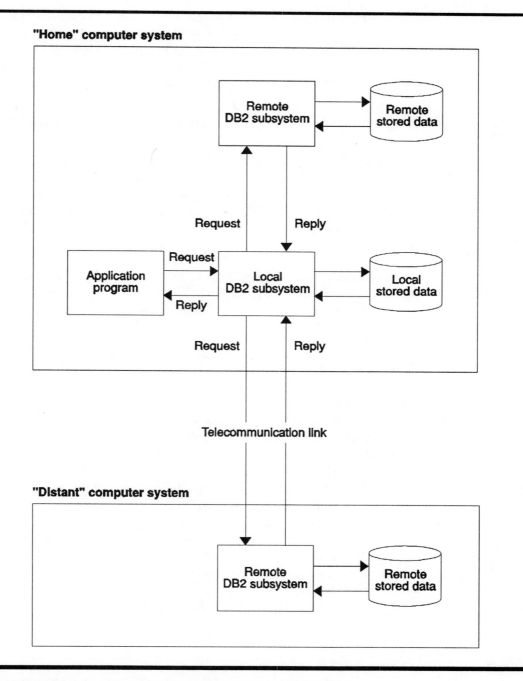

Figure 4-3 DB2 distributed data processing on two different computer systems

subsystems to communicate with each other. VTAM is a complicated product that can interact with virtually all of the major software components running on an MVS system. As such, covering it in detail is beyond the scope of this book. All you need to know is that VTAM is there and someone has configured it to support the distributed processing you do.

Programming considerations for processing distributed data

Because so much of the overhead that's necessary to do distributed processing is shielded from you, it's surprisingly easy to access distributed data. To do so, you need to know: (1) how to refer to remote objects, (2) what restrictions on SQL are in force when programs process remote data, (3) how application performance is affected by distributed processing, and (4) what some of the data problems are that can occur when you do distributed processing.

How to identify remote objects in your SQL statements   All of the SQL statements I've shown you so far have identified local objects with *two-level names*, also called *two-part names*. For instance, the two-level name

    MMADBV.CUST

identifies a customer table. A two-part name consists of an *authorization-id* and an *object name*. Here, MMADBV is the authorization-id (that is, the id of the user who created or owns the object), and CUST is the name of the object to be processed (here, a table). To identify an object that your local subsystem owns, a two-part name is sufficient.

To access a remote object, all you have to do is add another high-level qualifier to the two-level name to create a *three-level name*, also called a *three-part name*. The third level is a *location name* that a systems programmer assigned to the subsystem you want to access.

Here's an example. Suppose the CUST table is "owned" by a DB2 subsystem running on a computer system located in San Diego. The location name for San Diego is SAN. Users who access DB2 through the San Diego subsystem (that is, for whom the San Diego subsystem is the local subsystem) can refer to the CUST table with the two-part name I just showed you. However, a user on a remote subsystem would have to specify

    SAN.MMADBV.CUST

to access the CUST table.

I think you'll agree that it's simple to identify a remote object. However, you should realize that to be able to process a remote object, all of the right preliminary work needs to have been done already. That means that the communication mode between the two subsystems must have already been specified. Proper telecommunication links must be in place and active. And the DDF needs to be active for both subsystems.

Also, you need to have proper authorization at the remote site for the processing you will do with its data. With DB2 distributed processing, each site maintains control over its data and manages who may and may not access it. So, even if you know the complete three-part name for a remote object, you may not be able to access it.

Although three-part names are easy to code, they can become cumbersome. And they can present a more serious programming problem. If a table is moved from one subsystem to another, every statement that refers to it by its three-part name will have to be changed to reflect the new location name. That means all programs that specify the three-part name would have to be edited to specify the new name and put through the program preparation process. If many programs are affected, this can be a big job.

System designers can avoid this problem if they use DB2's alias feature. An *alias* is an object a DBA or systems programmer can generate with the SQL CREATE ALIAS statement. An alias associates a symbolic name with the complete three-part name that identifies an object. Application programs can use the alias rather than the complete three-part name in their SQL statements. Then, if an object is moved, only its alias needs to be changed. The programs that use the alias will be unaffected.

Because an alias is an object, its name has the same two parts as a table name: an authorization-id and an object name. When you use an alias someone else created, you have to specify both. For example, suppose a company has three data centers: one in San Diego (location SAN), one in Boston (BOS), and one in Houston (HOU). To access a table in San Diego named MMADBV.CUST without an alias, a user in Houston would have to qualify the object name as SAN.MMADBV.CUST. However, suppose a DBA at Houston, whose authorization-id is REMOTEDBA, issued this CREATE ALIAS statement to assign an alias to the CUST table:

```
CREATE ALIAS CUSTOMERS FOR SAN.MMADBV.CUST
```

Then, instead of coding a statement like

```
DELETE FROM SAN.MMADBV.CUST
    WHERE CUSTNO < '015000'
```

a programmer writing a program to be run at Houston could code

```
DELETE FROM REMOTEDBA.CUSTOMERS
    WHERE CUSTNO < '015000'
```

Notice that the statement qualifies the alias object name with the authorization-id of its creator.

As this example shows, aliases promote *location transparency.* That means that a program that accesses a table like CUST doesn't need to specify exactly where it is. That's handled within DB2, through the alias, instead of within the application program.

So, imagine the CUST table has been moved from the San Diego site to the subsystem in Boston, with a location-name of BOS. The DBA would issue the statement

```
CREATE ALIAS CUSTOMERS FOR BOS.MMADBV.CUST
```

to allow local programs to access the table that now resides on the Boston system. Because the same alias name is used, no programs have to be changed. DB2 will properly route any SQL statement that contains a reference to that alias to the Boston subsystem.

Aliases let installations standardize object names from a central point of control. As a result, application programmers usually aren't involved in creating and maintaining them. It takes special authorities to issue CREATE ALIAS statements.

Don't make the mistake of thinking that because you can use an alias created by another user that you inherit that user's authorizations. When you issue a statement that contains an alias, DB2 translates the statement before sending it to the remote subsystem. In other words, it modifies the statement by substituting the actual name of the object for the alias. Then, *your* authorizations are verified for that object, not the authorizations of the creator of the alias.

Processing restrictions on distributed data   You can use most of the SQL statements you're already familiar with when you process distributed data. However, there are a few restrictions that you need to be aware of. Figure 4-4 summarizes them for DB2 version 2.2.

First, you can't refer to data from more than one subsystem in the same statement. Unfortunately, that prevents you from using the union or join feature to combine data from two or more sites.

You can issue *different* SQL statements that retrieve data from multiple sites. But, if you're updating, inserting, or deleting data, you need to know that you can't issue statements that change tables at more than one location in the same unit of work. That's because the current release of DB2 isn't able to coordinate its rollback facility so it works properly at more than one location.

Problems coordinating recovery operations between subsystems constrain distributed processing in another way too. Programs that run under

---

You may not use SQL in distributed processing that:

- refers to data from more than one subsystem in the same statement

- changes data at more than one subsystem in the same unit of work

- changes data on *any* remote subsystem from a program that runs under CICS or IMS

- does data definition operations (e.g., creates or drops tables or grants authorizations) on remote subsystems

---

Figure 4-4   Processing restrictions on distributed data under DB2 2.2

CICS or IMS can't issue statements to change remote data at all. Of course, they can still issue INSERT, DELETE and UPDATE statements to change local objects.

Also, because each subsystem location controls its own data, you can't issue DDL (Data Definition Language) statements for any remote subsystems. That means you can't create or alter remote tables. It also means that you can't issue SQL GRANT statements to gain the authorizations you need to access remote data. Those privileges have to be granted by the DBA staff at the remote site.

Performance issues related to distributed data   As you can probably guess, processing distributed data uses more system resources than the same operations on local data. At the least, the control and coordination information that the two subsystems have to pass back and forth adds to the processing load. Worse, under DB2 version 2.2, all statements that are executed at a remote site are processed dynamically instead of statically. That means the processing costs associated with translating and binding dynamic statements are added as well.

Above and beyond these processing costs are the costs of sending large amounts of data over telecommunication links. For statements that generate and return large results tables, these costs can be substantial. Fortunately, DB2 includes a performance feature called *block fetch* that reduces this cost.

Without block fetch, each row that a remote SELECT statement generates is transmitted to the local subsystem separately. This involves not just the time (which is the same as cost) of transmitting the data itself, but also the time it takes for the two subsystems to synchronize their transmission and reception. In contrast, with block fetch, the remote system packages a group of rows together into a block and sends it as a unit to the local system. This avoids the start-stop effect of standard data retrieval, and it dramatically reduces transmission times.

As with most of the other details of distributed processing through DB2, you don't have to know that block fetch is happening to take advantage of it. When it can, DB2 automatically uses block fetch. So, although the DECLARE CURSOR statement includes an explicit option that lets you specify block fetch (FOR FETCH ONLY) you don't need to code it.

DB2 can't use block fetch when there's a chance that the data it's retrieving will be modified. That's the case when you code FOR UPDATE OF on the DECLARE CURSOR statement. So, just be sure you don't code FOR UPDATE OF unless you intend to modify data.

Data problems that can occur when you do distributed processing

There are two unusual processing conditions that you may have to deal with when you work with distributed data. First, DB2 doesn't do any character conversions when it sends data from one subsystem another. That means that if you access data on a subsystem that uses a different character set than yours, such as one that operates in a different native language, you may find yourself retrieving meaningless data. And, perhaps worse, if you issue INSERT, UPDATE, or DELETE statements for objects on such remote subsystems, you can save meaningless data and corrupt the information on the other subsystem.

Second, when you specify the special registers CURRENT DATE, CURRENT TIME, and CURRENT TIMESTAMP in an SQL statement, DB2 gets those values from the system that processes the statement. So, when you work with remote data, statements that affect it use the values of these registers from the remote system, not your local system.

Both of these problems are unlikely to cause you difficulty. But if they are an issue for you, they have the potential to be real trouble. Fortunately, DBAs are sensitive to these kinds of problems and will be able to suggest approaches you can take to avoid them in your programs.

Changes to distributed processing with DB2 version 2.3

You might expect that DB2 version 2.3's support for distributed processing would be in the form of enhancements to version 2.2's support. Unfortunately, that's not the case. Instead, it will be based on open, standard protocols that will be the basis for IBM's *DRDA*, or *Distributed Relational Data Architecture*. Although the long-term plans for DRDA are that it will be able to support full-function distributed processing, the implementation in version 2.3 falls short of that.

A disadvantage of DB2 version 2.3's support for distributed processing is that it will allow a program to access only one location during a single unit of work. In contrast, version 2.2 allows access to multiple locations, as long as changes to stored data are limited to one location.

An advantage of version 2.3's distributed processing is that it will support static SQL on the remote subsystem. This will involve a different approach to program binding in which the execution locations of remotely processed statements will have to be specified at bind-time on the local subsystem. Or, the program will have to specify the location name explicitly. Both approaches are a step backward from the location transparency DB2 version 2.2 aliases provide, but the performance gains are probably worth it.

Terms

distributed data
subsystem
object
local subsystem
local table
remote subsystem
remote table
Distributed Data Facility
DDF
Communication Data Base
CDB
VTAM
Virtual Telecommunications Access Method
two-level name
two-part name
authorization-id
object name
three-level name
three-part name
location name
alias
location transparency
block fetch
DRDA
Distributed Relational Data Architecture

Objectives

1. Describe how DB2 provides support for distributed data processing.

2. Given the name of a remote object and the location name for the subsystem where the object resides, code an SQL statement that processes the object.

3. Given the alias for a remote object, code an SQL statement that processes the object.

4. List the restrictions on processing distributed data under DB2 Version 2 Release 2.

5. Describe the advantage the block fetch feature offers for processing distributed data.

Chapter 5

How to maximize locking efficiency and concurrency

DB2 supports a high degree of program *concurrency*. That means that DB2 lets multiple programs running at the same time access shared tables. In such an environment, it's inevitable that from time to time, two programs will try to access the same data at the same time. To protect that shared data, DB2 uses a sophisticated set of *locking* features. A DB2 *lock* insures that while one user is in the middle of a process that depends on the consistent state of a resource, that resource is locked to other users. That means another program can't change it.

DB2's locking operations are usually transparent to programs, and most of the options that affect locking are specified by DBAs. However, programmers do need to understand basic locking concepts. For example, some bind options, which you may be responsible for specifying, can affect locking operations in dramatic ways. And, you may need to use a couple of simple programming techniques related to locking. In this chapter, I'll present those concepts, options, and techniques.

As you read this chapter, you should keep in mind two conflicting goals DB2 constantly tries to meet. The first goal is to allow immediate, unrestricted access to stored data for authorized users. The second goal is to maintain the accuracy and consistency of stored data. One of the major tasks of data base administrators is to balance the factors that affect these goals. In this chapter, you'll learn what those factors are.

DB2 locking facilities

DB2 locks determine whether other users can access the table data your program is using and, if so, what they can do with it. The details of how DB2 locks work are complicated. However, the basic principles are simple. Whenever a program accesses data from a DB2 table, DB2 creates a lock. That lock indicates which program is using the data and whether or not the program intends to update the data. Whenever a program attempts to access data that is already locked, DB2 determines whether or not it's safe to allow the access. In this way, DB2 can insure that other programs won't interfere with a program that is in the process of updating table data.

To understand how locking works, you should think about three attributes of locks: mode, size, and duration. Figure 5-1 lists those attributes. It presents what each means, what options are available for each, and how DB2 determines the options it uses.

Mode of a lock

The first of the three attributes of a lock is its *mode* or *state*. The mode of a lock determines how restrictive the lock is. As you can see in the first column in figure 5-1, a lock's mode determines what the program that owns the lock and what other programs can do with the locked resource. The mode of a lock is determined by the SQL statement that caused the lock to be applied. There are three basic types of lock modes: share, update, and exclusive.

The least restrictive kind of lock is a *share lock*, or *S lock*. When DB2 processes a data retrieval statement (SELECT or FETCH), it applies a share lock to the stored data it accesses. The owner of a share lock can retrieve, but not change, the stored data. As a result, you'll sometimes see S locks referred to as *read-only locks*.

Because the program that holds an S lock can't change the locked data, it can't interfere with other programs. So, multiple users can acquire S locks on the same resource. In other words, multiple programs can issue SELECT statements for the same rows, and DB2 can support all of them at the same time.

	Lock mode (state)	Lock size (granularity)	Lock duration
Meaning	What the lock owner and other users can do with the locked data	How much stored data is actually locked	How long the lock is held
Options	Share Update Exclusive	Page Table Table space	When locks are placed and removed
Determined by	SQL statement issued against the object and other locks already in place Lock promotion	Bind option (ACQUIRE) Options specified for DB2 objects by DBAs SQL LOCK TABLE statement issued by a program Lock escalation	Bind options (ISOLATION, ACQUIRE, and RELEASE)

Figure 5-1   Attributes of DB2 locks

On first thought, it may seem to you that a lock isn't necessary at all if a program isn't going to change stored data. However, when a resource is locked with an S lock, DB2 knows that it shouldn't allow another program to *change* that data until the S lock is released. That insures that the data the first program holds will be consistent through a unit of work.

The second category of lock is the *update lock*, or *U lock*. You can think of this kind of lock as a *read-for-update lock*. DB2 applies a U lock to a resource when a program issues an UPDATE or DELETE statement against it or when a program retrieves data from a cursor-controlled results table whose DECLARE CURSOR statement specified FOR UPDATE OF. After it has applied a U lock to a resource, DB2 still lets other programs access the stored data in read-only mode. However, none may acquire a second update lock on the resource.

Before DB2 actually changes the stored data, it waits until all other S locks on the resource are released. Then, in a process called *lock promotion*, DB2 changes the update lock to a third kind of lock, an *exclusive lock*, or *X lock*. You can also call an X lock a *change lock*. An exclusive lock is the most restrictive kind of lock. When DB2 applies this kind of lock to a resource, no other programs can access it. After DB2 protects the resource

Multiple programs can access the same resource at the same time to retrieve (SELECT or FETCH) data. DB2 assigns a share (S) lock to the resource for each program.

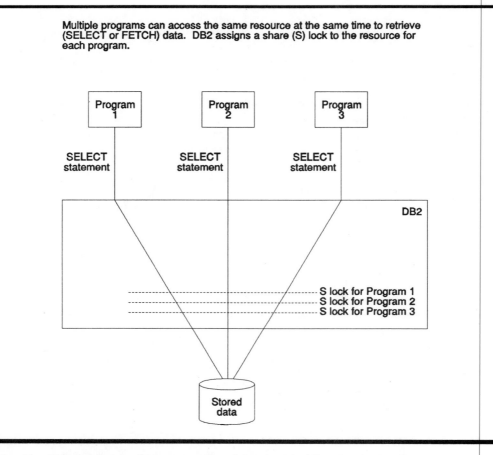

Figure 5-2 How DB2 uses lock modes to protect shared data (part 1 of 5)

from being accessed by other programs, it performs the update. (You might like to think of U and X locks as two kinds of "update" locks, where U means "update pending" and X means "update in progress.")

Figure 5-2 illustrates how DB2 might use lock modes to manage the data accesses requested by three programs. In part 1 of the figure, all three programs are accessing the same stored data. Here, each program issued a SELECT statement to retrieve data. As a result, DB2 applied an S lock to the resource for each program. Because S locks are compatible with one another, the three programs can access the stored data at the same time.

In part 2 of figure 5-2, Program 1 issued an UPDATE statement to make a change to the data it is sharing with the other two programs. This statement causes DB2 to apply a U lock to the resource for Program 1.

If a program tries to change data that other programs hold S locks on, DB2
assigns that program an update (U) lock. The specified data is accessed,
but the update is deferred until the other programs' locks are released.

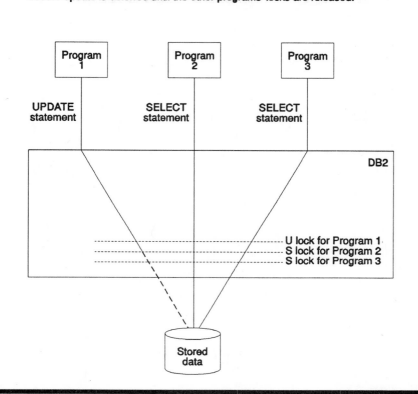
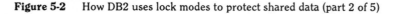

Figure 5-2   How DB2 uses lock modes to protect shared data (part 2 of 5)

Because U and S locks are compatible, Program 2 and Program 3 can continue their retrieval operations. But because Program 1's changes may interfere with the operations of the programs that hold the S locks, DB2 won't
change the data until Program 2 and Program 3 finish their retrieval
operations. When their S locks are released, DB2 can complete the
UPDATE request Program 1 made. But before it actually makes the change
to the stored data, DB2 promotes Program 1's U lock on the resource to an
X lock, as you can see in part 3 of figure 5-2.

   If a program holds an X lock on a resource, no other programs can
access the data. In part 4 of figure 5-2, Program 2 and Program 3 each
issued another SELECT statement for the locked resource. However, this
time, they have to wait for Program 1's operation to finish.

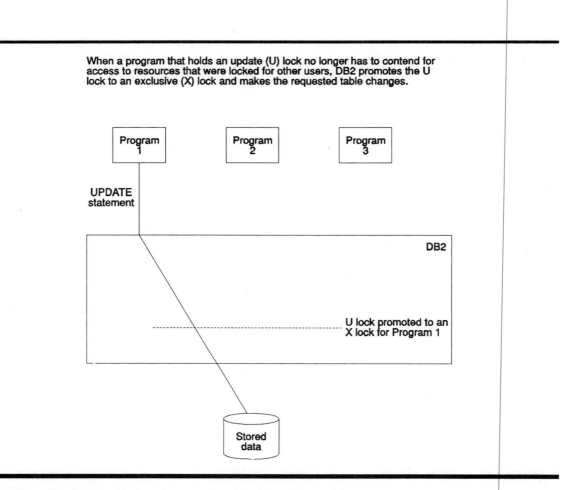

When a program that holds an update (U) lock no longer has to contend for access to resources that were locked for other users, DB2 promotes the U lock to an exclusive (X) lock and makes the requested table changes.

Figure 5-2   How DB2 uses lock modes to protect shared data (part 3 of 5)

When the UPDATE operation Program 1 requested finishes and the unit of work in which it executed is complete, DB2 releases the X lock. Then, as part 5 of figure 5-2 shows, the pending SELECT statements for the data can be satisfied, and DB2 establishes new S locks on the resource for Program 2 and Program 3.

Size of a lock

The size of a lock (that is, the amount of stored data DB2 locks) can vary from one situation to another. The DB2 literature uses the term *granularity* to describe this attribute of locking. Here, I'll describe the three different units of storage DB2 can lock, how DB2 automatically selects the size

When programs try to access resources that another program holds an
exclusive lock on, they have to wait until that program completes its
operation and the lock is released.

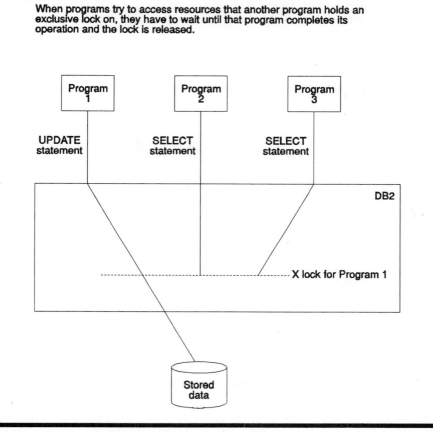

Figure 5-2   How DB2 uses lock modes to protect shared data (part 4 of 5)

for a lock, and how you can use the LOCK TABLE statement to override
DB2's automatic locking operations.

Lock units   You might expect DB2 to lock individual table rows as programs access them, but that's not the case. Instead, locks are applied at
three higher levels: page, table, and table space. To understand these lock
units, you need to know what table spaces, segments, and pages are.
     A *table space* is a group of 1 to 64 VSAM data sets that contain DB2
data. Table spaces vary in size from small to huge, and a single DB2 subsystem can own many table spaces. It's common for DBAs to define system
resources so one table space contains data for just one table. However,
that's not a requirement: A single table space can contain data for many

After an exclusive lock on a resource is released, DB2 can allow other
programs to access the data.

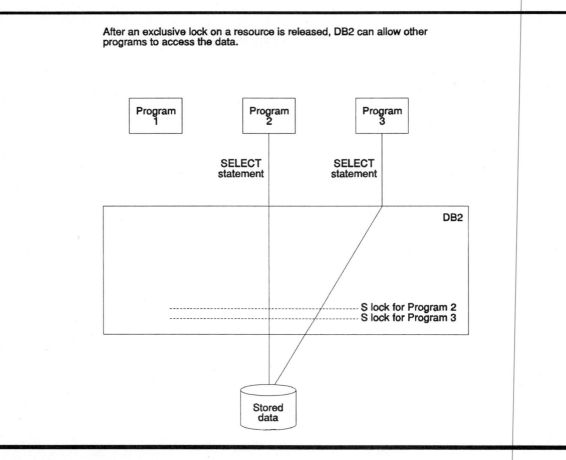

Figure 5-2   How DB2 uses lock modes to protect shared data (part 5 of 5)

tables. The table space is the largest unit of storage DB2 can lock. When a
lock is applied at the table space level, it applies to all of the data in the
table space, regardless of the number of tables or data sets involved.

The disk storage that makes up a table space is divided into smaller
units called *pages*. Because disk I/O to read or write table data is done at
the page level, the page is the lowest level where DB2 can apply a lock. A
single table space can contain thousands of pages. Each page is a fixed-size
unit, either 4K or 32K. (The DBA specifies the page size when she defines
the table space.) Each page can contain data from more than one table,
unless the table space is segmented.

In a *segmented table space*, the allocated storage is divided into units
called *segments*. Each segment can contain from 4 to 64 pages. Since the

pages in a segmented table space can contain data from only one table, DB2 is able to lock entire tables without also locking data for other tables that reside in the same table space. In contrast, the data for a single table in a *non-segmented table space* can't be locked independently of the data for other tables in the table space.

Figure 5-3 illustrates different lock sizes with small, simple table spaces. Each of these table spaces contains four pages and stores data for two tables, Table 1 and Table 2. Table 1 has six rows, and Table 2 has five rows.

Examples 1 and 2 in figure 5-3 show the effects of lock size in a non-segmented table space. Both examples illustrate locking when a program accesses Row 1 in Table 2. As you can see, the page that contains the data for that row, Page 2, contains rows not just from Table 2, but also from Table 1.

As example 1 shows, with page-level locking, accessing that row causes DB2 to lock the entire page that contains it. (The dark rectangle represents the size of the lock.) On the other hand, when locking is done at the table-space level, as in example 2, more data is involved. In this example, even though the target of the operation is just one row, DB2 locks all of the data in Table 2 plus all of the data in Table 1. Here, that's only four pages, but imagine the effect of table-space locking for a table space with 4,000 pages.

Examples 3 and 4 in figure 5-3 illustrate the effects of lock size in a segmented table space. (For simplicity, the segments in examples 3 and 4 each contain only two pages. In reality, they would contain a minimum of four pages.) Here, because the data from the two tables isn't mixed in a single page, the data for Row 1 of Table 2 is in Page 3 in examples 3 and 4, not Page 2. That means that a page-level lock can't affect data in more than one table, as you can see in example 3. And when data is stored in a segmented table space, the DBA can specify locking at the table level, as the lock in example 4 illustrates.

How DB2 selects the size for a lock   The storage unit DB2 uses for a lock depends on a bind option (RESOURCE ACQUISITION TIME, which I'll describe when I discuss lock duration) and on how the DBA defined the table space that contains the data being accessed. The LOCKSIZE clause of the Data Definition Language statements CREATE TABLESPACE and ALTER TABLESPACE specifies the default lock size for the table space. If a DBA knows that one size will be best for a given table space, she can explicitly specify PAGE, TABLE, or TABLESPACE on the LOCKSIZE clause.

Because the PAGE option restricts access to the smallest possible amount of stored data, it allows the greatest concurrency. As a result, the DBA will probably define table spaces that will contain shared data with page-level locking. However, for batch programs that access much stored

Example 1   Locking at the page level in a non-segmented table space can affect data for more than one table.

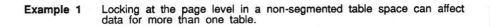
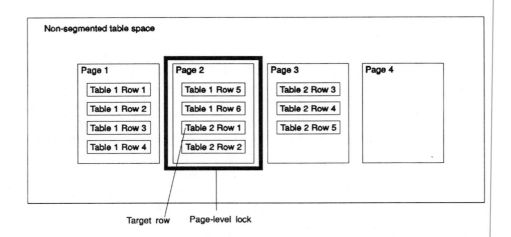

Target row   Page-level lock

Example 2   Locking at the table-space level locks much data and can dramatically reduce concurrency.

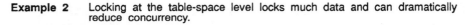
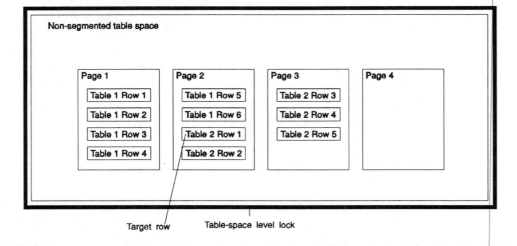

Target row   Table-space level lock

Figure 5-3   Lock sizes (part 1 of 2)

data, the CPU time and storage requirements for using page locks can be excessive. In that case, it may be more desirable for the DBA to specify TABLE or TABLESPACE on the LOCKSIZE clause. But, as you can imagine, such a lock may restrict access to a large amount to data. That can dramatically reduce concurrency because it allows one program to monopolize

Example 3   Locking at the page level in a segmented table space affects data for only one table.

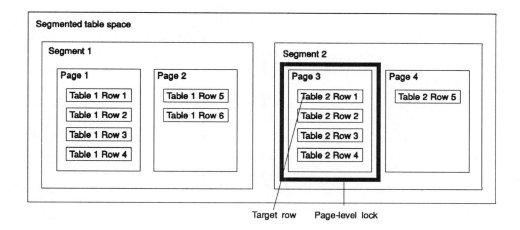

Target row   Page-level lock

Example 4   Locking at the table level is possible only in a segmented table space.

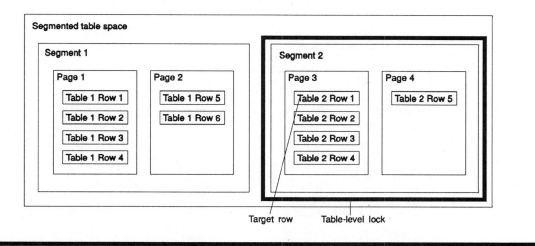

Target row   Table-level lock

Figure 5-3   Lock sizes (part 2 of 2)

all of the data in the table space. As a result, a DBA will be reluctant to define a table space with table or table-space locking as its default.

Fortunately, DB2 doesn't require the DBA to choose one of these three options for the LOCKSIZE clause. Instead, the DBA may specify a fourth option: ANY. ANY directs DB2 to select the most appropriate lock size for each processing situation. With ANY, DB2 usually uses page locks. But, if the number of pages that are locked exceeds an installation default, DB2 does a *lock escalation* and automatically locks a larger unit. For processing in a non-segmented table space, that means the lock is escalated to the table-space level; for processing in a segmented table space, that means the lock is escalated to the table level. DBAs can rely on the lock escalation feature to balance the performance requirements of specific applications with over-all system concurrency.

How to override lock unit defaults with the LOCK TABLE statement   If you *know* that a program you're developing is likely to cause a lock escala-tion, you may want to take control of the locking done on its behalf. If you do, you'll improve program performance by avoiding the many individual page locks DB2 would normally apply before escalating the lock. Your pro-gram can explicitly specify that DB2 use table (or table-space) locking for a resource, even though the DBA defined the table space with page-level lock-ing as its default.

You can do that with the LOCK TABLE statement. Figure 5-4 presents its syntax. As you can see, you specify two items on the statement: the name of the table you want to lock and the mode you want to use for the lock. For example,

```
EXEC SQL
    LOCK TABLE MMADBV.CUST
        IN EXCLUSIVE MODE
END-EXEC.
```

specifies that DB2 should apply an X (exclusive) lock to the table MMADBV.CUST.

The size of the lock DB2 applies when you issue a LOCK TABLE state-ment depends on whether or not the table resides in a segmented table space. If it does, DB2 applies a table lock, so just the pages for that table are locked. However, if you name a table that resides in a non-segmented table space, DB2 locks all of the tables stored in it, even though you named only one on the statement. This has the potential to affect many users.

The SHARE and EXCLUSIVE options of the LOCK TABLE statement determine the mode for the explicit lock. If you specify IN EXCLUSIVE MODE, DB2 applies an X lock to the table or table space, and if you specify IN SHARE MODE, DB2 applies an S lock. Note that you can't request DB2 to apply a U lock using the LOCK TABLE statement.

When a program issues the LOCK TABLE statement, it may have to wait to have the lock applied. That's the case if other programs already hold U or X locks that affect the table. Those programs have to complete their

The SQL LOCK TABLE statement

```
EXEC SQL
    LOCK TABLE table-name
        IN {SHARE    } MODE
           {EXCLUSIVE}
END-EXEC.
```

Explanation

table-name	The name of the table to be locked. You may not specify a view for *table-name*. If the table resides in a segmented table space, just the table is locked. If the table resides in a non-segmented table space, the entire table space is locked.
SHARE	Applies a share (S) lock.
EXCLUSIVE	Applies an exclusive (X) lock.

Figure 5-4   The SQL LOCK TABLE statement

operations and release their locks before DB2 will satisfy your program's LOCK TABLE statement.

Remember, when DB2 applies a lock at the table or table-space level, overall concurrency is likely to suffer. However, concurrency may not be an issue if your program runs in batch during off-hours or if it processes tables that aren't accessed by the on-line system. In fact, in those situations, locking at the table or table-space level may actually improve overall performance.

Duration of a lock

The third attribute of a lock that you need to understand is its *duration*, or how long it's held over a resource. For overall system performance reasons, it's desirable to keep resources locked for as short a time as possible. That's especially true in an on-line transaction processing environment. The length of time DB2 holds a resource depends on a number of factors related to the processing currently being done on the system. For the most part, these factors are out of your control.

One way you *can* control the duration of locks is through bind options. The three options I've shaded in the Bind panel in figure 5-5 are the ones whose settings affect the duration of a lock: ISOLATION LEVEL,

```
                               BIND
    ===>

    Enter DBRM data set name(s):
     1  LIBRARY(s)   ===> TEMP.DBRM
     2  MEMBER(s)    ===> CUSTINQ
     3  PASSWORD(s)  ===>

     4  MORE DBRMS?  ===> NO                    (YES to list more DBRMs)

    Enter options as desired:
     5  PLAN NAME ................ ===> CUSTINQ     (Required to create a plan)
     6  ACTION ON PLAN ........... ===> REPLACE     (REPLACE or ADD)
     7  RETAIN EXECUTION AUTHORITY ===> YES         (YES to retain user list)
     8  ISOLATION LEVEL .......... ===> CS          (RR or CS)
     9  PLAN VALIDATION TIME ..... ===> BIND        (RUN or BIND)
    10  RESOURCE ACQUISITION TIME  ===> ALLOCATE    (USE or ALLOCATE)
    11  RESOURCE RELEASE TIME .... ===> DEALLOCATE  (COMMIT or DEALLOCATE)
    12  EXPLAIN PATH SELECTION ... ===> NO          (NO or YES)
    13  OWNER OF PLAN (AUTHID).... ===> MMA002      (Leave blank for your primary ID
    14  DEFER PREPARE ............ ===> NO          (NO or YES)

    F1=HELP       F2=SPLIT      F3=END       F4=RETURN    F5=RFIND     F6=RCHANGE
    F7=UP         F8=DOWN       F9=SWAP      F10=LEFT     F11=RIGHT    F12=RETRIEVE
```

Figure 5-5   Bind panel options related to locking and concurrency

RESOURCE ACQUISITION TIME, and RESOURCE RELEASE TIME. If programmers in your shop are responsible for binding production programs, you should understand these options and know what values to use for them.

The ISOLATION LEVEL option applies to page locks. The RR (Repeatable Read) isolation level causes DB2 to hold all page locks a program acquires until the program reaches the end of a unit of work. This option insures that DB2 creates the same results table each time your program performs a retrieval operation during the same unit of recovery. As you might expect, RR isolation can cause one program to monopolize stored data and can significantly reduce concurrency. So don't use RR isolation unless your program must process multiple rows to make an update decision or unless retrieved rows must not be changed until the end of the unit of work.

On the other hand, when DB2 services a program bound with the CS (Cursor Stability) isolation level, it releases locks on pages that were not changed when the program acquires a lock on a different page. CS isolation improves overall concurrency. With CS isolation, the current row is protected from update by other programs, but when the program moves forward, the row is available to other programs. However, if the program makes a change to a row in a given page, DB2 doesn't release the lock on that page until the unit of work ends.

The RESOURCE ACQUISITION TIME option determines when DB2 locks a resource and at what level it's locked. You can specify either ALLOCATE or USE for this option. ALLOCATE means *all* DB2 resources that *may* be affected by a program are automatically locked at the table-space level when the program starts. The alternate value, USE, causes DB2 to lock a resource only when a program actually uses it and to use the smallest possible lock size.

The RESOURCE RELEASE TIME option determines when DB2 releases a locked resource. You can specify either DEALLOCATE or COMMIT for this option. DEALLOCATE means that DB2 will retain any locks it applies during the execution of a program until the program ends. COMMIT means that DB2 will release locks at the end of a unit of work. If a program doesn't issue COMMIT statements to partition its execution into separate units of work, it doesn't matter which release option you use.

The RESOURCE ACQUISITION TIME and RESOURCE RELEASE TIME options you select have a combined effect on locking efficiency and concurrency. Figure 5-6 shows the performance effects different combinations produce. The ALLOCATE/DEALLOCATE combination reduces CPU costs because it requires less locking. However, it drastically reduces concurrency because it affects entire table spaces for the entire duration of the program. Even so, for batch programs that run during off-hours or that update data not involved in on-line transaction processing, using this combination may be a performance advantage.

For on-line applications, USE/COMMIT is almost sure to be a more acceptable combination than ALLOCATE/DEALLOCATE because it allows much greater concurrency. But, the USE/COMMIT combination causes more locking activity. As a result, you should code programs that access data defined with this combination of options so they execute as quickly as possible or so they issue COMMIT statements frequently to release locked resources.

The third valid combination, USE/DEALLOCATE, causes DB2 to acquire locks only when they're necessary, but to maintain them even after commit points are reached. As a result, it can cause data to be tied up longer than is probably necessary. For that reason, it's unlikely to be the best choice in many situations.

What happens when locks conflict with each other?

In busy on-line processing environments where users contend for access to the same data, two kinds of conflicts are likely to arise: timeouts and deadlocks. DB2 provides facilities to handle both of these conflicts.

A *timeout* occurs when DB2 can't fulfill a program's data base request in a set amount of time. This amount of time depends on specifications made by the DBA through the software product that manages locking, the *IMS Resource Lock Manager*, or *IRLM*. (The same software product manages locking activities for both IMS and DB2.)

When the IRLM detects a timeout, it sends a message to that effect to DB2. DB2, in turn, informs the program of the timeout by returning -911 or -913 as the SQLCODE value. The first, -911, means DB2 automatically rolled back your program's current unit of work. The second, -913, means that a ROLLBACK was not issued for your program.

Although it's obvious, it's worth mentioning that timeouts are more likely to happen on a busy system than on a slow system. And they can frustrate users and reduce their productivity. So, as you might imagine, shops invest substantial effort in tuning their systems to reduce the number of timeouts that occur. Careful placement and organization of heavily used data items, for instance, can make a big difference.

A *deadlock* occurs when two or more programs need to access locked resources held by one another. In the absence of intervention by DB2, the deadlocked programs would wait forever. As a result, another more colorful term for deadlock that you'll see in DB2 literature is *deadly embrace*. DB2 handles deadlocks by rolling back the work done by one of the programs to clear the way for the other. DB2 literature calls the program that gets rolled back the *victim*. The victim in a deadlock situation receives -911 as the SQLCODE value.

When on-line programs are written so they perform limited, "small" tasks, their execution times are short. As a result, deadlocks and timeouts are unlikely. And, if an on-line program does encounter a deadlock or timeout, it probably will execute successfully if the user runs it a second time. That's because the program that interfered with it probably will have ended by then. Batch programs that run during off-hours or that process tables that don't have to be shared with other users are also unlikely to encounter timeouts and deadlocks.

However, there are some situations where timeout and deadlock conditions can, and will, occur. Programmers have two choices for dealing with these situations. The first approach is simply to treat the error as unrecoverable and end the program. That may or may not mean explicitly issuing a ROLLBACK statement to reverse the current unit of work. (Remember,

	ALLOCATE	USE
DEALLOCATE	Maximum impact on concurrency Minimum CPU requirements for locking	Intermediate impact on concurrency
COMMIT	Not allowed	Minimum impact on concurrency Maximum CPU requirements for locking

Figure 5-6   Combinations of RESOURCE ACQUISITION TIME and RESOURCE RELEASE TIME options

SQLCODE -911 means DB2 automatically performed a rollback, and -913 means it did not.)

The other approach is to code programs that reissue failed statements, in hope that the conditions that led to the deadlock or timeout will simply "go away" as other programs finish their processing. If you plan to use this technique, your programs must respond differently to the two SQLCODE values DB2 can return to report a deadlock or timeout. If DB2 automatically performed a rollback (that is, if the value of SQLCODE is -911) and the current unit of work involved more than one transaction, all of those transactions will have to be processed again. The programming logic necessary to implement this type of processing can be challenging.

Which of these two approaches you use to handle timeout and deadlock conditions depends on the particular program and your shop standards. Ask your DBA if you're not sure which approach is appropriate.

Discussion

The recommendations I've made in this chapter are for general cases for typical program types. Some problem situations require compromise solutions. For example, some batch programs are run at the same time as on-line transaction processing applications. In that situation, it's just not reasonable for the batch program to lock an entire table or table space. So, the batch program won't use LOCK TABLE. Instead, it will commit its work often, and it will probably be bound with the USE/COMMIT options for resource acquisition and release time. Although the processing costs of using page-level locks for a batch operation are great, they're necessary when the batch program must run concurrently with on-line transaction processing programs.

Terms

concurrency	granularity
locking	table space
lock	page
mode	segmented table space
state	segment
share lock	non-segmented table space
S lock	lock escalation
read-only lock	duration
update lock	timeout
U lock	IMS Resource Lock Manager
read-for-update lock	IRLM
lock promotion	deadlock
exclusive lock	deadly embrace
X lock	victim
change lock	

Objectives

1. Describe the three attributes of a DB2 lock.

2. Describe the effects lock mode, lock size, and lock duration options can have on program concurrency.

3. Use the SQL LOCK TABLE statement to raise DB2's locking for a resource from the page level to the table or table-space level.

4. Bind a program with the most appropriate combination of lock duration options.

5. Describe the difference between a timeout and a deadlock.

Section

2

DB2 in CICS programs

Most interactive application programs on IBM mainframe systems run under CICS. Because new program development work is typically for interactive environments, the chances are good that you'll face the challenge of developing CICS/DB2 programs. You can easily access DB2 data from programs that run under CICS. The chapters in this section show you how to do that.

Chapter 6 introduces CICS concepts and terminology for DB2 programmers. Even if you're an experienced CICS programmer, you should read this chapter. That's because it describes how using DB2 services from a CICS program changes the program development process. And it explains how the connection between CICS and DB2 is defined.

Chapters 7 and 8 illustrate programming techniques for processing DB2 data in CICS programs. Chapter 7 covers basics you have to know to access DB2 data from any CICS program. Chapter 8 presents more advanced programming techniques you can use to develop CICS programs that process multi-row results tables.

Although this section will show you how to access DB2 data through CICS programs, it won't present all you need to know to develop CICS programs. For a complete CICS course, you can turn to Doug Lowe's *CICS for the COBOL Programmer*, a two-book set. You'll find ordering information at the end of this book.

Chapter 6

CICS concepts and terminology for DB2 programmers

CICS (Customer Information Control System) is an IBM software product that lets computer systems support many terminal users who run a range of interactive application programs. CICS loads those programs, coordinates their execution, manages data transmissions between the programs and terminals, controls the programs' accesses to stored data (not just DB2 tables, but also IMS data bases and VSAM data sets), and maintains the integrity of stored data. So, to develop application programs that access DB2 data under CICS, you have to understand not just DB2, but also CICS.

In this chapter, I'll begin by introducing how CICS works. If you're already an experienced CICS programmer, you can skim over most of this material. Then, I'll outline basic CICS program development considerations and discuss how you define a CICS/DB2 program to CICS. You should read this material even if you're experienced with CICS. It relates specifically to the CICS/DB2 interface and discusses some features you may be expected to use.

How CICS works

Like DB2, CICS operates as an MVS *subsystem*. As such, CICS provides a variety of services that it uses to process application programs. In this section, I'll introduce you to those services and show you how application programs use them. Then, I'll describe one of the services, Basic Mapping Support, in more detail. As an application programmer, you'll need to know how to use this service directly. But before I present any of these services, you need to understand CICS transactions.

CICS transactions   Simply put, the function of the CICS subsystem is to manage transactions. A *transaction* is a predefined unit of work that a terminal user can invoke. An inquiry or order-processing application, for example, runs as a CICS transaction.

A CICS terminal user can invoke a transaction in two ways. First, he can enter a four-character code called a *transaction identifier* (or just *trans-id*) at his terminal. Alternatively, he can make a selection from a CICS menu program. Menus make access to programs easier because they supply trans-ids to CICS in a way that's transparent to the user.

CICS uses the trans-id to select the application to run. For example, to run an inquiry application, the operator might enter a trans-id like DIN1. Then, CICS would retrieve the main load module for the application associated with the trans-id DIN1, load it into storage, and execute it.

In general, CICS applications are small, single-function programs that execute quickly. There's often a one-to-one relationship between a CICS application and a CICS program, and, therefore, between a CICS program and a CICS transaction. However, that doesn't have to be the case. It's also common for an application to be designed as a set of small, related programs that perform subfunctions and that pass control back and forth as necessary to process a transaction.

How application programs use CICS services   An interactive program that operates under CICS actually executes *within* CICS. The storage it uses is CICS storage. To understand, consider figure 6-1. It shows a CICS subsystem that's running programs for four users. Because CICS provides the storage these programs occupy and services their requests, it insulates them from the operating system. In fact, as far as the operating system is concerned, CICS is the only program running in the CICS subsystem.

To access DB2 data, a program that runs under CICS issues SQL statements. As you can see in figure 6-1, the CICS subsystem passes the data request to the DB2 subsystem. DB2 does the table processing the program requests, then passes the result back to the program through CICS.

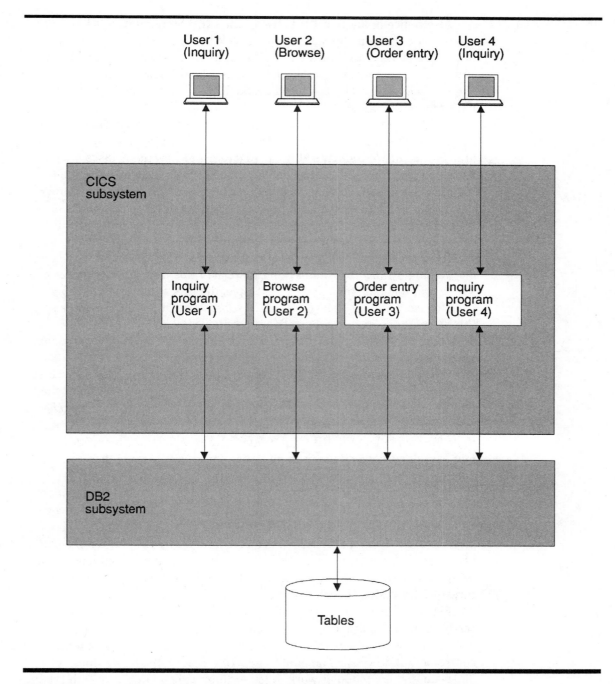

Figure 6-1   Interactive application programs executing within CICS can request DB2 services

Also notice in figure 6-1 that two of the CICS terminal users (1 and 4) are running the same transaction: inquiry. When a user invokes a transaction, CICS starts a *task* for the user. The difference between a transaction and a task is that while several users may invoke the same transaction, CICS creates a separate task for each. So, in figure 6-1, User 1 and User 4 have separate tasks.

CICS provides distinct data areas for different tasks, even when they're associated with the same program. However, it loads only one copy of a program's *executable* code into storage, regardless of how many tasks are using the program. If CICS loaded the same program code into storage for multiple tasks, it would waste valuable virtual storage. Imagine the storage that would be required if a CICS system had to support not just two users running the same inquiry program, but hundreds. Fortunately, the facility CICS uses so that only one copy of a program is loaded into storage is transparent to you as an application programmer.

To support the application program related to a task, CICS provides a variety of functional modules. For example, the task control module controls the execution of tasks in the CICS subsystem. Other CICS modules that support application programs are terminal control, file control, transient data control, temporary storage control, journal control, program control, interval control, and Basic Mapping Support.

When DB2 is used with CICS, special DB2 interface modules are loaded into storage along with the CICS modules, and they're executed under the control of CICS. These interface modules make up the *CICS/DB2 attachment facility*. Although there are some systems programming considerations for controlling the DB2/CICS interface, as an application programmer, you don't have to worry about them. You simply include the appropriate SQL statements in your program.

When your program issues an SQL statement, CICS requests the attachment facility to establish a connection with DB2 called a *thread*. Once the connection is made, the attachment facility uses it to pass the SQL statement, and any subsequent SQL statements issued by your program, to DB2. From the DB2 perspective, the SQL statement could just as well have come from a program running in batch or under TSO. I'll have more to say about threads later in this chapter.

Figure 6-2 shows in more detail how application programs use CICS services. In this figure, I've shown some of the important CICS modules. Notice that two modules control interactions with display stations: terminal control and BMS (Basic Mapping Support). Although the figure doesn't illustrate it, these modules work together to provide an interface with the operating system's telecommunications access method. The telecommunications access method, in turn, provides support for the terminal devices.

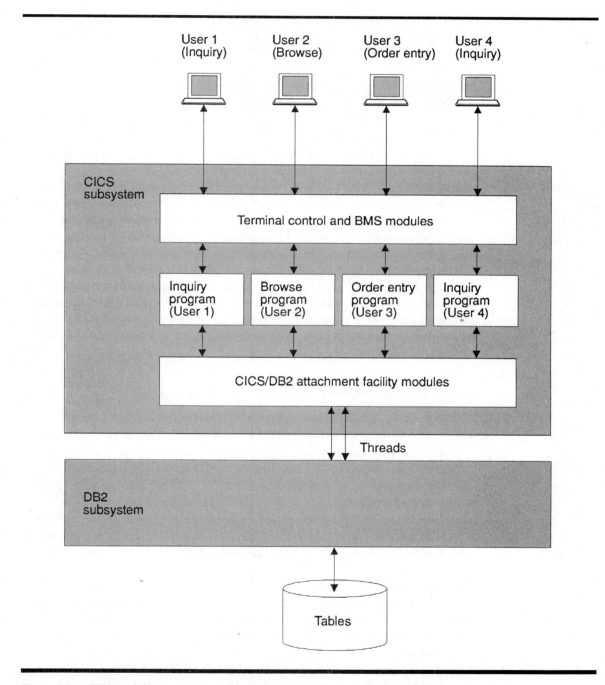

Figure 6-2   CICS modules provide terminal and data base I/O services for application programs

Basic Mapping Support   It's possible for a CICS program to interact directly with the terminal control module. However, it's more likely that you'll use *Basic Mapping Support,* or *BMS,* as an interface between your program and terminal control. BMS provides a simplified way of formatting terminal displays. So, to receive data from or send data to a terminal, an application program requests BMS services.

When you use BMS, you can exercise a high degree of control over the format of data displayed on and retrieved from a terminal. To do that, you code a special kind of assembler language program called a *mapset.* When you assemble the mapset, the assembler creates both a physical map and a symbolic map. A *physical map* is a module BMS uses to determine the screen locations and attributes of data sent to and received from the terminal. A *symbolic map,* in COBOL, is a COPY library member that defines the format of data sent to or received from the terminal.

When an application program requests that a map be sent to a terminal, BMS takes data from the symbolic map, formats, or *maps,* it according to the physical map, and sends it to the terminal. Likewise, when an application program requests that data be retrieved from a terminal, BMS uses the physical map to map the data from the screen into the symbolic map. In the next two chapters, I'll show you the BMS mapsets and the related symbolic maps for two sample programs.

Program development for a CICS/DB2 program

Figure 6-3 presents the steps in the preparation of a CICS/DB2 program. As you can see, the process is much like that for developing a DB2 program that doesn't execute under CICS. However, programming for the CICS environment requires you to add one step to the process: CICS translation. It also requires you to make some changes to other steps in the process. And it usually requires you to use a special program design technique called pseudo-conversational programming. In this section, then, I'll describe how developing a DB2 program for the CICS environment is different from developing one that will execute in batch or under TSO.

Pseudo-conversational program design   Most CICS application programs have to be written so they don't tie up valuable virtual storage resources. Although a single CICS system can support hundreds of terminals, it can't operate efficiently if many programs remain in storage while they wait for data from terminals. As a result, most CICS programs are written using the *pseudo-conversational* programming technique.

With pseudo-conversational programming, a program ends after it sends data to a terminal. Then, CICS restarts it when the operator

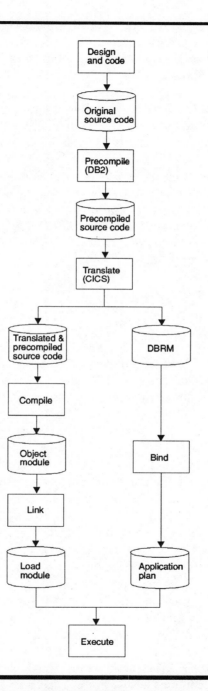

Figure 6-3   The steps required to prepare a CICS/DB2 COBOL program for execution

completes an entry. This is called "pseudo-conversational" because although the program *appears* to be carrying on a conversation with the terminal user, it may not be present in storage.

Much of the difficulty in developing a CICS program is in implementing pseudo-conversational design. This programming technique can be confusing for CICS novices because your program has to be able to figure out what it should do when it's restarted. In the next two chapters, I'll show you two inquiry programs that use the pseudo-conversational technique.

Coding the program   Obviously, just as with a non-CICS program, you have to develop a source program before you can proceed with the steps in the program preparation process. When you code a CICS program, you request CICS services by issuing *CICS commands*. To do that, you use an EXEC-level coding interface, just like you do for DB2 SQL statements.

For example, the CICS command

```
EXEC CICS
    RECEIVE MAP('DINMAP1')
            MAPSET('DINSET1')
            INTO(DINMAP1I)
END-EXEC.
```

directs CICS to receive data from the terminal screen formatted according to the specifications in a BMS mapset named DINSET1. Because a mapset can contain more than one map, this command must also specify the name of the map. In this case, it's DINMAP1. This command also directs CICS to return the terminal data to the program's Working-Storage group item named DINMAP1I.

CICS provides a number of commands. Figure 6-4 lists some of the most commonly used ones. As you can see, these commands let you request services from the CICS modules. For example, the BMS-related commands RECEIVE MAP and SEND MAP let you accept and display formatted data on the user's terminal. Although I won't present the syntax of the CICS commands, I will use several of them in the program examples in the next two chapters. And, as I describe the source code for the programs, I'll describe how the CICS commands operate.

A CICS program can also issue the full range of SQL DML statements to process data owned by the local DB2 subsystem. And, a CICS program can retrieve data owned by remote DB2 subsystems, but it can't change that data. So, don't code a CICS program that issues SQL statements like INSERT or UPDATE for data in remote tables.

As I mentioned earlier in this chapter, on-line transaction-processing programs need to be small and quick in their execution. Because of that, it makes sense to minimize the number of different SQL statements you use,

CICS commands for doing BMS-controlled screen interactions

> RECEIVE MAP
> SEND MAP

CICS commands for passing control from one program to another

> LINK
> RETURN
> XCTL

CICS commands for using temporary storage

> DELETEQ TS
> READQ TS
> WRITEQ TS

CICS commands for processing VSAM data sets

> DELETE
> ENDBR
> READ
> READNEXT
> READPREV
> RESETBR
> REWRITE
> STARTBR
> WRITE

CICS commands for handling exceptions

> HANDLE ABEND
> HANDLE AID
> HANDLE CONDITION

CICS command for maintaining data integrity

> SYNCPOINT

Figure 6-4   Commonly used CICS commands

to code the simplest statements you can, and to minimize the number of different tables a program processes. That leads to more efficient program execution.

You may also be able to improve performance by grouping SQL statements as closely as you can and deferring them to near the end of the execution of a program. Doing that can reduce the amount of time a program controls a thread, since the CICS/DB2 attachment facility doesn't create a thread for a transaction until the program makes its first DB2 request.

Just as with programs that process DB2 data in batch or under TSO, CICS/DB2 programs should commit their work often. Doing so reduces the amount of data DB2 has to maintain during a unit of work, and it makes the data available to other programs sooner. In addition, under CICS, committing a unit of work causes threads to be released and made available to other users.

Your programs won't use SQL COMMIT statements to do that. And they won't use SQL ROLLBACK statements to reverse uncommitted table changes. Because CICS serves as the transaction manager for programs it controls, it coordinates recovery operations for the different subsystems it uses. So instead of COMMIT and ROLLBACK, you request recovery services through CICS with its SYNCPOINT command.

In CICS, a commit point is called a *synchronization point,* or *sync point.* A CICS sync point occurs when a transaction ends or when the program explicitly issues a SYNCPOINT command. The SYNCPOINT command with the ROLLBACK option achieves the same result as an SQL ROLLBACK statement: It causes CICS to direct DB2 to reverse uncommitted table changes.

Translating the program   Before you compile a CICS COBOL program, you first must process your source code with the *CICS command-level translator* (often called just the CICS *translator*). The CICS translator converts CICS commands to a form that's meaningful to the COBOL compiler. The source code in figure 6-5 illustrates what the translator does.

The top section of figure 6-5 shows a typical CICS command; it's the BMS RECEIVE MAP command I've already shown you. The CICS translator converts each CICS command in a source program into a series of COBOL MOVE statements followed by a CALL statement. You can see these statements in the bottom section of figure 6-5. The MOVE statements assign values to the program fields that are the arguments of the CALL statement's USING clause. The CALL statement activates the CICS command-level interface to invoke the required CICS services. The translator also includes the source code for the original command as comments in

Original source code

```
EXEC CICS
    RECEIVE MAP('INQMAP1')
            MAPSET('INQSET1')
            INTO(INQMAP1I)
END-EXEC.
```

Translated source code

```
*
*EXEC CICS
*    RECEIVE MAP('INQMAP1')
*            MAPSET('INQSET1')
*            INTO(INQMAP1I)
*END-EXEC.
     MOVE '..}............00061   ' TO DFHEIVO
     MOVE 'INQMAP1' TO DFHC0070
     MOVE 'INQSET1' TO DFHC0071
     CALL 'DFHEI1' USING DFHEIVO  DFHC0070 INQMAP1I DFHDUMMY
     DFHC0071.
```

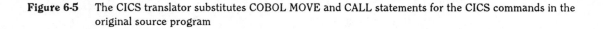

Figure 6-5   The CICS translator substitutes COBOL MOVE and CALL statements for the CICS commands in the original source program

the translated version of the program. These comments can help you read the translated program.

Besides converting all CICS commands to MOVE and CALL statements, the translator inserts other code in your program's Working-Storage and Linkage Sections. Most of it isn't directly relevant to you. However, one segment of code that the translator inserts contains definitions for a storage area called the *Execute Interface Block*, or *EIB*. CICS returns several pieces of useful information to programs through the EIB fields. You'll see examples of how to use EIB data in the programs in chapters 7 and 8.

Note that before you run the CICS translator, you should run the DB2 precompiler. (If you do your program development work through DB2I's panels, this is the sequence you'll use.) If you don't, the CICS translator will return a series of diagnostic messages because it doesn't recognize SQL statements. In contrast, the DB2 precompiler recognizes CICS commands and ignores them.

Finally, when you translate your program, you need to be careful that you specify the same delimiter character (quote or apostrophe) for strings as you do for the precompiler and the COBOL compiler. The defaults for the precompiler and the COBOL compiler are different from the default for the CICS translator.

Link-editing the program   The link-edit step of the CICS/DB2 program development process has a special requirement. To issue SQL statements from a CICS program, you must link-edit the program so it includes an interface to the CICS/DB2 attachment facility. The module that provides that interface is DSNCLI. If your shop uses a cataloged procedure for CICS/DB2 program development, it almost certainly contains the INCLUDE for this module. (You may recall from *Part 1: An Introductory Course* that you have to specify a similar interface module, DSNELI, for DB2 programs that will execute under TSO.)

Binding the program   The bind process uses the data base request module (DBRM) the precompiler produces and creates an application plan. The plan specifies the optimal paths DB2 should use to satisfy the program's data base access requests. In the examples I've shown you so far, the application plans have been simple: a single plan for a single program. However, because CICS applications are often designed as sets of multiple, related programs, the bind process can be more complicated.

When a CICS transaction involves multiple programs, the DBRMs for all of them should be available when a user invokes the transaction. If the necessary DBRMs aren't available, DB2 errors (SQLCODE -805 or -818) can result when the transaction issues an SQL statement. These errors can also result if an old version of a DBRM is used.

To include multiple DBRMs in a single application plan, just specify them on the MEMBER keyword when you bind the plan. For example, suppose I was developing an application that used three related programs whose DBRM names are PROGA, PROGB, and PROGC. Then, I'd create an application plan by coding a DSN BIND subcommand like the one in figure 6-6.

You should also notice the RESOURCE ACQUISITION TIME, RESOURCE RELEASE TIME, and ISOLATION LEVEL bind options I specified in the example in figure 6-6. For a transaction-processing program, the RESOURCE ACQUISITION TIME and RESOURCE RELEASE TIME options should probably be USE and COMMIT. That insures that data the program doesn't need won't be locked unnecessarily to other users.

The ISOLATION LEVEL bind option for on-line programs should probably be CS (Cursor Stability) rather than RR (Repeatable Read). RR may be appropriate if a program must insure that none of the data it retrieves through a cursor-controlled results table will change during a unit of work, even after it has read past a specific row. However, because CICS programs

```
DSN SYSTEM(DSNB)
BIND MEMBER      (PROGA,PROGB,PROGC) -
     PLAN        (PLANABC) -
     LIBRARY     (DB2PROG.DBRMS) -
     ACTION      (REPLACE) -
     RETAIN -
     ISOLATION (CS) -
     VALIDATE    (BIND) -
     ACQUIRE     (USE) -
     RELEASE     (COMMIT) -
     EXPLAIN     (NO) -
     OWNER       (MMA002) -
     NODEFER
END
```

Figure 6-6   A BIND statement that creates an application plan for a three-program CICS application

typically accomplish their tasks and end quickly, it's unlikely that many CICS programs will require this bind option.

The three-DBRM bind example in figure 6-6 is simple. But in production environments, application plans can involve many DBRMs. Under older releases of DB2, this has presented serious problems. The biggest problem is that an entire application plan, involving *all* of its DBRMs, had to be rebound if *any* of the DBRMs in it change. For large plans, this could take a significant amount of time. And during that time, CICS users were unable to run the transaction.

More recent releases of DB2 provide two ways to get around this problem: *Dynamic Plan Selection* and *plan packages*. Since these facilities are complex, and since application programmers aren't typically responsible for creating production application plans for the CICS environment, I'm not going to describe these facilities here. If you need advice on the right approach to take to preparing application plans, you should check with your shop's DBA or CICS-administration staff.

Defining a CICS/DB2 program to CICS

Even after you've worked through the program development process that figure 6-3 illustrates, you still can't run your program under CICS. For a program to access DB2 data from CICS, the connection between its CICS transaction and DB2 must be defined. That's done by making an entry in the CICS Resource Control Table (*RCT*).

The RCT contains the names of all CICS transactions that request DB2 services. For each transaction, the RCT contains the name of the DB2 application plan that's used with it. In addition, the RCT also specifies the threads that connect DB2 with CICS and the DB2 authorizations for CICS transactions. Although the systems programmer in your shop is probably responsible for updating the RCT, it's worth knowing what information related to threads and DB2 authorizations she can specify.

Threads   Every CICS program that requests DB2 services does so through a thread. The RCT specifies the total number of threads that will be available to connect CICS and DB2. The default maximum is 12. However, most shops specify a larger number. Even so, the number of threads is a limited resource, and contention for threads can affect overall system performance.

The RCT also specifies the type of thread CICS uses to connect to DB2. For transactions that are heavily used, *entry threads* can improve overall performance. An entry thread is one that's dedicated to a specific transaction. It can be either protected or unprotected. CICS automatically releases an *unprotected entry thread* when the program it was allocated to ends. The only exception to this is if another transaction bound with the same application plan is waiting to access DB2 data. Then, CICS uses the thread it allocated to the first transaction for the second transaction. In contrast, CICS automatically maintains a *protected entry thread* for up to a minute after the program it was allocated to ends. If another transaction bound with the same application plan is initiated within that time, CICS assigns that thread to it. Otherwise, it releases the thread.

Transactions that aren't heavily used are probably better off if they're defined so they use *pool threads*. A pool thread is one that's shared among transactions that may have different application plans. It's possible for many infrequently used transactions to operate effectively sharing a small number of pool threads. If CICS assigned entry threads to them instead, system resources would be wasted.

DB2 authorizations for CICS transactions   For a CICS program to access table data, CICS must pass an appropriate authorization to DB2. DB2 uses that value to verify that the program has authority to perform the function it requests with SQL statements. The systems programmer is typically responsible for defining to DB2 the functions a program can perform.

In the simplest case, the RCT entry for a transaction specifies an explicit authorization ID. But the CICS systems programmer may also specify through the RCT that the authorization passed to DB2 should be (1) the CICS operator id, (2) the id of the terminal where the transaction was initiated, (3) the trans-id, or (4) a USERID authorized by RACF, IBM's Resource Acquisition Control Facility.

Discussion

Developing programs that run under CICS requires you to know a number of concepts and programming techniques. Besides what I presented in this chapter, you have to know how to use CICS commands to request the functions your program needs; you have to know how to code and prepare BMS mapsets; and you have to know how to implement pseudo-conversational programs. In the next two chapters, I'll present sample CICS programs that process DB2 data, and I'll cover the considerations DB2 imposes on CICS program development. However, as I mentioned at the start of this section, you'll need to learn more skills and techniques than this section presents to be able to work at a professional level as a CICS programmer.

Terms

CICS
Customer Information Control System
subsystem
transaction
transaction identifier
trans-id
task
CICS/DB2 attachment facility
thread
Basic Mapping Support
BMS
mapset
physical map
symbolic map
pseudo-conversational programming
CICS command
synchronization point
sync point
CICS command-level translator
CICS translator
Execute Interface Block
EIB
Dynamic Plan Selection
plan package
Resource Control Table
RCT
entry thread
unprotected entry thread

protected thread
pool thread

Objectives

1. Describe how CICS lets interactive programs request DB2 services.

2. Describe the function of Basic Mapping Support.

3. List and describe the steps required to prepare a CICS/DB2 program for execution.

4. Explain why you must use the pseudo-conversational programming technique for most CICS programs.

5. Explain why you don't use SQL COMMIT or ROLLBACK statements in a CICS/DB2 program.

6. Explain why application plans for CICS/DB2 transactions are often more complicated than application plans for batch DB2 programs.

7. Describe the information that can be specified in the RCT to define a CICS/DB2 program to CICS.

Chapter 7

Basic CICS/DB2 programming techniques

In this chapter, I'll describe how a CICS program that accesses DB2 data works. To illustrate the required programming techniques, I'll present a simple CICS inquiry program. This program is a CICS version of CUSTINQ, the first program example I presented in *Part 1: An Introductory Course*.

The CUSTINQ program from *Part 1* is an interactive inquiry application that runs under TSO. It accepts a customer number from a terminal user, retrieves the corresponding row from the customer table, and displays the contents of the row. The CICS version of the program this chapter presents does the same things. However, the requirements of CICS make the programming more complicated.

I'll begin this chapter by showing you a simple terminal session from the CICS customer inquiry program. Then, I'll show you the BMS mapset that defines the screen it uses. Finally, I'll present and explain the program's design and source code.

The operation of the CICS/DB2 customer inquiry program

Figure 7-1 presents the screen displays from a session with the CICS version of the customer inquiry program. Notice that the CICS program uses screens that are more complicated that those the TSO version uses. These screen designs follow the rules of IBM's *Common User Access*, or *CUA*. CUA provides sets of standards that insure that programs interact with users in consistent ways. For more information about CUA, you can refer to the IBM manual *Common User Access Basic Interface Design Guide*.

When I started this program, CICS responded by retrieving the program's load module and executing it. During its first execution, the program issues a CICS command to display the screen in part 1 of figure 7-1. This screen shows the name of the map from the BMS mapset, "DINMAP1," the name of the program, "Customer Inquiry," and directions for the user, "Type a customer number. Then press Enter." From this screen, the user can enter the number for the customer whose information he wants to see. The number is entered into the field that appears on the screen as a series of underscores following the label "Customer number."

Notice at the bottom of the screen that the user can press either of two PF (Program Function) keys to end the program. In this example, Exit (F3) and Cancel (F12) accomplish the same thing: They end the program. In other programs, these two keys may do different things. And more complicated applications may offer other PF key options.

In part 2 of figure 7-1, I entered the customer number 400001 and pressed the Enter key. The program responded by displaying the data for the specified customer, as part 3 shows. At this point, I can enter a different customer number to retrieve and display data for that customer. Or, I can press F3 or F12 to end the program.

The BMS mapset and symbolic map for the CICS/DB2 customer inquiry program

CICS's Basic Mapping Support (BMS) manages formatted displays like the ones in figure 7-1. As you'll remember from the last chapter, BMS is a CICS module that works with the terminal control module to support terminal interactions. BMS uses specifications contained in a mapset to prepare and display formatted data on a terminal screen.

Figure 7-2 presents the BMS mapset for the displays in figure 7-1. Although this mapset specifies a number of options, I'm not going to discuss all of them here. For a full treatment of BMS, you should refer to Doug Lowe's *CICS for the COBOL Programmer, Part 1*. However, I think

Part 1

The inquiry program
displays its initial screen.

```
DINMAP1              Customer Inquiry

Type a customer number.  Then press Enter.

Customer number. . . . . _____

Name and address . . . :












F3=Exit    F12=Cancel
```

Part 2

The user enters
customer number
400001 and presses the
Enter key.

```
DINMAP1              Customer Inquiry

Type a customer number.  Then press Enter.

Customer number. . . . . 400001

Name and address . . . :












F3=Exit    F12=Cancel
```

Figure 7-1   The operation of the CICS customer inquiry program

Part 3

The program retrieves the data for customer 400001 and displays it on the screen.

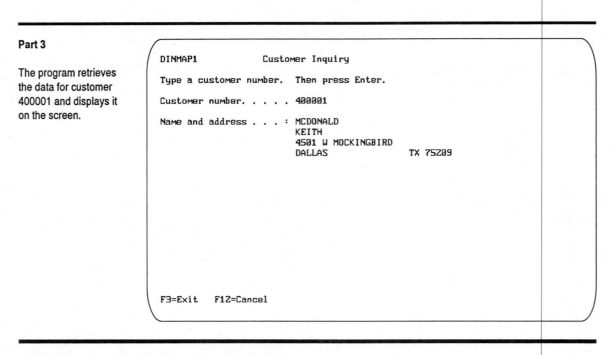

```
DINMAP1              Customer Inquiry

Type a customer number.  Then press Enter.

Customer number. . . . . 400001

Name and address . . . : MCDONALD
                         KEITH
                         4501 W MOCKINGBIRD
                         DALLAS              TX 75209









F3=Exit    F12=Cancel
```

Figure 7-1   The operation of the CICS customer inquiry program (continued)

you'll be able to understand much of the mapset, even though it may look intimidating.

First, notice the lines near the beginning of the mapset that specify values for the macro called DFHMSD. They specify that the symbolic map that BMS generates from this mapset should be in COBOL (LANG=COBOL), that the symbolic map should include fields for both input and output (MODE=INOUT), and that the mapset should work with a standard 3270-type display station (TERM=3270-2).

The next macro, DFHMDI, defines a map (that is, a screen display) within the mapset. It specifies that the size of the screen display is 24 lines of 80 characters each (SIZE=(24,80)). In this example, the mapset consists of just one map, so it contains just one DFHMDI macro. More complicated mapsets can include multiple maps.

The other macros in the mapset are DFHMDF macros. They define the fields on the display screen. For example,

```
DFHMDF POS=(1,1)
       LENGTH=7,
       ATTRB=(NORM,PROT),
       COLOR=BLUE,
       INITIAL='DINMAP1'
```

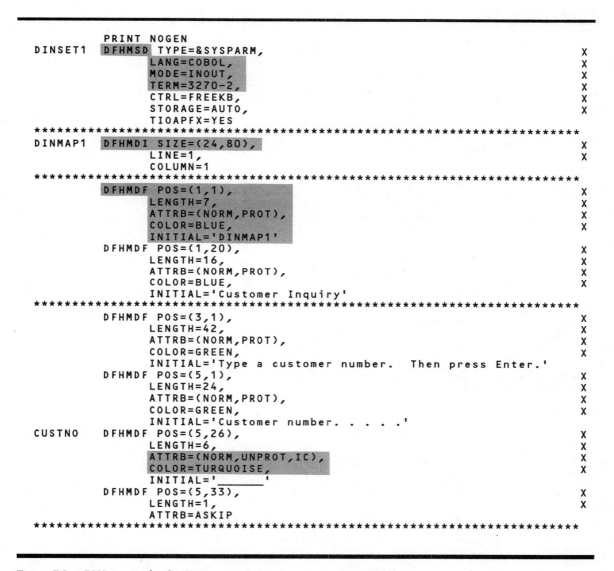

```
            PRINT NOGEN
DINSET1  DFHMSD  TYPE=&SYSPARM,                                             X
                 LANG=COBOL,                                                X
                 MODE=INOUT,                                                X
                 TERM=3270-2,                                               X
                 CTRL=FREEKB,                                               X
                 STORAGE=AUTO,                                              X
                 TIOAPFX=YES
*****************************************************************************
DINMAP1  DFHMDI  SIZE=(24,80),                                             X
                 LINE=1,                                                    X
                 COLUMN=1
*****************************************************************************
         DFHMDF  POS=(1,1),                                                X
                 LENGTH=7,                                                  X
                 ATTRB=(NORM,PROT),                                         X
                 COLOR=BLUE,                                                X
                 INITIAL='DINMAP1'
         DFHMDF  POS=(1,20),                                               X
                 LENGTH=16,                                                 X
                 ATTRB=(NORM,PROT),                                         X
                 COLOR=BLUE,                                                X
                 INITIAL='Customer Inquiry'
*****************************************************************************
         DFHMDF  POS=(3,1),                                                X
                 LENGTH=42,                                                 X
                 ATTRB=(NORM,PROT),                                         X
                 COLOR=GREEN,                                               X
                 INITIAL='Type a customer number.  Then press Enter.'
         DFHMDF  POS=(5,1),                                                X
                 LENGTH=24,                                                 X
                 ATTRB=(NORM,PROT),                                         X
                 COLOR=GREEN,                                               X
                 INITIAL='Customer number. . . . .'
CUSTNO   DFHMDF  POS=(5,26),                                               X
                 LENGTH=6,                                                  X
                 ATTRB=(NORM,UNPROT,IC),                                    X
                 COLOR=TURQUOISE,                                           X
                 INITIAL='_____'
         DFHMDF  POS=(5,33),                                               X
                 LENGTH=1,                                                  X
                 ATTRB=ASKIP
*****************************************************************************
```

Figure 7-2   BMS mapset for the CICS customer inquiry program (part 1 of 2)

defines the literal value that appears in the upper left corner of the screen.
As you can see, I used several parameters to define this field.

The POS parameter determines the location of the field. Actually, POS
determines the location of the *attribute byte* for field. An attribute byte is a
single-character value that takes up a screen position and specifies the

```
          DFHMDF POS=(7,1),                                              X
                 LENGTH=24,                                              X
                 ATTRB=(NORM,PROT),                                      X
                 COLOR=GREEN,                                            X
                 INITIAL='Name and address . . . :'
LNAME     DFHMDF POS=(7,26),                                             X
                 LENGTH=30,                                              X
                 COLOR=TURQUOISE,                                        X
                 ATTRB=(NORM,PROT)
FNAME     DFHMDF POS=(8,26),                                             X
                 LENGTH=20,                                              X
                 COLOR=TURQUOISE,                                        X
                 ATTRB=(NORM,PROT)
ADDR      DFHMDF POS=(9,26),                                             X
                 LENGTH=30,                                              X
                 COLOR=TURQUOISE,                                        X
                 ATTRB=(NORM,PROT)
CITY      DFHMDF POS=(10,26),                                            X
                 LENGTH=20,                                              X
                 COLOR=TURQUOISE,                                        X
                 ATTRB=(NORM,PROT)
STATE     DFHMDF POS=(10,47),                                            X
                 LENGTH=2,                                               X
                 COLOR=TURQUOISE,                                        X
                 ATTRB=(NORM,PROT)
ZIPCODE   DFHMDF POS=(10,50),                                            X
                 LENGTH=10,                                              X
                 COLOR=TURQUOISE,                                        X
                 ATTRB=(NORM,PROT)
***********************************************************************
MESSAGE   DFHMDF POS=(23,1),                                            X
                 LENGTH=79,                                             X
                 ATTRB=(BRT,PROT),                                      X
                 COLOR=YELLOW
          DFHMDF POS=(24,1),                                            X
                 LENGTH=20,                                             X
                 ATTRB=(NORM,PROT),                                     X
                 COLOR=BLUE,                                            X
                 INITIAL='F3=Exit    F12=Cancel'
DUMMY     DFHMDF POS=(24,79),                                           X
                 LENGTH=1,                                              X
                 ATTRB=(DRK,PROT,FSET),                                 X
                 INITIAL=' '
***********************************************************************
          DFHMSD TYPE=FINAL
          END
```

Figure 7-2   BMS mapset for the CICS customer inquiry program (part 2 of 2)

characteristics of a field. In this example, since the attribute byte is in column 1, the field will appear starting at column 2.

The next parameter, LENGTH, specifies the maximum number of characters the field can contain. In this case, the field can hold up to seven characters. If you combine the information the POS and LENGTH options provide, you can figure out that this field will appear on the screen in columns 2 through 8 of line 1.

The ATTRB and COLOR parameters specify the attributes for the screen field. The NORM option of the ATTRB parameter means the field should be displayed in normal (rather than bright) intensity; PROT means that the field should be protected so the user can't change its contents. The COLOR parameter specifies that the field should be displayed in blue, the CUA standard for a screen title.

Finally, the INITIAL parameter supplies the starting value for the field: DINMAP1. Because this is a protected field, the user can't change this value. That's appropriate for a screen's name. If you count the number of characters in the INITIAL value, you'll see that the number is the same as the value for LENGTH: 7.

Most of the fields the mapset in figure 7-2 defines have the same combination of options in the ATTRB parameter: normal display intensity and protected from change. However, the fields named CUSTNO and MESSAGE specify different options for this parameter. Also, many of the fields have different colors. All these fields follow the CUA standards.

CUSTNO is the field where the user will enter the number of the customer to be displayed. It's defined with the UNPROT attribute, which means the user can change its value. A third option, IC (Initial Cursor), is also included on the ATTRB parameter. This option specifies that the cursor should be positioned at this field when the screen is displayed. Its color, turquoise, is also different.

The MESSAGE field is where error messages will be displayed. It uses the BRT attribute instead of NORM. This insures that any error message values that appear in this field display in high intensity characters rather than normal intensity characters. Also, its color is yellow.

Figure 7-3 presents the symbolic map the assembler produced from the mapset in figure 7-2. You'll recall from chapter 6 that the symbolic map is stored as a COBOL copy book. Then, the COBOL compiler includes that copy book when it processes the translated source program.

Notice that the symbolic map uses the same data area for both terminal input and output. The input fields are subordinate to the 01-level item DINMAP1I, and the output fields are subordinate to the 01-level item DINMAP1O, which is a redefinition of DINMAP1I. The symbolic map defines separate fields for input and output so that you can specify different PICTURE clauses for them. You may want to do that if you're working with numeric data.

For each screen field that's named in the mapset, the symbolic map contains a data field, a length field, and an attribute field. Since the fields that

```
01  DINMAP1I.
    02    FILLER     PIC X(12).
    02    CUSTNOL    PIC S9(4) COMP.
    02    CUSTNOF    PIC X.
    02    FILLER REDEFINES CUSTNOF.
     03   CUSTNOA    PIC X.
    02    CUSTNOI    PIC X(0006).
    02    LNAMEL     PIC S9(4) COMP.
    02    LNAMEF     PIC X.
    02    FILLER REDEFINES LNAMEF.
     03   LNAMEA     PIC X.
    02    LNAMEI     PIC X(0030).
    02    FNAMEL     PIC S9(4) COMP.
    02    FNAMEF     PIC X.
    02    FILLER REDEFINES FNAMEF.
     03   FNAMEA     PIC X.
    02    FNAMEI     PIC X(0020).
    02    ADDRL      PIC S9(4) COMP.
    02    ADDRF      PIC X.
    02    FILLER REDEFINES ADDRF.
     03   ADDRA      PIC X.
    02    ADDRI      PIC X(0030).
    02    CITYL      PIC S9(4) COMP.
    02    CITYF      PIC X.
    02    FILLER REDEFINES CITYF.
     03   CITYA      PIC X.
    02    CITYI      PIC X(0020).
    02    STATEL     PIC S9(4) COMP.
    02    STATEF     PIC X.
    02    FILLER REDEFINES STATEF.
     03   STATEA     PIC X.
    02    STATEI     PIC X(0002).
    02    ZIPCODEL   PIC S9(4) COMP.
    02    ZIPCODEF   PIC X.
    02    FILLER REDEFINES ZIPCODEF.
     03   ZIPCODEA   PIC X.
    02    ZIPCODEI   PIC X(0010).
    02    MESSAGEL   PIC S9(4) COMP.
    02    MESSAGEF   PIC X.
    02    FILLER REDEFINES MESSAGEF.
     03   MESSAGEA   PIC X.
    02    MESSAGEI   PIC X(0079).
    02    DUMMYL     PIC S9(4) COMP.
    02    DUMMYF     PIC X.
    02    FILLER REDEFINES DUMMYF.
     03   DUMMYA     PIC X.
    02    DUMMYI     PIC X(0001).
```

Figure 7-3   Symbolic map for the CICS customer inquiry program (part 1 of 2)

define headings, labels, and instructions aren't named in the mapset, they don't appear in the symbolic map. Typically, you'll name only those fields in a mapset that your program needs to access.

```
01  DINMAP1O REDEFINES DINMAP1I.
    02    FILLER     PIC  X(12).
    02    FILLER     PIC  X(3).
    02    CUSTNOO    PIC  X(0006).
    02    FILLER     PIC  X(3).
    02    LNAMEO     PIC  X(0030).
    02    FILLER     PIC  X(3).
    02    FNAMEO     PIC  X(0020).
    02    FILLER     PIC  X(3).
    02    ADDRO      PIC  X(0030).
    02    FILLER     PIC  X(3).
    02    CITYO      PIC  X(0020).
    02    FILLER     PIC  X(3).
    02    STATEO     PIC  X(0002).
    02    FILLER     PIC  X(3).
    02    ZIPCODEO   PIC  X(0010).
    02    FILLER     PIC  X(3).
    02    MESSAGEO   PIC  X(0079).
    02    FILLER     PIC  X(3).
    02    DUMMYO     PIC  X(0001).
```

Figure 7-3   Symbolic map for the CICS customer inquiry program (part 2 of 2)

For the example program in this chapter, I'll use the symbolic map produced by BMS without any changes. However, notice that the data names in the symbolic map BMS produced aren't as meaningful as they could be. Also, the format of the code in the BMS-created symbolic map makes it harder to read and use than it needs to be. In the next chapter, I'll show you a customized symbolic map you can use instead of the BMS-generated one.

The design of the CICS/DB2 customer inquiry program

You should remember from the last chapter that most CICS programs are pseudo-conversational. That means that although it seems like a CICS program is waiting to interact with the user when a screen is displayed, it really has ended. Then, when the user does something to signal that the program should respond, CICS starts the program again.

Pseudo-conversational programming complicates program design and coding. That's because each time CICS starts a program, the program has to determine if it should start from scratch or if it's in the middle of an interaction. As a result, programs that run under CICS have designs that are different from what you may expect. For example, consider the structure chart in figure 7-4 for the CICS customer inquiry program.

Each time the program starts, it evaluates the conditions surrounding its execution to determine what to do. In a moment, when I discuss the program source code, I'll describe each of those conditions. For now, assume that the condition is that the user just entered a customer number and pressed the Enter key. In that case, the top level module invokes module 1000 to process the input map.

To do that, the program first retrieves the customer-number entry from the screen (module 1100) and edits it (module 1200). If the edit doesn't detect any problems with the customer number, the program issues an SQL statement to retrieve the requested row from the table (module 1300). If DB2 retrieves the row successfully, it passes it back to the program through CICS. Then, the program sends the output map to the screen with the data from the row (module 1400). On the other hand, if either module 1200 or module 1300 detects an error condition, module 1000 sends an error message to the terminal user (module 1500).

The program execution I just described depends on the program detecting a "normal" condition. If the program's top level module detects some other condition, it can do one of three things. First, it can send an error message to the user (module 1500 invoked from 0000). Second, it can send a "fresh" data entry screen to the terminal to let the user start a new inquiry (module 2000). Or third, it can end. (There isn't a separate module for this function.)

This is different from the design for the first version of the program I presented in *Part 1: An Introductory Course*. That program was structured around a PERFORM-UNTIL loop. It prompted the user for a customer number, retrieved the row for that customer, and displayed the data from it. It repeated that process until the user signalled that the program should end. So, for example, even if a user wanted to review data for six customers, the program would run only once. That one execution would work through the loop six times, once for each display request. This program was conversational, not pseudo-conversational.

In contrast, a session with the CICS version of the program to retrieve and display six rows from the table would involve at least eight separate executions of the program. The first execution would display the entry screen, then end. The second through the seventh executions would use the customer number the user entered on the screen to retrieve the requested row from the customer table, then display the data from it and end. If any of the iterations of this process detected an error, such as an invalid key entered by the operator or a customer number value that didn't correspond to a row in the customer table, the number of executions would be even greater. The last execution of the program would detect the use of the F3 or F12 key and end.

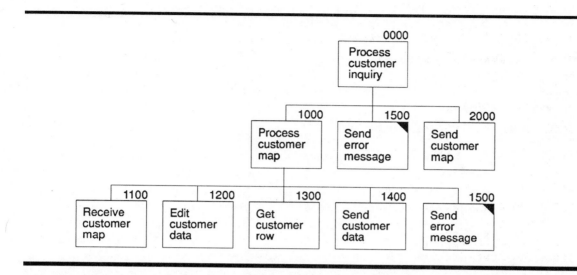

Figure 7-4   Structure chart for the CICS customer inquiry program

The source code for the CICS/DB2 customer inquiry program

Figure 7-5 presents the source code for the CICS version of the customer inquiry program. I'll discuss this program in three parts. First, I'll describe its data areas. Then, I'll discuss how its Procedure Division code processes a "normal" transaction request. In that context, I'll describe the CICS commands that do screen operations and the SQL statement the program issues. Third, I'll describe how the program's Procedure Division implements the pseudo-conversational design.

How the program's data areas are defined   Like the other DB2 program examples I've shown you, this program's Identification, Environment, and Data Divisions are simple. Just as you don't have to include any Environment Division entries for the DB2 tables your programs process, you also don't need to include any entries for the CICS-controlled screens they use. So, this program has an Environment Division header with no subordinate items. However, the Data Division contains entries in both its Working-Storage and Linkage Sections.

The Working-Storage Section contains several items. The first 01-level item, SWITCHES, contains one control field: VALID-DATA-SW. You'll see how the program uses this switch when I show you its Procedure Division code.

The next field is for data related to a special CICS storage area called the *communication area*. The communication area provides a place where

```
000100 IDENTIFICATION DIVISION.
000200*
000300 PROGRAM-ID.  DB2DIN1.
000400*
000500 ENVIRONMENT DIVISION.
000600*
000700 DATA DIVISION.
000800*
000900 WORKING-STORAGE SECTION.
001000*
001100 01  SWITCHES.
001200*
001300     05  VALID-DATA-SW            PIC X     VALUE 'Y'.
001400         88 VALID-DATA                      VALUE 'Y'.
001500*
001600 01  COMMUNICATION-AREA           PIC X.
001700*
001800     EXEC SQL
001900         INCLUDE CUST
002000     END-EXEC.
002100*
002200     EXEC SQL
002300         INCLUDE SQLCA
002400     END-EXEC.
002500*
002600 COPY DINSET1.
002700*
002800 COPY DFHAID.
002900*
003000 LINKAGE SECTION.
003100*
003200 01  DFHCOMMAREA                  PIC X.
003300*
```

Figure 7-5   COBOL source code for the CICS customer inquiry program (part 1 of 4)

a program can move data that it will use in its next execution. That's necessary because, when a pseudo-conversational program ends, the contents of
its Working-Storage fields are lost.

To use the communication area, you need to provide two definitions for
it in your program: one in the Working-Storage Section and one in the Linkage Section. I named the Working-Storage definition COMMUNICATION-
AREA in the program example in figure 7-5. The Linkage Section definition
is named DFHCOMMAREA. Although you can use any name for the
Working-Storage field, you must use the name DFHCOMMAREA for the
Linkage Section field. I'll show you how the customer inquiry program uses
the communication area when I discuss the Procedure Division code that
implements the pseudo-conversational design.

```
003400 PROCEDURE DIVISION.
003500*
003600 0000-PROCESS-CUSTOMER-INQUIRY.
003700*
003800     EVALUATE TRUE
003900
004000         WHEN EIBCALEN = ZERO
004100             PERFORM 2000-SEND-CUSTOMER-MAP
004200
004300         WHEN EIBAID = DFHCLEAR
004400             PERFORM 2000-SEND-CUSTOMER-MAP
004500
004600         WHEN EIBAID = DFHPA1 OR DFHPA2 OR DFHPA3
004700             CONTINUE
004800
004900         WHEN EIBAID = DFHPF3 OR DFHPF12
005000             EXEC CICS
005100                 XCTL PROGRAM('DB2MENU')
005200             END-EXEC
005300
005400         WHEN EIBAID = DFHENTER
005500             PERFORM 1000-PROCESS-CUSTOMER-MAP
005600
005700         WHEN OTHER
005800             MOVE 'Invalid key pressed.' TO MESSAGEO
005900             PERFORM 1500-SEND-ERROR-MESSAGE
006000
006100     END-EVALUATE.
006200
006300     EXEC CICS
006400         RETURN TRANSID('DIN1')
006500                 COMMAREA(COMMUNICATION-AREA)
006600     END-EXEC.
006700*
```

Figure 7-5   COBOL source code for the CICS customer inquiry program (part 2 of 4)

You should recognize the next two items in the Working-Storage Section: SQL INCLUDE statements. The first statement causes the DB2 precompiler to include the DCLGEN-generated host variable definitions for the customer table. Figure 7-6 presents the DCLGEN output. The second statement causes the precompiler to include the SQLCA fields.

Next are two COBOL COPY statements. The first one causes the COBOL compiler to include the symbolic map for the mapset DINSET1. The second COPY statement causes the compiler to include a member called DFHAID in the program. Figure 7-7 presents the DFHAID copy book, which IBM supplies. It contains literal values that correspond to the AID (attention identifier) keys. These are the keys the user can press to

```
006800 1000-PROCESS-CUSTOMER-MAP.
006900*
007000     PERFORM 1100-RECEIVE-CUSTOMER-MAP.
007100     PERFORM 1200-EDIT-CUSTOMER-DATA.
007200     IF VALID-DATA
007300         PERFORM 1300-GET-CUSTOMER-ROW.
007400     IF VALID-DATA
007500         PERFORM 1400-SEND-CUSTOMER-DATA
007600     ELSE
007700         PERFORM 1500-SEND-ERROR-MESSAGE.
007800*
007900 1100-RECEIVE-CUSTOMER-MAP.
008000*
008100     EXEC CICS
008200         RECEIVE MAP('DINMAP1')
008300                 MAPSET('DINSET1')
008400                 INTO(DINMAP1I)
008500     END-EXEC.
008600*
008700 1200-EDIT-CUSTOMER-DATA.
008800*
008900     IF        CUSTNOL = ZERO
009000         OR CUSTNOI = SPACE
009100        MOVE 'N' TO VALID-DATA-SW
009200        MOVE 'You must enter a customer number.' TO MESSAGEO.
009300*
009400 1300-GET-CUSTOMER-ROW.
009500*
009600     EXEC SQL
009700         SELECT CUSTNO,     FNAME,      LNAME,
009800                ADDR,       CITY,       STATE,
009900                ZIPCODE
010000         INTO  :CUSTNO,     :FNAME,     :LNAME,
010100               :ADDR,       :CITY,      :STATE,
010200               :ZIPCODE
010300         FROM    MMADBV.CUST
010400         WHERE CUSTNO=:CUSTNOI
010500     END-EXEC.
010600     IF SQLCODE = 0
010700         MOVE LNAME          TO LNAMEO
010800         MOVE FNAME          TO FNAMEO
010900         MOVE ADDR           TO ADDRO
011000         MOVE CITY           TO CITYO
011100         MOVE STATE          TO STATEO
011200         MOVE ZIPCODE        TO ZIPCODEO
011300         MOVE SPACE          TO MESSAGEO
```

Figure 7-5   COBOL source code for the CICS customer inquiry program (part 3 of 4)

communicate with the system. In figure 7-7, I've highlighted the keys that the customer inquiry program in figure 7-5 tests.

When the user presses one of the AID keys, CICS passes the corresponding one-byte value in the DFHAID member to the program through a field in the EIB (Execute Interface Block). That field is EIBAID. Figure 7-8

```
011400                    ELSE IF SQLCODE = 100
011500                    MOVE 'N' TO VALID-DATA-SW
011600                    MOVE 'That customer does not exist.' TO MESSAGEO
011700                    MOVE SPACE TO LNAMEO
011800                                 FNAMEO
011900                                 ADDRO
012000                                 CITYO
012100                                 STATEO
012200                                 ZIPCODEO
012300              ELSE
012400                  EXEC CICS
012500                      ABEND
012600                  END-EXEC.
012700*
012800 1400-SEND-CUSTOMER-DATA.
012900*
013000      EXEC CICS
013100          SEND MAP('DINMAP1')
013200               MAPSET('DINSET1')
013300               FROM(DINMAP1O)
013400               DATAONLY
013500      END-EXEC.
013600*
013700 1500-SEND-ERROR-MESSAGE.
013800*
013900      EXEC CICS
014000          SEND MAP('DINMAP1')
014100               MAPSET('DINSET1')
014200               FROM(DINMAP1O)
014300               DATAONLY
014400               ALARM
014500      END-EXEC.
014600*
014700 2000-SEND-CUSTOMER-MAP.
014800*
014900      MOVE LOW-VALUE TO DINMAP1O.
015000      EXEC CICS
015100          SEND MAP('DINMAP1')
015200               MAPSET('DINSET1')
015300               FROM(DINMAP1O)
015400               ERASE
015500      END-EXEC.
```

Figure 7-5   COBOL source code for the CICS customer inquiry program (part 4 of 4)

presents the definitions of the other EIB fields. The CICS translator automatically includes this code in the Linkage Section of your program, so you don't need to code it yourself. The two fields I've highlighted, EIBAID and EIBCALEN, are the only fields the customer inquiry program uses.

To illustrate how the DFHAID fields and EIBAID work, suppose the user presses F12. Then, CICS stores "@," the value of DFHPF12, in

```
************************************************************************
* DCLGEN TABLE(MMADBV.CUST)                                           *
*        LIBRARY(MMA002.DCLGENS.COBOL(CUST))                          *
*        ACTION(REPLACE)                                              *
*        STRUCTURE(CUSTOMER-ROW)                                      *
*        APOST                                                        *
* ... IS THE DCLGEN COMMAND THAT MADE THE FOLLOWING STATEMENTS        *
************************************************************************
     EXEC SQL DECLARE MMADBV.CUST TABLE
     ( CUSTNO                        CHAR(6) NOT NULL,
       FNAME                         CHAR(20) NOT NULL,
       LNAME                         CHAR(30) NOT NULL,
       ADDR                          CHAR(30) NOT NULL,
       CITY                          CHAR(20) NOT NULL,
       STATE                         CHAR(2) NOT NULL,
       ZIPCODE                       CHAR(10) NOT NULL
     ) END-EXEC.
************************************************************************
* COBOL DECLARATION FOR TABLE MMADBV.CUST                             *
************************************************************************
 01  CUSTOMER-ROW.
     10 CUSTNO              PIC X(6).
     10 FNAME               PIC X(20).
     10 LNAME               PIC X(30).
     10 ADDR                PIC X(30).
     10 CITY                PIC X(20).
     10 STATE               PIC X(2).
     10 ZIPCODE             PIC X(10).
************************************************************************
* THE NUMBER OF COLUMNS DESCRIBED BY THIS DECLARATION IS 7            *
************************************************************************
```

Figure 7-6   DCLGEN output for the CUST table

EIBAID. Your program can check for F12 explicitly by using an IF statement like

```
IF EIBAID = '@'
```

However, if you use the literal data name from the DFHAID copy member in an IF statement like

```
IF EIBAID = DFHPF12
```

your program will be easier to read and understand.

How the program handles a "normal" transaction   Now, turn to the start of the program's Procedure Division in part 2 of figure 7-5. Frankly, the hardest part of this program to understand is the first module,

```
****************************************************************
*  CONTROL BLOCK NAME= DFHAID                                  *
*                                                              *
*  NAME OF MATCHING ASSEMBLER CONTROL BLOCK = NONE             *
*                                                              *
*  DESCRIPTIVE NAME = 3270 AID VALUES                          *
*                                                              *
*  COPYRIGHT          =              5688-101                  *
*                                    COPYRIGHT = NONE          *
*                                                              *
*  STATUS          RELEASE 1.2                                 *
*                                                              *
*  FUNCTION =  Provides the values for AIDs supplied by        *
*     the BMS support in CICS OS/2                             *
*                                                              *
****************************************************************
   01      DFHAID.
     02    DFHNULL     PIC  X   VALUE IS ' '.
     02    DFHENTER    PIC  X   VALUE IS ''''.
     02    DFHCLEAR    PIC  X   VALUE IS '_'.
     02    DFHCLRP     PIC  X   VALUE IS '('.
     02    DFHPEN      PIC  X   VALUE IS '='.
     02    DFHOPID     PIC  X   VALUE IS 'W'.
     02    DFHMSRE     PIC  X   VALUE IS 'X'.
     02    DFHSTRF     PIC  X   VALUE IS 'h'.
     02    DFHTRIG     PIC  X   VALUE IS '''.
     02    DFHPA1      PIC  X   VALUE IS '%'.
     02    DFHPA2      PIC  X   VALUE IS ''.
     02    DFHPA3      PIC  X   VALUE IS ','.
     02    DFHPF1      PIC  X   VALUE IS '1'.
     02    DFHPF2      PIC  X   VALUE IS '2'.
     02    DFHPF3      PIC  X   VALUE IS '3'.
     02    DFHPF4      PIC  X   VALUE IS '4'.
     02    DFHPF5      PIC  X   VALUE IS '5'.
     02    DFHPF6      PIC  X   VALUE IS '6'.
     02    DFHPF7      PIC  X   VALUE IS '7'.
     02    DFHPF8      PIC  X   VALUE IS '8'.
     02    DFHPF9      PIC  X   VALUE IS '9'.
     02    DFHPF10     PIC  X   VALUE IS ':'.
     02    DFHPF11     PIC  X   VALUE IS '#'.
     02    DFHPF12     PIC  X   VALUE IS 'a'.
     02    DFHPF13     PIC  X   VALUE IS 'A'.
     02    DFHPF14     PIC  X   VALUE IS 'B'.
     02    DFHPF15     PIC  X   VALUE IS 'C'.
     02    DFHPF16     PIC  X   VALUE IS 'D'.
     02    DFHPF17     PIC  X   VALUE IS 'E'.
     02    DFHPF18     PIC  X   VALUE IS 'F'.
     02    DFHPF19     PIC  X   VALUE IS 'G'.
     02    DFHPF20     PIC  X   VALUE IS 'H'.
     02    DFHPF21     PIC  X   VALUE IS 'I'.
     02    DFHPF22     PIC  X   VALUE IS X'5B'.
     02    DFHPF23     PIC  X   VALUE IS '.'.
     02    DFHPF24     PIC  X   VALUE IS ''.
```

Figure 7-7 The DFHAID copy book

0000-PROCESS-CUSTOMER-INQUIRY. It contains the logic required to
implement the pseudo-conversational design. The EVALUATE statement
specifies actions for different conditions the program may encounter when
it's started.

In a moment, I'll describe each of the conditions the EVALUATE statement checks. But first, I want to describe how the program deals with the
basic case: receiving a customer number, retrieving the associated row from
the customer table, and displaying the data from that row. If the user
entered a customer number and pressed the Enter key, the condition in the
fifth WHEN clause in the EVALUATE statement is satisfied:

```
WHEN EIBAID = DFHENTER
    PERFORM 1000-PROCESS-CUSTOMER-MAP
```

So, the program performs module 1000. (DFHENTER is one of the literal
values in the DFHAID copy member in figure 7-7.)

In contrast to module 0000, module 1000 is easy to understand. You'll
recognize what it does from my discussion of the program structure chart.
First, module 1000 executes module 1100 to get the data the user entered
on the screen. Then, it executes module 1200 to edit that data. If the edit
doesn't detect an error, the program executes module 1300 to retrieve the
requested row from the customer table. If that function is successful, the
program displays the retrieved data by invoking module 1400. On the other
hand, if an error is detected, the program executes module 1500 to display
an error message.

Module 1100 contains a single CICS command: RECEIVE MAP. You'll
recall from chapter 6 that this command receives data from the terminal. It
names the map and the mapset CICS will use for the operation (DINMAP1
in DINSET1, the mapset in figure 7-2). And it identifies the program field
where CICS will return the data from the screen (DINMAP1I, the input component of the symbolic map in figure 7-3). So, after CICS processes the
RECEIVE MAP command in module 1100, the number for the customer
whose table row the user wants to retrieve is returned in the appropriate
field in the symbolic map: CUSTNOI.

The only editing requirement in this program is that the user must
enter a customer number. Module 1200 checks the customer-number entry
with this compound condition:

```
IF      CUSTNOL = ZERO
    OR CUSTNOI = SPACE
    MOVE 'N' TO VALID-DATA-SW
    MOVE 'You must enter a customer number.' to MESSAGEO.
```

```
01    DFHEIBLK.
02      EIBTIME  PIC S9(7) COMP-3.
02      EIBDATE  PIC S9(7) COMP-3.
02      EIBTRNID PIC X(4).
02      EIBTASKN PIC S9(7) COMP-3.
02      EIBTRMID PIC X(4).
02      DFHEIGDI COMP PIC S9(4).
02      EIBCPOSN COMP PIC S9(4).
02      EIBCALEN COMP PIC S9(4).
02      EIBAID   PIC X(1).
02      EIBFN    PIC X(2).
02      EIBRCODE PIC X(6).
02      EIBDS    PIC X(8).
02      EIBREQID PIC X(8).
02      EIBRSRCE PIC X(8).
02      EIBSYNC  PIC X(1).
02      EIBFREE  PIC X(1).
02      EIBRECV  PIC X(1).
02      EIBFIL01 PIC X(1).
02      EIBATT   PIC X(1).
02      EIBEOC   PIC X(1).
02      EIBFMH   PIC X(1).
02      EIBCOMPL PIC X(1).
02      EIBSIG   PIC X(1).
02      EIBCONF  PIC X(1).
02      EIBERR   PIC X(1).
02      EIBERRCD PIC X(4).
02      EIBSYNRB PIC X(1).
02      EIBNODAT PIC X(1).
02      EIBRESP  COMP PIC S9(8).
02      EIBRESP2 COMP PIC S9(8).
02      EIBRLDBK PIC X(1).
```

Figure 7-8   COBOL code the CICS translator inserts into a program's Linkage Section for the EIB
(Execute Interface Block)

The second part of this condition is easy to understand. It checks the customer number entry field for spaces. If the user keyed spaces into this field, the entry is invalid. However, this condition isn't satisfied if the field was blank and the user didn't enter anything or if the user erased the field using the ERASE-EOF key. In both of these cases, no data is transmitted back to CICS. And, after CICS processes the RECEIVE MAP command, the CUSTNOI field will contain low-values, and low-values and spaces are different. So, to test for these conditions, the IF statement also checks the symbolic map's length field for CUSTNO (CUSTNOL) for a value of zero. A value of zero indicates that no data was transmitted.

If either of the two error conditions the IF statement tests is true, module 1200 sets the value of VALID-DATA-SW to "N." As you'll see in a minute, the program uses this switch to determine the processing it does next. This module also moves the text of an error message to the output field in the symbolic map for the screen's MESSAGE field.

Execution of the code in module 1000 continues when module 1200 finishes. If module 1200 didn't set the VALID-DATA-SW to "N," module 1000 invokes module 1300 to issue the SQL statement necessary to retrieve the requested row from the customer table. This SELECT statement is the same as the one in the non-CICS version of the program from *Part 1: An Introductory Course*.

If the SQL statement doesn't produce a DB2 error, the value of SQLCODE will be zero. Then, module 1300 moves the values returned from DB2 (through the fields in the DCLGEN-generated host variable definitions) into the corresponding output fields in the BMS symbolic map:

```
MOVE LNAME    TO LNAMEO
MOVE FNAME    TO FNAMEO
MOVE ADDR     TO ADDRO
MOVE CITY     TO CITYO
MOVE STATE    TO STATEO
MOVE ZIPCODE  TO ZIPCODEO
```

It also moves space to the output field used for messages. On the other hand, if the SELECT statement isn't successful, the program does one of two things depending on the value of SQLCODE. If SQLCODE is 100, which indicates that the row wasn't found, the program issues the statements

```
MOVE 'N' TO VALID-DATA-SW
MOVE 'That customer does not exist.' TO MESSAGEO
MOVE SPACE TO LNAMEO
             FNAMEO
             ADDRO
             CITYO
             STATEO
             ZIPCODEO
```

to set the control switch, prepare an error message, and clear the output fields. If SQLCODE is any non-zero value other than 100, the program issues a CICS ABEND command. The ABEND command terminates the task and returns control to CICS.

Finally, module 1000 sends data back to the terminal. It invokes module 1400 if it didn't find errors as it processed the transaction. If it did find an error, it invokes module 1500 instead.

Modules 1400 and 1500 both issue a CICS SEND MAP command. The only difference between them is that the SEND MAP command in module 1500 specifies the ALARM option. ALARM causes an audio beep to sound at the terminal to call the user's attention to the error. Notice that these two SEND MAP commands, like the RECEIVE MAP command in module

1100, specify the mapset DINSET1 and the map DINMAP1. However, instead of the INTO option, SEND MAP uses the FROM option. The FROM option specifies the source of the data to be sent to the terminal. In this case, the source is the output fields in the symbolic map.

The SEND MAP commands in both of these modules specify the DATAONLY option. That means that only the variable data, that is, only the data in the symbolic map, is sent to the terminal; the literals that make up the headings, labels, and instructions don't need to be sent again because they're already there from the previous execution. Using this option improves performance because it reduces the amount of data transmitted between CICS and users' terminals.

How the program uses the pseudo-conversational programming technique   Most of the executions of the inquiry program will follow the pattern I just described. However, the program has to be able to deal with other conditions as well. All of these conditions relate to the processing required by pseudo-conversational programming. That processing is managed by the EVALUATE statement in module 0000.

The operation of the EVALUATE statement depends on values CICS makes available to the program through the Execute Interface Block. Remember, the CICS translator automatically includes the EIB field definitions in the Linkage Section of your program. In this program, the EVALUATE statement uses two of the EIB fields: EIBCALEN and EIBAID.

Consider the first condition in the EVALUATE statement:

```
WHEN EIBCALEN = ZERO
      PERFORM 2000-SEND-CUSTOMER-MAP
```

The field named EIBCALEN contains the length of the data passed to the program through its communication area. If the length is zero, that means that no data was passed to the program. By implication, that means there was no previous execution of the program. As a result, the screen needs to be initialized.

Note that this program uses the communication area only to determine whether it's executing for the first time. Other programs also pass data elements from one execution to the next through the communication area. The program example I'll present in the next chapter uses the communication area for both purposes.

To prepare the terminal to accept the data it needs, the program invokes module 2000. First, module 2000 moves LOW-VALUE to the symbolic map. Then, it issues a SEND MAP command, much like the ones I just described for modules 1400 and 1500. However, the command in module 2000 contains a different set of options. Instead of DATAONLY, the command in module 2000 specifies ERASE. That causes CICS to clear the screen so any data it contained is removed. Then, because the command does not contain DATAONLY, both literals and variable data fields are sent to the screen.

The next four conditions the EVALUATE statement in module 0000 specifies depend on the EIBAID field. Its value indicates which attention key the user last pressed. Each condition uses data names from the DFHAID copy member I presented in figure 7-7. The program checks EIBAID so it can avoid retrieving data from the terminal if the function it's about to perform doesn't call for it. That reduces network use and improves overall system performance.

For the first of these conditions, the program compares the value of EIBAID to the DFHAID field named DFHCLEAR:

```
WHEN EIBAID = DFHCLEAR
     PERFORM 2000-SEND-CUSTOMER-MAP
```

If the values in these fields are the same, that means the user pressed the Clear key, and the program should restart with a fresh screen. So, the program executes module 2000, the same module that's executed the first time through the program.

The next condition,

```
WHEN EIBAID = DFHPA1 OR DFHPA2 OR DFHPA3
    .CONTINUE
```

specifies how the program should react if the user pressed one of the program attention (PA) keys. In this program, no special action is taken. So the CONTINUE statement causes program execution to proceed after the EVALUATE statement.

Then, the third condition,

```
WHEN EIBAID = DFHPF3 OR DFHPF12
    EXEC CICS
        XCTL PROGRAM('DB2MENU')
    END-EXEC
```

checks for the two keys the user can press to leave the program: F3 and F12. If the user pressed either of these keys, the program issues a CICS XCTL command, which causes the program to end. In this case, CICS passes control to the menu named DB2MENU.

I've already described the next condition:

```
WHEN EIBAID = DFHENTER
    PERFORM 1000-PROCESS-CUSTOMER-MAP
```

It determines if the user pressed the Enter key. If so, the program performs module 1000 to receive the customer map and process it.

If none of the other conditions the EVALUATE statement specifies are true, the last condition

```
WHEN OTHER
     MOVE 'Invalid key pressed." TO MESSAGEO
     PERFORM 1500-SEND-ERROR-MESSAGE
```

is reached. It causes the program to display the customer map with the error message it supplies.

Unless the XCTL command was executed in response to F3 or F12, program execution continues following the EVALUATE statement. The next statement is a CICS command:

```
EXEC CICS
     RETURN TRANSID('DIN1')
             COMMAREA(COMMUNICATION-AREA)
END-EXEC.
```

This CICS RETURN command causes CICS to invoke the same trans-id (DIN1) the next time the user presses one of the AID keys. It also contains the code necessary to save data from one execution of the program to another in the communication area. In the COMMAREA option, it names the Working-Storage field (COMMUNICATION-AREA) whose contents should be passed forward to the next execution of the program through the CICS communication area. Note that the program never establishes the value of this field. That's because it doesn't matter what its value is. The program checks only its length.

Discussion

Although the DB2 processing this program does is trivial, it should be clear to you that there's little difference between DB2 processing in a CICS program and in a batch program. The point of this program was to show you that CICS programming is a complicated subject. In the next chapter, I'll present a more challenging CICS/DB2 programming problem: How to browse a multi-row results table.

Terms

Common User Access
CUA
attribute byte
communication area

Objective

Given program specifications, a BMS mapset, and a symbolic map for a CICS program that retrieves a single row from a DB2 table, design and code the program.

Chapter 8

How to browse DB2 data in a CICS program

The program in the last chapter retrieved and displayed table data from a single row to reply to a user inquiry. As a result, it was relatively simple. However, some CICS applications let users make inquiries that return multiple rows. In CICS, this is called *browsing*. Browsing a multi-row results table through a CICS program can present performance and programming challenges.

This chapter starts with an example of a terminal session with a CICS/DB2 browse program. Then, the chapter describes the basic problems involved in CICS/DB2 browse operations, and it presents strategies programmers can use to code browse programs. Finally, it presents the mapset, symbolic map, design, and source code for the example browse program.

Operation of the CICS/DB2 customer browse program

A browse program lets a user retrieve a number of items of stored data and examine all of them. Usually, a browse operation involves more data than will fit on a terminal screen at one time. Browsing implies that the user can move, or *scroll*, from one screen to another and review all of them. As a result, a single browse operation can involve many CICS displays.

Figure 8-1 illustrates part of a session with a CICS browse program that lets a user retrieve and scroll through information for all customers who live in a specific state. (This example uses a different version of the customer table that contains more rows than the table I've used in previous examples.) Part 1 of the figure shows the first screen the program displays. It prompts the user to enter the state code to be used for the browse. Here, the user entered CA to direct the program to retrieve data for all customers who live in California.

After the user pressed the Enter key, the program displayed the screen in part 2 of the figure. It shows data for 14 customers. If you look at the right side of the screen, you'll see the program reported that it's displaying the first 14 of a total of 75 rows that contain CA as the state code. The message

```
Lines     1 to     14 of     75
```

follows IBM's CUA (Common User Access) standard for displaying information about scrollable data. The line beneath the count information,

```
More:    +
```

is also CUA scroll information. It advises the user that there is more data he can scroll. The plus sign indicates that the user can read more data by scrolling forward (down).

The CUA standard keys for scrolling data are F7 (for scrolling backward, or up) and F8 (for scrolling forward, or down). The bottom line of the screen reminds the user of these options.

When the user pressed the F8 key on the screen in part 2 of figure 8-1, the screen in part 3 appeared. The scroll information lines here report that the rows on this screen are lines 14 to 27 of 75. Notice that both a minus sign and a plus sign follow "More:" in this screen. They indicate that the user can scroll both forward and backward from this screen. Also notice that the last line of data displayed in part 2 of figure 8-1 is the first line of data displayed in part 3. That's because CUA standards suggest that when data scrolls in blocks, one item from the previous group should remain on the screen to orient the user.

Part 1

The browse program displays its initial screen. The user keys in CA to view a list of customers from California.

```
  DINMAPZ            Customer Browse

  Type the state whose customers you want to browse.  Then press Enter.

  State. . CA


  Number   Last name, first initial          City










  F3=Exit    F7=Bkwd    F8=Fwd    F12=Cancel
```

Part 2

Information for the first 14 of 75 rows retrieved for California customers is displayed. The user can specify another state or press F8 to scroll forward.

```
  DINMAPZ            Customer Browse

  Type the state whose customers you want to browse.  Then press Enter.

  State. . CA
                                          Lines    1 to   14 of   75
                                                          More:    +
  Number   Last name, first initial        City
  400254   ALLEN, H.                       LOS ANGELES
  400577   AVILLA, S.                      OAKLAND
  400270   BAILEY, P.                      OAKLAND
  400566   BERTHOLD, K.                    SANTA CRUZ
  400371   BOESE, A.                       LOS ANGELES
  400615   BURNS, M.                       VENTURA
  400097   CHU, J.                         INVERNESS
  400285   CLARK, V.                       MERCED
  400589   DONALDSON, N.                   SAN FRANCISCO
  400590   DOYLE, K.                       RICHMOND
  400156   DULMAGE, D.                     POWAY
  400178   DURHAM, J.                      SAN BERNARDINO
  400433   ENNIS, S.                       SACRAMENTO
  400584   ERICKSON, M.                    REDWOOD CITY

  F3=Exit    F7=Bkwd    F8=Fwd    F12=Cancel
```

Figure 8-1   The operation of the CICS customer browse program

Part 3

When the user pressed
F8, the next group of
rows was displayed.

```
  DINMAPZ              Customer Browse

  Type the state whose customers you want to browse.  Then press Enter.

  State. . CA
                                              Lines   14 to   27 of   75
                                                           More: - +

  Number   Last name, first initial          City
  400584   ERICKSON, M.                       REDWOOD CITY
  400289   FOGEL, H.                          DALY CITY
  400543   FORBES, T.                         BURBANK
  400079   FULLER, S.                         LOS ANGELES
  400044   GREEN, W.                          EL CENTRO
  400179   HALL, C.                           LOS ANGELES
  400251   HARRISON, W.                       PALO ALTO
  400029   HOMEN, T.                          MILBRAE
  400006   HONG, P.                           SAN FRANCISCO
  400003   HOWARD, S.                         REDWOOD CITY
  400611   HUSS, I.                           LOS ANGELES
  400600   HYDE, R.                           LOS ANGELES
  400606   IRELAND, T.                        EUREKA
  400592   KENNEDY, L.                        CHICO

  F3=Exit    F7=Bkwd    F8=Fwd    F12=Cancel
```

Figure 8-1   The operation of the CICS customer browse program (continued)

From the screen in part 3, the user was able to press F8 four more times to display more sets of rows. When he reached the end of the data, he used F7 and F8 several times to scroll backward and forward to browse the data. When he had finally seen all of the customer rows he wanted, he pressed F3 to end the program.

The CICS/DB2 conflict and programming strategies for browsing DB2 data

Unfortunately, the way you code efficient CICS programs and the way DB2 operates conflict with one another when a browse is involved. In this section, I'll describe how they conflict, and I'll present some strategies you can use to code your CICS/DB2 browse programs.

How CICS and DB2 operations conflict with each other

As the customer browse program illustrates, a single browse operation can involve many CICS displays. And, if the program is written using pseudo-conversational programming, the operation may involve many separate executions of the program.

Strategy 1	Do a separate query for each execution of the program.
Strategy 2	Do a single query and browse in a conversational program.
Strategy 3	Do a single query and save the results in: • a DB2 work table • a VSAM data set • CICS temporary storage

Figure 8-2   Strategies you can use to browse table data in a CICS program

Unfortunately, DB2 operations and CICS operations come into conflict when multi-row results tables need to be browsed. That's because when a pseudo-conversational program ends, DB2 drops the results table it was using for the browse operation. Although the program could recreate the results table each time it's executed, the system resources required to do this can be excessive. On the other hand, if the program were written using conversational programming so the results table was created only once, the whole CICS subsystem would suffer.

The conflict between the operating modes of CICS and DB2 is so serious that some shops prohibit CICS/DB2 browse programs or limit their number and operations. For applications that could involve huge numbers of rows, limiting CICS/DB2 browsing is certainly reasonable. For example, if an on-line table contains millions of rows, it would be unreasonable *not* to prohibit browse operations. However, for results tables that contain modest numbers of rows, browsing with a CICS program may be reasonable if you adopt an appropriate programming strategy.

Programming strategies for CICS/DB2 browse programs

Here, I'd like to discuss three programming strategies for CICS/DB2 browse programs. Figure 8-2 lists these strategies. As you'll see, all of them are costly. They differ largely by how the CICS and DB2 subsystems share the processing burden.

Although I'll discuss the three strategies separately, you should realize that you can use them together and in different combinations to meet your specific application requirements. And, you can reduce the burden browse operations impose by following two general guidelines that apply regardless of which strategy you adopt. First, you should minimize the number of rows DB2 includes in the results table it produces. That means that if you know the limiting key values for the rows you want to select, you should specify them through host variables you use in the WHERE clause of the DECLARE CURSOR statement. Second, you should display as much data on each screen as you can. Doing that reduces the number of screen interactions required for a browse operation.

Strategy 1: Do a separate query for each execution of the program   If the number of rows that will be browsed is small, it may be acceptable to recreate the results table each time the CICS program executes. To implement this strategy, the CICS program would need to store values between executions to indicate the scroll position. An execution of the program would use that data to determine which rows to retrieve, format, and display. In effect, that means that the CICS program starts the browse from scratch each time it runs.

This strategy is the most efficient from the CICS perspective, but it imposes a real burden on DB2. Remember, browse programs typically execute in busy interactive systems. Contention for access to stored data is high, and the overhead of having to recreate interim results tables over and over is probably unacceptable. That's because this kind of process lets a browse program monopolize a thread longer and more often than an average program. Also, it can cause extensive DB2 locking activity, another kind of access bottleneck.

Strategy 2: Do a single query and browse in a conversational program Another way to address the CICS/DB2 conflict is to avoid pseudo-conversational programming altogether. Instead, it may occasionally be acceptable to write a *conversational program.*

A conversational program is one that doesn't end and pass control back to CICS with each operator interaction. It operates more like the TSO version of the inquiry program I presented in chapter 2 of *Part 1: An Introductory Course.* It continues to run (and occupy CICS storage and use CICS resources) while it waits for a user to make a terminal entry. The program would require the operator to make a special entry to signal that execution should end.

This approach may be in order when (1) the DB2 costs for doing browse operations are so great in a pseudo-conversational program that they're excessive and (2) the browse application is critical. It makes the CICS subsystem pay much of the cost of the browse operation. So, it's a trade-off between DB2 efficiency and CICS efficiency. You should realize, though, that this would be an unusual approach. That's because long browses implemented in this way tie up resources in both the CICS and DB2 subsystems.

Strategy 3: Do a single query and save the results   Another way to improve access to shared data when you have to do browse operations is to create a temporary working subset of the base table. Then, the data you need for the browse is saved between program executions. The bulleted list under Strategy 3 in figure 8-2 lists three approaches you can take to use this strategy.

The first approach is to use a DB2 work table. With this approach, your program would perform a mass insert at the beginning of a browse operation to construct the work table. On the INSERT statement, you would specify a subselect so that data from the base table is inserted into the work table only if it satisfies your selection condition.

To scroll through the data in the work table, separate executions of the program could create a cursor-controlled results table from the work table, not the base table. Then, the program would fetch the appropriate rows from that cursor-controlled results table. When the browse was completed, the program would delete the data from the temporary work table.

By itself, this strategy doesn't reduce the number of SQL operations the program performs. However, it can improve efficiency because it reduces access to the base tables that many other users may be accessing. Also, the DB2 locks your program's SQL statements generate won't block other programs' requests. Your program is the only one that will access your temporary work table.

The disadvantage of this approach is the extra overhead it requires, both in terms of disk space and processor time. And, it still doesn't eliminate the fundamental conflict between CICS and DB2. Browsing data in a temporary work table still requires the program to create a cursor-controlled results table each time it's executed.

Two other approaches to this strategy involve creating a working set of the selected table data outside DB2. To do this, your program would fetch each row from a cursor-controlled results table at the start of a browse operation, then write its contents at another location that's accessible to CICS. One option is to use a VSAM data set. Then, after you transfer the data into the VSAM data set, you can use CICS's browse commands (STARTBR, READNEXT, READPREV, ENDBR, and RESETBR) to retrieve the data for display. This approach is much more efficient in terms of processor time because it's less costly to browse VSAM data than it is to browse DB2 data. Still, this approach may be unacceptable for performance reasons.

A variation of this approach is to store the contents of the results table in a CICS storage area called *temporary storage*. CICS provides temporary storage for your programs through a VSAM data set it manages for you. CICS also provides special commands for saving and retrieving data from temporary storage. Because this approach is simple and straightforward, I'll use it in the program example I'll show you in a moment.

A CICS/DB2 browse program

To illustrate how you can implement a browse application in CICS, I'd like to present a program that does the customer browse I described at the start of this chapter. This program prompts the user for a state code, then retrieves data from all the rows in the customer table for customers who live in that state. As it retrieves the data, it stores it in CICS temporary storage. Then, the program formats and displays the data in groups of 14 rows. The user can scroll forward and backward from group to group to view all of the data that satisfied the selection request.

In this section, I'll first show you the BMS mapset and symbolic map for the application. Then, I'll describe the program's design. Finally, I'll discuss the program's source code.

The BMS mapset for the CICS/DB2 customer browse program

The BMS mapset for the browse program is more complicated than the one for the inquiry program you saw in the last chapter. However, the difference isn't in the complexity of the features it uses; it's just in the number of fields it defines. In fact, the entries in part 1 of figure 8-3 are much like the ones I described for the inquiry application's mapset.

In contrast to the first part of figure 8-3, the second part of this mapset is significantly different from the one for the inquiry program. The first two DFHMDF macros in part 2 of the figure define the fields that contain the scrolling messages that appear on the right side of the display. The one at the top of part 2, named LINEMSG, is used for the messages like

```
Lines    14 to    27 of    75
```

and the one beneath it, MOREMSG, is used for the messages like

```
More: - +
```

Neither of these fields has an initial value. The application program provides their values each time it sends this map to the terminal.

```
          PRINT NOGEN
DINSET2   DFHMSD TYPE=&SYSPARM,                                          X
                 LANG=COBOL,                                             X
                 MODE=INOUT,                                             X
                 TERM=3270-2,                                            X
                 CTRL=FREEKB,                                            X
                 STORAGE=AUTO,                                           X
                 TIOAPFX=YES
*********************************************************************
DINMAP2   DFHMDI SIZE=(24,80),                                           X
                 LINE=1,                                                 X
                 COLUMN=1
*********************************************************************
          DFHMDF POS=(1,1),                                             X
                 LENGTH=7,                                              X
                 ATTRB=(NORM,PROT),                                     X
                 COLOR=BLUE,                                            X
                 INITIAL='DINMAP2'
          DFHMDF POS=(1,20),                                           X
                 LENGTH=15,                                            X
                 ATTRB=(NORM,PROT),                                    X
                 COLOR=BLUE,                                           X
                 INITIAL='Customer Browse'
*********************************************************************
          DFHMDF POS=(3,1),                                            X
                 LENGTH=39,                                           X
                 ATTRB=(NORM,PROT),                                   X
                 COLOR=GREEN,                                         X
                 INITIAL='Type the state whose customers you want'
          DFHMDF POS=(3,41),                                          X
                 LENGTH=29,                                           X
                 ATTRB=(NORM,PROT),                                   X
                 COLOR=GREEN,                                         X
                 INITIAL='to browse.  Then press Enter.'
          DFHMDF POS=(5,1),                                           X
                 LENGTH=8,                                            X
                 ATTRB=(NORM,PROT),                                   X
                 COLOR=GREEN,                                         X
                 INITIAL='State. .'
STATE     DFHMDF POS=(5,10),                                          X
                 LENGTH=2,                                            X
                 ATTRB=(NORM,UNPROT,IC),                              X
                 COLOR=TURQUOISE,                                     X
                 INITIAL='__'
          DFHMDF POS=(5,13),                                          X
                 LENGTH=1,                                            X
                 ATTRB=ASKIP
```

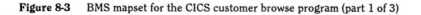

Figure 8-3   BMS mapset for the CICS customer browse program (part 1 of 3)

The third and fourth DFHMDF macros in part 2 of figure 8-3 define the column headings for the lines of customer information the screen displays. Then, the mapset contains 14 groups of macros, one for each of the

```
****************************************************************
LINEMSG  DFHMDF POS=(6,53),                                    X
                LENGTH=26,                                     X
                ATTRB=(NORM,PROT),                             X
                COLOR=BLUE
MOREMSG  DFHMDF POS=(7,69),                                    X
                LENGTH=9,                                      X
                ATTRB=(NORM,PROT),                             X
                COLOR=WHITE
****************************************************************
         DFHMDF POS=(8,1),                                     X
                LENGTH=33,                                     X
                ATTRB=(NORM,PROT),                             X
                COLOR=BLUE,                                    X
                INITIAL='Number   Last name, first initial'
         DFHMDF POS=(8,48),                                    X
                LENGTH=4,                                      X
                ATTRB=(NORM,PROT),                             X
                COLOR=BLUE,                                    X
                INITIAL='City'
*        Customer line 1      ********************************
CUST1    DFHMDF POS=(9,1),                                     X
                LENGTH=6,                                      X
                COLOR=TURQUOISE,                               X
                ATTRB=(NORM,PROT)
NAME1    DFHMDF POS=(9,10),                                    X
                LENGTH=34,                                     X
                COLOR=TURQUOISE,                               X
                ATTRB=(NORM,PROT)
CITY1    DFHMDF POS=(9,48),                                    X
                LENGTH=20,                                     X
                COLOR=TURQUOISE,                               X
                ATTRB=(NORM,PROT)
*        Customer line 2      ********************************
CUST2    DFHMDF POS=(10,1),                                    X
                LENGTH=6,                                      X
                COLOR=TURQUOISE,                               X
                ATTRB=(NORM,PROT)
NAME2    DFHMDF POS=(10,10),                                   X
                LENGTH=34,                                     X
                COLOR=TURQUOISE,                               X
                ATTRB=(NORM,PROT)
CITY2    DFHMDF POS=(10,48),                                   X
                LENGTH=20,                                     X
                COLOR=TURQUOISE,                               X
                ATTRB=(NORM,PROT)
```

Figure 8-3   BMS mapset for the CICS customer browse program (part 2 of 3)

customer data lines that appear on the screen. Each group contains three
DFHMDF macros. The first macro defines the customer number field, the
second defines the name field, and the third defines the city field. I've only
shown the first 3 of these 14 groups in figure 8-3.

```
*               Customer line 3      ***************************************
CUST3      DFHMDF POS=(11,1),                                              X
                  LENGTH=6,                                                X
                  COLOR=TURQUOISE,                                         X
                  ATTRB=(NORM,PROT)
NAME3      DFHMDF POS=(11,10),                                             X
                  LENGTH=34,                                               X
                  COLOR=TURQUOISE,                                         X
                  ATTRB=(NORM,PROT)
CITY3      DFHMDF POS=(11,48),                                             X
                  LENGTH=20,                                               X
                  COLOR=TURQUOISE,                                         X
                  ATTRB=(NORM,PROT)
                  .
                  .
                  .
           Eleven more sets of field definitions for customer lines 4 through 14.
                  .
                  .
                  .
***************************************************************************
MESSAGE    DFHMDF POS=(23,1),                                             X
                  LENGTH=79,                                              X
                  ATTRB=(BRT,PROT),                                       X
                  COLOR=YELLOW
           DFHMDF POS=(24,1),                                            X
                  LENGTH=39,                                             X
                  ATTRB=(NORM,PROT),                                    X
                  COLOR=BLUE,                                           X
                  INITIAL='F3=Exit    F7=Bkwd    F8=Fwd    F12=Cancel'
DUMMY      DFHMDF POS=(24,79),                                          X
                  LENGTH=1,                                            X
                  ATTRB=(DRK,PROT,FSET),                               X
                  INITIAL=' '
***************************************************************************
           DFHMSD TYPE=FINAL
           END
```

Figure 8-3　　BMS mapset for the CICS customer browse program (part 3 of 3)

The last three macros in the mapset are similar to those in the mapset for the inquiry program you saw in the last chapter. The only difference is the initial value of the second field, which contains instructions for the user. Here, the instructions include the functions of the F7 and F8 keys.

The symbolic map for the CICS/DB2 customer browse program

In the last chapter, I mentioned that you can code your own symbolic map instead of using the symbolic map BMS generates. That's what I did in this program. If you code your own symbolic maps, you should use the BMS-generated maps as a guide. That way, you'll be sure to include the same number and types of fields.

Figure 8-4 presents the BMS-generated symbolic map for the browse program, and figure 8-5 presents the customized map I coded. I think you'll agree that the customized map is much easier to read than the BMS version.

In the customized map, I gave the 01-level item a meaningful name (STATE-INQUIRY-MAP). Then, I used an abbreviation of that name as the prefix for all of the data names subordinate to it: SIM. For each of the map fields, I coded three data names in the symbolic map: one for the length field, one for the attribute field, and one for the data field itself. To distinguish these three fields, I included the characters -L- for the length field, -A- for the attribute field, and -D- for the data field. These names parallel the ones in the BMS-generated map in figure 8-4, but they're more understandable.

You'll recall from the last chapter that BMS provides separate data names in its symbolic maps for input and output operations. The output area is a redefinition of the input area. You can see the output area for the BMS-generated symbolic map in part 3 of figure 8-4. I chose not to include separate input and output field names in my customized symbolic map because they're unnecessary for this program.

The biggest difference between the customized symbolic map in figure 8-5 and the BMS-generated map in figure 8-4 is in how the fields are defined for the customer data lines. In the BMS-generated version, separate data names are used for the elements in each of those lines. (Figure 8-4 shows only the fields for the first three of these lines.) I chose to use an OCCURS structure instead, which made the symbolic map shorter. But more important, it makes it easier for me to code the program statements that move data to the symbolic map. I'll show you that code in a moment.

The design of the CICS/DB2 customer browse program

Figure 8-6 presents the structure chart for the browse program. Like the inquiry program in the last chapter, the browse program is pseudo-conversational. So each time the program is executed, it has to figure out what it should do. Most of the possibilities are the same as those I presented in the last chapter. I'll review those possibilities in a moment when I describe the program's source code.

Two of the execution possibilities in the browse program are different from those in the inquiry program: (1) start a new browse or (2) scroll the browse display. If the user presses the Enter key, the program starts a new browse. But if the user presses the F7 or F8 key, the program displays another screen of data from the current browse.

```
01   DINMAP2I.
     02    FILLER      PIC X(12).
     02    STATEL      PIC S9(4) COMP.
     02    STATEF      PIC X.
     02    FILLER REDEFINES STATEF.
      03   STATEA      PIC X.
     02    STATEI      PIC X(0002).
     02    LINEMSGL    PIC S9(4) COMP.
     02    LINEMSGF    PIC X.
     02    FILLER REDEFINES LINEMSGF.
      03   LINEMSGA    PIC X.
     02    LINEMSGI    PIC X(0026).
     02    MOREMSGL    PIC S9(4) COMP.
     02    MOREMSGF    PIC X.
     02    FILLER REDEFINES MOREMSGF.
      03   MOREMSGA    PIC X.
     02    MOREMSGI    PIC X(0009).
     02    CUST1L      PIC S9(4) COMP.
     02    CUST1F      PIC X.
     02    FILLER REDEFINES CUST1F.
      03   CUST1A      PIC X.
     02    CUST1I      PIC X(0006).
     02    NAME1L      PIC S9(4) COMP.
     02    NAME1F      PIC X.
     02    FILLER REDEFINES NAME1F.
      03   NAME1A      PIC X.
     02    NAME1I      PIC X(0034).
     02    CITY1L      PIC S9(4) COMP.
     02    CITY1F      PIC X.
     02    FILLER REDEFINES CITY1F.
      03   CITY1A      PIC X.
     02    CITY1I      PIC X(0020).
     02    CUST2L      PIC S9(4) COMP.
     02    CUST2F      PIC X.
     02    FILLER REDEFINES CUST2F.
      03   CUST2A      PIC X.
     02    CUST2I      PIC X(0006).
     02    NAME2L      PIC S9(4) COMP.
     02    NAME2F      PIC X.
     02    FILLER REDEFINES NAME2F.
      03   NAME2A      PIC X.
     02    NAME2I      PIC X(0034).
     02    CITY2L      PIC S9(4) COMP.
     02    CITY2F      PIC X.
     02    FILLER REDEFINES CITY2F.
      03   CITY2A      PIC X.
     02    CITY2I      PIC X(0020).
```

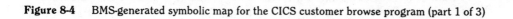

Figure 8-4   BMS-generated symbolic map for the CICS customer browse program (part 1 of 3)

```
02     CUST3L     PIC S9(4) COMP.
02     CUST3F     PIC X.
02     FILLER REDEFINES CUST3F.
 03    CUST3A     PIC X.
02     CUST3I     PIC X(0006).
02     NAME3L     PIC S9(4) COMP.
02     NAME3F     PIC X.
02     FILLER REDEFINES NAME3F.
 03    NAME3A     PIC X.
02     NAME3I     PIC X(0034).
02     CITY3L     PIC S9(4) COMP.
02     CITY3F     PIC X.
02     FILLER REDEFINES CITY3F.
 03    CITY3A     PIC X.
02     CITY3I     PIC X(0020).
 .
 .
 .
```

Eleven more sets of field definitions for customer lines 4 through 14 .

```
 .
 .
 .
02     MESSAGEL   PIC S9(4) COMP.
02     MESSAGEF   PIC X.
02     FILLER REDEFINES MESSAGEF.
 03    MESSAGEA   PIC X.
02     MESSAGEI   PIC X(0079).
02     DUMMYL     PIC S9(4) COMP.
02     DUMMYF     PIC X.
02     FILLER REDEFINES DUMMYF.
 03    DUMMYA     PIC X.
02     DUMMYI     PIC X(0001).
```

Figure 8-4   BMS-generated symbolic map for the CICS customer browse program (part 2 of 3)

How the program starts a new browse   To start a new browse, the program must retrieve all the customers who live in the specified state and display the first group of them. Module 1000 performs that function. The first thing module 1000 does is invoke module 1100 to delete the program's CICS temporary storage area, called a *temporary storage queue*, or *TS queue*. The program deletes this queue so it doesn't contain data from a previous browse. (There's no way to delete the data from a queue without deleting the queue.) Then, module 1200 receives the screen map to get the state code that will be used for the browse. And module 1300 checks to make sure the user entered an acceptable state code value.

```
01   DINMAP2O REDEFINES DINMAP2I.
     02    FILLER      PIC X(12).
     02    FILLER      PIC X(3).
     02    STATEO      PIC X(0002).
     02    FILLER      PIC X(3).
     02    LINEMSGO    PIC X(0026).
     02    FILLER      PIC X(3).
     02    MOREMSGO    PIC X(0009).
     02    FILLER      PIC X(3).
     02    CUST1O      PIC X(0006).
     02    FILLER      PIC X(3).
     02    NAME1O      PIC X(0034).
     02    FILLER      PIC X(3).
     02    CITY1O      PIC X(0020).
     02    FILLER      PIC X(3).
     02    CUST2O      PIC X(0006).
     02    FILLER      PIC X(3).
     02    NAME2O      PIC X(0034).
     02    FILLER      PIC X(3).
     02    CITY2O      PIC X(0020).
     02    FILLER      PIC X(3).
     02    CUST3O      PIC X(0006).
     02    FILLER      PIC X(3).
     02    NAME3O      PIC X(0034).
     02    FILLER      PIC X(3).
     02    CITY3O      PIC X(0020).
              .
              .
              .
```

Eleven more sets of field definitions for customer lines 4 through 14 .

```
              .
              .
              .
     02    FILLER      PIC X(3).
     02    MESSAGEO    PIC X(0079).
     02    FILLER      PIC X(3).
     02    DUMMYO      PIC X(0001).
```

Figure 8-4   BMS-generated symbolic map for the CICS customer browse program (part 3 of 3)

If the user did enter an acceptable state code value, the program invokes module 1400 to retrieve all the rows from the customer table whose state column contains that value. Module 1400 generates the appropriate results table by first opening the cursor using the new state code value (module 1410). Then, if that was successful, module 1400 performs module 1420 repeatedly to fetch the current row from the results table (module 1430) and store the data it contains in the temporary storage queue (module 1440). When module 1430 tries to fetch a row beyond the last row in the results table, module 1400 stops invoking 1420 and closes

```
 01   STATE-INQUIRY-MAP.
 *
      05   FILLER                     PIC X(12).
 *
      05   SIM-L-STATE                PIC S9(4)      COMP.
      05   SIM-A-STATE                PIC X.
      05   SIM-D-STATE                PIC XX.
 *
      05   SIM-L-LINEMSG              PIC S9(4)      COMP.
      05   SIM-A-LINEMSG              PIC X.
      05   SIM-D-LINEMSG              PIC X(26).
 *
      05   SIM-L-MOREMSG              PIC S9(4)      COMP.
      05   SIM-A-MOREMSG              PIC X.
      05   SIM-D-MOREMSG              PIC X(9).
 *
      05   SIM-CUSTOMER-LINE          OCCURS 14.
 *
           10   SIM-L-CUSTNO          PIC S9(4)      COMP.
           10   SIM-A-CUSTNO          PIC X.
           10   SIM-D-CUSTNO          PIC X(6).
 *
           10   SIM-L-NAME            PIC S9(4)      COMP.
           10   SIM-A-NAME            PIC X.
           10   SIM-D-NAME            PIC X(34).
 *
           10   SIM-L-CITY            PIC S9(4)      COMP.
           10   SIM-A-CITY            PIC X.
           10   SIM-D-CITY            PIC X(20).
 *
      05   SIM-L-MESSAGE              PIC S9(4)      COMP.
      05   SIM-A-MESSAGE              PIC X.
      05   SIM-D-MESSAGE              PIC X(79).
 *
      05   SIM-L-DUMMY                PIC S9(4)      COMP.
      05   SIM-A-DUMMY                PIC X.
      05   SIM-D-DUMMY                PIC X.
 *
```

Figure 8-5   Customized symbolic map for the CICS customer browse program

the cursor (module 1450). Since all the data needed to perform the browse operation is now stored outside of DB2, DB2's work is complete.

The next step is for module 1500 to prepare the first screen of data for the new browse. It invokes module 1510 14 times to fill in the symbolic map fields with data for the first 14 records retrieved from the TS queue. After it has prepared the symbolic map, module 1500 performs module 1520 to issue the CICS SEND MAP command to display the data.

If one of module 1000's subordinates detects a processing error, module 1000 performs module 1600 to send an error message to the

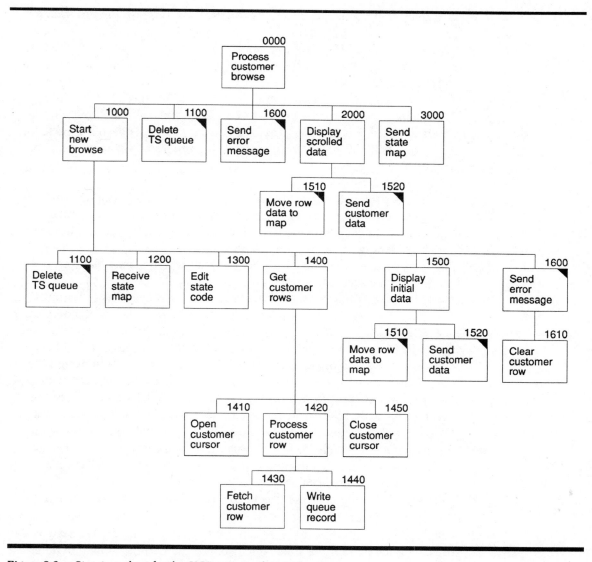

Figure 8-6   Structure chart for the CICS customer browse program

terminal. It does that by issuing a CICS SEND MAP command. But first, it performs module 1610 14 times to clear the customer line fields in the symbolic map. That insures that no data remains on the screen.

How the program scrolls the display   If the program has already retrieved the data for a browse, the user may enter F7 or F8 to scroll the customer lines on the screen. To process a scroll request, the program performs module 2000. It uses the same subordinates as module 1500. First, it invokes module 1510 14 times to move the appropriate data from the temporary storage queue to the symbolic map. Then, it performs module 1520 to send the map.

Module 0000 also invokes modules 1100, 1600, and 3000. Module 1100 deletes the TS queue before the program ends. Module 1600 displays an error message if the user presses a key the program doesn't provide for. And module 3000 sends a fresh screen if the program is executing for the first time or if the user pressed the Clear key.

Other approaches to the design of the program   As I designed this program, I tried to keep it as easy to understand as possible. In particular, I wanted to use simple operations and implement them in a straightforward and obvious way. (Even so, the program design and code can *still* seem confusing.) Because I took this approach, I didn't include some features in the program that could make it operate more efficiently.

First, I could have designed the program so it stored larger "chunks" of data in temporary storage. As this program's design suggests, it stores each row it fetches in a single temporary storage record. Then, to display scrolled data, it retrieves the proper 14 records from temporary storage in 14 separate operations. A more efficient approach would have been to design the temporary storage record so it contains data from 14 rows: all the customer data that would appear on the screen at one time. That would reduce the number of CICS requests the program would have to make to store data in temporary storage and retrieve it. However, that would also impose a fixed scroll size: a full screen. By using separate temporary storage records for each customer line, the program could easily be adjusted to let the user scroll a specific number of lines.

Second, I could have designed the program so that if the user presses the Enter key without changing the state code, the program doesn't start a new browse. To do that, the program would have to compare the state code the user entered with the state code used for the current browse to determine what processing it would do next. This would be more efficient and wouldn't penalize the user, in terms of response time, for a simple keying error.

Third, I could have combined the functions of modules 1400 and 1500. Under the design in figure 8-6, the program first fetches and stores all of the retrieved data (module 1400). Then it goes back to the temporary storage queue to get the data for the first 14 rows to format the display (module 1500). I used this approach because I think it makes it easier to understand the programming techniques that accomplish these two tasks.

However, a more efficient approach would have been for the program to prepare the symbolic map fields for the first screen of a new browse as it loads the temporary storage queue.

If you put your mind to it, I'm sure you can think of still other ways the program could operate. In practice, CICS program development depends on a high degree of finesse that varies with the specifics of the application, the users, the execution environment, and the data itself. So, what may be the best approach in one situation may not be the best in another. For more perspective on CICS design issues, I recommend Doug Lowe's *CICS for the COBOL Programmer, Part 1* and *Part 2*. Here, I want to present *one* example that uses *one* approach. You can take it from there.

How the browse program selects the appropriate execution option

Figure 8-7 presents the source code for the browse program. Its top-level module is much like that of the inquiry program from the last chapter. An EVALUATE statement determines which of several functions the current execution of the program should perform.

The first two conditions in the EVALUATE statement cause the program to invoke module 3000 to send a fresh screen to the terminal. This happens the first time the program is executed during a terminal session (EIBCALEN = ZERO) and when the user presses the Clear key to reset the screen display (EIBAID = DFHCLEAR). Module 3000 moves LOW-VALUE to the symbolic map, STATE-INQUIRY-MAP, then issues a SEND MAP command with the ERASE option.

The third condition in the EVALUATE statement in module 0000 (EIBAID = DFHPA1 OR DFHPA2 OR DFHPA3) is the same as in the inquiry program in the last chapter. It specifies literal values from the DFHAID copy member to detect if the user pressed one of the program attention keys (PA1, PA2, or PA3). CONTINUE directs the program to skip the rest of the EVALUATE structure and continue execution with the next statement.

The fourth condition (EIBAID = DFHPF3 OR DFHPF12) causes the program to issue a CICS XCTL command to pass control back to the menu program named DB2MENU when the user presses either F3 or F12. Before it does that, though, it performs module 1100. This module deletes the TS queue the program used for previous browse operations.

The fifth EVALUATE condition (EIBAID = DFHPF7 OR DFHPF8) was *not* present in the inquiry program. It causes the program to invoke module 2000 to scroll the lines displayed on the screen. The same module handles

```
000100 IDENTIFICATION DIVISION.
000200*
000300 PROGRAM-ID.   DB2DIN2.
000400*
000500 ENVIRONMENT DIVISION.
000600*
000700 DATA DIVISION.
000800*
000900 WORKING-STORAGE SECTION.
001000*
001100 01  SWITCHES.
001200*
001300     05  VALID-DATA-SW            PIC X      VALUE 'Y'.
001400         88 VALID-DATA                       VALUE 'Y'.
001500     05  END-OF-CUSTOMERS-SW      PIC X      VALUE 'N'.
001600         88  END-OF-CUSTOMERS               VALUE 'Y'.
001700     05  CLEAR-CUSTOMER-ROWS-SW   PIC X      VALUE 'N'.
001800         88  CLEAR-CUSTOMER-ROWS            VALUE 'Y'.
001900*
002000 01  COMMUNICATION-AREA.
002100*
002200     05  CA-STATE-CODE            PIC XX.
002300     05  CA-TS-RECORD-COUNT       PIC S9(4)    COMP.
002400     05  CA-FIRST-RECORD-ON-DISPLAY PIC S9(4)  COMP.
002500*
002600 01  RESPONSE-CODE                PIC S9(8)    COMP.
002700*
002800 01  TEMPORARY-STORAGE-FIELDS.
002900*
003000     05  TS-QUEUE-NAME.
003100         10  TS-TERMINAL-ID       PIC X(4).
003200         10  FILLER               PIC X(4)     VALUE 'DIN2'.
003300     05  TS-ITEM-NUMBER           PIC S9(4)    COMP
003400                                               VALUE ZERO.
003500     05  TS-CUSTOMER-ROW.
003600         10 TS-CUSTNO             PIC X(6).
003700         10 TS-CNAME              PIC X(34).
003800         10 TS-CITY              PIC X(20).
003900*
004000 01  POSITION-MESSAGE.
004100*
004200     05  FILLER                   PIC X(6)
004300                                              VALUE 'Lines '.
004400     05  PM-START                 PIC ZZZ9.
004500     05  FILLER                   PIC X(4)
004600                                              VALUE ' to '.
004700     05  PM-END                   PIC ZZZ9.
004800     05  FILLER                   PIC X(4)
004900                                              VALUE ' of '.
005000     05  PM-TOTAL                 PIC ZZZ9.
005100*
005200 01  WORK-FIELDS.
005300*
005400     05  TOP-ROW-PLUS-13          PIC S9(4)    COMP.
005500     05  STATE-MAP-ROW            PIC S9(4)    COMP.
005600*
```

Figure 8-7   COBOL source code for the CICS customer browse program (part 1 of 7)

```
005700 01   CUSTOMER-ROW.
005800*
005900      05   CUSTNO                      PIC X(6).
006000      05   CNAME                       PIC X(34).
006100      05   CITY                        PIC X(20).
006200*
006300      EXEC SQL
006400          INCLUDE SQLCA
006500      END-EXEC.
006600*
006700 COPY DINSET2.
006800*
006900 COPY DFHAID.
007000*
007100      EXEC SQL
007200          DECLARE CUST CURSOR FOR
007300              SELECT CUSTNO,
007400                  (LNAME || ', ' ||
007500                  SUBSTR(FNAME,1,1) || '.'),
007600                  CITY
007700                FROM MMADBV.CUST
007800                WHERE STATE = :SIM-D-STATE
007900              ORDER BY 2
008000      END-EXEC.
008100
008200 LINKAGE SECTION.
008300*
008400 01   DFHCOMMAREA                      PIC X(6).
008500*
008600 PROCEDURE DIVISION.
008700*
008800 0000-PROCESS-CUSTOMER-BROWSE.
008900*
009000      EVALUATE TRUE
009100
009200          WHEN EIBCALEN = ZERO
009300              PERFORM 3000-SEND-STATE-MAP
009400
009500          WHEN EIBAID = DFHCLEAR
009600              PERFORM 3000-SEND-STATE-MAP
009700
009800          WHEN EIBAID = DFHPA1 OR DFHPA2 OR DFHPA3
009900              CONTINUE
010000
010100          WHEN EIBAID = DFHPF3 OR DFHPF12
010200              PERFORM 1100-DELETE-TS-QUEUE
010300              EXEC CICS
010400                  XCTL PROGRAM('DB2MENU')
010500              END-EXEC
010600          WHEN EIBAID = DFHPF7 or DFHPF8
010700              PERFORM 2000-DISPLAY-SCROLLED-DATA
010800
010900          WHEN EIBAID = DFHENTER
011000              PERFORM 1000-START-NEW-BROWSE
011100
```

Figure 8-7   COBOL source code for the CICS customer browse program (part 2 of 7)

```
011200          WHEN OTHER
011300              MOVE DFHCOMMAREA TO COMMUNICATION-AREA
011400              MOVE LOW-VALUE TO STATE-INQUIRY-MAP
011500              MOVE 'Invalid key pressed.' TO SIM-D-MESSAGE
011600              MOVE CA-STATE-CODE TO SIM-D-STATE
011700              PERFORM 1600-SEND-ERROR-MESSAGE
011800
011900      END-EVALUATE.
012000
012100      EXEC CICS
012200          RETURN TRANSID('DIN2')
012300                  COMMAREA(COMMUNICATION-AREA)
012400      END-EXEC.
012500*
012600 1000-START-NEW-BROWSE.
012700*
012800      MOVE LOW-VALUE TO STATE-INQUIRY-MAP.
012900      MOVE SPACE      TO SIM-D-MESSAGE.
013000      PERFORM 1100-DELETE-TS-QUEUE.
013100      PERFORM 1200-RECEIVE-STATE-MAP.
013200      PERFORM 1300-EDIT-STATE-CODE.
013300      IF VALID-DATA
013400          MOVE ZERO TO CA-TS-RECORD-COUNT
013500          PERFORM 1400-GET-CUSTOMER-ROWS.
013600      IF VALID-DATA
013700          IF CA-TS-RECORD-COUNT > 0
013800              PERFORM 1500-DISPLAY-INITIAL-DATA
013900          ELSE
014000              MOVE 'There are no customers in that state.'
014100                      TO SIM-D-MESSAGE
014200              MOVE SPACE TO SIM-D-LINEMSG
014300                           SIM-D-MOREMSG
014400              MOVE 'Y'   TO CLEAR-CUSTOMER-ROWS-SW
014500              MOVE 'N'   TO VALID-DATA-SW.
014600      IF NOT VALID-DATA
014700          PERFORM 1600-SEND-ERROR-MESSAGE.
014800*
014900 1100-DELETE-TS-QUEUE.
015000*
015100      MOVE EIBTRMID TO TS-TERMINAL-ID.
015200      EXEC CICS
015300          DELETEQ TS QUEUE(TS-QUEUE-NAME)
015400                     RESP(RESPONSE-CODE)
015500      END-EXEC.
015600      IF          RESPONSE-CODE NOT = DFHRESP(NORMAL)
015700          AND RESPONSE-CODE NOT = DFHRESP(QIDERR)
015800          EXEC CICS
015900              ABEND
016000          END-EXEC.
016100*
```

Figure 8-7   COBOL source code for the CICS customer browse program (part 3 of 7)

```
016100 1200-RECEIVE-STATE-MAP.
016200*
016300     EXEC CICS
016400         RECEIVE MAP('DINMAP2')
016500                 MAPSET('DINSET2')
016600                 INTO(STATE-INQUIRY-MAP)
016700     END-EXEC.
016800*
016900 1300-EDIT-STATE-CODE.
017000*
017100     IF         SIM-L-STATE = ZERO
017200             OR SIM-D-STATE = SPACE
017300         MOVE 'N' TO VALID-DATA-SW
017400         MOVE 'Y' TO CLEAR-CUSTOMER-ROWS-SW
017500         MOVE 'You must enter a state code.' TO SIM-D-MESSAGE
017600     ELSE
017700         MOVE SIM-D-STATE TO CA-STATE-CODE.
017800*
017900 1400-GET-CUSTOMER-ROWS.
018000*
018100     PERFORM 1410-OPEN-CUSTOMER-CURSOR.
018200     IF VALID-DATA
018300         PERFORM 1420-PROCESS-CUSTOMER-ROW
018400             UNTIL END-OF-CUSTOMERS
018500         PERFORM 1450-CLOSE-CUSTOMER-CURSOR.
018600*
018700 1410-OPEN-CUSTOMER-CURSOR.
018800*
018900     EXEC SQL
019000         OPEN CUST
019100     END-EXEC.
019200     IF SQLCODE NOT = 0
019300         MOVE 'Y' TO CLEAR-CUSTOMER-ROWS-SW
019400         MOVE 'DB2 open error.' TO SIM-D-MESSAGE
019500         MOVE 'N' TO VALID-DATA-SW.
019600*
019700 1420-PROCESS-CUSTOMER-ROW.
019800*
019900     PERFORM 1430-FETCH-CUSTOMER-ROW.
020000     IF NOT END-OF-CUSTOMERS
020100         PERFORM 1440-WRITE-QUEUE-RECORD.
020200*
020300 1430-FETCH-CUSTOMER-ROW.
020400*
020500     EXEC SQL
020600         FETCH CUST
020700             INTO :CUSTNO, :CNAME, :CITY
020800     END-EXEC.
020900     IF SQLCODE NOT= 0
021000         MOVE 'Y' TO END-OF-CUSTOMERS-SW
021100         IF SQLCODE NOT = 100
021200             MOVE 'Y' TO CLEAR-CUSTOMER-ROWS-SW
021300             MOVE 'DB2 fetch error.' TO SIM-D-MESSAGE
021400             MOVE 'N' TO VALID-DATA-SW.
021500*
```

Figure 8-7   COBOL source code for the CICS customer browse program (part 4 of 7)

```
021600 1440-WRITE-QUEUE-RECORD.
021700*
021800      ADD 1        TO CA-TS-RECORD-COUNT.
021900      MOVE CUSTNO TO TS-CUSTNO.
022000      MOVE CNAME   TO TS-CNAME.
022100      MOVE CITY    TO TS-CITY.
022200      EXEC CICS
022300          WRITEQ TS QUEUE(TS-QUEUE-NAME)
022400                      FROM(TS-CUSTOMER-ROW)
022500      END-EXEC.
022600*
022700 1450-CLOSE-CUSTOMER-CURSOR.
022800*
022900      EXEC SQL
023000          CLOSE CUST
023100      END-EXEC.
023200      IF SQLCODE NOT = 0
023300          MOVE 'Y' TO CLEAR-CUSTOMER-ROWS-SW
023400          MOVE 'DB2 close error.' TO SIM-D-MESSAGE
023500          MOVE 'N' TO VALID-DATA-SW.
023600*
023700 1500-DISPLAY-INITIAL-DATA.
023800*
023900      MOVE SPACE TO SIM-D-MESSAGE.
024000      MOVE 1 TO CA-FIRST-RECORD-ON-DISPLAY
024100                TS-ITEM-NUMBER.
024200      PERFORM 1510-MOVE-ROW-DATA-TO-MAP
024300          VARYING STATE-MAP-ROW FROM 1 BY 1
024400          UNTIL STATE-MAP-ROW > 14.
024500      MOVE 1 TO PM-START.
024600      MOVE CA-TS-RECORD-COUNT TO PM-TOTAL.
024700      IF CA-TS-RECORD-COUNT > 14
024800          MOVE 14 TO PM-END
024900          MOVE 'More:    +' TO SIM-D-MOREMSG
025000      ELSE
025100          MOVE CA-TS-RECORD-COUNT TO PM-END
025200          MOVE SPACE TO SIM-D-MOREMSG.
025300      MOVE POSITION-MESSAGE TO SIM-D-LINEMSG.
025400      PERFORM 1520-SEND-CUSTOMER-DATA.
025500*
025600 1510-MOVE-ROW-DATA-TO-MAP.
025700*
025800      IF TS-ITEM-NUMBER <= CA-TS-RECORD-COUNT
025900          EXEC CICS
026000              READQ TS QUEUE(TS-QUEUE-NAME)
026100                      INTO(TS-CUSTOMER-ROW)
026200                      ITEM(TS-ITEM-NUMBER)
026300          END-EXEC
026400          MOVE TS-CUSTNO TO SIM-D-CUSTNO(STATE-MAP-ROW)
026500          MOVE TS-CNAME  TO SIM-D-NAME(STATE-MAP-ROW)
026600          MOVE TS-CITY   TO SIM-D-CITY(STATE-MAP-ROW)
026700          ADD 1 TO TS-ITEM-NUMBER
026800      ELSE
026900          MOVE SPACE TO SIM-D-CUSTNO(STATE-MAP-ROW)
027000                        SIM-D-NAME(STATE-MAP-ROW)
027100                        SIM-D-CITY(STATE-MAP-ROW).
027200*
```

Figure 8-7   COBOL source code for the CICS customer browse program (part 5 of 7)

```
027200 1520-SEND-CUSTOMER-DATA.
027300*
027400     EXEC CICS
027500         SEND MAP('DINMAP2')
027600              MAPSET('DINSET2')
027700              FROM(STATE-INQUIRY-MAP)
027800              DATAONLY
027900     END-EXEC.
028000*
028100 1600-SEND-ERROR-MESSAGE.
028200*
028300     IF CLEAR-CUSTOMER-ROWS
028400         PERFORM 1610-CLEAR-CUSTOMER-ROW
028500             VARYING STATE-MAP-ROW FROM 1 BY 1
028600             UNTIL STATE-MAP-ROW > 14.
028700     EXEC CICS
028800         SEND MAP('DINMAP2')
028900              MAPSET('DINSET2')
029000              FROM(STATE-INQUIRY-MAP)
029100              DATAONLY
029200              ALARM
029300     END-EXEC.
029400*
029500 1610-CLEAR-CUSTOMER-ROW.
029600*
029700     MOVE SPACE TO SIM-D-CUSTNO(STATE-MAP-ROW)
029800                   SIM-D-NAME(STATE-MAP-ROW)
029900                   SIM-D-CITY(STATE-MAP-ROW).
030100*
030200 2000-DISPLAY-SCROLLED-DATA.
030300*
030400     MOVE DFHCOMMAREA    TO COMMUNICATION-AREA.
030500     MOVE EIBTRMID       TO TS-TERMINAL-ID.
030600     MOVE LOW-VALUE      TO STATE-INQUIRY-MAP.
030700     MOVE SPACE          TO SIM-D-MESSAGE.
030800     MOVE CA-STATE-CODE TO SIM-D-STATE.
030900     IF CA-TS-RECORD-COUNT = 0
031000         MOVE 'No customers selected.' TO SIM-D-MESSAGE
031100     ELSE
031200         IF EIBAID = DFHPF7
031300             IF CA-FIRST-RECORD-ON-DISPLAY > 13
031400                 SUBTRACT 13 FROM CA-FIRST-RECORD-ON-DISPLAY
031500             END-IF
031600           ELSE
031700             IF CA-FIRST-RECORD-ON-DISPLAY <
031800                     CA-TS-RECORD-COUNT - 13
031900                 ADD 13 TO CA-FIRST-RECORD-ON-DISPLAY
032000             END-IF
032100           END-IF
```

Figure 8-7   COBOL source code for the CICS customer browse program (part 6 of 7)

```
032100           MOVE CA-FIRST-RECORD-ON-DISPLAY TO TS-ITEM-NUMBER
032200           PERFORM 1510-MOVE-ROW-DATA-TO-MAP
032300               VARYING STATE-MAP-ROW FROM 1 BY 1
032400               UNTIL STATE-MAP-ROW > 14
032500           MOVE CA-FIRST-RECORD-ON-DISPLAY TO PM-START
032600           MOVE CA-TS-RECORD-COUNT          TO PM-TOTAL
032700           ADD 13 TO CA-FIRST-RECORD-ON-DISPLAY
032800               GIVING TOP-ROW-PLUS-13
032900           IF CA-FIRST-RECORD-ON-DISPLAY = 1
033000               IF TOP-ROW-PLUS-13 < CA-TS-RECORD-COUNT
033100                   MOVE TOP-ROW-PLUS-13     TO PM-END
033200                   MOVE 'More:    +'         TO SIM-D-MOREMSG
033300               ELSE
033400                   MOVE CA-TS-RECORD-COUNT TO PM-END
033500                   MOVE SPACE               TO SIM-D-MOREMSG
033600               END-IF
033700           ELSE
033800               IF TOP-ROW-PLUS-13 < CA-TS-RECORD-COUNT
033900                   MOVE TOP-ROW-PLUS-13     TO PM-END
034000                   MOVE 'More: - +'         TO SIM-D-MOREMSG
034100               ELSE
034200                   MOVE CA-TS-RECORD-COUNT TO PM-END
034300                   MOVE 'More: - '          TO SIM-D-MOREMSG
034400               END-IF
034500           END-IF
034600           MOVE POSITION-MESSAGE TO SIM-D-LINEMSG.
034700       PERFORM 1520-SEND-CUSTOMER-DATA.
034800*
034900 3000-SEND-STATE-MAP.
035000*
035100       MOVE LOW-VALUE TO STATE-INQUIRY-MAP.
035200       EXEC CICS
035300           SEND MAP('DINMAP2')
035400               MAPSET('DINSET2')
035500               FROM(STATE-INQUIRY-MAP)
035600               ERASE
035700       END-EXEC.
```

Figure 8-7   COBOL source code for the CICS customer browse program (part 7 of 7)

forward *and* backward scrolls. I'll describe how it works later in this chapter.

The sixth condition (EIBAID = DFHENTER) causes the program to start a new browse. To do that, it invokes module 1000. As the structure chart shows, module 1000 has several subordinates. All of the program's DB2 operations occur under the control of module 1000. I'll describe it in detail later in this chapter too.

Finally, if none of the preceding six EVALUATE conditions are true, the program reaches the WHEN OTHER clause. This happens if the user pressed an AID key other than those the EVALUATE conditions specify.

The program treats that as an error, but not one that erases the data on the screen or starts another browse operation.

The first thing the WHEN OTHER segment of code does is get the contents of the communication area from the previous execution of the program. To do that, it issues the statement

```
MOVE DFHCOMMAREA TO COMMUNICATION-AREA
```

DFHCOMMAREA is the name of the Linkage Section field where CICS makes communication area data available; COMMUNICATION-AREA is a Working-Storage field I defined. You can see it in part 1 of figure 8-7.

Unlike the inquiry program from the last chapter, this program *does* pass data elements from one execution to the next through the communication area. The first of the three data items the program saves in the communication area is the code for the state currently being browsed. The other two items are the total number of records stored in the TS queue and the number of the record that appears at the top of the list of customers on the current display.

The next statement in the last EVALUATE group moves LOW-VALUE to the symbolic map. That insures that CICS doesn't transmit data to the screen for most of its fields. However, after it moves LOW-VALUE to the entire map, it moves other values to two specific fields. It sets the value of the map's error message field to "Invalid key pressed." to advise the operator of the error. And, it moves the state code value for the current browse to the state field in the symbolic map. That way, if the user changed the state code before pressing an invalid key, the state code for the customer rows currently on display will reappear when the map is sent to the terminal. Finally, the program performs module 1600 to send the map to the terminal. Module 1600 contains a SEND MAP command with the ALARM option.

Unless the user pressed F3 or F12, program execution continues with the statement that follows EVALUATE. This statement is a CICS RETURN command:

```
EXEC CICS
    RETURN TRANSID('DIN2')
            COMMAREA(COMMUNICATION-AREA)
END-EXEC.
```

It passes control back to CICS and causes the current execution of the program to end. However, it specifies that the next time the terminal user presses an AID key, CICS should execute the program associated with the transaction identifier DIN2. That's the browse program this chapter presents. The RETURN command also specifies that the contents of the

Working-Storage field COMMUNICATION-AREA should be retained in the CICS communication area. So, the next time this program runs, that data will be available through DFHCOMMAREA.

How the program starts a new browse

Whenever the terminal user presses the Enter key, the program interprets that as a request to start a new browse. As I've already described, that causes the program to perform module 1000. The code for module 1000 is in part 3 of figure 8-7. Its functions fall into five categories: (1) clearing data stored by a previous browse, (2) getting a valid state code for the new browse, (3) retrieving all the data for the new browse into temporary storage, (4) preparing and displaying the first screen of browse data, and (5) displaying an error message, if necessary.

How the program clears data stored from a previous browse   To get rid of the customer data from the previous execution of the program, module 1000 invokes module 1100. It uses a CICS command I haven't shown you yet: DELETEQ TS. This command causes CICS to delete the temporary storage queue the statement names.

Because your program names the TS queue it uses, you should use a unique identifier as part of the name. That way, you'll avoid naming conflicts with other users' temporary storage queues. Although in many cases an application can benefit by sharing the data in a single TS queue among its users, the customer browse program needs exclusive use of the storage area where it keeps the data it retrieves.

A simple, effective way to create a unique queue name is to combine the CICS identification for the terminal where the user is running the transaction with the name of the transaction itself. To create that name, I defined a Working-Storage field called TS-QUEUE-NAME. It's a group item that has two subordinates:

```
05   TS-QUEUE-NAME.
     10   TS-TERMINAL-ID      PIC X(4).
     10   FILLER              PIC X(4)  VALUE 'DIN2'.
```

The name of the transaction, DIN2, is easy to code as a literal. However, the name of the terminal will vary. The program can get the identification of the terminal where the user started the program from one of the Execute Interface Block fields, EIBTRMID. So, module 1100 starts by moving that value to the terminal-id component of the TS-QUEUE-NAME field.

After formatting the name for the temporary storage queue, module 1100 executes the statement

```
EXEC CICS
     DELETEQ TS QUEUE(TS-QUEUE-NAME)
                    RESP(RESPONSE-CODE)
END-EXEC.
```

to delete it. The RESP option specifies a Working-Storage field that will contain a response-code value CICS returns to report the success or failure of the command. The compound IF statement that immediately follows the command checks the response code.

Although the details of this error checking are beyond the scope of this book, you should know what the IF statement in module 1100 checks for. First, it checks to be sure no errors occurred (DFHRESP(NORMAL)). If an error did occur, it checks to see if the error was an invalid queue name (DFHRESP(QIDERR)). This condition will occur for the first browse request, since no queue was previously created. (A TS queue is created automatically when your program writes to it.) If an error occurred and the queue name wasn't invalid, it indicates that a more serious error occurred. Then, module 1100 issues a CICS ABEND command to end the program immediately.

How the program gets a valid state code for the new browse   After module 1100 deletes the program's temporary storage queue, execution continues as module 1000 invokes module 1200. Module 1200 issues a CICS RECEIVE MAP command to get the data the user entered to start the browse. It is much like the RECEIVE MAP command I showed you in the inquiry program in the last chapter. However, notice that I specified the name of the customized symbolic map I created (STATE-INQUIRY-MAP) for the INTO option.

Next, module 1000 performs module 1300 to edit the state code value the user entered. Again, the browse program is similar here to the inquiry program. If the length of the user's entry (returned in the symbolic map field SIM-L-STATE) is greater than zero and the entry itself (the value of SIM-D-STATE) isn't spaces, the entry is valid. A more sophisticated version of this program might include a table look-up to verify that a non-blank entry really *is* a valid state code.

If the state code isn't valid, the program sets VALID-DATA-SW to "N" and CLEAR-CUSTOMER-ROWS-SW to "Y." You'll see how the program uses these switches when I show you how it deals with errors. The program also moves an error message to the message field in the symbolic map (SIM-D-MESSAGE).

After module 1300 finishes, module 1000 checks the setting of VALID-DATA-SW to determine if the program should proceed to retrieve data from the customer table using the state code value the user entered. If VALID-DATA is true, module 1000 performs module 1400.

How the program retrieves the data for a new browse into temporary storage   Module 1400 manages all of this program's SQL operations. First, it performs module 1410 to open a cursor for the browse. The SQL OPEN statement in module 1410 names CUST as the cursor. You can look back to part 2 of the figure to see the DECLARE CURSOR statement that specifies CUST:

```
EXEC SQL
    DECLARE CUST CURSOR FOR
        SELECT CUSTNO,
               (LNAME || ', ' ||
                SUBSTR(FNAME,1,1) || '.'),
               CITY
            FROM MMADBV.CUST
            WHERE STATE = :SIM-D-STATE
        ORDER BY 2
END-EXEC.
```

I'd like you to notice several things about this statement. First, it returns a three-column results table. One of those columns, the second, won't be in the exact form of the original data in the customer table. It's a concatenation that starts with the entire last name value (a variable-length item in this version of the CUST table) from a selected row, adds a comma and a space after it, then appends the first letter of the customer's first name and a period to it. As a result, the maximum length of the second column in this results table is 34 characters (up to 30 characters for LNAME data, 2 characters for a comma and a space, 1 character for the first letter of FNAME, and 1 character for the trailing period).

Because this isn't compatible with the data definitions in the DCLGEN output for the CUST table, I didn't include that output in the Working- Storage Section of the program. Instead, I created my own host variables. They're subordinate to the group item CUSTOMER-ROW in part 2 of figure 8-7. I used the familiar names CUSTNO and CITY for the host variables that will contain those data items, but I made up a new name (CNAME) for the concatenated last name/first initial variable.

The next thing you should notice in the DECLARE CURSOR statement is the SELECT component's WHERE clause:

```
WHERE STATE = :SIM-D-STATE
```

It specifies that data should be selected from rows in the CUST table where the value of the STATE column is equal to the value of the program host variable SIM-D-STATE. SIM-D-STATE contains the state code the user entered. Remember that you can select data based on the contents of columns that you don't retrieve into the results table. In this case, the STATE column isn't one of the three column specifications in the SELECT component.

Finally, notice that the DECLARE CURSOR statement includes an ORDER BY clause. It specifies that the rows in the cursor-controlled results table should be put into ascending sequence by the contents of the second column. Because that column contains the last name/first initial concatenation, the results table will be in alphabetical order.

If the OPEN statement in module 1410 returns a non-zero SQLCODE value, it indicates some serious processing error occurred. In that case, module 1410 supplies an appropriate error message and sets switches whose values control later processing. Otherwise, the cursor-controlled results table is ready for the program to access. Then, module 1400 continues.

Module 1400 uses a PERFORM UNTIL statement to execute module 1420 repeatedly. Module 1420 has two subordinates of its own. Module 1430 issues an SQL FETCH statement to retrieve a row from the cursor-controlled results table. The INTO clause of the FETCH statement in module 1430 names the three fields I created in the host structure for the operation: CUSTNO, CNAME, and CITY. Module 1430 also performs error checking similar to module 1410's.

If the FETCH succeeds, module 1420 performs module 1440. This module begins by incrementing the counter field that keeps track of how many rows are returned through the cursor-controlled results table:

```
ADD 1        TO CA-TS-RECORD-COUNT.
```

Then, it moves the fetched data into Working-Storage fields:

```
MOVE CUSTNO TO TS-CUSTNO.
MOVE CNAME  TO TS-CNAME.
MOVE CITY   TO TS-CITY.
```

These fields make up a record that will be stored in the temporary storage queue. Finally, module 1440 issues the CICS command to write the record to the temporary storage queue:

```
EXEC CICS
    WRITEQ TS QUEUE(TS-QUEUE-NAME)
              FROM(TS-CUSTOMER-ROW)
END-EXEC.
```

This command's first option, TS-QUEUE-NAME, is the same name the program used in module 1100. The second option, TS-CUSTOMER-ROW, is the name of the group item that contains the data this command writes to the temporary storage queue.

After the program fetches all the rows in the CUST table that have the specified state code and writes them to the TS queue, module 1400 executes module 1450. Module 1450 issues an SQL CLOSE statement to close the CUST cursor. Then, it performs some error checking. From this point on, the program manages all the interactions for the browse without issuing another DB2 statement.

How the program prepares and displays the first screen of browse data
If no unexpected errors occur during the processing of module 1400, module 1000 invokes module 1500 to display the first screen of data for the new browse. This module performs module 1510 14 times, once for each customer row on the screen. Module 1510 issues a CICS READQ TS command to retrieve a stored record from the temporary storage queue:

```
EXEC CICS
     READQ TS QUEUE(TS-QUEUE-NAME)
              INTO(TS-CUSTOMER-ROW)
              ITEM(TS-ITEM-NUMBER)
END-EXEC
```

I've already discussed the first two of the three options this command specifies. TS-QUEUE-NAME contains the queue name the program constructed using the EIB terminal-id. TS-CUSTOMER-ROW is the Working-Storage data area where the program prepared the queue data for storage. The third option, ITEM, names a program field whose value specifies the record number in the queue that should be returned into TS-CUSTOMER-ROW. You can think of this as a sort of key field. The first record written to the queue is item 1, the second is item 2, and so on. Module 1500 sets the value of TS-ITEM-NUMBER to 1 before it executes module 1510. And module 1510 increments its value each time it retrieves a record from the queue.

Notice that module 1510 issues the CICS READQ TS command only if the number of the queue item that's about to be read is not greater than the total number of rows that were fetched from the CUST table and saved in the TS queue. Then, after it retrieves the item, it moves the data to the appropriate fields in the symbolic map. Otherwise, it moves spaces to those fields.

After it performs module 1510 to format each of the 14 customer lines in the symbolic map, module 1500 prepares the contents of the scroll information lines:

```
MOVE 1 TO PM-START.
MOVE CA-TS-RECORD-COUNT TO PM-TOTAL.
IF CA-TS-RECORD-COUNT > 14
    MOVE 14 TO PM-END
    MOVE 'More:   +' TO SIM-D-MOREMSG
ELSE
    MOVE CA-TS-RECORD-COUNT TO PM-END
    MOVE SPACE TO SIM-D-MOREMSG.
MOVE POSITION-MESSAGE TO SIM-D-LINEMSG.
```

Here, the program stores the information for the first line in a group item named POSITION-MESSAGE. It sets the value of the first row displayed (PM-START) to 1 and the value of the total number of rows retrieved (PM-TOTAL) to the value of CA-TS-RECORD-COUNT. Then, if the program stored more than 14 records in the TS queue for the browse, it sets the value of the last row displayed (PM-END) to 14. If the program stored 14 or fewer records in the TS queue, it sets the value of PM-END to CA-TS-RECORD-COUNT.

Module 1500 also provides a literal value for the scrolling direction message field in the symbolic map (SIM-D-MOREMSG). If the program stored 14 or fewer records in the TS queue, it sets the value of SIM-D-MOREMSG to space; no scrolling is possible, either up or down. Otherwise, it sets the value of SIM-D-MOREMSG to indicate that the user can scroll forward. After the condition ends, the program moves the entire line-count message (POSITION-MESSAGE) to the SIM-D-LINEMSG field in the symbolic map.

After it has prepared the entire symbolic map, module 1500 performs module 1520. This module issues a CICS SEND MAP command with the DATAONLY option. The command transmits the contents of the symbolic map to the terminal without headings and captions. Those literal values are already present on the screen.

How the program deals with errors generated as it starts a new browse
If one of module 1000's subordinates detects an unmanageable error condition, it sets the value of VALID-DATA-SW to "N." The last thing module 1000 does is check the value of that switch. If it indicates an error, module 1000 invokes module 1600 to send an error message. Module 1600 performs its own subordinate, module 1610, 14 times to clear the contents of the customer lines in the symbolic map. Notice that this module is executed only if the CLEAR-CUSTOMER-ROWS switch is true. That's the case if any errors occur in a module subordinate to module 1000. The only time this condition isn't true is when module 1600 is executed from module 0000.

After module 1600 performs module 1610, it issues a SEND MAP command with the ALARM option to advise the user of the error.

How the program scrolls the display

When a browse is in progress, the user may be able to press F7 or F8 to scroll backward or forward on the screen. If the EVALUATE statement in module 0000 detects either of those PF keys, it performs module 2000 to scroll the display as indicated by the user.

The operation of module 2000 depends on the values CICS passed to the current execution of the program from the previous execution through the communication area. So, the first thing module 2000 does is move the contents of DFHCOMMAREA to the Working-Storage item named COMMUNICATION-AREA. The scroll operations in this module depend on two of the three values from the communication area. CA-TS-RECORD-COUNT contains the total number of records in temporary storage. And CA-TS-FIRST-RECORD-ON-DISPLAY contains the number of the temporary storage record that's currently the first customer line on the screen.

Although the code in module 2000 may look intimidating, it's simple. In essence, it displays the 13 rows that precede those currently on the screen if the user pressed F7 or the 13 rows that follow those currently on the screen if the user pressed F8. Remember, the program scrolls the display 13 rows rather than 14 so that one item from the previous group remains on the screen to orient the user.

After module 2000 sets the values of some data items, it determines which record in the temporary storage queue should appear at the top of the screen after the scroll operation is completed. To do that, it processes this condition:

```
IF EIBAID = DFHPF7
    IF CA-FIRST-RECORD-ON-DISPLAY > 13
        SUBTRACT 13 FROM CA-FIRST-RECORD-ON-DISPLAY
    END-IF
ELSE
    IF CA-FIRST-RECORD-ON-DISPLAY <
            CA-TS-RECORD-COUNT - 13
        ADD 13 TO CA-FIRST-RECORD-ON-DISPLAY
    END-IF
END-IF
```

For "typical" scrolls, this condition simply subtracts 13 from CA-FIRST-RECORD-ON-DISPLAY to move backward or adds 13 to it to move forward. The condition is more complicated because it also has to recognize and handle "atypical" scroll requests: those that would reference a record that doesn't exist in temporary storage. For a backward scroll, that means an attempt to scroll before the first record; for a forward scroll, that means an attempt to scroll beyond the last record. For simplicity, the program leaves the value of CA-FIRST-RECORD-ON-DISPLAY unchanged in these situations.

After it determines what queue record should appear in the first line on the next screen of data, the program moves the number of that record to the Working-Storage field named TS-ITEM-NUMBER. Then, it uses a PERFORM VARYING statement to invoke module 1510 repeatedly. I described this module in detail when I showed you how the program formats and displays the initial screen for a browse. It retrieves records from temporary storage and moves the data they contain to the proper fields in the symbolic map.

The rest of the code in module 2000 prepares the contents of the scroll information lines so they contain the proper line numbers and the right scrolling message for the new screen. Then, the symbolic map is complete, and module 2000 performs module 1520 to send the data to the terminal.

Discussion

The approach to browsing this program uses is appropriate when the amount of data to be browsed is modest. The number of rows in my example, 75, is probably acceptable. However, ten times that many probably isn't, and 10 times more certainly isn't. The approach you adopt depends on the application, the needs of end users, how predictable the data you're accessing is, and a host of other factors. But, regardless of the techniques you use to code a browse program, you should always remember that browses are costly, and they can degrade the overall performance of an on-line transaction processing system.

Terms

browsing
scroll
conversational program
temporary storage
temporary storage queue
TS queue

Objectives

1. Explain why the operating modes of CICS and DB2 conflict with one another.

2. Describe programming strategies you can use to perform CICS/DB2 browse operations.

3. Given program specifications, design and code a CICS/DB2 browse program.

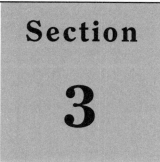

Section

3

Data base administration

To design and develop application programs that process DB2 data, you don't need a thorough understanding of data base administration. That's because most programmers aren't responsible for designing, defining, and administering the DB2 tables their programs process. Those tasks are usually the responsibilities of DBAs. However, I'm convinced that you'll be able to work more productively and professionally as a programmer if you have a basic understanding of several topics related to data base administration. The chapters in this section present those topics.

Chapter 9 presents concepts for designing DB2 data structures. Chapter 10 presents the SQL Data Definition Language (DDL) statements you can use to create and manage DB2 objects as you test your programs. Chapter 11 describes the information you can get from some of the system tables that comprise the DB2 catalog. And chapter 12 covers an SQL statement you can use to get performance analysis data about your programs: EXPLAIN.

My intention in this section is to give you a basic understanding of DB2 concepts and practices related to data base administration. Because you may never need to use the features this section presents, the chapters give only an overview of them. However, this information should be enough to get you started if you ever need to use any of these features. And, where it's appropriate, I'll point you to other resources you can use to learn more about them.

Chapter 9

DB2 relational data base design concepts

Data base administrators are usually responsible for designing and implementing production tables. However, you'll be able to work more effectively and confidently as a programmer if you have a basic understanding of DB2 data base design concepts. This chapter takes a closer look at these concepts and how they affect the way you design a data base.

I'll begin this chapter by describing the source document for the invoice application I've used throughout this book. This document contains all the information that will be stored for invoices. So, I can use it to develop a preliminary data structure. Then, using the elements in this data structure, I'll describe the four ways data elements can be associated with each other. And I'll tell you how you can implement these associations in a data base design. Finally, I'll show you how to refine the data structure using a design methodology called normalization.

After you've finished this chapter, you'll be able to design simple test tables for your programs. You may even be able to plan out the data base requirements for a production application if you understand the application thoroughly. However, I want you to realize that there is plenty more to learn about data base design than what this chapter presents. For more information, refer to the IBM manuals. Some manuals that are especially useful are *IBM Database 2 Version 2 Application Programming and SQL Guide* and the three-volume set *IBM Database 2 Version 2 Administration Guide*.

An overview of the invoice application

Figure 9-1 shows a sample of the invoice form I used to design the invoice data structure. The information this form contains falls into three groups. The first group contains identifying information for the invoice (a unique invoice number and the invoice date) and for the customer associated with the invoice (number, name, and address). The second group contains one line item for each product sold. Each line item specifies the product, the quantity sold, and the dollar amount billed. Finally, the third group contains total dollar amounts for the transaction and a marketing promotion code associated with it.

The most straightforward way to begin designing a data structure is to map all the data elements into a record description. Figure 9-2 illustrates the starting data structure I created for the invoice application. Figure 9-3 presents the COBOL record description for this data structure.

I want you to notice two things about these "invoices." First, the structure contains a data element, invoice number, that is unique for each invoice. Because it's unique, the invoice number can serve as a key. Keys let you establish relationships between data elements in different tables.

Second, notice that I included the line items within the invoice data structure as a repeating group. In figure 9-3, I defined the repeating group with a COBOL OCCURS clause. For applications that use standard data sets, this approach is acceptable. However, DB2 can operate only with "flat" tables; it doesn't support repeating groups. As a result, it's necessary to change the data structure in figures 9-2 and 9-3. But before I show you how to do that, you need to recognize the relationships between the elements in this data structure.

Four ways data elements can be associated with each other

The data elements in figures 9-2 and 9-3 are related to one another in various ways. These four kinds of relationships, or associations, are illustrated in figure 9-4. The first kind is called a *one-to-one association*. For example, a specific customer number relates to one and only one customer name and address. Conversely, a customer name and address relates to one and only

| Invoice number | 999999 |
| Invoice date | 99-99-99 |

Customer Number	999999
Name	XXXXXXXXXXXXXXXXXX XXXXXXXXXXXXXXXXXXXXXXXXXXXX
Address	XXXXXXXXXXXXXXXXXXXXXXXXXXXXXX
City State Zip	XXXXXXXXXXXXXXXXXX XX 99999-9999

Product	Description	Quantity	Unit price	Discount	Extension
XXXXXXXXXX	XXXXXXXXXXXXXXXXXXXXXXXXXXXXXX	9999999	99999.99	99999.99	99999.99
XXXXXXXXXX	XXXXXXXXXXXXXXXXXXXXXXXXXXXXXX	9999999	99999.99	99999.99	99999.99
XXXXXXXXXX	XXXXXXXXXXXXXXXXXXXXXXXXXXXXXX	9999999	99999.99	99999.99	99999.99
XXXXXXXXXX	XXXXXXXXXXXXXXXXXXXXXXXXXXXXXX	9999999	99999.99	99999.99	99999.99
XXXXXXXXXX	XXXXXXXXXXXXXXXXXXXXXXXXXXXXXX	9999999	99999.99	99999.99	99999.99
XXXXXXXXXX	XXXXXXXXXXXXXXXXXXXXXXXXXXXXXX	9999999	99999.99	99999.99	99999.99
XXXXXXXXXX	XXXXXXXXXXXXXXXXXXXXXXXXXXXXXX	9999999	99999.99	99999.99	99999.99
XXXXXXXXXX	XXXXXXXXXXXXXXXXXXXXXXXXXXXXXX	9999999	99999.99	99999.99	99999.99
XXXXXXXXXX	XXXXXXXXXXXXXXXXXXXXXXXXXXXXXX	9999999	99999.99	99999.99	99999.99
XXXXXXXXXX	XXXXXXXXXXXXXXXXXXXXXXXXXXXXXX	9999999	99999.99	99999.99	99999.99
XXXXXXXXXX	XXXXXXXXXXXXXXXXXXXXXXXXXXXXXX	9999999	99999.99	99999.99	99999.99
XXXXXXXXXX	XXXXXXXXXXXXXXXXXXXXXXXXXXXXXX	9999999	99999.99	99999.99	99999.99
XXXXXXXXXX	XXXXXXXXXXXXXXXXXXXXXXXXXXXXXX	9999999	99999.99	99999.99	99999.99
XXXXXXXXXX	XXXXXXXXXXXXXXXXXXXXXXXXXXXXXX	9999999	99999.99	99999.99	99999.99
XXXXXXXXXX	XXXXXXXXXXXXXXXXXXXXXXXXXXXXXX	9999999	99999.99	99999.99	99999.99
XXXXXXXXXX	XXXXXXXXXXXXXXXXXXXXXXXXXXXXXX	9999999	99999.99	99999.99	99999.99

Subtotal	9999999.99
Shipping	99999.99
Sales tax	99999.99
TOTAL DUE	9999999.99
Promotion	XXXXXXXXXX

Figure 9-1 Sample invoice for the data base design example

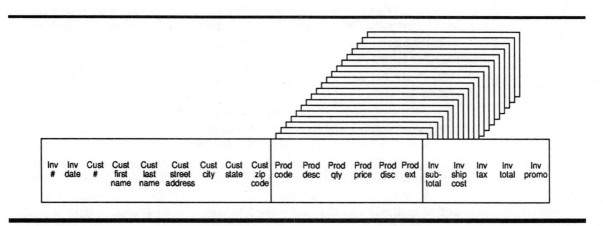

Figure 9-2 Starting structure for unnormalized invoice data

```
*
 01  INVOICE-RECORD.
*
     05   IR-INVNO           PIC X(6).
     05   IR-INVDATE         PIC X(8).
     05   IR-CUSTNO          PIC X(6).
     05   IR-FNAME           PIC X(20).
     05   IR-LNAME           PIC X(30).
     05   IR-ADDR            PIC X(30).
     05   IR-CITY            PIC X(20).
     05   IR-STATE           PIC XX.
     05   IR-ZIPCODE         PIC X(10).
     05   IR-LINE-ITEM  OCCURS 20 TIMES.
          10   IR-PCODE      PIC X(10).
          10   IR-DESC       PIC X(30).
          10   IR-QTY        PIC S9(7)       COMP-3.
          10   IR-PRICE      PIC S9(5)V99    COMP-3.
          10   IR-DISC       PIC S9(5)V99    COMP-3.
          10   IR-EXT        PIC S9(5)V99    COMP-3.
     05   IR-INVSUBT         PIC S9(7)V99    COMP-3.
     05   IR-INVSHIP         PIC S9(5)V99    COMP-3.
     05   IR-INVTAX          PIC S9(5)V99    COMP-3.
     05   IR-INVTOTAL        PIC S9(7)V99    COMP-3.
     05   IR-INVPROM         PIC X(10).
```

Figure 9-3   COBOL record description for an unnormalized invoice file

one customer number. When data elements have one-to-one relationships, it often makes sense to store them together in the same row of a table.

On the other hand, a customer has a *one-to-many association* with invoices, because there can be many invoices for a single customer. If you look at this one-to-many association from the opposite point of view, it's a *many-to-one association*. There may be many invoices associated with a single customer. To implement one-to-many and many-to-one associations with DB2 data, you use two separate tables that tie the related items together with keys.

Finally, because each invoice can contain line items for many products and each product can be included in many invoices, there is a *many-to-many association* between invoices and products. Implementing a many-to-many association usually requires an intermediate table that contains the key values for both of the associated elements.

In the simplest cases, you may be able to design an efficient data structure based on the associations you identify. In most cases, however, you'll need to use a more sophisticated method to refine the data structure. The design methodology that has come into wide use for relational data bases is *normalization*.

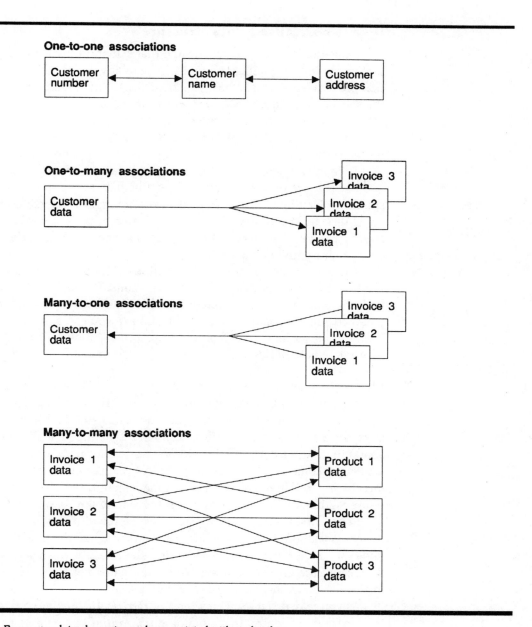

Figure 9-4   Four ways data elements can be associated with each other

How to normalize a data structure

Normalization results in a data design that's appropriate for DB2 tables, that's easy to understand, and that will be relatively efficient. The normalization process has several steps. The table design that results from each of the steps is called a *normal form*. For example, the result of the first step is called the first normal form, the result of the second step is called the second normal form, and so on. Data base designers often use five levels of normalization, and theoreticians have proposed even more. For the purpose of this chapter, it's sufficient that you understand the first three.

The essence of normalization is that the data stored in a row of a table should be identifiable by a key, and all the columns in the table should relate directly to that key. For example, customer table key values identify specific rows in the table, and all the data elements in a row relate to the entity represented by the key value.

To illustrate normalization, I'll continue with the invoice example. I want to stress that this example is a simple one. Production projects are typically much more complicated than this. But this simple example will let you focus on the concepts of normalization so you can apply them in more complicated settings. After I present the normalization process, I'll explain why a data base designer may sometimes want to denormalize data.

First normal form   When I presented the COBOL record description for the unnormalized invoice data structure, I mentioned that DB2 doesn't support repeating groups. To create a data structure in *first normal form*, you store the elements of a repeating group in a separate table. Figure 9-5 shows the invoice data structure in first normal form. As you can see, I've labeled its components as "tables." That's because you can implement them directly in DB2. In contrast, you can't implement the data structure in figure 9-2 in DB2 because it contains a repeating group.

In this first normal form, a single invoice row can be related (in a one-to-many association) to multiple line item rows. Each of the line item rows contains the unique *primary key* value that identifies the invoice row related to it. Because the invoice numbers stored in the line item table identify rows in another table, they're called *foreign keys*.

As you may recall from chapter 4 of *Part 1: An Introductory Course*, foreign keys are central to maintaining *referential integrity*. Referential integrity means that references from one table to another (such as from the line item table to the invoice table) are valid. DBAs can specify that DB2 should automatically enforce referential integrity rules when they define related tables. Or, application programs may be responsible for maintaining referential integrity.

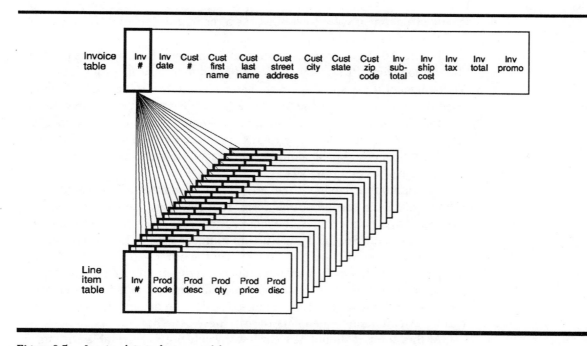

Figure 9-5   Invoice data in first normal form

By including the invoice number in a line item row, I implemented the association between a line item and its related invoice. However, the invoice number by itself isn't enough to identify a line item row uniquely. That's because each invoice may contain several line items. As a result, I added the product code for a specific line item to the invoice number to create a *composite key*. The combination of the invoice number and product code values uniquely identifies a specific line item row.

Also notice that I excluded the extension data item from the structures in figure 9-5. Because the extension can be calculated based on other data elements in the row, it would be redundant to include it. It's more efficient to omit it.

Second normal form   The next step in the normalization process is to separate data items from a table with a composite key if the items depend only on part of the key. For example, the complete key for the line item table in figure 9-5 consists of both the invoice number and the product code. However, one of the line item data elements, product description, depends only on the product code component of the composite key. It doesn't depend on the invoice number component because its value doesn't change from one invoice to another. As a result, this table needs to be modified to be in *second normal form*.

Figure 9-6 shows the second normal form. Here, I removed the product description from the line item table and put it in a separate product table. To implement the association from the line item table to the product table, I used the product code as the primary key for the product table. Now, all of the data elements in the line item table depend on the complete composite key. If you reflect on the data structure in figure 9-6, you'll notice that the line item table is an implementation of the many-to-many association between invoices and products.

You should realize that there are performance trade-offs involved in refining a table to second normal form. That's because the more you split the data into separate tables, the more system resources it takes to retrieve and join the data. So, the data structure in figure 9-6 will be less efficient than the simpler structure in figure 9-5. On the other hand, with the second normal form design in figure 9-6, product description information is stored in just one place. That saves storage space, makes maintenance easier, and reduces the chances of storing inconsistent data. In general, it's worth the extra cost of joining related data to reap these benefits.

At this point, it should be clear how heavily normalized table structures rely on associations implemented through keys. I want to stress that it's essential for equal key values to represent the same entity. Although that may sound obvious, remember that DB2 can join data elements even if they don't make sense in the context of the application. Just keep this point in mind.

Third normal form   The data structure in figure 9-6 can be improved further by taking it to *third normal form*. In third normal form, the data in non-key columns must depend *only* on the key. In other words, they must have a one-to-one association with the key. If a non-key data item depends on another non-key data item, the structure isn't in third normal form.

In figure 9-6, the name and address information for the customer associated with an invoice isn't dependent on the invoice number. It's dependent on the customer number. As a result, the invoice table in figure 9-6 isn't in third normal form. The problem with this is that if a customer had two invoices, the name and address information could be changed in one invoice, but not the other. And this would result in inconsistency.

To avoid this problem, I moved the customer name and address data from the invoice table into a customer table. Figure 9-7 shows the data structure after this change. The primary key for the customer table is the customer number. The customer number remains in the invoice table, but as a foreign key that identifies the associated row in the customer table.

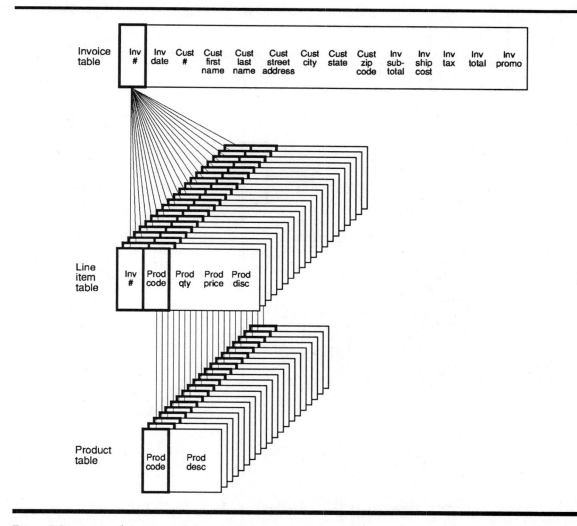

Figure 9-6   Invoice data in second normal form

As you look at the structure in figure 9-7, keep in mind that this is the structure from the perspective of a single invoice. But you can look at the structure from other perspectives too. If you looked at it from the perspective of a customer, for example, the structure would show that many invoices can be associated with a single customer. And the structure from the perspective of a line item or a product would be still different. The important thing to note is that, from any of these perspectives, the individual tables would contain the same data and keys.

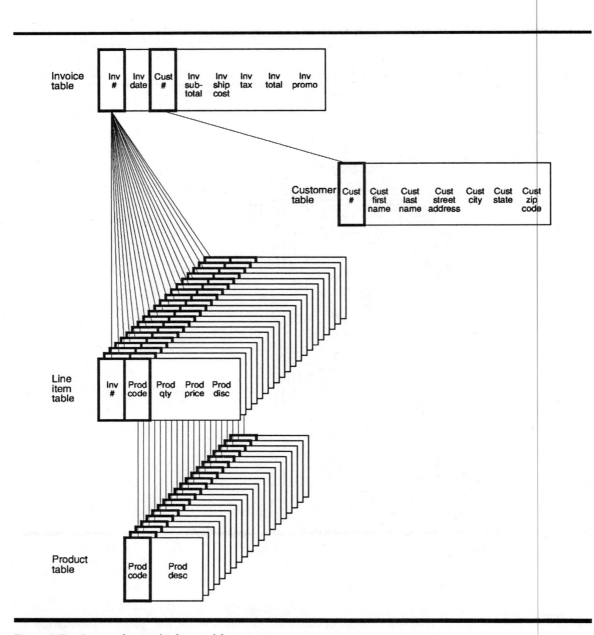

Figure 9-7   Invoice data in third normal form

The tables in figure 9-7 should look familiar. They're the ones I adopted for the test tables I've used in this book and in *Part 1: An Introductory Course*. Figure 9-8 shows the host structure definitions for the rows of these tables.

Customer table

```
01   CUSTOMER-ROW.
     10   CUSTNO              PIC  X(6).
     10   FNAME               PIC  X(20).
     10   LNAME               PIC  X(30).
     10   ADDR                PIC  X(30).
     10   CITY                PIC  X(20).
     10   STATE               PIC  X(2).
     10   ZIPCODE             PIC  X(10).
```

Invoice table

```
01   INVOICE-ROW.
     10   INVCUST             PIC  X(6).
     10   INVNO               PIC  X(6).
     10   INVDATE             PIC  X(10).
     10   INVSUBT             PIC  S9(7)V99    COMP-3.
     10   INVSHIP             PIC  S9(5)V99    COMP-3.
     10   INVTAX              PIC  S9(5)V99    COMP-3.
     10   INVTOTAL            PIC  S9(7)V99    COMP-3.
     10   INVPROM             PIC  X(10).
```

Line item table

```
01   LINE-ITEM-ROW.
     10   LIINVNO             PIC  X(6).
     10   LIPCODE             PIC  X(10).
     10   LIQTY               PIC  S9(7)       COMP-3.
     10   LIPRICE             PIC  S9(5)V99    COMP-3.
     10   LIDISC              PIC  S9(5)V99    COMP-3.
```

Product table

```
01   PRODUCT-ROW.
     10   PCODE               PIC  X(10).
     10   PDESC               PIC  X(30).
```

Figure 9-8   COBOL host structures for the tables created to store invoice data

Denormalization   Data base designers can continue the normalization process beyond third normal form. The *fourth* and *fifth normal forms* may be appropriate when a data structure involves one-to-many and many-to-many associations. However, few situations require the fourth and fifth normal forms. Moreover, these forms can result in fragmented data structures that consist of many small tables, all related by keys.

Often, the performance costs of normalization beyond third normal form are too high for the benefits they yield. And in some cases, even normalizing data completely to the second or third normal form will lead to an inefficient design. As a result, DBAs sometimes chose to *denormalize* stored data. A DBA who denormalizes data does it by choosing *not* to normalize data as far a possible.

Although denormalized data structures involve fewer tables, fewer rows, and fewer keys than fully normalized structures, they have their drawbacks too. Denormalization results in greater redundancy of stored data, the need for extra storage for the redundant data, and the potential for inconsistency because of the redundant data. So weighing the costs of normalizing against the risks of denormalizing is a critical system design concern. And designers and programmers need to understand the decisions made and their implications.

Discussion

Planning a set of related tables is easy, as long as the number of tables is small. However, in real world applications, the number of tables required can be large, and the relationships among them can be complicated. As a result, data base design is typically more difficult for real-world applications than for a simple textbook example.

Different sources (books, manuals, articles, and courses) recommend different approaches to data base design. And different shops follow different design practices. However, all have one requirement in common: A data base designer must have a thorough understanding of the meaning of the data that will be stored. For programmers to understand the design decisions that underlie the structures of the tables their programs will process, designers need to share that understanding with them.

Terms

one-to-one association
one-to-many association
many-to-one association
many-to-many association
normalization
normal form
first normal form
primary key
foreign key
referential integrity

composite key
second normal form
third normal form
fourth normal form
fifth normal form
denormalize

Objectives

1. Describe the four different kinds of data associations you can implement with DB2 tables.

2. Describe the normalization process.

3. Explain why completely normalizing data structures isn't always appropriate.

Chapter 10

How to manage DB2 objects with SQL's Data Definition Language

To create and modify tables, as well as all other DB2 objects, you use DB2's *Data Definition Language*, or *DDL*. DDL is a subset of SQL just like DB2's Data Manipulation Language, or DML. Figure 10-1 lists all of the SQL DDL statements. If you look at all the variations of the CREATE statement, you'll see that these statements operate on eight different kinds of objects. In the first part of this chapter, I'll describe each of them.

Data base administrators are likely to use each of the statements in figure 10-1 from time to time. Programmers, however, don't use as many even when they're responsible for creating test tables and other objects. In the second part of this chapter, I'll show you how to use the few you may need. They're the ones I shaded in figure 10-1.

DDL statements to create, modify, and delete objects

CREATE DATABASE	Defines a new database.
CREATE STOGROUP	Defines a new storage group.
CREATE TABLESPACE	Defines a new tablespace.
CREATE TABLE	Defines a new table.
CREATE INDEX	Defines a new index.
CREATE VIEW	Defines a new view.
CREATE SYNONYM	Defines a new synonym.
CREATE ALIAS	Defines a new alias.
ALTER STOGROUP	Modifies the attributes of a specified storage group.
ALTER TABLESPACE	Modifies the attributes of a specified table space.
ALTER TABLE	Modifies the attributes of a specified table.
ALTER INDEX	Modifies the attributes of a specified index.
DROP	Deletes a specified object.

DDL statements to add comments or labels to catalog definitions of objects

COMMENT ON	Specifies an informational text string, up to 254 characters, for an object.
LABEL ON	Specifies an informational text string, up to 80 characters, for an object.

DDL statements to manage authorizations and ids

GRANT	Grants specified processing privileges to specified authorization-ids.
REVOKE	Revokes specified processing privileges for specified authorization-ids.
SET CURRENT SQLID	Changes the authorization-id of the current user.

Figure 10-1   DDL statements

DB2 objects

An *object* is anything that can be created and manipulated with SQL. DB2 uses eight kinds of objects: databases, storage groups, table spaces, tables, indexes, views, synonyms, and aliases. However, programmers rarely have to work directly with objects other than tables, views, and indexes. But because I think you can benefit from understanding the other object types, I'll describe all of them here.

Databases

A DB2 *database* is simply a named entity that can contain *other* DB2 objects. A DBA defines a database with the SQL CREATE DATABASE statement. What a specific database contains depends on how a DBA creates, names, and manages objects like tables. In other words, installation strategies for using DB2 databases vary.

One installation may opt to use a single database for all of its production DB2 data and a second database for all of its test data. Another shop may use many individual databases for its different applications and may allocate still other databases to different program development teams. And, a third installation may allow many users to process data stored in a few shared, common databases, but restrict access to other databases to specific users. For example, the database that contains the tables I've used for examples in this book was defined for my exclusive use.

Figure 10-2 illustrates a simple database named BILLDB. It contains four tables: the customer, invoice, line item, and product tables I used as examples in the last chapter. In addition to these four tables, the database also contains four indexes, one for each table. (I'll describe indexes in more detail later in this chapter.)

It may surprise you, but databases don't have storage space allocated to them directly. Instead, DB2 provides disk storage as necessary as users add data to and delete data from objects "owned" by a database. That storage space is provided on disk volumes that are specified in a second type of DB2 object, a storage group. When a DBA creates a database, he can specify the storage group that should be used for the objects it will contain. But as far as users are concerned, allocation of disk space for the objects is automatic and transparent.

Storage groups

A *storage group* is a set of disk volumes that contain the VSAM data sets where the objects associated with a database are stored. Figure 10-3 shows the storage group that contains the objects that belong to the BILLDB

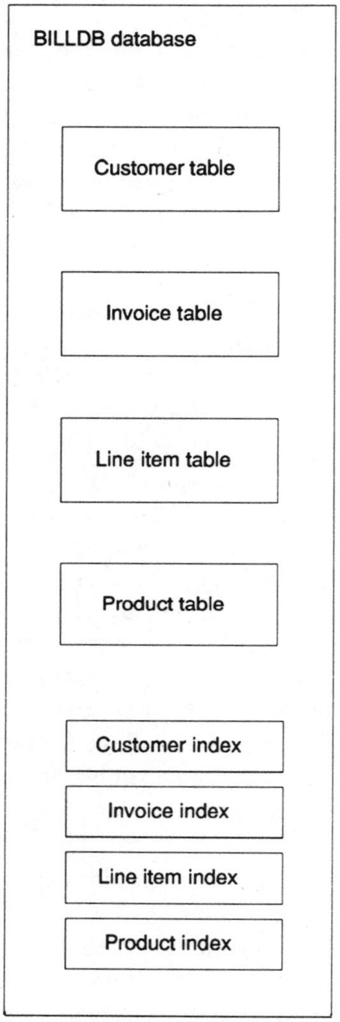

Figure 10-2   Tables and indexes are defined within a database

database. In this example, the storage group, named BILLSG, consists of two disk volumes. The maximum number of volumes that a storage group may use is 133. For nearly all applications, that's plenty.

A DBA defines a storage group with the SQL CREATE STOGROUP statement. On this statement, he names the disk volumes that will comprise the new storage group. To add or remove disk volumes from an existing storage group, the DBA uses the ALTER STOGROUP statement.

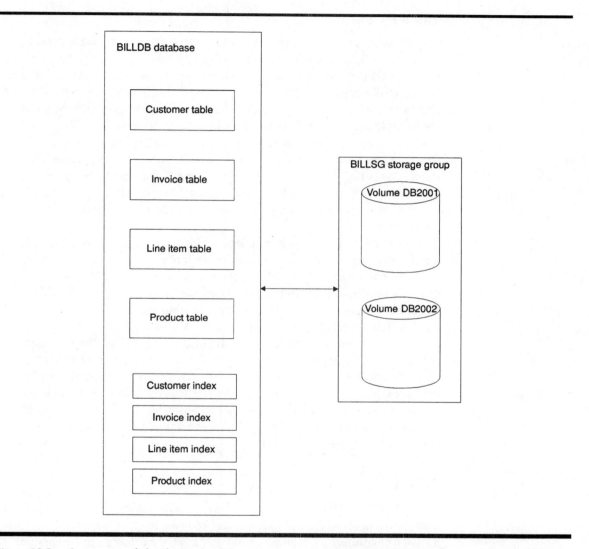

Figure 10-3   One or more disk volumes that belong to a storage group provide the storage required for the objects in a database

Within the disk volume(s) associated with a storage group, DB2 automatically defines and manages VSAM data sets to provide storage for objects like tables and indexes. After a DBA defines a storage group, DB2 is able to insulate users from the details of data management. Users don't have to know either the database or the storage group associated with a table to access the table.

Table spaces

There's another object "layer" between a table and the database and storage group where it resides: the table space. A *table space* consists of one or more VSAM data sets that reside on the volumes associated with a storage group. DB2 supports different kinds of table spaces, and they have different effects on system operations, particularly locking. For more information about table spaces and locking, you can refer to chapter 5.

Figure 10-4 shows how table spaces relate to the objects in the BILLDB database and the disk volumes in the BILLSG storage group. Here, table space 1 uses two data sets, table space 2 uses three, and table space 3 uses one. Each of the data sets that comprise a table space is a sequential file. As an application programmer, you never need to know the format of the stored data.

Regardless of the number of data sets it requires, a single table space may be defined so it contains one or more tables. For example, in figure 10-4, the customer table resides in its own table space (table space 1) and so does the product table (table space 3). However, the invoice and line item tables both reside in the same table space (table space 2).

To create a table space explicitly, a DBA uses the CREATE TABLE-SPACE statement. It specifies the name of the table space, the storage group where it will reside, the database that will own it, its locking characteristics, and several other attributes. To change the characteristics of an existing table space, a DBA issues an ALTER TABLESPACE statement.

DB2 can also create table spaces implicitly. If a DBA doesn't specify the name of a table space when he creates a table, DB2 automatically creates a new table space for it.

Tables

Of all of DB2's objects, you're most familiar with tables. As you know, DB2 uses tables to store data. Tables consist of rows, each containing a specific number of columns. The number of rows a table contains can be small or can range into the millions.

Because you've seen examples of tables throughout this book, I don't need to say more about them here. Later in this chapter, I'll show you how to use the SQL CREATE TABLE, ALTER TABLE, and DROP statements to define, change, and delete tables.

Indexes

An *index* is a DB2 object that contains a set of pointers to rows in a related table. The pointers are based on the values in the table's primary key

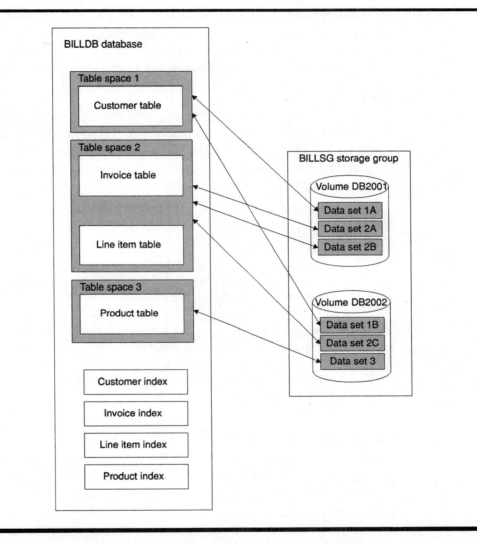

Figure 10-4 Table spaces map to VSAM data sets on the disk volumes in a storage group

column(s). Indexes make it easier for DB2 to retrieve specific rows, and they let DB2 enforce uniqueness and referential integrity.

Indexes occupy their own *index spaces*, just as tables occupy table spaces. Like table spaces, index spaces consist of one or more VSAM data sets. Unlike table spaces, DB2 manages index spaces in a way that's completely transparent to you.

Users typically don't know when indexes are present and in use. For that matter, programmers don't need to know either, most of the time. However, when you create a table and specify a primary key, you must also define an index for it. If you try to process a table you defined with a primary key, but you haven't created an index for the key, DB2 will return SQLCODE -625.

To manage indexes, you can use the SQL CREATE INDEX, ALTER INDEX, and DROP statements. In this chapter, I'll show you how to use CREATE INDEX and DROP. When you need to change an index in a program testing environment, it's usually simplest just to delete the old index and recreate it with new specifications. So I won't show you ALTER INDEX.

Views

A *view* is a DB2 object that provides an alternative representation of data stored in one or more tables, which I'll call base tables. You can include some or all of the columns in the base tables in a view. The columns you include depend on the specific application.

Although processing restrictions affect what you can do with some views, for most purposes, you can use a view just like a table. For example, you can specify a view name instead of a table name on an SQL statement like SELECT. In the second part of this chapter, I'll show you how to use the SQL CREATE VIEW statement to define a view and how to use the view in a SELECT statement.

Synonyms

A *synonym* is an alternative name for a table or view. Although I'm not going to present it in this chapter, you should know that you can use the CREATE SYNONYM statement to assign a new name to a table or view. If you assign a shorter or more meaningful name to a table or view you access often, you can simplify your SQL statements. However, only the user who creates a synonym can use it.

Aliases

An *alias* is like a synonym: It's an alternative name for a table or view. However, unlike a synonym, an alias is available to all users. As with CREATE SYNONYM, I'm not going to present CREATE ALIAS in this chapter. If you'd like more information about it, you can refer back to my discussion of it in chapter 4.

DDL statements programmers may need to use

In this section, I'll present the syntax of the few DDL statements you may need to use to test your DB2 COBOL programs, and I'll show you examples of each. Specifically, I'll show you how to define tables (with CREATE TABLE), how to define indexes (with CREATE INDEX), how to change existing tables (with ALTER TABLE), how to define views (with CREATE VIEW), and how to delete tables, indexes, and views (with DROP).

How to use the CREATE TABLE statement

To define a new table, you use the CREATE TABLE statement. Figure 10-5 presents two formats for CREATE TABLE that represent two different approaches to defining a new table. You use the first format to create a table that has the same characteristics as an existing table. That means the new table will have the same number of columns with the same data types and names as the existing table and the same keys. You use the second format to create a new table that isn't exactly like an existing table. As you can see, this format is much more complicated.

The formats in figure 10-5 present basic options. The complete format for the CREATE TABLE statement lets users specify more exotic options like edit procedures and auditing actions. But, for program testing purposes, these options are likely to be unnecessary. As a result, I'll skip them and focus on the basic ones.

I want you to notice in figure 10-5 that I included EXEC SQL and END-EXEC delimiters for the CREATE TABLE statement. That's appropriate, because you can code CREATE TABLE as an embedded statement in an application program. You might want to do that to create a temporary work table from an application program. However, it's more likely that you'll use CREATE TABLE interactively through SPUFI. When you do, you don't code EXEC SQL and END-EXEC. That's the approach I'll use in the examples in this chapter.

How to create a table that's modeled after an existing table   You can "clone" a table's structure using the first format of the CREATE TABLE statement in figure 10-5. On this statement, you specify three things: the name for the new table, the name of the table that you want to model the new one after, and the database that will own the new table. For example, the statement in figure 10-6 defines a new table called CUSTCOPY. It will have the same characteristics as the CUST table.

Often, programmers need to create test tables that have the same structure as production tables. That's when this technique comes in handy.

The SQL CREATE TABLE statement

Format 1: To create a table with a structure copied from an existing table

```
EXEC SQL
    CREATE TABLE table-name
        LIKE existing-table
        IN  { DATABASE database-name
            { [database-name.]tablespace-name }
END-EXEC.
```

Format 2: To create a table with a structure *not* copied from an existing table

```
EXEC SQL
    CREATE TABLE table-name
        (column-name data-type [{NOT NULL
                                 {NOT NULL WITH DEFAULT}]
        [,column-name data-type [{NOT NULL
                                 {NOT NULL WITH DEFAULT}] ...]
        [PRIMARY KEY (pkey-column-name[,pkey-column-name...])]

        FOREIGN KEY (fkey-column-name[,fkey-column-name...])
            REFERENCES parent-table-name
                       {RESTRICT}
            ON DELETE  {CASCADE }
                       {SET NULL}

        [,FOREIGN KEY (fkey-column-name[,fkey-column-name...])
            REFERENCES parent-table-name
                       {RESTRICT}
            ON DELETE  {CASCADE }           ]  ...        )
                       {SET NULL}

        IN  { DATABASE database-name
            { [database-name.]tablespace-name }
END-EXEC.
```

Figure 10-5   The SQL CREATE TABLE statement (part 1 of 2)

When you use it, you can be sure that your test table is identical to the production table.

How to create a table that's *not* modeled after an existing table   You'll use the second format of the CREATE TABLE statement in figure 10-5 to create a table that's not exactly like one that already exists. As with the first format, you give a name to the table you're creating. But then, you have to

Explanation

table-name	The name DB2 will use for the new table.
existing-table	The name of an existing table whose structure will be copied for the new table.
database-name	The database that will contain the new table.
tablespace-name	The table space that will contain the new table. If you don't specify a table space, DB2 creates one implicitly. If you name a table space, it must be owned by the database you specify or by your DB2 system's default database.
column-name	The name of a column that will be included in the table. The value you supply for *column-name* may be no longer than 18 characters.
data-type	The type of data the column will contain. The value you supply for *data-type* must one of those in figure 10-7.
NOT NULL NOT NULL WITH DEFAULT	Specifies how DB2 will handle nulls. If you specify NOT NULL for a column, DB2 prevents the column from having null values. If you specify NOT NULL WITH DEFAULT, DB2 substitutes a default value for the column when it is presented as null. The defaults are 0 for numeric columns, spaces for fixed-length strings, strings with length 0 for variable-length strings, and the current date, time, or timestamp for columns with those data types. If you don't specify either option for a column, DB2 will allow nulls in it.
pkey-column-name	The name of a column whose value is to be used as the primary key or a part of the primary key. The columns you use must be defined with NOT NULL or NOT NULL WITH DEFAULT. You may specify up to 16 column names to define a composite primary key.
fkey-column-name	The name of a column whose value is to be used as a foreign key or a part of a foreign key. You may specify up to 16 column names to define a composite foreign key.
parent-table-name	The name of a table that is the parent of the new table.
RESTART CASCADE SET NULL	Specifies the referential constraint for the relationship the FOREIGN KEY clause defines. Refer to chapter 4 of *Part 1: An Introductory Course* for more information.

Figure 10-5   The SQL CREATE TABLE statement (part 2 of 2)

specify *all* of the columns that will make up the new table, and you have to define all the keys the table will include.

For each column in the table, you must specify a name and a data type. Figure 10-7 lists the different values you can specify for a column's data type. You can also specify how DB2 should handle nulls for each column. If you specify NOT NULL for a column, DB2 won't allow a program or user to store nulls in it. If you specify NOT NULL WITH DEFAULT, DB2 allows a user to request that nulls be stored in a column, but it substitutes a

```
CREATE TABLE MMADBV.CUSTCOPY
       LIKE MMADBV.CUST
       IN DATABASE MMADB
```

Figure 10-6   A statement that creates a new table that's modeled after an existing table

standard default for it (such as 0 for numeric columns or spaces for CHAR columns). If you don't specify either of these two options for a column, you can store nulls in it.

To define a primary key for a table, you include the PRIMARY KEY clause on its CREATE TABLE statement. On this clause, you name the column, or columns, that comprise the key. Remember, DB2 supports composite, multi-column keys. Although you can specify up to 16 columns for a primary key, few primary keys involve more than two columns.

You use a similar approach to define a table's foreign keys. (Remember, a foreign key contains a value that's the same as the value of the primary key column(s) in the parent table.) Although you can specify only one primary key for a table, you can create multiple foreign keys. For each foreign key, you specify three things on the FOREIGN KEY clause. First, you name the column or columns (up to 16) that comprise the key. Then, for REFERENCES, you specify the name of the parent table. Finally, for ON DELETE, you specify how DB2 should handle requests to delete a row in the parent table whose primary key value matches the foreign key value of one or more rows in the table you're creating. This is necessary to maintain the referential integrity of the two tables. (Refer to chapter 4 of *Part 1: An Introductory Course* to refresh your memory about referential constraints.)

The last item in format 2 in figure 10-5 is the IN clause. As with the simpler format of CREATE TABLE, you specify the name of the database that will own the table on this clause.

Figure 10-8 presents a typical CREATE TABLE statement that uses this format. It defines the line item table I described in the last chapter. The name of the table I specified in this statement is LITEM, qualified with my authorization-id, MMADBV. This table will be owned by the database named MMADB.

As you can see, the table consists of five columns, and none of them can contain nulls. The primary key for the LITEM table is a composite key: It consists of both an invoice number (LIINVNO) and a product code (LIPCODE). Both of these data elements are also foreign keys. The value of LIINVNO identifies a row in the INV table, and the value of LIPCODE identifies a row in the PRODUCT table.

Value	Description
CHARACTER(n) CHAR(n)	Fixed-length string column, where *n* is its length
VARCHAR(n)	Variable-length string column, where *n* is its maximum length
LONG VARCHAR	Variable-length string column whose maximum length can be determined by the amount of space available in the page where a row is stored
DATE	Date column
TIME	Time column
TIMESTAMP	Timestamp column
INTEGER INT	Large integer column
SMALLINT	Small integer column
DECIMAL(p,s) DEC(p,s) NUMERIC(p,s)	Packed-decimal numeric column, where *p* is its precision and *s* is its scale
FLOAT(21) REAL	Single-precision floating-point numeric column
FLOAT(53) FLOAT DOUBLE PRECISION	Double-precision floating-point numeric column
GRAPHIC(n)	Fixed-length graphic (Double-Byte Character Set) column, where *n* is its length
VARGRAPHIC(n)	Variable-length DBCS column, where *n* is its maximum length
LONG VARGRAPHIC	Variable-length DBCS column whose maximum length can be determined by the amount of space available in the page where a row is stored

Figure 10-7   Data-type values you can specify for a column

How to use the CREATE INDEX statement

Figure 10-9 presents the basic syntax of the SQL CREATE INDEX statement. As with CREATE TABLE, I'm not presenting some elements of CREATE INDEX. The options I didn't include are related to optimizing the performance of the index, a responsibility that's in the domain of the DBA, not the programmer.

Figure 10-10 shows a typical CREATE INDEX statement. It creates an index for the line item table defined in figure 10-8. The first line of the

```
CREATE TABLE MMADBV.LITEM
   (LIINVNO   CHAR(6)       NOT NULL,
    LIPCODE   CHAR(10)      NOT NULL,
    LIQTY     DECIMAL(7)    NOT NULL,
    LIPRICE   DECIMAL(7,2) NOT NULL,
    LIDISC    DECIMAL(7,2) NOT NULL,
    PRIMARY KEY(LIINVNO,LIPCODE),
    FOREIGN KEY(LIINVNO)
       REFERENCES MMADBV.INV ON DELETE RESTRICT,
    FOREIGN KEY(LIPCODE)
       REFERENCES MMADBV.PRODUCT ON DELETE RESTRICT)
    IN DATABASE MMADB
```

Figure 10-8   A statement that creates a new table that is not modeled after an existing table

statement specifies that a unique index named LITEMX (qualified with my authorization-id) should be created "ON" the table named LITEM. The UNIQUE keyword insures that no duplicate key values occur. To create an index for a primary key, you must specify UNIQUE.

The second line identifies the columns that will make up the index. Notice that these are the same columns I specified in the PRIMARY KEY clause of the CREATE TABLE statement in figure 10-8, and they're in the same order. That makes sense because the index pointers are based on the values in the table's primary key column(s).

How to use the ALTER TABLE statement

One way to change the definition of an existing object is to delete it (with the DROP statement) and recreate it with an updated definition. In fact, for objects like indexes and views, that's the approach I suggest you take. And, I recommend it for most simple test tables as well. However, when you delete an object, you loose any data it contains. To make an adjustment to a table's structure without deleting its contents, you can use the ALTER TABLE statement.

Figure 10-11 presents the syntax of ALTER TABLE for three functions I think you may need to use. These three functions let you add a column, a primary key, or a foreign key to a table. If you look back at the CREATE TABLE statement in figure 10-5, you'll see that the same values are required to create a column or key in a table as are required to add a column or key to a table. So you shouldn't have any problem using the ALTER TABLE statement.

The SQL CREATE INDEX statement

```
EXEC SQL
    CREATE [UNIQUE] INDEX index-name ON table-name
        (column-name[,column name...])
END-EXEC.
```

Explanation

UNIQUE	Specifies that the table should not contain more than one row with a given value of the index column(s).
index-name	The name DB2 will use for the index you want to create.
table-name	The name of the table that's associated with the index.
column-name	The name of a column from the table specified by *table-name* whose value will be used as the index, or as part of the index. You may specify up to 16 columns for the index.

Figure 10-9   The SQL CREATE INDEX statement

```
CREATE UNIQUE INDEX MMADBV.LITEMX ON MMADBV.LITEM
    (LIINVNO,LIPCODE)
```

Figure 10-10   A statement that creates an index

Figure 10-12 presents two ALTER TABLE statements you can use to add a column named INVCOMMENTS to the INV table. This column will be used to store notes entered by users. In both examples, I specified a variable-length character column with a maximum length of 254 bytes. You can refer back to figure 10-7 for a list of the valid data types.

If you use ALTER TABLE to add a column to a table, you need to tell DB2 what the initial value of the column will be. You do that by specifying, or not specifying, the NOT NULL WITH DEFAULT option. In the first example in figure 10-12, I omitted this option. So the value of the new column in each row is set to null. To insure that the new column has a non-null value, you would specify NOT NULL WITH DEFAULT, as in the second

The SQL ALTER TABLE statement to add elements to a table definition

```
EXEC SQL
    ALTER TABLE table-name
      ⎧ADD column-name data-type [NOT NULL WITH DEFAULT]      ⎫
      ⎪ADD PRIMARY KEY (pkey-column-name[,pkey-column-name...])⎪
      ⎨ADD FOREIGN KEY (fkey-column-name[,fkey-column-name...])⎬
      ⎪    REFERENCES parent-table-name                        ⎪
      ⎪                        ⎧RESTRICT⎫                      ⎪
      ⎩    ON DELETE          ⎨CASCADE ⎬                       ⎭
                              ⎩SET NULL⎭

    END-EXEC.
```

Explanation

table-name	The name of the table you want to change.
column-name	The name to be used for a new column. The value you supply for *column-name* may be no longer than 18 characters.
data-type	The data type to be used for the new column. The value you supply for *data-type* must one of those in figure 10-7.
NOT NULL WITH DEFAULT	Causes DB2 to substitute a default value for the new column. The defaults are 0 for numeric columns, spaces for fixed-length strings, strings with length 0 for variable-length strings, and the current date, time, or timestamp for columns with those data types. If this option is omitted, the column is initialized to nulls.
pkey-column-name	The name of a column whose value is to be used as the primary key or as a part of the primary key. You may specify up to 16 column names to define a composite primary key.
fkey-column-name	The name of a column whose value is to be used as a foreign key or a part of a foreign key. You may specify up to 16 column names to define a composite foreign key.
parent-table-name	The name of a table that is the parent of the table you're changing.
RESTRICT CASCADE SET NULL	Specifies the referential constraint for the relationship the FOREIGN KEY clause defines. Refer to chapter 4 of *Part 1: An Introductory Course* for more information.

Figure 10-11 The SQL ALTER TABLE statement to add elements to a table definition

example in figure 10-12. That causes DB2 to store a string with length 0 in each row of the invoice table. (That's the default for variable-length data.)

Adding a primary key to a table is just as simple. For example, if I had forgotten to define a PRIMARY KEY column for the invoice table when I created it, I could issue the statement in figure 10-13 to add one. Then, I'd

Example 1

```
ALTER TABLE MMADBV.INV
    ADD INVCOMMENTS VARCHAR(254)
```

Example 2

```
ALTER TABLE MMADBV.INV NOT NULL WITH DEFAULT
    ADD INVCOMMENTS VARCHAR(254)
```

Figure 10-12 Two statements that add a column to an existing table

```
ALTER TABLE MMADBV.INV
    ADD PRIMARY KEY (INVNO)
```

Figure 10-13 A statement that specifies a primary key for an existing table that was defined without one

have to issue a CREATE INDEX statement to create an index for the new primary key.

If you've ever had to add a field to a standard file, you'll appreciate the simplicity of using ALTER TABLE. With a standard file, you have to move all the data stored in the old file to a file with the new definition. Then, at the least, you'd have to recompile every program that uses that file. Using ALTER TABLE, you simply issue the statement and DB2 does the rest for you.

How to use the CREATE VIEW statement

To understand views, I'd like you to think about an example. Imagine what you would have to do if you were given a programming assignment that called for generating a display of the names of all customers who have purchased a specific product. The display should also include the invoice number and date for the sales of that product.

This display requires related data from the customer, invoice, line item, *and* product tables I've used in previous examples. One way to extract this data is to use a join operation to create a results table. Figure 10-14 shows a SELECT statement to do that. As you can see, the results table will contain information for the product with product code SLE40025XL. Specifically, the table will contain the customer number and name for each customer (from the customer table) that has purchased the specified product, matched with the invoice number and date for a specific sale (from the invoice table), the product code and sale amount for a specific sale (from the line item table), and the description of the product (from the product table).

Although the SELECT statement in figure 10-14 isn't difficult to construct, you'd have to code it every time you needed the information it provides. You can avoid having to do that by creating a view instead. Then, you can use the view as if it was a single table that contains exactly the information this application needs.

To define a view, you use the SQL CREATE VIEW statement. Figure 10-15 presents its syntax. On this statement, you specify the name for the view and the names for the columns it will contain. Then, you code a subselect to identify the table data the view will provide to the user.

The statement in figure 10-16 generates the view for the application I described above. The name I used for the view is CUSTPROD. (I tried to create a name that suggests CUSTomers and the PRODucts they have purchased.) The second line of the statement lists the names I want to use for the columns the view will contain. To help you identify these names, I used the original column names from the base tables, but added the prefix V (for View) to each.

The next part of the statement is the subselect that defines what should be extracted from the base tables to generate the view. As you can see, it's similar to the SELECT statement in figure 10-14. The only difference is that the WHERE clause doesn't contain a specific value for PCODE. So the view will contain information for all the products in the product table.

To retrieve data patterned according to the view, you code a SELECT statement that uses the view name. For example, the SELECT in figure 10-17 retrieves data from the CUSTPROD view for the product whose code is SLE40025XL. The result of this statement is the same as the result of the SELECT statement in figure 10-14 that does an explicit join.

If you perform the same join operation often, it should be clear how views can simplify the procedure. Without a view, you'd have to issue a SELECT statement like the one in figure 10-14 to retrieve the data each time you needed it. However, with a view, you define the information you need once, then issue a simple SELECT statement like the one in figure 10-17 to retrieve specific data.

Views can also be useful because they insulate users from some of the complexities of SQL. For instance, an end user might access the

```
SELECT CUSTNO, FNAME, LNAME, PCODE,
       PDESC, PQTY, INVNO, INVDATE
   FROM MMADBV.CUST, MMADBV.INV, MMADBV.LITEM, MMADBV.PRODUCT
   WHERE CUSTNO = INVCUST AND
         INVNO  = LIINVNO AND
         LIPCODE = PCODE AND
         PCODE   ='SLE40025XL'
```

Figure 10-14 A SELECT statement that does an explicit join

The SQL CREATE VIEW statement

```
EXEC SQL
    CREATE VIEW view-name [column-name,[column-name...]]
        AS subselect
END-EXEC.
```

Explanation

view-name	The name DB2 will use for the view.
column-name	The name of a column in the view. If you specify column names, you must include the same number that the subselect returns. If you omit the list of column names, DB2 uses the names from the subselect.
subselect	A SELECT statement that defines the contents of the view. The subselect may not name more than 16 base tables.

Figure 10-15 The SQL CREATE VIEW statement

CUSTPROD view and not even know it *is* a view. He might think that there really is a table named CUSTPROD.

If you use views, you should know that not all SQL operations are allowed for all views. DB2 won't process INSERT, UPDATE, or DELETE statements issued against a read-only view. A *read-only view* is one that involves more than one base table (like the example I just showed you), or one whose definition included a column function, a GROUP BY clause, a HAVING clause, or a DISTINCT clause.

```
CREATE VIEW CUSTPROD
             VCUSTNO,  VFNAME,  VLNAME,  VPCODE,
             VPDESC,   VPQTY,   VINVNO,  VINVDATE
     AS SELECT     CUSTNO,   FNAME,   LNAME,   PCODE,
             PDESC,    PQTY,    INVNO,   INVDATE
         FROM  MMADBV.CUST,
               MMADBV.INV,
               MMADBV.LITEM,
               MMADBV.PRODUCT
         WHERE CUSTNO  = INVCUST AND
               INVNO   = LIINVNO AND
               LIPCODE = PCODE
```

Figure 10-16   A statement that creates a view

```
SELECT VCUSTNO, VFNAME, VLNAME, VPCODE,
       VPDESC,  VPQTY,  VINVNO, VINVDATE
    FROM CUSTPROD
    WHERE VPCODE = 'SLE40025XL'
```

Figure 10-17   A SELECT statement that accesses a view

How to use the DROP statement

The simplest DDL statement this chapter presents is DROP. It lets authorized users delete DB2 objects. You'll be authorized to delete objects you create, and perhaps others as well. Figure 10-18 presents the syntax of DROP for table, view, and index objects. As you can see, all you need to know to delete an object is its type and its name. When you delete an object, all of the data associated with it is deleted too. So, be careful when you use the DROP statement.

Discussion

With what you've learned in this chapter about DB2's Data Definition Language, you should be able to create and manage tables, indexes, and views that you need as you test application programs. Realize, though, that you could learn more about data base administration. For example, DBAs spend much time and energy working with indexes to optimize system performance. Usually, that means balancing the performance improvements indexes offer with what are often substantial costs of maintaining them. For more

The SQL DROP statement to delete a table, index, or view

```
EXEC SQL
              (TABLE table-name)
      DROP    {INDEX index-name}
              (VIEW view-name )
END-EXEC.
```

Explanation

table-name	The name of the table you want DB2 to delete.
index-name	The name of the index you want DB2 to delete.
view-name	The name of the view you want DB2 to delete.

Figure 10-18   The SQL DROP statement to delete a table, index, or view

information about indexes and other objects, you can turn to the same IBM manuals I recommended in the last chapter: *IBM Database 2 Version 2 Application Programming and SQL Guide* and the three-volume set *IBM Database 2 Version 2 Administration Guide*.

Terms

Data Definition Language
DDL
object
database
storage group
table space
index
index space
view
synonym
alias
read-only view

Objectives

1. Describe the relationships among the eight kinds of SQL objects: databases, storage groups, table spaces, tables, indexes, views, synonyms, and aliases.

2. Code and issue a CREATE TABLE statement to define a new table modeled after an existing one.

3. Code and issue a CREATE TABLE statement to define a new table that is not modeled after an existing one.

4. Code and issue a CREATE INDEX statement to define an index for a table's primary key.

5. Code and issue an ALTER TABLE statement to add a column or key to an existing table.

6. Code and issue a CREATE VIEW statement to define a view.

7. Code and issue a DROP statement to delete a table, index, or view.

Chapter 11

How to extract information from DB2's catalog tables

The *DB2 catalog* is a set of related tables, called *catalog tables*. DB2 records information about objects, application plans, and resource usage in its catalog tables. Most of the time, programmers don't need to use the catalog or even know about it. However, you may want to turn to it occasionally as a source of information about DB2 objects.

In this chapter, I'll briefly describe the catalog and the tables it contains. Then, I'll take a closer look at five of the catalog tables. For each, I'll present its structure and show you an example of how to extract information from it. Finally, I'll show you how to join columns from multiple catalog tables to get more useful information.

An introduction to the DB2 catalog tables

Figure 11-1 lists all of DB2's catalog tables and presents a brief description of each. Note that the full name of each catalog table starts with the authorization-id SYSIBM as a high-level qualifier. So, the complete name of the first table in the figure, SYSCOLAUTH, is actually SYSIBM. SYSCOLAUTH.

Many of the catalog tables are associated with one another in parent/ dependent relationships, also known as parent/child relationships. For example, SYSTABLESPACE is the parent of SYSTABLES. That makes sense, because tables "belong" to table spaces. Similarly, SYSTABLES is the parent of SYSCOLUMNS. The DB2 term for a parent/child relationship between catalog items is a *link*. DB2 stores information about links in one of its catalog tables: SYSLINKS.

Although catalog tables have structures like non-catalog tables, you can't issue DELETE, INSERT, and UPDATE statements to make changes to their contents. Instead, DB2 makes changes to these tables when you issue DDL statements, like the ones I described in the last chapter. However, DB2 does allow direct access for retrieval operations. So if you have the proper authorizations, you can issue SELECT statements through SPUFI to retrieve data from the catalog tables. Catalog information can help you design and manage the objects you'll use as you test your programs.

You can find complete descriptions of the contents of all the tables figure 11-1 lists in the manual *IBM Database 2 Version 2 SQL Reference*. In this chapter, I want to present the structures of the catalog tables I think you're most likely to use. They're the ones I shaded in figure 11-1: SYSCOLUMNS, SYSINDEXES, SYSKEYS, SYSRELS, and SYSTABLES. Their contents are complicated and technical, so I won't discuss all of it in detail. Instead, I'll cover the columns in each of those five tables that contain information you might want to use. As you read the descriptions of these tables, you'll get an idea of the kind of information all the tables contain and how they're related to each other.

How to extract column information from the SYSCOLUMNS catalog table

The SYSCOLUMNS table contains one row for each column of every table and view in the DB2 subsystem. Figure 11-2 presents its structure. The columns I've shaded are the ones that contain data you might find useful.

To understand how you extract information from this table, suppose I didn't remember the exact names of the columns in the tables related to invoicing. Then, I could issue a SELECT statement to access SYSCOLUMNS to refresh my memory. Figure 11-3 shows two screens from a session I had with SPUFI to do just that.

Table name (all with SYSIBM high-level qualifier)	Contents
SYSCOLAUTH	Privileges held by users over columns for updates
SYSCOLUMNS	One row for each column in every table and view
SYSCOPY	DB2 recovery information
SYSDATABASE	One row for each database
SYSDBAUTH	Privileges held by users over databases
SYSDBRM	One row for each data base request module in every application plan
SYSFIELDS	One row for every column defined with a field procedure
SYSFOREIGNKEYS	One row for each column of every foreign key
SYSINDEXES	One row for each index
SYSINDEXPART	Components of partitioned and unpartitioned indexes
SYSKEYS	One row for each column of every index key
SYSLINKS	One row for each link in the DB2 catalog
SYSPLAN	One row for each application plan
SYSPLANAUTH	Privileges held by users over application plans
SYSPLANDEP	Dependencies of application plans on objects
SYSRELS	One row for each referential constraint
SYSRESAUTH	Privileges held by users over storage resources
SYSSTMT	Information about each SQL statement in every DBRM
SYSSTOGROUP	One row for each storage group
SYSSYNONYMS	One row for each synonym
SYSTABAUTH	Privileges held by users over tables and views
SYSTABLEPART	Components of partitioned and unpartitioned table spaces
SYSTABLES	One row for each table, view, or alias
SYSTABLESPACE	One row for each table space
SYSUSERAUTH	Privileges held by users for system operation and use
SYSVIEWDEP	Dependencies of views
SYSVIEWS	One or more rows for each view
SYSVLTREE	Additional information for view "trees"
SYSVOLUMES	One row for each volume of every storage group
SYSVTREE	One row for each view with information about its "tree"

Figure 11-1   DB2 catalog tables

Column	Type	Contents
NAME	VARCHAR(18)	Name of the column
TBNAME	VARCHAR(18)	Name of the table or view that contains the column
TBCREATOR	CHAR(8)	Authorization-id of the table or view's owner
COLNO	SMALLINT	Position of the column in the table or view
COLTYPE	CHAR(8)	Type of data in the column
LENGTH	SMALLINT	Length of the data component of the column; precision for a DECIMAL column
SCALE	SMALLINT	Scale for a DECIMAL column
NULLS	CHAR(1)	"Y" if the column may contain nulls; "N" if it may not
COLCARD	INTEGER	Number of distinct values represented in the column (estimated for non-indexed columns)
HIGH2KEY	CHAR(8)	Second highest value stored in the column
LOW2KEY	CHAR(8)	Second lowest value stored in the column
UPDATES	CHAR(1)	"Y" if the column may be updated; "N" if it may not
IBMREQD	CHAR(1)	"Y" if the row came from an IBM tape ; "N" if it did not
REMARKS	VARCHAR(254)	Character string specified by the user with a COMMENT ON statement
DEFAULT	CHAR(1)	"Y" if the column has a default that is substitutable for null; "N" if it does not
KEYSEQ	SMALLINT	Position of the column in the table's primary key
FOREIGNKEY	CHAR(1)	"B" if the column contains foreign-key related bit data
FLDPROC	CHAR(1)	"Y" if the column has a field procedure; "N" if it does not
LABEL	VARCHAR(30)	Character string specified by the user with a LABEL ON statement

Figure 11-2   Structure of the SYSCOLUMNS table

In part 1 of figure 11-3, you can see the SELECT statement I used at the top of the SPUFI output:

```
SELECT TBNAME, COLNO, NAME, COLTYPE, LENGTH, SCALE, NULLS
    FROM SYSIBM.SYSCOLUMNS
        WHERE TBNAME LIKE 'INV%' AND
            TBCREATOR = 'MMADBV'
    ORDER BY TBNAME, COLNO;
```

I named seven columns from the SYSCOLUMNS table on this statement. They identify the tables and columns I'm interested in (TBNAME, COLNO, and NAME), the data type and size of those columns (COLTYPE, LENGTH, and SCALE), and whether or not the columns can contain nulls (NULLS).

Part 1

The first half of the
SPUFI output for a
query against the
SYSCOLUMNS table.

```
 BROWSE -- MMA002.DB2.OUTPUT ------------------------- LINE 00000000 COL 001 080
 COMMAND ===>                                                   SCROLL ===> PAGE
 ************************************* TOP OF DATA ****************************************
 --------+---------+---------+---------+---------+---------+---------+---------+
 SELECT TBNAME, COLNO, NAME, COLTYPE, LENGTH, SCALE, NULLS                  00000100
     FROM SYSIBM.SYSCOLUMNS                                                 00000200
         WHERE TBNAME LIKE 'INV%' AND                                       00000300
             TBCREATOR = 'MMADBU'                                           00000400
     ORDER BY TBNAME, COLNO;                                                00000500
 --------+---------+---------+---------+---------+---------+---------+---------+
 TBNAME              COLNO  NAME             COLTYPE  LENGTH  SCALE  NULLS
 --------+---------+---------+---------+---------+---------+---------+---------+
 INV                   1    INVCUST          CHAR        6      0    N
 INV                   2    INVNO            CHAR        6      0    N
 INV                   3    INVDATE          DATE        4      0    N
 INV                   4    INVSUBT          DECIMAL     9      2    N
 INV                   5    INVSHIP          DECIMAL     7      2    N
 INV                   6    INVTAX           DECIMAL     7      2    N
 INV                   7    INVTOTAL         DECIMAL     9      2    N
 INV                   8    INVPROM          CHAR       10      0    N
 INVHIST               1    INVCUST          CHAR        6      0    N
 INVHIST               2    INVNO            CHAR        6      0    N
 F1=HELP      F2=SPLIT      F3=END       F4=RETURN    F5=RFIND     F6=RCHANGE
 F7=UP        F8=DOWN       F9=SWAP      F10=LEFT     F11=RIGHT    F12=RETRIEVE
```

Part 2

The second half of the
SPUFI output for a
query against the
SYSCOLUMNS table.

```
 BROWSE -- MMA002.DB2.OUTPUT ------------------------- LINE 00000020 COL 001 080
 COMMAND ===>                                                   SCROLL ===> PAGE
 INVHIST               3    INVDATE          DATE        4      0    N
 INVHIST               4    INVSUBT          DECIMAL     9      2    N
 INVHIST               5    INVSHIP          DECIMAL     7      2    N
 INVHIST               6    INVTAX           DECIMAL     7      2    N
 INVHIST               7    INVTOTAL         DECIMAL     9      2    N
 INVHIST               8    INVPROM          CHAR       10      0    N
 INVMASTER             1    INVCUST          CHAR        6      0    N
 INVMASTER             2    INVNO            CHAR        6      0    N
 INVMASTER             3    INVDATE          DATE        4      0    N
 INVMASTER             4    INVSUBT          DECIMAL     9      2    N
 INVMASTER             5    INVSHIP          DECIMAL     7      2    N
 INVMASTER             6    INVTAX           DECIMAL     7      2    N
 INVMASTER             7    INVTOTAL         DECIMAL     9      2    N
 INVMASTER             8    INVPROM          CHAR       10      0    N
 DSNE610I NUMBER OF ROWS DISPLAYED IS 24
 DSNE616I STATEMENT EXECUTION WAS SUCCESSFUL, SQLCODE IS 100
 --------+---------+---------+---------+---------+---------+---------+---------+
 --------+---------+---------+---------+---------+---------+---------+---------+
 DSNE617I COMMIT PERFORMED, SQLCODE IS 0
 DSNE616I STATEMENT EXECUTION WAS SUCCESSFUL, SQLCODE IS 0
 F1=HELP      F2=SPLIT      F3=END       F4=RETURN    F5=RFIND     F6=RCHANGE
 F7=UP        F8=DOWN       F9=SWAP      F10=LEFT     F11=RIGHT    F12=RETRIEVE
```

Figure 11-3   A query against the SYSCOLUMNS table to retrieve information about columns in tables I created and
whose names start with "INV"

To generate the output I wanted, I used a compound selection condition in the WHERE clause. First, I specified that rows should be selected only when their table-name value starts with the letters "INV" (TBNAME LIKE 'INV%'). Also, I restricted the selection to tables I created (TBCREATOR = 'MMADBV'). If I hadn't included the second condition, the results table would have included information for all tables the subsystem manages whose names begin with "INV," regardless of who created them. To make the results table easier to read, I specified that it should be sorted by column number within table name (ORDER BY TBNAME, COLNO).

As you can see in the results table, three tables I created have names that start with INV: INV, INVHIST, and INVMASTER. If you examine the displays, you'll see that all three tables consist of eight columns. And, corresponding columns in each table have the same names, data types, and lengths. In fact, the structures of the INVHIST and INVMASTER tables are identical to the structure of the INV table I've used in so many examples. I used the INVHIST table in *Part 1: An Introductory Course* to hold inactive invoice data. INVMASTER is a table I used to restore the contents of the INV table to its starting conditions as I tested sample programs.

How to extract table information from the SYSTABLES catalog table

In addition to SYSCOLUMNS, you might find some information in SYSTABLES useful. It contains one row for each table, alias, and view in your DB2 subsystem. Like SYSCOLUMNS, it includes a column for the authorization-id of the user who owns a table. You can use that value to retrieve information for objects you own.

Figure 11-4 presents the structure of the SYSTABLES table. Again, I've highlighted the columns I think you'll find most useful. Figure 11-5 shows a SPUFI session where I issued a SELECT against SYSTABLES.

In figure 11-5, I retrieved information about all the tables I created that are involved in parent/child relationships. To do that, I specified the six columns you can see in the SELECT statement at the top of the display: NAME, TYPE, COLCOUNT, PARENTS, CHILDREN, and KEYCOLUMNS. Then, I coded a compound selection condition that retrieves data only for my tables (CREATOR = 'MMADBV') and for tables that are a parent, a child, or both (PARENTS > 0 OR CHILDREN > 0). The PARENTS column specifies how many parents a table has, and the CHILDREN column specifies how many children it has.

As you can see, the SELECT returned four rows: one each for the CUST, INV, LITEM, and PRODUCT tables I've used for examples in this section. The "T" values in the TYPE column report that all four rows are for

Column	Type	Contents
NAME	VARCHAR(18)	Name of the table
CREATOR	CHAR(8)	Authorization-id of the table's owner
TYPE	CHAR(1)	"T" for a table, "A" for an alias, or "V" for a view
DBNAME	CHAR(8)	Name of the database that contains the table space for the object
TSNAME	CHAR(8)	Name of the table space that contains the table
DBID	SMALLINT	Internal identifier for the database
OBID	SMALLINT	Internal identifier for the table
COLCOUNT	SMALLINT	Number of columns in the table or view
EDPROC	CHAR(8)	Name of the edit procedure specified for the table, if any
VALPROC	CHAR(8)	Name of the validation procedure specified for the table, if any
CLUSTERTYPE	CHAR(1)	Not used
CLUSTERID	INTEGER	Not used
CARD	INTEGER	Number of rows in the table
NPAGES	INTEGER	Number of storage pages that contain rows for this table
PCTPAGES	SMALLINT	Percent of the total number of pages in the table space that contain rows for this table
IBMREQD	CHAR(1)	"Y" if the row came from an IBM tape ; "N" if it did not
REMARKS	VARCHAR(254)	Character string specified by the user with a COMMENT ON statement
PARENTS	SMALLINT	Number of relationships in which the table is a parent
CHILDREN	SMALLINT	Number of relationships in which the table is a child
KEYCOLUMNS	SMALLINT	Number of columns in the table's primary key
RECLENGTH	SMALLINT	Maximum length in bytes of the data for a row
STATUS	CHAR(1)	" " if the table doesn't have a primary key; "X" if the table does have a primary key; "I" if the definition of the table is incomplete because an index hasn't been created for its primary key
KEYOBID	SMALLINT	Internal identifier for the table's primary key index
LABEL	VARCHAR(30)	Character string specified by the user with a LABEL ON statement
CHECKFLAG	CHAR(1)	Indicator for the table's state of referential integrity
CHECKRID	CHAR(4)	Indicator for the table's state of referential integrity
AUDITING	CHAR(1)	Audit option
CREATEDBY	CHAR(8)	Authorization-id of the table's creator
LOCATION	CHAR(16)	Blank, except for an alias defined for a remote object
TBCREATOR	CHAR(8)	Blank, except for an alias, when it contains the authorization-id of the owner of the referenced table
TBNAME	VARCHAR(18)	Blank, except for an alias, when it contains the name of the referenced table

Figure 11-4   Structure of the SYSTABLES table

```
   BROWSE -- MMA00Z.DBZ.OUTPUT ---------------------- LINE 00000000 COL 001 080
   COMMAND ===>                                              SCROLL ===> PAGE
   ************************************** TOP OF DATA ***********************************
   ---------+---------+---------+---------+---------+---------+---------+---------+
   SELECT NAME, TYPE, COLCOUNT, PARENTS, CHILDREN, KEYCOLUMNS              00000100
       FROM SYSIBM.SYSTABLES                                               00000200
           WHERE CREATOR = 'MMADBV' AND                                    00000300
               (PARENTS > 0 OR CHILDREN > 0)                              00000310
       ORDER BY NAME;                                                      00000400
   ---------+---------+---------+---------+---------+---------+---------+---------+
   NAME              TYPE  COLCOUNT  PARENTS  CHILDREN  KEYCOLUMNS
   ---------+---------+---------+---------+---------+---------+---------+---------+
   CUST               T        7        0        1         1
   INV                T        8        1        1         1
   LITEM              T        5        2        0         2
   PRODUCT            T        2        0        1         1
   DSNE610I NUMBER OF ROWS DISPLAYED IS 4
   DSNE616I STATEMENT EXECUTION WAS SUCCESSFUL, SQLCODE IS 100
   ---------+---------+---------+---------+---------+---------+---------+---------+
   ---------+---------+---------+---------+---------+---------+---------+---------+
   DSNE617I COMMIT PERFORMED, SQLCODE IS 0
   DSNE616I STATEMENT EXECUTION WAS SUCCESSFUL, SQLCODE IS 0
    F1=HELP     FZ=SPLIT    F3=END      F4=RETURN   F5=RFIND    F6=RCHANGE
    F7=UP       F8=DOWN     F9=SWAP     F10=LEFT    F11=RIGHT   F12=RETRIEVE
```

Figure 11-5   A query against the SYSTABLES table to retrieve information about parent/child relationships

tables rather than for aliases or views. The COLCOUNT value shows how many columns each table contains.

The information in the results table also shows that the CUST table has no parents, but one child; that INV has one parent and one child; that LITEM has two parents, but no children; and that PRODUCT, like CUST, has one child, but no parents. The last column in the SPUFI output in figure 11-5, KEYCOLUMNS, shows how many columns comprise the primary key for each table. All of the tables in this figure have single-column keys except LITEM; its primary key is a composite of two columns.

This query shows that the CUST, INV, LITEM, and PRODUCT tables are all involved in parent/child relationships of some kind. However, it doesn't list the specifics of the relationships. For example, although the query reports that the CUST table is a parent and the INV table is a child, it doesn't show that CUST and INV have a parent/child relationship with each other. For that information, you can look to another catalog table: SYSRELS.

Column	Type	Contents
CREATOR	CHAR(8)	Authorization-id of the owner of the child table
TBNAME	VARCHAR(18)	Name of the child table
RELNAME	CHAR(8)	Referential constraint name
REFTBNAME	VARCHAR(18)	Name of the parent table
REFTBCREATOR	CHAR(8)	Authorization-id of the owner of the parent table
COLCOUNT	SMALLINT	Number of columns in the foreign key
DELETERULE	CHAR(1)	"C" if the delete rule is cascade; "R" if it's restrict; "N" if it's set to null
IBMREQD	CHAR(1)	"Y" if the row came from an IBM tape ; "N" if it did not
RELOBID1	SMALLINT	Internal identifier for the database that contains the parent table
RELOBID2	SMALLINT	Internal identifier for the database that contains the child table
TIMESTAMP	TIMESTAMP	Date and time the constraint was defined

Figure 11-6   Structure of the SYSRELS table

How to extract parent/child relationship information from the SYSRELS catalog table

SYSRELS contains one row for every referential constraint in the subsystem. Figure 11-6 presents its contents, and figure 11-7 shows a SPUFI inquiry against it. This query simply retrieves the names of child tables (TBNAME) and their parents (REFTBNAME). The third column I retrieved from the SYSRELS table, RELNAME, specifies a referential constraint name DB2 assigns to each parent/child relationship. You can specify your own constraint name when you define a foreign key; if you don't, DB2 uses the name of the foreign key column in the child table as the constraint name. That's the case with the three relationships the results table in figure 11-7 shows. For example, you can read the data in the first line of the results table in figure 11-7 as "the child table LITEM's column LIPCODE is a foreign key to its parent table, PRODUCT." If a foreign key consists of multiple columns, DB2 makes up an appropriate constraint name.

How to extract index information from the SYSINDEXES catalog table

The SYSINDEXES table contains one row for each index in the DB2 subsystem. Figure 11-8 shows its contents. Like many of the other catalog tables, SYSINDEXES contains much technical information. Although this

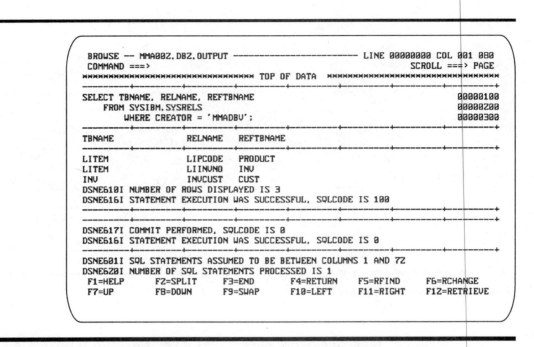

```
  BROWSE -- MMA002.DB2.OUTPUT ------------------------ LINE 00000000 COL 001 080
  COMMAND ===>                                             SCROLL ===> PAGE
*************************** TOP OF DATA ****************************************
--------+---------+---------+---------+---------+---------+---------+---------+
SELECT TBNAME, RELNAME, REFTBNAME                                     00000100
    FROM SYSIBM.SYSRELS                                               00000200
        WHERE CREATOR = 'MMADBV';                                     00000300
--------+---------+---------+---------+---------+---------+---------+---------+
TBNAME              RELNAME    REFTBNAME
--------+---------+---------+---------+---------+---------+---------+---------+
LITEM               LIPCODE    PRODUCT
LITEM               LIINVNO    INV
INV                 INVCUST    CUST
DSNE610I NUMBER OF ROWS DISPLAYED IS 3
DSNE616I STATEMENT EXECUTION WAS SUCCESSFUL, SQLCODE IS 100
--------+---------+---------+---------+---------+---------+---------+---------+
--------+---------+---------+---------+---------+---------+---------+---------+
DSNE617I COMMIT PERFORMED, SQLCODE IS 0
DSNE616I STATEMENT EXECUTION WAS SUCCESSFUL, SQLCODE IS 0
--------+---------+---------+---------+---------+---------+---------+---------+
DSNE601I SQL STATEMENTS ASSUMED TO BE BETWEEN COLUMNS 1 AND 72
DSNE620I NUMBER OF SQL STATEMENTS PROCESSED IS 1
  F1=HELP     F2=SPLIT    F3=END      F4=RETURN   F5=RFIND    F6=RCHANGE
  F7=UP       F8=DOWN     F9=SWAP     F10=LEFT    F11=RIGHT   F12=RETRIEVE
```

Figure 11-7   A query against the SYSRELS table to retrieve information about parent/child relationships

information is vital to DBAs, most of it isn't important for programmers. The columns you might be interested in are the ones I've shaded in the figure.

Probably the only time you'll work directly with indexes is when you create them for your test tables. So it's easy to forget what you named them. If you need to, you can access the SYSINDEXES table to list the indexes you've created. Figure 11-9 shows a SELECT that does that.

In figure 11-9, I retrieved four columns from SYSINDEXES. The first, NAME, contains the name of the index. The second, TBNAME, contains the name of the table associated with the index. UNIQUERULE is a one-character column that indicates whether the index is or isn't unique and, if it is, if it's associated with a primary key. Finally, the fourth column, COLCOUNT, contains the number of columns that make up the index key.

As you can see, I haven't created many indexes for the test tables I've used for this book. For those I did create, I used a simple naming convention: An index name is the name of the table it's related to combined with the suffix "X." All the indexes in the table in figure 11-9 are for primary keys ("P" in the UNIQUERULE column). And, except for the LITEMX index, all are based on single-column keys.

Column	Type	Contents
NAME	VARCHAR(18)	Name of the index
CREATOR	CHAR(8)	Authorization-id of the owner of the index
TBNAME	VARCHAR(18)	Name of the table the index is related to
TBCREATOR	CHAR(8)	Authorization-id of the owner of the related table
UNIQUERULE	CHAR(1)	"D" if duplicates are allowed; "U" if the index is unique; "P" if the index is a unique primary index
COLCOUNT	SMALLINT	Number of columns in the key
CLUSTERING	CHAR(1)	"Y" if clustering was specified for the index; "N" if it was not
CLUSTERED	CHAR(1)	"Y" if most of the table's rows are clustered; "N" if they are not
DBID	SMALLINT	Internal identifier for the database that contains the index
OBID	SMALLINT	Internal identifier for an index component
ISOBID	SMALLINT	Internal identifier for an index component
DBNAME	CHAR(8)	Name of the database that contains the index
INDEXSPACE	CHAR(8)	Name of the index space that contains the index
FIRSTKEYCARD	INTEGER	Number of distinct values in the first column of the key
FULLKEYCARD	INTEGER	Number of distinct values in the entire key
NLEAF	INTEGER	Number of "leaf" pages in the index
NLEVELS	SMALLINT	Number of levels in the index tree
BPOOL	CHAR(8)	Size of the buffer pool used for the index
PGSIZE	SMALLINT	Size of subpages in the index
ERASERULE	CHAR(1)	"Y" if index data sets should be erased when dropped; "N" if they should not
DSETPASS	CHAR(8)	Password for index data sets
CLOSERULE	CHAR(1)	"Y" if the index data sets should be closed when they're not in use; "N" if they should not
SPACE	INTEGER	Amount of disk storage allocated to the index
IBMREQD	CHAR(1)	"Y" if the row came from an IBM tape ; "N" if it did not
CLUSTERRATIO	SMALLINT	Percent of rows that are in clustering order
CREATEDBY	CHAR(8)	Authorization-id of the creator of the index

Figure 11-8   Structure of the SYSINDEXES table

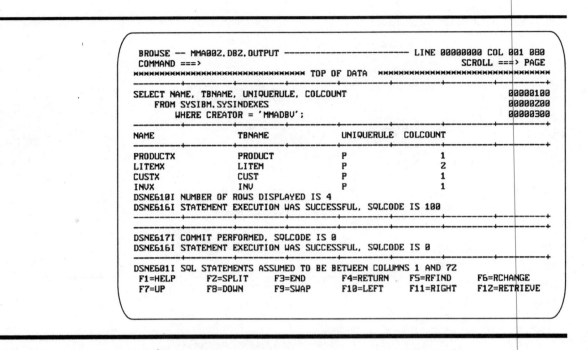

```
 BROWSE -- MMA002.DB2.OUTPUT --------------------- LINE 00000000 COL 001 080
   COMMAND ===>                                              SCROLL ===> PAGE
 **************************** TOP OF DATA *******************************
 ---------+---------+---------+---------+---------+---------+---------+---------+
 SELECT NAME, TBNAME, UNIQUERULE, COLCOUNT                             00000100
     FROM SYSIBM.SYSINDEXES                                            00000200
         WHERE CREATOR = 'MMADBV';                                     00000300
 ---------+---------+---------+---------+---------+---------+---------+---------+

 NAME                 TBNAME              UNIQUERULE  COLCOUNT
 ---------+---------+---------+---------+---------+---------+---------+---------+

 PRODUCTX             PRODUCT             P                  1
 LITEMX               LITEM               P                  2
 CUSTX                CUST                P                  1
 INVX                 INV                 P                  1
 DSNE610I NUMBER OF ROWS DISPLAYED IS 4
 DSNE616I STATEMENT EXECUTION WAS SUCCESSFUL, SQLCODE IS 100
 ---------+---------+---------+---------+---------+---------+---------+---------+

 ---------+---------+---------+---------+---------+---------+---------+---------+
 DSNE617I COMMIT PERFORMED, SQLCODE IS 0
 DSNE616I STATEMENT EXECUTION WAS SUCCESSFUL, SQLCODE IS 0
 ---------+---------+---------+---------+---------+---------+---------+---------+

 DSNE601I SQL STATEMENTS ASSUMED TO BE BETWEEN COLUMNS 1 AND 72
   F1=HELP      F2=SPLIT     F3=END      F4=RETURN    F5=RFIND     F6=RCHANGE
   F7=UP        F8=DOWN      F9=SWAP     F10=LEFT     F11=RIGHT    F12=RETRIEVE
```

Figure 11-9   A query against the SYSINDEXES table to retrieve information about existing indexes

How to extract column information for keys from the SYSKEYS catalog table

Although the results table in figure 11-9 shows the number of columns in each key, it doesn't show the names of those columns. To get that information, you can do a query against the SYSKEYS catalog table. Figure 11-10 presents the contents of this table. It contains one row for each column of every index in the DB2 subsystem. So for an index like LITEMX, the SYSKEYS table contains two rows.

Figure 11-11 shows a SELECT statement that extracts column information for keys from the SYSKEYS table. The results table includes the name of the index, the name of each column that makes up an index key, and the position of that column in the key. Notice that I sorted the output by column sequence for each index. So the two columns that make up the key for the LITEMX index are in the same order as they are in the LITEM table.

Column	Type	Contents
IXNAME	VARCHAR(18)	Name of the index
IXCREATOR	CHAR(8)	Authorization-id of the owner of the index
COLNAME	VARCHAR(18)	Name of the key column
COLNO	SMALLINT	Position of the column in the row
COLSEQ	SMALLINT	Position of the column in the key
ORDERING	CHAR(1)	"A" if the order of the column values in the index is ascending; "D" if the order is descending
IBMREQD	CHAR(1)	"Y" if the row came from an IBM tape ; "N" if it did not

Figure 11-10   Structure of the SYSKEYS table

How to extract information from multiple catalog tables

Although the information you can extract from any one catalog table can be useful, you need to combine information from multiple tables to really make use of the catalog. For example, if you wanted to know the names of the columns that comprise the primary keys of all of your tables, you'd need to look at three different tables.

Figure 11-12 shows a SELECT that joins data from the SYSTABLES, SYSINDEXES, and SYSKEYS tables to provide that information. This SELECT retrieves a table name from SYSTABLES and the names and positions of the columns that make up that table's primary key from SYSKEYS. To do that, it has to access SYSINDEXES to identify the primary index for each table it selects from SYSTABLES. The UNIQUERULE column of SYSINDEXES identifies the indexes that are associated with primary keys.

Figure 11-13 presents an even more complicated SELECT that uses these three tables. This statement returns the names of tables that have children. (Notice that one of the selection conditions specifies that the value of the CHILDREN column of the SYSTABLES row must be greater than zero for a row to be included in the join.) Each row in the results table includes the name of the column(s) that make up the table's primary key (COLNAME) and the position of the column in the key. Then, it includes the name of the table's child (TBNAME). The last column in each row is the name of the foreign key column in the child table that points to the parent.

```
  BROWSE -- MMA002.DB2.OUTPUT -------------------------- LINE 00000000 COL 001 080
  COMMAND ===>                                              SCROLL ===> PAGE
*********************************** TOP OF DATA *********************************
---------+---------+---------+---------+---------+---------+---------+---------+
SELECT IXNAME, COLNAME, COLSEQ                                         00000100
   FROM SYSIBM.SYSKEYS                                                 00000200
       WHERE IXCREATOR = 'MMADBV'                                      00000300
   ORDER BY IXNAME, COLSEQ;                                            00000400
---------+---------+---------+---------+---------+---------+---------+---------+
IXNAME              COLNAME              COLSEQ
---------+---------+---------+---------+---------+---------+---------+---------+
CUSTX               CUSTNO                  1
INVX                INVNO                   1
LITEMX              LIINVNO                 1
LITEMX              LIPCODE                 2
PRODUCTX            PRNO                    1
DSNE610I NUMBER OF ROWS DISPLAYED IS 5
DSNE616I STATEMENT EXECUTION WAS SUCCESSFUL, SQLCODE IS 100
---------+---------+---------+---------+---------+---------+---------+---------+

DSNE617I COMMIT PERFORMED, SQLCODE IS 0
DSNE616I STATEMENT EXECUTION WAS SUCCESSFUL, SQLCODE IS 0
 F1=HELP      F2=SPLIT     F3=END      F4=RETURN   F5=RFIND    F6=RCHANGE
 F7=UP        F8=DOWN      F9=SWAP     F10=LEFT    F11=RIGHT   F12=RETRIEVE
```

Figure 11-11   A query against the SYSKEYS table to retrieve information about the columns that make up keys

```
  BROWSE -- MMA002.DB2.OUTPUT -------------------------- LINE 00000000 COL 001 080
  COMMAND ===>                                              SCROLL ===> PAGE
*********************************** TOP OF DATA *********************************
---------+---------+---------+---------+---------+---------+---------+---------+
SELECT T.NAME, K.COLNAME, K.COLSEQ                                     00000100
   FROM SYSIBM.SYSKEYS K,                                              00000200
       SYSIBM.SYSINDEXES I,                                           00000300
       SYSIBM.SYSTABLES T                                             00000400
   WHERE I.UNIQUERULE  = 'P'       AND                                00000700
       K.IXNAME      = I.NAME    AND                                  00000800
       I.TBNAME      = T.NAME    AND                                  00000900
       T.CREATOR     = 'MMADBV'                                       00001100
   ORDER BY 1, 3;                                                     00001200
---------+---------+---------+---------+---------+---------+---------+---------+
NAME                COLNAME              COLSEQ
---------+---------+---------+---------+---------+---------+---------+---------+
CUST                CUSTNO                  1
INV                 INVNO                   1
LITEM               LIINVNO                 1
LITEM               LIPCODE                 2
PRODUCT             PRNO                    1
DSNE610I NUMBER OF ROWS DISPLAYED IS 5
 F1=HELP      F2=SPLIT     F3=END      F4=RETURN   F5=RFIND    F6=RCHANGE
 F7=UP        F8=DOWN      F9=SWAP     F10=LEFT    F11=RIGHT   F12=RETRIEVE
```

Figure 11-12   A query that joins data from the SYSKEYS, SYSINDEXES, and SYSTABLES tables to list the columns that make up all of my tables' primary keys

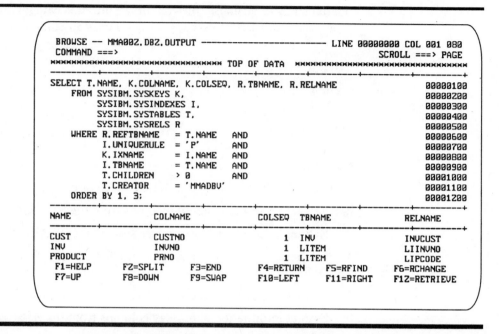

```
BROWSE -- MMA002.DB2.OUTPUT --------------------------- LINE 00000000 COL 001 080
COMMAND ===>                                                SCROLL ===> PAGE
XXXXXXXXXXXXXXXXXXXXXXXXXXXXXXXX TOP OF DATA XXXXXXXXXXXXXXXXXXXXXXXXXXXXXXXXX
----------+---------+---------+---------+---------+---------+---------+--------+
SELECT T.NAME, K.COLNAME, K.COLSEQ, R.TBNAME, R.RELNAME            00000100
    FROM SYSIBM.SYSKEYS K,                                         00000200
         SYSIBM.SYSINDEXES I,                                      00000300
         SYSIBM.SYSTABLES T,                                       00000400
         SYSIBM.SYSRELS R                                          00000500
   WHERE R.REFTBNAME   = T.NAME    AND                             00000600
         I.UNIQUERULE  = 'P'       AND                             00000700
         K.IXNAME      = I.NAME    AND                             00000800
         I.TBNAME      = T.NAME    AND                             00000900
         T.CHILDREN    > 0         AND                             00001000
         T.CREATOR     = 'MMADBU'                                  00001100
    ORDER BY 1, 3;                                                 00001200
----------+---------+---------+---------+---------+---------+---------+--------+
NAME                  COLNAME                COLSEQ  TBNAME            RELNAME
----------+---------+---------+---------+---------+---------+---------+--------+
CUST                  CUSTNO                      1  INV               INVCUST
INV                   INVNO                       1  LITEM             LIINVNO
PRODUCT               PRNO                        1  LITEM             LIPCODE
    F1=HELP      F2=SPLIT     F3=END     F4=RETURN    F5=RFIND    F6=RCHANGE
    F7=UP        F8=DOWN      F9=SWAP    F10=LEFT     F11=RIGHT   F12=RETRIEVE
```

Figure 11-13   A query that joins data from the SYSKEYS, SYSINDEXES, SYSTABLES, and SYSRELS tables to list the tables that have children and the columns that link parents to their children

Discussion

As I've mentioned, only a small portion of the information in the catalog tables is useful for programmers. It's more likely for DBAs to need the information in these tables. The kinds of questions DBAs can answer by retrieving catalog data relate to performance, locking, authorizations, disk use, and binding.

However, if you need to extract information from the catalog tables, the SELECT examples I've presented in this chapter should give you an idea of the type of information they contain. With only minor changes, you'll be able to use these statements as models for queries of your own. If you need information other than what I've presented in the catalog tables in this chapter, you can review the descriptions of all of the catalog tables in the manual *IBM Database 2 Version 2 SQL Reference*.

In addition, some shops use other tables that provide extensions to the DB2 catalog tables. For example, a shop might use a set of tables its staff has defined to store information for data base design or administration. Information about the nature of entities, their dependencies, and their relationships to business rules might fall into this category. Be sure to check with your DBA to see if your shop uses any tables like this.

Terms

catalog
catalog table
link

Objectives

1. Describe the types of information DB2 stores in its catalog tables.

2. Extract information about columns from the SYSCOLUMNS table.

3. Extract information about tables from the SYSTABLES table.

4. Extract information about referential constraints from the SYSRELS table.

5. Extract information about indexes from the SYSINDEXES table.

6. Extract information about key columns from the SYSKEYS table.

Chapter 12

How to get performance analysis data using the EXPLAIN statement

You may recall from *Part 1: An Introductory Course* that the application plan for a program specifies how DB2 will access the data to process the program's SQL statements. The approach DB2 takes to processing an SQL statement is called an *access path*. When more than one access path is possible, a component of DB2, called the *optimizer*, tries to select the best one. In the first part of this chapter, I'll give you some insight into how the optimizer selects an access path.

In the second part of this chapter, I'll show you how to use the EXPLAIN statement to display information about the access paths DB2 uses as it executes your I/O requests. Because much of this information is technical, it's more likely for system administrators to use it as they fine-tune the performance of a DB2 system than it is for programmers to use it. So I'll present only a small portion of it in this chapter.

DB2 access paths and the optimizer

To select an access path, the optimizer estimates the processing costs of the I/O operations each will require. These costs depend on many factors, including whether indexes are available for the affected tables and whether a join operation is required. After it assesses each possible access path, the optimizer chooses the one that seems as if it will have the lowest cost.

Usually, indexes improve performance. So, when an appropriate index is available, the optimizer will typically use it. But that isn't always the case. If a table is small, the optimizer may determine that it would cost less to look at all the data directly. If a selection is to be done on a column that has duplicate values, an index may not reduce costs either. (Remember, only a table's primary key values must be unique.)

If the optimizer decides to use an index, it must then choose the best strategy for using it. Sometimes, DB2 can satisfy a statement by looking at the index and not the related table. The technical term for this type of processing is an *index scan*. For an index scan to be possible, all the data referenced in the statement must be part of the index. Most situations require accesses to both the index and the table. If DB2 needs to access a table, it processes the data using a *table space scan*. That means that it looks at the pages that make up the table. Obviously, if the optimizer decides *not* to use an index, DB2 will use a table space scan. You'll see examples of both types of scans later in this chapter.

As you might guess, a statement that requires a join can be costly. DB2 uses one of two methods to perform a join operation: a *merge scan join* or a *nested loop join*. Because the details of how these two methods work are complicated, I won't describe them here. If you want more information, you can refer to the manual *IBM Database 2 Version 2 Administration Guide, Volume III*.

How to use the EXPLAIN statement

The EXPLAIN statement lets you "ask" DB2 to explain the access path(s) it will use to process SQL statements. The factors that EXPLAIN reports for a given statement depend on the nature of the data the statement will access and on the availability of indexes. Those factors are usually outside your control, so you probably won't be able to do much with the information you collect with EXPLAIN. However, you may be expected to supply EXPLAIN output for some SQL statements you create. And, at the least, looking at what EXPLAIN does will give you some insight into how DB2 works.

DB2 stores the output produced by an EXPLAIN statement in a special table named PLAN_TABLE. Before you use EXPLAIN for the first time, you

```
CREATE TABLE PLAN_TABLE
       (QUERYNO           INTEGER          NOT NULL,
        QBLOCKNO          SMALLINT         NOT NULL,
        APPLNAME          CHAR(8)          NOT NULL,
        PROGNAME          CHAR(8)          NOT NULL,
        PLANNO            SMALLINT         NOT NULL,
        METHOD            SMALLINT         NOT NULL,
        CREATOR           CHAR(8)          NOT NULL,
        TNAME             CHAR(18)         NOT NULL,
        TABNO             SMALLINT         NOT NULL,
        ACCESSTYPE        CHAR(2)          NOT NULL,
        MATCHCOLS         SMALLINT         NOT NULL,
        ACCESSCREATOR     CHAR(8)          NOT NULL,
        ACCESSNAME        CHAR(18)         NOT NULL,
        INDEXONLY         CHAR(1)          NOT NULL,
        SORTN_UNIQ        CHAR(1)          NOT NULL,
        SORTN_JOIN        CHAR(1)          NOT NULL,
        SORTN_ORDERBY     CHAR(1)          NOT NULL,
        SORTN_GROUPBY     CHAR(1)          NOT NULL,
        SORTC_UNIQ        CHAR(1)          NOT NULL,
        SORTC_JOIN        CHAR(1)          NOT NULL,
        SORTC_ORDERBY     CHAR(1)          NOT NULL,
        SORTC_GROUPBY     CHAR(1)          NOT NULL,
        TSLOCKMODE        CHAR(3)          NOT NULL,
        TIMESTAMP         CHAR(16)         NOT NULL,
        REMARKS           VARCHAR(254)     NOT NULL,
        PREFETCH          CHAR(1)          NOT NULL WITH DEFAULT,
        COLUMN_FN_EVAL    CHAR(1)          NOT NULL WITH DEFAULT,
        MIXOPSEQ          SMALLINT         NOT NULL WITH DEFAULT)
   IN DATABASE MMADB;
```

Figure 12-1   A CREATE TABLE statement to generate PLAN_TABLE for use with the EXPLAIN statement

need to create this table. I'll show you how to do that next. Then, I'll show you the format of the EXPLAIN statement and some sample output.

How to create PLAN_TABLE   The name of the table where DB2 stores the access path descriptions produced by EXPLAIN *must* be PLAN_TABLE, qualified by your authorization-id. Figure 12-1 presents a CREATE TABLE statement you can issue to define PLAN_TABLE. Figure 12-2 lists and describes each of its columns.

DB2 stores one row in PLAN_TABLE for each access path that's required to satisfy a statement. As I mentioned earlier, most of the data in PLAN_TABLE is highly technical. For detailed descriptions of the data elements, you can turn to *IBM Database 2 Version 2 Administration Guide*. In this chapter, I'll discuss and illustrate just a few of its columns.

Column	Contents
QUERYNO	A number you can assign to the EXPLAIN output (with the SET option of the EXPLAIN statement) to identify it in your table
QBLOCKNO	A number that identifies a subquery's order of processing
APPLNAME	Name of the application plan associated with the program that issued the statement; blank if not issued from a program
PROGNAME	Name of the program that issued the statement; blank if not issued from a program
PLANNO	A number that identifies the order that the steps of the application plan were executed
METHOD	Join method used for the current step of the plan: 0 for the first table accessed; 1 for a nested loop join; 2 for a merge scan join; 3 not for accessing a new table, but for sorting a table to meet the requirements of ORDER BY, GROUP BY, or DISTINCT.
CREATOR	Creator of a table accessed for the first time in the current step of the statement
TNAME	Name of the table accessed for the first time in the current step of the statement
TABNO	A number that identifies references to tables
ACCESSTYPE	Method used to access a table: "I" for an index scan, "R" for a table space page scan
MATCHCOLS	Number of index keys used in an index scan
ACCESSCREATOR	Creator of an index used in an index scan
ACCESSNAME	Name of an index used in an index scan
INDEXONLY	"Y" if access to the index alone was sufficient to process the statement; "N" if data had to be accessed
SORTN_UNIQ	"Y" if an intermediate sort was required to remove duplicate rows; "N" if it was not
SORTN_JOIN	"Y" if an intermediate sort was required in a merge scan join; "N" if it was not
SORTN_ORDERBY	"Y" if an intermediate sort was required to process an ORDER BY clause; "N" if it was not
SORTN_GROUPBY	"Y" if an intermediate sort was required to process a GROUP BY clause; "N" if it was not
SORTC_UNIQ	"Y" if an intermediate sort was required to remove duplicate rows; "N" if it was not
SORTC_JOIN	"Y" if an intermediate sort was required in a merge scan join; "N" if it was not
SORTC_ORDERBY	"Y" if an intermediate sort was required to process an ORDER BY clause; "N" if it was not
SORTC_GROUPBY	"Y" if an intermediate sort was required to process a GROUP BY clause; "N" if it was not
TSLOCKMODE	Lock mode used for the table space
TIMESTAMP	Date and time the EXPLAIN was processed
REMARKS	User-supplied text
PREFETCH	An indicator of a prefetch method used to retrieve data
COLUMN_FN_EVAL	An indicator of when column functions are processed
MIXOPSEQ	Sequence of steps in a multiple-index operation

Figure 12-2   Columns in PLAN_TABLE

The SQL EXPLAIN statement

```
EXEC SQL
    EXPLAIN ALL [SET QUERYNO = query-number] FOR
        sql-statement
END-EXEC.
```

Explanation

query-number	An integer you want EXPLAIN to assign to the rows it adds to PLAN_TABLE for the current run. The value is stored in the QUERYNO column of PLAN_TABLE.
sql-statement	A SELECT, INSERT, UPDATE, or DELETE statement. If you issue EXPLAIN from an application program, *sql-statement* may not be a host variable.

Figure 12-3   The SQL EXPLAIN statement

The format of the EXPLAIN statement   You can use the EXPLAIN statement in two ways. The first is to enable the EXPLAIN option of the BIND command. If you use this approach, DB2 stores the access paths for all SELECT, DELETE, UPDATE, and INSERT statements that are part of the application plan you're creating in PLAN_TABLE.

The second way to use EXPLAIN is to invoke the EXPLAIN statement directly. When you use this technique, the result is an explanation of a single statement, which you specify as part of the EXPLAIN statement. I'll present this approach in this chapter.

Figure 12-3 presents the syntax of the EXPLAIN statement. Although you can code it in an application program, it's not particularly useful there. Instead, you're more likely to issue it interactively under SPUFI. When you do, you don't code the EXEC SQL and END-EXEC delimiters I included in the figure.

You need to supply two variable items when you invoke EXPLAIN. The first is an integer "label" that will identify the explanation it produces. DB2 stores the label you specify in the QUERYNO column for each row it adds to PLAN_TABLE. The value you specify for QUERYNO should be a new value that you haven't already used. If it's not, you'll have no way to identify the rows for a particular statement. You should delete rows from PLAN_TABLE often to avoid duplicate values in QUERYNO.

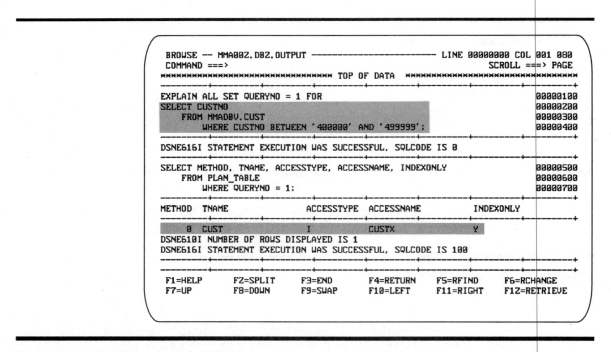

Figure 12-4   EXPLAIN analysis of a SELECT that retrieves customer data from only the customer index

The second variable of EXPLAIN is the SQL statement to be explained.
It may be a SELECT, DELETE, UPDATE, or INSERT statement, which you
code as a literal. For example,

```
EXPLAIN ALL SET QUERYNO = 12345 FOR
    SELECT * FROM MMADBV.CUST
        WHERE STATE = 'CA'
```

specifies that EXPLAIN should report the access path(s) for the SELECT in
the second and third lines of the statement. It also specifies that the
information should be identified with the number 12345.

Sample output produced by EXPLAIN   Figures 12-4 through 12-8 present SPUFI output displays for EXPLAIN statements for five different
SELECTs. The statements illustrate the variety of access paths DB2 can use
when it retrieves table data.

The example in figure 12-4 requests an explanation of a SELECT that
will access the customer table and return all customer numbers between
400000 and 499999:

```
EXPLAIN ALL SET QUERYNO = 1 FOR
SELECT CUSTNO
    FROM MMADBV.CUST
        WHERE CUSTNO BETWEEN '400000' AND '499999';
```

Notice that I coded the SELECT as part of the EXPLAIN statement. Also, I specified that DB2 should store the value 1 in the QUERYNO column in rows it adds to PLAN_TABLE during this execution.

After the first line of the EXPLAIN statement in figure 12-4, I coded a SELECT to examine some of the data in PLAN_TABLE:

```
SELECT METHOD, TNAME, ACCESSTYPE, ACCESSNAME, INDEXONLY
    FROM PLAN_TABLE
        WHERE QUERYNO = 1;
```

Here, the WHERE clause uses the value I specified for QUERYNO in the EXPLAIN statement. As you can see, only one row satisfied this request.

I selected five columns to be displayed in figure 12-4. The first column, METHOD, reports the method the optimizer selects to accomplish a join. This statement doesn't involve a join, so the value of METHOD is "0." TNAME reports the name of the table that was processed: CUST. The value of ACCESSTYPE, "I," means that the access will be through an index, which is identified in ACCESSNAME as CUSTX. Finally, the value "Y" for INDEXONLY means that this statement will be processed using an index scan. In other words, only the index will be accessed. That makes sense, because the statement requests only the value of the primary key column: CUSTNO.

Figure 12-5 shows another example. This SELECT also processes the CUST table. However, it retrieves *all* columns from the table, not just the key column. Notice that the EXPLAIN output for this statement shows the value "R" for ACCESSTYPE. That means that DB2 won't use an index scan for this statement. Instead, it will use a table space scan. Notice also that ACCESSNAME is blank; that means DB2 won't use the index CUSTX at all for this statement. Again, this approach makes sense. DB2 figured out that it will have to read most of the rows in the table to satisfy this SELECT statement. So working through the index doesn't offer any benefit.

The situation is different with the example in figure 12-6. This time, I specified a narrow range of key values on the WHERE clause. DB2 will use the index for this statement, as you can tell by the value "I" in the ACCESSTYPE column and the index name CUSTX in the ACCESSNAME column. However, it will also have to retrieve data from the table, so the value of INDEXONLY is "N."

Figure 12-7 shows an explanation for a SELECT statement that names a view. (You can look back to chapter 10 for a description of the CUSTPROD view.) Although the SELECT statement names only one object, the processing it requires involves data from four tables. The four lines DB2 generated for this statement represent the steps it will go through as it does the join necessary for the CUSTPROD view. The values in the

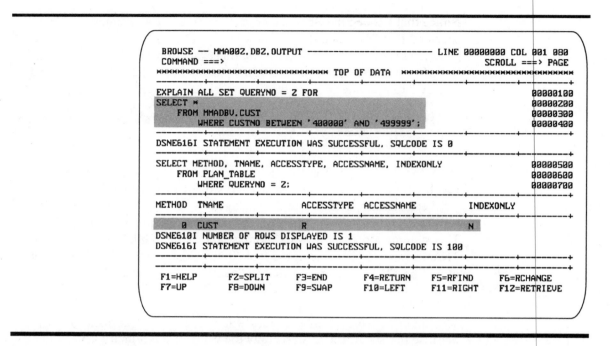

Figure 12-5   EXPLAIN analysis of a SELECT that retrieves customer data from only the customer table

Figure 12-6   EXPLAIN analysis of a SELECT that retrieves customer data from the customer table and the customer
index

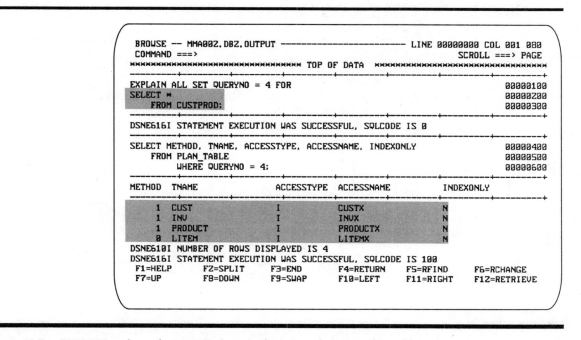

```
   BROWSE -- MMA002.DB2.OUTPUT ----------------------------- LINE 00000000 COL 001 080
   COMMAND ===>                                                       SCROLL ===> PAGE
   ********************************** TOP OF DATA ***********************************
   ----------+---------+---------+---------+---------+---------+---------+---------+
EXPLAIN ALL SET QUERYNO = 4 FOR                                          00000100
  SELECT *                                                               00000200
     FROM CUSTPROD;                                                      00000300
   ----------+---------+---------+---------+---------+---------+---------+---------+
DSNE616I STATEMENT EXECUTION WAS SUCCESSFUL, SQLCODE IS 0
   ----------+---------+---------+---------+---------+---------+---------+---------+
SELECT METHOD, TNAME, ACCESSTYPE, ACCESSNAME, INDEXONLY                  00000400
     FROM PLAN_TABLE                                                     00000500
         WHERE QUERYNO = 4;                                              00000600
   ----------+---------+---------+---------+---------+---------+---------+---------+
METHOD  TNAME              ACCESSTYPE  ACCESSNAME        INDEXONLY
   ----------+---------+---------+---------+---------+---------+---------+---------+
     1  CUST                 I          CUSTX             N
     1  INV                  I          INVX              N
     1  PRODUCT              I          PRODUCTX          N
     0  LITEM                I          LITEMX            N
DSNE610I NUMBER OF ROWS DISPLAYED IS 4
DSNE616I STATEMENT EXECUTION WAS SUCCESSFUL, SQLCODE IS 100
  F1=HELP        F2=SPLIT      F3=END        F4=RETURN    F5=RFIND     F6=RCHANGE
  F7=UP          F8=DOWN       F9=SWAP       F10=LEFT     F11=RIGHT    F12=RETRIEVE
```

Figure 12-7   EXPLAIN analysis of a SELECT that specifies a view that names four tables

METHOD column indicate how DB2 will perform each part of the join operation. Here, DB2 will use nested loop joins to combine data from the CUST, INV, and PRODUCT tables with data from the LITEM table. Notice that all four tables are accessed through their indexes (the value "I" in the ACCESSTYPE column and specific index names in the ACCESSNAME column), and all require access to data in the base tables (the value "N" for INDEXONLY).

Figure 12-8 shows a simpler join that names the tables it will process explicitly. In this example, the only information required from the LITEM table is the product code value (LIPCODE). Because this item is part of the table's primary key, DB2 can retrieve it's value from the index; it doesn't need to access the table.

Discussion

If you need to dig into the details of DB2 internals, EXPLAIN is a good place to start. For example, you can determine when sorts are necessary to process a statement. And, its output includes information on the locking a

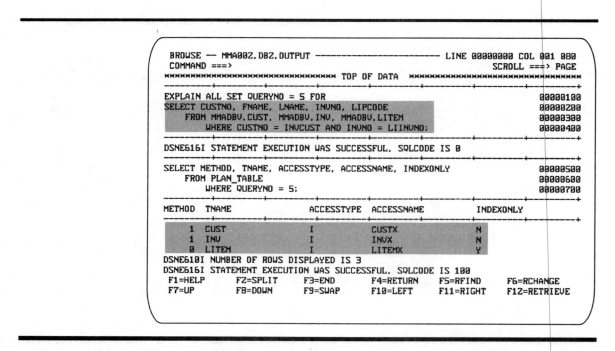

Figure 12-8   EXPLAIN analysis of a SELECT that performs an explicit join of data from three tables

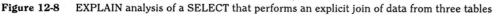

statement can cause. But again, programmers aren't likely to need most of this information.

In spite of the wealth of information EXPLAIN provides, a statement can incur costs that EXPLAIN doesn't report. In particular, the processing DB2 has to do to enforce referential constraints isn't reported by EXPLAIN. Also, EXPLAIN returns information only about accesses to data stored at the local site. You can't get an explanation of access paths for data stored at remote sites.

Terms

access path
optimizer
index scan
table space scan
merge scan join
nested loop join

Objectives

1. Create a version of PLAN_TABLE for your use.

2. Issue an EXPLAIN statement and examine its output to determine the access path the DB2 optimizer will choose to satisfy a SELECT, DELETE, INSERT, or UPDATE statement.

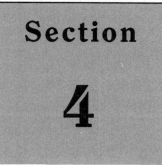

Section

4

Query Management Facility

IBM's Query Management Facility, or QMF, is an interactive software product that lets users access data stored in DB2 tables. QMF is targeted at a wide range of users, from those with no data processing experience to experts. This section presents basic QMF concepts and skills for programmers.

The first chapter in this section, chapter 13, introduces QMF and the concepts and terms you need to know to use it. It also gives an overview of how you can work with QMF. Chapter 14 describes how to use QMF to do queries against DB2 tables. It presents three techniques: standard SQL, Query by Example (QBE), and Prompted SQL. Then, chapter 15 shows you how to define and produce reports that contain data extracted from DB2 tables. You should read the chapters in this section in sequence.

Chapter 13

An introduction to QMF

Query Management Facility, or *QMF,* is an IBM software product that supplements IBM's relational data base management systems. (Of course, under MVS, that's DB2; another version of QMF works in the VM environment with SQL/DS.) QMF lets users issue queries against stored data, and it generates formatted reports based on the results of those queries. In addition, QMF lets users create objects, insert, update, and delete rows, and save query and report specifications for later use.

QMF is like SPUFI because it lets you enter directives to process DB2 data and see the results immediately on your terminal. However, QMF can be easier to use than SPUFI. And, it gives you more flexibility for formatting output. When you're testing programs, these features can be a big advantage. In this chapter, I'll describe how QMF works and present basic skills you need to know to use it.

QMF was planned, and is marketed, as an "end-user" product. That means it's intended to let unsophisticated users retrieve useful data from DB2 tables. It does that by allowing prepackaged queries (in QMF procedures) to be made available to end users. However, developing queries for end users or for program testing purposes requires an understanding of the

stored data, of the capabilities of the relational data base system, and of
QMF.

Understanding QMF items and QMF storage

To work effectively with QMF, you need to understand two basic concepts:
QMF items and QMF storage. This section describes both of them.

QMF items   QMF's operations center around several basic kinds of
items. Figure 13-1 lists them. The first type of item, a *query*, is an instruc-
tion to DB2 that describes what data elements you want to access and what
you want to do with them. You can code a query in the form of an SQL
statement, such as SELECT. Although the word "query" suggests data
retrieval, that's not always the case. QMF queries can issue SQL statements
other than SELECT, such as INSERT and DELETE. But SELECT is the
most common by far.

The second item is the data itself. When QMF processes a SELECT, it
passes it to DB2, and DB2 does the processing necessary to satisfy it. Then,
DB2 passes a copy of the results table back to QMF. QMF treats that data
as an item.

The third QMF item is a form. A *form* specifies how data retrieved by a
SELECT should be presented to the user. When data is structured according to the specifications in a form, it's called a *report*. In other words, QMF
lets you issue queries against data and lets you view the results in reports
that are organized according to forms.

In addition to queries, data, and forms, QMF uses two other kinds of
items: procedures and profiles. A *procedure* is a series of QMF commands
packaged together to accomplish a task. You can create and save procedures to simplify QMF use. A *profile* is a description of how a user interacts
with QMF. To do the kinds of operations this chapter illustrates, you won't
need to worry about your profile. In the next chapter, I'll show you how to
make a change to your profile so you can issue QMF queries in different
ways.

QMF storage   QMF uses two distinct kinds of storage. For the immediate
work you're doing, QMF uses *temporary storage*. (Temporary storage is a
QMF term, and you shouldn't confuse it with the same term used with
other products, like CICS.) Temporary storage can contain only one query,
one form, one report, one table, and one procedure at a time. To be able to
work with any item, you need to bring it into temporary storage.

Temporary storage really *is* temporary. Your temporary storage areas
are empty at the start of a QMF session. When you end a QMF session, the

Query	An instruction to DB2. Queries are often SELECTs. However, a query may also be an INSERT, UPDATE, or DELETE statement or a DDL statement.
Data	Data elements retrieved by DB2 in response to a SELECT and passed to QMF.
Form	Specifications for how data should be presented in a report.
Procedure	A set of QMF commands you can execute as a package.
Profile	The options that define your interactions with QMF.

Figure 13-1   QMF items

contents of temporary storage are lost. And, the one-item-of-a-kind limit means that when you want to work with a new item, like a new query, QMF replaces an existing item.

Fortunately, QMF provides another area, called a *database*, where you can store items permanently. Don't confuse this with a DB2 database. Database in this context is a QMF term. In a moment, I'll describe the QMF commands you can use to move items between temporary storage and the database.

Basic skills for working with QMF

Using QMF is simple. Here, I'll show you two basic skills you need to master to work with QMF. First, I'll describe how to access QMF. Then, I'll show you two ways you can issue QMF commands.

How to access QMF   Most shops let users access QMF through ISPF menu options. On my system, the ISPF Primary Option Menu includes a choice for QMF, as you can see in figure 13-2. Here, I entered the choice for QMF, Q, in the command area. The chances are that your shop's ISPF menu system includes QMF. If you can't find it, ask a co-worker or your supervisor where it is.

The first panel QMF displays when you access it is the Home panel, presented in figure 13-3. It displays copyright and license information at the top of the screen and the QMF logo in the middle of the screen. The bottom third of the screen, beneath the logo, contains the information you need to interact with QMF.

Notice the message

```
OK, you may enter a command.
```

```
-------------------------  ISPF/PDF PRIMARY OPTION MENU  --------------------
OPTION  ===> Q
                                                        USERID   - MMA002
      0  ISPF PARMS  - Specify terminal and user parameters    TIME     - 10:21
      1  BROWSE      - Display source data or output listings   TERMINAL - 3278
      2  EDIT        - Create or change source data             PF KEYS  - 24
      3  UTILITIES   - Perform utility functions
      4  FOREGROUND  - Invoke language processors in foreground
      5  BATCH       - Submit job for language processing
      6  COMMAND     - Enter TSO command or CLIST
      7  DIALOG TEST - Perform dialog testing
      8  LM UTILITIES- Perform library administrator utility functions
      9  IBM PRODUCTS- Additional IBM program development products
     10  SCLM        - Software Configuration and Library Manager
      C  CHANGES     - Display summary of changes for this release
      D  DB2 V2      - Perform DATABASE 2 V2 interactive functions
      Q  QMF 2.4     - QMF Version 2.4
      M  QMFMTOOL    - QMF Message Tool
      S  SDSF        - Spool Display and Search Facility
      T  TUTORIAL    - Display information about ISPF/PDF
      X  EXIT        - Terminate ISPF using log and list defaults

F1=HELP       F2=SPLIT      F3=END        F4=RETURN     F5=RFIND      F6=RCHANGE
F7=UP         F8=DOWN       F9=SWAP       F10=LEFT      F11=RIGHT     F12=RETRIEVE
```

Figure 13-2   A QMF option that appears on the ISPF Primary Option Menu

```
IBM*     Licensed Materials - Property of IBM
5668-721 5668-AAA (c) Copyright IBM Corp. 1982, 1989.  All rights reserved.
US Government Users Restricted Rights - Use, duplication
or disclosure restricted by GSA ADP Schedule Contract with IBM Corp.
* Trademark of International Business Machines Corp.


QMF HOME PANEL
Version 2                          ******   **   **   **********
Release 4.0                      **   **  ***  ***   **
                                 **   **  ****  ****  *******
Query                            **   **  ** ** ** **  **
Management                       **  * **  **  ****  **  **
Facility                         ******   **   **   ** **
                                     *

Type command on command line or use PF keys. For help, press PF1 or type HELP.

1=Help        2=List        3=End        4=Show      5=Chart      6=Query
7=Retrieve    8=Edit Table  9=Form       10=Proc     11=Profile   12=Report
OK, you may enter a command.
COMMAND ===>
```

Figure 13-3   The QMF Home panel

F1=Help	Get context-sensitive information about the panel you're viewing.
F2=List	Show a list of QMF items of a specific type.
F3=End	End the current operation and return to the next higher-level panel.
F4=Show	Present a sequence of prompts for a QMF function.
F5=Chart	Produce a graphic representation of a query.
F6=Query	View, change, and execute the query in temporary storage.
F7=Retrieve	Get a copy of a QMF command you recently entered.
F8=Edit Table	Make changes to stored data.
F9=Form	View and change the form in temporary storage.
F10=Proc	View, change, and execute the procedure in temporary storage.
F11=Profile	View and change your user profile.
F12=Report	View the result of the current SELECT formatted according to the current form.

Figure 13-4   Functions associated with program function keys on the QMF Home panel

on the second line from the bottom of the screen. The designers of QMF tried to make messages conversational, so you'll see lots of "OKs" as you work with QMF. At this point, you have to issue a command to request the QMF service you want.

How to request QMF services   You can issue commands to request QMF services in two ways: by using the function keys that appear at the bottom of each screen or by typing in a QMF command. Most of the heavily used QMF functions, like accessing the query or form in temporary storage, are assigned to function keys. When a function is available through a function key, you'll probably use it that way.

The specific function keys that are enabled at any given time and the functions they perform depend on what you're doing. For example, from the Home panel in figure 13-3, F1 through F12 are active. Figure 13-4 describes the functions assigned to each of these keys. In this section, I'll illustrate how to use the QUERY (F6), REPORT (F12), and FORM (F9) commands. Then, near the end of this chapter, I'll discuss the HELP (F1) option.

Although you can usually accomplish your QMF work by issuing commands with function keys, you sometimes have to type a command directly into the *command line*. The command line is the one with the label

```
COMMAND ===>
```

at the bottom of the screen. When you use this technique, you have to know the correct syntax for the command you're issuing.

Figure 13-5 lists the commands you're most likely to need to enter in the command line. They relate to moving items between the QMF database and temporary storage: LIST, SAVE, DISPLAY, ERASE, and RUN.

The LIST command displays a list of the items stored in the database of the type you request. You can issue it directly or by using F2. However, if you use F2, you have to enter the item type you want to list in the command line first. You'll see an example of this later in this chapter.

The DISPLAY command lets you move an item from the QMF database into temporary storage so you can view it or work with it. For example, if I had stored a query named INVQ, I could retrieve it by entering

```
DISPLAY QUERY INVQ
```

in the command line and pressing Enter.

To save an item from temporary storage to the QMF database, you issue the SAVE command. For example, to save the INVQ item I just retrieved with DISPLAY with a different name, I could enter a command like

```
SAVE QUERY NEWINVQ
```

When you issue the SAVE command, QMF stores the contents of the item you name (QUERY) with the name you supply (NEWINVQ). If you want other users to be able to access an item you save, you can add the SHARE option to the command. For example,

```
SAVE QUERY NEWINVQ (SHARE=YES
```

would make this item available to other QMF users. (Notice the unusual way options are coded: A left parenthesis separates an option from the main part of the command.)

To delete an item you've saved in the QMF database, you use the ERASE command. For example,

```
ERASE QUERY NEWINVQ
```

deletes the query item named NEWINVQ I just saved.

To list queries or forms you've stored in the database:

```
LIST {FORMS  }
     {QUERIES}
```

To retrieve into temporary storage a form or query you've stored in the database:

```
DISPLAY {FORM }  object-name
        {QUERY}
```

To store a form or query from temporary storage in the database:

```
SAVE {FORM }  AS object-name [(SHARE=  {YES}]
     {QUERY}                           {NO }
```

To delete a form or query from the database:

```
ERASE {FORM }  object-name
      {QUERY}
```

To execute a saved query:

```
RUN query-name [(FORM=form-name]
```

Figure 13-5   Formats of the QMF commands to manage forms, queries, and reports

Finally, you can use the RUN command to invoke a query you've saved and format the data it returns according to a form. For example

```
RUN OLDINVQ (FORM=OLDINVF
```

retrieves the query OLDINVQ and the form OLDINVF from the QMF database, issues the query, and returns the result formatted according to the form. Using RUN can save you several steps.

If you find yourself working with QMF often, you may want to write QMF procedures for tasks you do repeatedly. In that case, you'll want to learn the syntax and details of other commands. To do that, you can use QMF's on-line help facility to get information about specific commands. (I'll show you how at the end of this chapter.) Or, you can turn to the QMF manuals for more information.

A simple QMF session

Now, I'd like to show you a typical QMF session: retrieving data and adjusting the format of the report that displays it. To start the sequence, I pressed F6 from the Home panel in figure 13-3. When I did, the panel in part 1 of figure 13-6 appeared: the SQL Query panel. Notice that some of the menu choices at the bottom of the screen are different on this panel than on the Home panel.

Because this was my first query during the current QMF session, the SQL Query screen is empty. If I had issued a query previously during the session, that query would have been displayed. In that case, I could either modify the current query or delete if from temporary storage and begin the new query from scratch. To delete a query from temporary storage, you issue the command

    RESET QUERY

To enter the new query, I moved the cursor to the beginning of the query area using the Home key and keyed in a SELECT statement. Part 2 of the figure shows the SELECT I entered: It joins data elements from the customer and invoice tables I've used in many examples in this book. Notice that I didn't end the statement with a semicolon. That's necessary with SPUFI, but not with QMF.

After I completed the entry, I pressed F2 to run the query. (Unlike SPUFI, you don't have to return to another menu to invoke the statement.) When QMF passed the query to DB2, it displayed the information screen in part 3 of figure 13-6. This screen shows an estimate of the relative processing cost of the statement. Your shop probably has guidelines, formal or informal, for determining what QMF processing costs are acceptable. If the number QMF displays is above your shop's recommended ceiling, you can cancel your query by pressing RESET followed by PA1. Because my test tables are small and the current SELECT is simple, this isn't a very costly query.

After a moment, the result of the query appeared on the screen, as you can see in part 4 of figure 13-6. Notice the title in the upper left corner of the screen: REPORT. QMF automatically displayed the Report panel to show the results of my query. Also notice that you can print a hard copy of the report from this panel by pressing PF4.

To produce a report, QMF requires a form. When it needs to, QMF generates a form automatically based on the characteristics of the data elements a query returns. As you can see in part 4 of figure 13-6, the default column labels in the report are the names of the table columns I retrieved.

Also, the columns of the report are sized so they're appropriate for the data they contain.

At this point, I can return to the SQL Query panel if I want to modify the SELECT statement and reissue it. It's an easy matter to adjust your queries as you experiment with them. In this case, I'm satisfied with the result of the query. However, I want to change the format of the report.

Because all the columns I requested in my query don't fit on the screen, I have to scroll horizontally to view all the data. (If you look back to the SELECT statement in part 2, you'll see that two of the columns I requested, CITY and STATE, didn't fit.) To do that, you can use the standard ISPF scroll keys: F10 to scroll left and F11 to scroll right. You can also use the standard scroll keys to scroll vertically: F7 to scroll up and F8 to scroll down.

An alternative to scrolling horizontally is to adjust the form used to create the report so the data fits on one screen. To modify the form in temporary storage, you can press F9. I did that from the screen in part 4, and the screen in part 5 appeared. Notice the panel name: FORM.MAIN. This is QMF's default form name.

The bottom half of the panel in part 5 of figure 13-6 contains several general reporting features. Here, you can specify text that will print at the top and bottom of each page and at the end of the report. You can also specify options related to control breaks, which I'll cover in chapter 15. For now, I want to focus on the specifications for the columns of the report in the top part of the panel. The panel in part 5 contains specifications for the first five of the eight columns in the report.

The first item for each report column is its sequence in the query's results table. The second item is the label QMF uses for a report column. In this example, the labels are the names of the table columns I specified in the SELECT statement that generated the report (INVNO, INVDATE, INVTOTAL, CUSTNO, and FNAME). The third item, USAGE, lets you specify special report formatting options, like control breaks and aggregation functions. I'll cover usage options in chapter 15. The fourth item, INDENT, specifies how many spaces should precede the data in a report column. The default is 2. The fifth item, WIDTH, specifies how many characters wide a report column should be. This number is taken from the description of the table columns. The sixth item, EDIT, specifies how values are to be presented in a column. For example, L2 for the INVTOTAL column specifies that data in this column should be displayed with two digits after a decimal point. The last item, SEQ, specifies the position for the column in the report. In this example, the report position and the result table column positions are the same for all five items. This is the default.

Part 1

When you press F6 on the
QMF Home panel, the
SQL Query panel appears.
When you access the SQL
Query panel for the first
time in a QMF session, it's
empty.

Part 2

You can enter an SQL
statement directly on the
SQL QUERY panel. To run
a query, press F2.

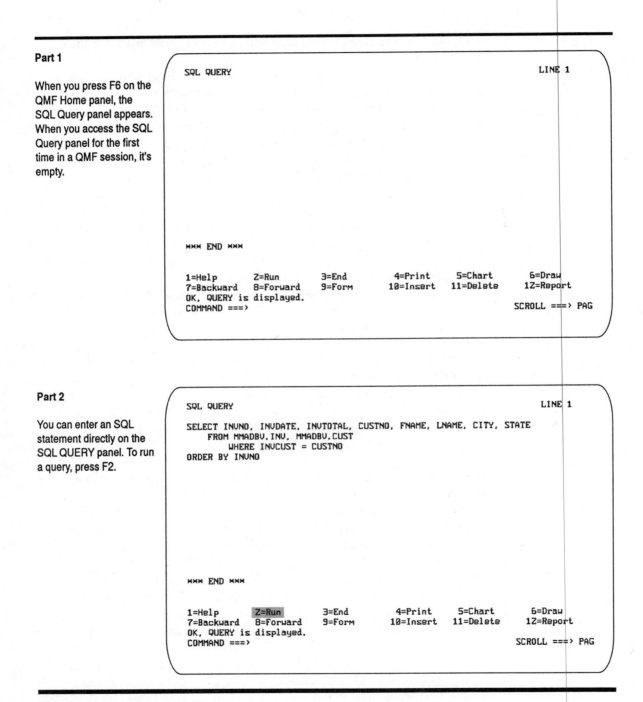

Figure 13-6   A simple QMF session

Part 3

QMF passes your query to
DB2 and displays an
estimate of its processing
cost.

```
                        DATABASE STATUS PANEL


      Your request is currently being processed by the Database Manager.

           The relative cost estimate for your request is: 1
```

Part 4

DB2 returns the results of
the query to QMF, and
QMF displays the results
as a report. If you want to
adjust the form used for
the report, press F9.

```
REPORT                                          LINE 1      POS 1     79


   INVNO    INVDATE           INVTOTAL  CUSTNO  FNAME                    LNAME
   ------   ----------        --------  ------  ------------------       --------------
   062308   1990-12-22          204.45  400012  S D                      HOEHN
   062309   1990-12-22           15.00  400011  WILLIAM C                FERGUSON
   062310   1991-02-22          147.50  400011  WILLIAM C                FERGUSON
   062311   1991-02-22          193.89  400014  R                        BINDER
   062312   1991-02-22          173.07  400002  ARREN                    ANELLI
   062313   1991-03-14           22.50  400011  WILLIAM C                FERGUSON
   062314   1991-03-14          149.80  400003  SUSAN                    HOWARD
   062315   1991-03-14          181.42  400004  CAROL ANN                EVANS
   062316   1991-03-14          147.50  400010  ENRIQUE                  OTHON
   062317   1991-03-17          298.00  400011  WILLIAM C                FERGUSON
   062318   1991-03-17          199.99  400012  S D                      HOEHN
   062319   1991-03-17          181.42  400015  VIVIAN                   GEORGE
   062320   1991-03-17         3405.00  400015  VIVIAN                   GEORGE
   062321   1991-04-03          219.60  400001  KEITH                    MCDONALD
1=Help         2=            3=End         4=Print        5=Chart         6=Query
7=Backward     8=Forward     9=Form        10=Left        11=Right        12=
OK, this is the REPORT from your RUN command.
COMMAND ===>                                               SCROLL ===> PAGE
```

Figure 13-6   A simple QMF session (continued)

Part 5

The FORM.MAIN panel
displays the specifications
for the current form and
lets you adjust them.

```
FORM.MAIN

COLUMNS:                    Total Width of Report Columns: 125
   NUM COLUMN HEADING                          USAGE   INDENT WIDTH EDIT  SEQ
   ---- -------------------------------------- ------- ------ ----- ----  ---
    1 INVNO                                             2      6    C     1
    2 INVDATE                                           2     10    TDY-  2
    3 INVTOTAL                                          2     12    L2    3
    4 CUSTNO                                            2      6    C     4
    5 FNAME                                             2     20    C     5

PAGE:     HEADING  ===>
          FOOTING  ===>
FINAL:    TEXT     ===>
BREAK1:   NEW PAGE FOR BREAK? ===> NO
          FOOTING  ===>
BREAK2:   NEW PAGE FOR BREAK? ===> NO
          FOOTING  ===>
OPTIONS:  OUTLINE? ===> YES             DEFAULT BREAK TEXT? ===> YES

1=Help    2=Check    3=End       4=Show       5=Chart       6=Query
7=Backward 8=Forward 9=          10=Insert    11=Delete     12=Report
OK, FORM is displayed.
COMMAND ===>                                   SCROLL ===> PAGE
```

Part 6

After I changed the
column specifications for
the first five columns, I
pressed F8 to scroll
forward to see the
specifications for the other
items on the report.

```
FORM.MAIN

COLUMNS:                    Total Width of Report Columns: 125
   NUM COLUMN HEADING                          USAGE   INDENT WIDTH EDIT  SEQ
   ---- -------------------------------------- ------- ------ ----- ----  ---
    1 INV #                                             2      6    C     1
    2 DATE                                              2     10    TDY-  2
    3 TOTAL                                             2     12    L2    3
    4 CUST #                                            2      6    C     4
    5                                                   2      1    C     6

PAGE:     HEADING  ===>
          FOOTING  ===>
FINAL:    TEXT     ===>
BREAK1:   NEW PAGE FOR BREAK? ===> NO
          FOOTING  ===>
BREAK2:   NEW PAGE FOR BREAK? ===> NO
          FOOTING  ===>
OPTIONS:  OUTLINE? ===> YES             DEFAULT BREAK TEXT? ===> YES

1=Help    2=Check    3=End       4=Show       5=Chart       6=Query
7=Backward 8=Forward 9=          10=Insert    11=Delete     12=Report
OK, FORM is displayed.
COMMAND ===>                                   SCROLL ===> PAGE
```

Figure 13-6   A simple QMF session (continued)

Part 7

The remaining entries for the current form appear with the their starting values.

```
FORM.MAIN                                              MODIFIED

COLUMNS:                    Total Width of Report Columns: 106
    NUM COLUMN HEADING                                 USAGE   INDENT WIDTH EDIT  SEQ
    --- ------------------------------------------     ------- ------ ----- ----  ---
      6 LNAME                                                    2      30   C     6
      7 CITY                                                     2      20   C     7
      8 STATE                                                    2       5   C     8
        *** END ***


    PAGE:    HEADING  ===>
             FOOTING  ===>
    FINAL:   TEXT     ===>
    BREAK1:  NEW PAGE FOR BREAK? ===> NO
             FOOTING  ===>
    BREAK2:  NEW PAGE FOR BREAK? ===> NO
             FOOTING  ===>
    OPTIONS: OUTLINE? ===> YES           DEFAULT BREAK TEXT? ===> YES

    1=Help     2=Check    3=End        4=Show       5=Chart      6=Query
    7=Backward 8=Forward  9=          10=Insert    11=Delete    12=Report
    OK, FORWARD performed. Please proceed.
    COMMAND ===>                                       SCROLL ===> PAGE
```

Part 8

After I entered the changes I wanted to make, I pressed F12 to redisplay the report.

```
FORM.MAIN                                              MODIFIED

COLUMNS:                    Total Width of Report Columns: 106
    NUM COLUMN HEADING                                 USAGE   INDENT WIDTH EDIT  SEQ
    --- ------------------------------------------     ------- ------ ----- ----  ---
      6 NAME                                                    2      10   C     5
      7 CITY                                                    2      10   C     7
      8 STATE                                                   2       5   C     8
        *** END ***


    PAGE:    HEADING  ===>
             FOOTING  ===>
    FINAL:   TEXT     ===>
    BREAK1:  NEW PAGE FOR BREAK? ===> NO
             FOOTING  ===>
    BREAK2:  NEW PAGE FOR BREAK? ===> NO
             FOOTING  ===>
    OPTIONS: OUTLINE? ===> YES           DEFAULT BREAK TEXT? ===> YES

    1=Help     2=Check    3=End        4=Show       5=Chart      6=Query
    7=Backward 8=Forward  9=          10=Insert    11=Delete    12=Report
    OK, FORWARD performed. Please proceed.
    COMMAND ===>                                       SCROLL ===> PAGE
```

Figure 13-6 A simple QMF session (continued)

Part 9

The report shows the
same data formatted
according to the new
specifications. Because I
was satisfied with the
appearance of the report, I
entered a SAVE command
to store the current form in
the database.

```
 REPORT                                        LINE 1      POS 1      79



  INV #   DATE            TOTAL   CUST #  NAME          CITY        STATE
 ------   ----------   ----------  ------  ----------  -  ----------  -----
  062308  1990-12-22       204.45  400012  HOEHN       S  RIDDLE      OR
  062309  1990-12-22        15.00  400011  FERGUSON    W  MIAMI       FL
  062310  1991-02-22       147.50  400011  FERGUSON    W  MIAMI       FL
  062311  1991-02-22       193.89  400014  BINDER      R  DEPEW       NY
  062312  1991-02-22       173.07  400002  ANELLI      A  DENVILLE    NJ
  062313  1991-03-14        22.50  400011  FERGUSON    W  MIAMI       FL
  062314  1991-03-14       149.80  400003  HOWARD      S  REDWOOD CI  CA
  062315  1991-03-14       181.42  400004  EVANS       C  GREAT LAKE  IL
  062316  1991-03-14       147.50  400010  OTHON       E  RICHMOND    VA
  062317  1991-03-17       298.00  400011  FERGUSON    W  MIAMI       FL
  062318  1991-03-17       199.99  400012  HOEHN       S  RIDDLE      OR
  062319  1991-03-17       181.42  400015  GEORGE      V  PHILADELPH  PA
  062320  1991-03-17      3405.00  400015  GEORGE      V  PHILADELPH  PA
  062321  1991-04-03       219.60  400001  MCDONALD    K  DALLAS      TX
 1=Help        2=          3=End         4=Print       5=Chart      6=Query
 7=Backward    8=Forward   9=Form       10=Left       11=Right     12=
 OK, REPORT is displayed.
 COMMAND ===> SAVE FORM AS ICJOINF                        SCROLL ===> PAGE
```

Part 10

After QMF finished the
save operation for the
current form, I issued
another SAVE command
for the current query.

```
 REPORT                                        LINE 1      POS 1      79



  INV #   DATE            TOTAL   CUST #  NAME          CITY        STATE
 ------   ----------   ----------  ------  ----------  -  ----------  -----
  062308  1990-12-22       204.45  400012  HOEHN       S  RIDDLE      OR
  062309  1990-12-22        15.00  400011  FERGUSON    W  MIAMI       FL
  062310  1991-02-22       147.50  400011  FERGUSON    W  MIAMI       FL
  062311  1991-02-22       193.89  400014  BINDER      R  DEPEW       NY
  062312  1991-02-22       173.07  400002  ANELLI      A  DENVILLE    NJ
  062313  1991-03-14        22.50  400011  FERGUSON    W  MIAMI       FL
  062314  1991-03-14       149.80  400003  HOWARD      S  REDWOOD CI  CA
  062315  1991-03-14       181.42  400004  EVANS       C  GREAT LAKE  IL
  062316  1991-03-14       147.50  400010  OTHON       E  RICHMOND    VA
  062317  1991-03-17       298.00  400011  FERGUSON    W  MIAMI       FL
  062318  1991-03-17       199.99  400012  HOEHN       S  RIDDLE      OR
  062319  1991-03-17       181.42  400015  GEORGE      V  PHILADELPH  PA
  062320  1991-03-17      3405.00  400015  GEORGE      V  PHILADELPH  PA
  062321  1991-04-03       219.60  400001  MCDONALD    K  DALLAS      TX
 1=Help        2=          3=End         4=Print       5=Chart      6=Query
 7=Backward    8=Forward   9=Form       10=Left       11=Right     12=
 OK, FORM was saved as ICJOINF in the database.
 COMMAND ===> SAVE QUERY AS ICJOINQ                       SCROLL ===> PAGE
```

Figure 13-6   A simple QMF session (continued)

Part 11

When QMF reported that
the query had been saved
in the database, I pressed
F3 to return to the Home
panel.

```
 REPORT                                             LINE 1      POS 1      79


   INV #   DATE          TOTAL   CUST # NAME           CITY          STATE
   -----   ----------   ------   ------ ----------  -  ----------    -----
   062308  1990-12-22   204.45   400012 HOEHN       S  RIDDLE        OR
   062309  1990-12-22    15.00   400011 FERGUSON    W  MIAMI         FL
   062310  1991-02-22   147.50   400011 FERGUSON    W  MIAMI         FL
   062311  1991-02-22   193.89   400014 BINDER      R  DEPEW         NY
   062312  1991-02-22   173.07   400002 ANELLI      A  DENVILLE      NJ
   062313  1991-03-14    22.50   400011 FERGUSON    W  MIAMI         FL
   062314  1991-03-14   149.80   400003 HOWARD      S  REDWOOD CI    CA
   062315  1991-03-14   181.42   400004 EVANS       C  GREAT LAKE    IL
   062316  1991-03-14   147.50   400010 OTHON       E  RICHMOND      VA
   062317  1991-03-17   298.00   400011 FERGUSON    W  MIAMI         FL
   062318  1991-03-17   199.99   400012 HOEHN       S  RIDDLE        OR
   062319  1991-03-17   181.42   400015 GEORGE      V  PHILADELPH    PA
   062320  1991-03-17  3405.00   400015 GEORGE      V  PHILADELPH    PA
   062321  1991-04-03   219.60   400001 MCDONALD    K  DALLAS        TX
 1=Help          2=           3=End        4=Print         5=Chart        6=Query
 7=Backward      8=Forward    9=Form      10=Left         11=Right       12=
 OK, QUERY was saved as ICJOINQ in the database.
 COMMAND ===>                                            SCROLL ===> PAGE
```

Part 12

To verify that the save
operation in part 11
worked properly, I entered
QUERIES on the
command line and
pressed F2 to list the
items of that type in the
database.

```
 IBM×    Licensed Materials - Property of IBM
 5668-721 5668-AAA (c) Copyright IBM Corp. 1982, 1989.  All rights reserved.
 US Government Users Restricted Rights - Use, duplication
 or disclosure restricted by GSA ADP Schedule Contract with IBM Corp.
 × Trademark of International Business Machines Corp.


   QMF HOME PANEL
   Version 2                              ××××××    ××    ××    ××××××××××
   Release 4.0                          ××    ××   ××××  ××××   ××
                                        ××    ××   ××××  ××××   ×××××××××
   Query                                ××    ××  ×× ×× ×× ××    ××
   Management                           ××  × ××   ××   ×××××  ××  ××
   Facility                             ××××××    ××    ××   ×× ××
                                            ×

 Type command on command line or use PF keys. For help, press PF1 or type HELP.

 1=Help         2=List       3=End        4=Show          5=Chart        6=Query
 7=Retrieve     8=Edit Table 9=Form      10=Proc         11=Profile     12=Report
 OK, END command executed successfully.
 COMMAND ===> QUERIES
```

Figure 13-6   A simple QMF session (continued)

Part 13

QMF listed information for
my stored queries. The
query I just saved,
ICJOINQ, is among them.
To return to the Home
panel, I pressed F3.

```
                        QMF Database Object List                  ROW 1 OF 7
  TYPE: QUERIES     OWNER: MMA00Z        NAME: ALL
  Enter a QMF command next to the name you want to specify and press ENTER.
  You may use a "/" to insert the object name into your command.

  QMF                          Object  Object  Object
  Command  Object Name         Owner   Type    Subtype  Model    Restricted
  -------  ------------------  ------  ------  -------  -------  ----------
           CUSTALL             MMA00Z  QUERY   SQL               Y
           CUSTINQZ            MMA00Z  QUERY   SQL               Y
           CUSTINQ3            MMA00Z  QUERY   QBE               Y
           ICJOINQ             MMA00Z  QUERY   SQL               Y
           INVALL              MMA00Z  QUERY   SQL               Y
           TESTA               MMA00Z  QUERY   SQL               Y
           TESTB               MMA00Z  QUERY   SQL               Y
  **************************** BOTTOM OF DATA ****************************



  OK, your database object list is displayed.
  ISPF Command ===>                                    SCROLL ===> PAGE
  F1=Help     F2=          F3=End List  F4=SortName  F5=SortOwnr  F6=SortType
  F7=Backward F8=Forward   F9=List ?    F10=Clear    F11=Refresh  F12=Comments
```

Figure 13-6   A simple QMF session (continued)

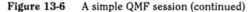

You can change the values of any of these items except the first one. To
do that, you simply type over the existing values. For example, in part 6 of
figure 13-6, I changed the titles of all five report columns. I also changed
the width of the first name column from 20 characters to 1. And, I wanted
to reverse the positions of the last name and first name columns in the
report. So, I changed the value of the SEQ item for the first name column
from 5 to 6.

To adjust the right-most columns of the report, I pressed F8 on the
panel in part 6, and the one in part 7 appeared. I made some changes to
this panel too, which you can see in part 8 of the figure. Here, I changed
the label for the LNAME column to NAME. I reduced the widths of the last
name and city columns to 10 characters each. And, I changed the report
column position for last name from 6 to 5.

To look at an updated version of the report based on the new form, I
pressed F12. Part 9 shows the new version of the report. Note that I didn't
have to reissue the query to produce this report. QMF maintained the data
the query returned and simply formatted it according to the new specifications in the form. Although some of the data items appear truncated in the

new report, this version is easier for me to use for testing purposes because all the columns are on a single screen.

I was satisfied with the report in part 9 of figure 13-6, so I wanted to save a copy of the form in the database. To do that, I entered a SAVE command at the bottom the screen in part 9 and pressed Enter. Notice in the SAVE command that I specified the kind of temporary storage item I wanted to save (FORM) and the name to be assigned to it in the database (ICJOINF).

QMF saved the form with the name I specified, as the message near the bottom of the screen in part 10 shows. I also wanted to save the query item, so I keyed in another SAVE command in part 10. I assigned the name ICJOINQ to the query. QMF reported in part 11 that it successfully saved the query.

To return to the Home panel, I pressed F3 from the screen in part 11. To double-check that the query was saved, I issued the LIST command by pressing F2 from the Home panel in part 12. But before I did that, I entered QUERIES in the command line to identify the kind of item I wanted to see.

QMF's response is in part 13 of the figure. As you can see, the ICJOINQ item was stored successfully. Its name appears with the names of several other queries I saved previously.

In a later QMF session, I can retrieve both of the items I saved. For example,

```
DISPLAY FORM ICJOINF
```

directs DB2 to retrieve the form ICJOINF from the database, move it to temporary storage, and display it on the Form panel. (Remember that if a form is already in temporary storage, this DISPLAY command will cause ICJOINF to replace it.) Once it's displayed, I can make additional changes to it.

I could also use the RUN command

```
RUN ICJOINQ (FORM ICJOINF
```

to invoke the saved query and display the results formatted according to the saved form. Note that although the query and form in this example depend on each other to an extent, they aren't linked directly. So, it's possible to generate a report with the ICJOINF form from data returned by another query. But if the data returned by the query doesn't match the form, QMF will display an error message.

How to use QMF HELP

You can access QMF's help facility to answer questions at any time by pressing F1. The information QMF provides depends on what you're doing when you press F1. As a result, it's called *context-sensitive help*.

For example, if you press F1 from the QMF Home panel, QMF displays the general help panel in part 1 of figure 13-7. From it, you can get answers to general questions about QMF features and operations. If you want information about the format of a specific command, you can key in 11 in the command area and press Enter. Then, QMF displays the panel in part 2 of figure 13-7. This panel is another menu you can use to select a specific command. If I wanted information about the SAVE command, for example, I would type the number associated with it, 30, and press Enter. Then, QMF would return a more detailed screen, as in part 3 of the figure. This is the same information you'd find in the QMF manual.

When you access help from other QMF panels, what you'll see will be different. In particular, if you access help when QMF has just displayed an error message, the reply will address the error. Don't hesitate to use QMF's help panels. They can put the information you need right at your fingertips, and they can save you much time digging through manuals.

Discussion

The interactions I went through to enter and test the SELECT statement in figure 13-6 are similar to what I'd have to do with SPUFI. However, QMF's display features are much more powerful than SPUFI's. Moreover, changing the form for a QMF report is relatively efficient. That's because the DB2 operations to retrieve the data only need to be done once. In contrast, with SPUFI, you'd have to issue the same SQL statement repeatedly to change the format of its output.

As with SPUFI, you can issue statements other than SELECT with QMF. Although I didn't illustrate it in this chapter, you can issue INSERT, UPDATE, and DELETE statements for your tables. I'll show you an example that uses these statements in the next chapter. If you have the proper authorizations, you can also issue DDL statements to create, modify, and delete objects like tables, indexes, and views.

Entering a query in SQL, as I did in the example in figure 13-6, is simple, especially because you've seen so many examples in this book and in *Part 1: An Introductory Course*. However, QMF provides two other approaches you can take to developing queries. In the next chapter, I'll present both and compare them to using basic SQL. Then, in chapter 15, I'll show you how to create and use special forms that take advantage of QMF's powerful report-generation features.

Part 1

When you press F1 on the
QMF Home panel, the
QMF Help: General panel
appears. To display a
menu of QMF commands,
type 11 on the command
line and press Enter.

```
                        QMF HELP:   GENERAL              Page 1 of 1

         To read about any topic, type its number after the arrow on the
         command line and press ENTER.

                 1    Using QMF HELP
                 2    Entering a QMF command
                 3    Interrupting a QMF command
                 4    Viewing a QMF panel
                 5    Scrolling a QMF panel
                 6    Temporary Storage
                 7    Prompted Query
                 8    Table Editor
                 9    About QMF applications
                 10   Features available with newer databases
                 11   Explanations of QMF commands


         To see all the topics in sequence, press ENTER repeatedly.



         ISPF Command ===> 11
         F3=End Help    F7=Up            F8=Skip         F10=Previous   F11=Next
```

Part 2

To display more
information about
a particular command,
type its number on the
command line and press
Enter.

```
                        QMF HELP:   COMMANDS             Page 1 of 1

         Explanations of QMF Commands

         For help, enter the number of the command on the command line.

             1    BACKWARD     14   FORWARD          27   RETRIEVE
             2    BOTTOM       15   IMPORT           28   RIGHT
             3    CHECK        16   INSERT           29   RUN
             4    CONVERT      17   INTERACT         30   SAVE
             5    DELETE       18   IRM              31   SET GLOBAL
             6    DISPLAY      19   LAYOUT           32   SET PROFILE
             7    DRAW         20   LEFT             33   SHOW
             8    EDIT         21   LIST             34   START
             9    END          22   MESSAGE          35   STATE
             10   ERASE        23   PRINT            36   TOP
             11   EXIT         24   QMF              37   TSO
             12   EXPORT       25   RESET GLOBAL
             13   EXTRACT      26   RESET objecttype



         ISPF Command ===> 30
         F3=End Help    F7=Up            F8=Skip         F10=Previous   F11=Next
```

Figure 13-7   Using QMF's Help panels

Part 3

If you select item 30 from the QMF Help: Commands panel, QMF displays detailed information about the SAVE command.

```
                          QMF HELP:   COMMANDS                 Page 1 of 4

          The SAVE command

          Use the SAVE command to store the contents of a temporary
          storage area into the database.  SAVE is not valid in the
          Table Editor.

          SAVE objecttype AS objectname    (CONFIRM=YES¦NO COMMENT='text'
                                             SHARE=YES¦NO

          objecttype is the name of the temporary storage area to be saved.
          It must be QUERY, FORM, PROFILE, PROC, or DATA.

          objectname is the name the object is to have in the database.


          (continued...)




          ISPF Command ===>
          F3=End Help    F7=Up          F8=Skip          F10=Previous  F11=Next
```

Figure 13-7   Using QMF's Help panels (continued)

Terms

Query Management Facility	profile
QMF	temporary storage
query	database
form	command line
report	context-sensitive help
procedure	

Objectives

1. Access QMF on your system.

2. Distinguish between QMF temporary storage and the QMF database.

3. Use function keys to access the Query, Form, and Report panels.

4. Enter, issue, and save an SQL query with QMF.

5. Modify the default form QMF creates for a query and save it.

6. Access and use QMF's context-sensitive help facility to answer questions you have as you work with QMF.

Chapter 14

How to issue QMF queries through SQL, QBE, and Prompted SQL

In the last chapter, I showed you how to use QMF to create, issue, and save an SQL query. For most of the program development work you'll do, that's sufficient. And from what you've already learned about SQL in this book and in *Part 1: An Introductory Course*, you should have no problem constructing SQL queries. But there is a command that can help you draft a query more easily: DRAW. In this chapter, I'll show you how to use the DRAW command not just for SELECT statements, but also for INSERT and UPDATE statements.

After I show you how to use DRAW, I'll present two other ways you can create queries: with QMF's QBE (Query By Example) feature and its Prompted SQL feature. Because you may never need to use either of these features, I'll present only the basics of each in this chapter. If you want to

---

To create a basic SQL query:

```
DRAW table-name [(TYPE={SELECT}
                        {INSERT}
                        {UPDATE})]
```

Figure 14-1   The QMF DRAW command

learn more about them, you can refer to the IBM manuals *Query Management Facility: Learner's Guide* and *Query Management Facility: User's Guide and Reference.*

The DRAW command

The QMF DRAW command can help you construct a query by retrieving catalog information for the table(s) you want to process. Then, it formats that information in a SELECT, INSERT, or UPDATE statement. The advantage of using DRAW is that you don't have to remember the names and descriptions of all the columns in a table.

Figure 14-1 shows the basic format of the QMF DRAW command. On this command, you name the table you want to process and the type of statement you want to issue: SELECT, INSERT, or UPDATE. The default for the TYPE option is SELECT, so you can omit this option for a retrieval operation. In this section, I'll show you how to use DRAW to prepare each of the three types of statements.

How to use the DRAW command to construct a SELECT statement

Figure 14-2 shows how I used DRAW to create a SELECT statement that joins data from the customer and invoice tables. In part 1, I started with a blank SQL Query panel. Then, I keyed

```
DRAW MMADBV.CUST
```

into the command line and pressed Enter. Because I didn't specify the TYPE option, QMF will use its default, SELECT.

Part 2 shows the result of the DRAW command. It created part of a SELECT statement that names all the columns in the customer table and identifies the table in the FROM clause. Notice that QMF added comments at the end of the two lines that contain column names. These comments specify the table the columns belong to. That way, if you draw information

Part 1

I entered a DRAW command to retrieve the column names from the CUST table for the first part of a SELECT statement.

```
SQL QUERY                                                          LINE 1




















*** END ***


1=Help        2=Run        3=End         4=Print     5=Chart      6=Draw
7=Backward    8=Forward    9=Form        10=Insert   11=Delete    12=Report
OK, QUERY is displayed.
COMMAND ===> DRAW MMADBV.CUST                              SCROLL ===> PAG
```

Part 2

QMF replied by constructing a partial SELECT statement with all of the column names for the CUST table. Then, I entered a second DRAW command to retrieve the column names for the INV table.

```
SQL QUERY                                              MODIFIED    LINE 1

SELECT CUSTNO, FNAME, LNAME, ADDR, CITY      -- MMADBV.CUST
     , STATE, ZIPCODE                        -- MMADBV.CUST
FROM MMADBV.CUST











*** END ***


1=Help        2=Run        3=End         4=Print     5=Chart      6=Draw
7=Backward    8=Forward    9=Form        10=Insert   11=Delete    12=Report
OK, select query for table MMADBV.CUST drawn.
COMMAND ===> DRAW MMADBV.INV                               SCROLL ===> PAG
```

Figure 14-2   Using the DRAW command to construct a SELECT statement

Part 3

QMF added the columns
for the INV table to the
SELECT statement.
Then, I added an
appropriate WHERE
clause.

```
SQL QUERY                                          MODIFIED     LINE 1

SELECT CUSTNO, FNAME, LNAME, ADDR, CITY    -- MMADBV.CUST
     , STATE, ZIPCODE                      -- MMADBV.CUST
     , INVCUST, INVNO, INVDATE, INVSUBT    -- MMADBV.INV
     , INVSHIP, INVTAX, INVTOTAL, INVPROM  -- MMADBV.INV
FROM MMADBV.CUST
   , MMADBV.INV
WHERE CUSTNO = INVCUST




*** END ***


1=Help      2=Run       3=End       4=Print    5=Chart     6=Draw
7=Backward  8=Forward   9=Form      10=Insert  11=Delete   12=Report
OK, select query for table MMADBV.INV drawn.
COMMAND ===>                                            SCROLL ===> PAG
```

Figure 14-2   Using the DRAW command to construct a SELECT statement (continued)

from more than one table, which I'll do in a moment, you'll know what
table each column belongs to.

   Once QMF formats a query according to a DRAW command, you can
edit the query any way you'd like. So, in part 2 of figure 14-2, I could
remove some column names. And, I'd almost certainly want to add a
WHERE clause to specify what customer rows QMF should retrieve.

   Because I want to perform a join operation, I need to add column
names from the invoice table to the SELECT statement in part 2 of figure
14-2. So, I keyed another DRAW command,

```
DRAW MMADBV.INV
```

into the command line in part 2 of the figure and pressed Enter. Part 3
shows the result. Here, QMF added the names of all the columns in the INV
table to the SELECT statement. And, it added the table name to the FROM
clause. At this point, I keyed in the WHERE clause to specify the join condition for the operation. To run the statement, all I would have to do is press
PF2.

How to use the DRAW command to construct an INSERT or UPDATE statement   It's just as easy to build an INSERT or UPDATE statement using DRAW. Figure 14-3 shows how to do that. This figure presents a series of screens from a QMF session where I created, changed, then deleted a customer row.

In part 1 of figure 14-3, I again started with a blank SQL Query panel. To build an INSERT, I keyed

```
DRAW MMADBV.CUST (TYPE=INSERT
```

in the command line and pressed Enter. QMF created the starting INSERT statement presented in part 2 of the figure. This statement looks quite different from the SELECT in figure 14-2. Here, QMF formatted the statement with one line for each column. To specify the columns' values, you simply enter them in the spaces at the left of each line. Notice that QMF supplied a comment on each of those lines that contains the name of the corresponding column, its data type and length, and whether it may contain nulls. This information can help you enter an appropriate value for each column.

In part 3, I keyed in the data for the new row. Because all seven columns have the CHAR data type, I enclosed the value for each in quotes. After I completed the data entry in part 3, I pressed F2 to run the query.

QMF responded by displaying its Run Confirmation panel, presented in part 4. This panel lets you verify a query request. If you decide you don't want to run a query, you can type NO in this panel. Otherwise, you can accept QMF's default value (YES) and QMF will execute the query. That's what I did in part 4.

After a moment, QMF returned to the SQL Query panel, as you can see in part 5. It displayed a message to advise me that the INSERT statement was successful. At this point, I wanted to start another query, so I typed the command

```
RESET QUERY
```

in the command line and pressed Enter. Part 6 shows that QMF cleared the INSERT statement from temporary storage and displayed a "fresh" SQL Query screen to let me key in a new query.

This time, I wanted to issue an UPDATE statement, so I entered

```
DRAW MMADBV.CUST (TYPE=UPDATE
```

on the command line. Then, QMF built the starting UPDATE statement in part 7. Again, the statement includes comments to remind me about the characteristics of the columns in the table. And, QMF again provided spaces

Part 1

I issued the DRAW
command to direct QMF to
build a starting INSERT
statement so I could issue
a query to add a row to the
CUST table.

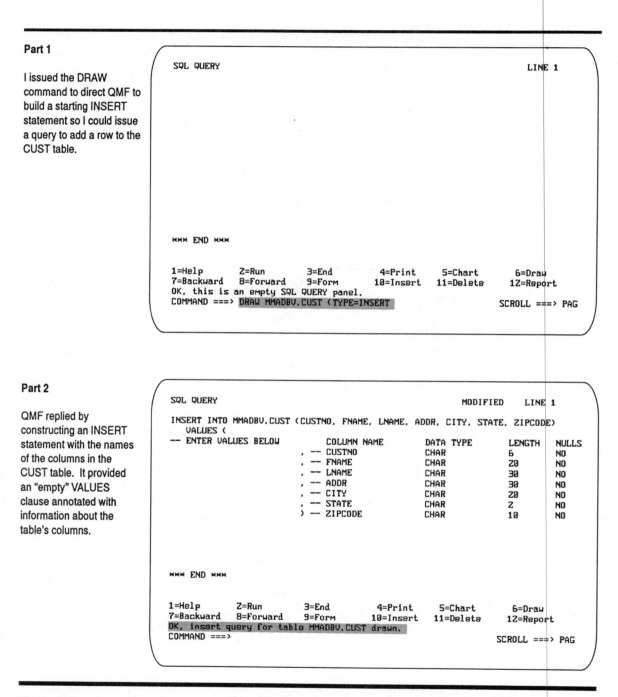

Part 2

QMF replied by
constructing an INSERT
statement with the names
of the columns in the
CUST table. It provided
an "empty" VALUES
clause annotated with
information about the
table's columns.

Figure 14-3   Using QMF to construct and issue INSERT, UPDATE, and DELETE statements

Part 3

I keyed in values for all
columns for the new row.
Then, I pressed F2 to run
the query.

```
SQL QUERY                                            MODIFIED    LINE 1

INSERT INTO MMADBV.CUST (CUSTNO, FNAME, LNAME, ADDR, CITY, STATE, ZIPCODE)
    VALUES (
-- ENTER VALUES BELOW          COLUMN NAME       DATA TYPE    LENGTH   NULLS
'400017'                   , -- CUSTNO           CHAR         6        NO
'MARTIN'                   , -- FNAME            CHAR         20       NO
'MANDELL'                  , -- LNAME            CHAR         30       NO
'654 SAN PABLO AVE'        , -- ADDR             CHAR         30       NO
'OAKLAND'                  , -- CITY             CHAR         20       NO
'CA'                       , -- STATE            CHAR         2        NO
'94618'                    ) -- ZIPCODE          CHAR         10       NO




*** END ***


1=Help        2=Run        3=End         4=Print      5=Chart      6=Draw
7=Backward    8=Forward    9=Form        10=Insert    11=Delete    12=Report
OK, insert query for table MMADBV.CUST drawn.
COMMAND ===>                                          SCROLL ===> PAG
```

Part 4

QMF displayed its Run
Confirmation panel to
verify that I wanted to
insert a new row. I
accepted its default value,
"YES," by pressing the
Enter key.

```
                        RUN CONFIRMATION

    WARNING -- Your RUN command will modify
              1        rows in the database.

    DO YOU WANT TO MAKE THIS CHANGE? ===> YES


                  YES -- The changes made by your query will be made
                         permanent in the database.

                  NO  -- The table will be restored to what it was before
                         the query was run.  No changes will be made.


              Press ENTER after answering the question.

              Press END at any time to cancel your QMF command
              and return to the original QMF panel.



    ISPF Command ===>
    F1=Help                            F3=End
```

Figure 14-3   Using QMF to construct and issue INSERT, UPDATE, and DELETE statements (continued)

Part 5

QMF reported that the
insert was successful.
Next, I entered the RESET
QUERY command to clear
the insert query from
temporary storage.

```
SQL QUERY                                          MODIFIED    LINE 1
INSERT INTO MMADBV.CUST (CUSTNO, FNAME, LNAME, ADDR, CITY, STATE, ZIPCODE)
    VALUES (
-- ENTER VALUES BELOW            COLUMN NAME      DATA TYPE     LENGTH   NULLS
'400017'                    ,  -- CUSTNO         CHAR          6        NO
'MARTIN'                    ,  -- FNAME          CHAR          20       NO
'MANDELL'                   ,  -- LNAME          CHAR          30       NO
'654 SAN PABLO AVE'         ,  -- ADDR           CHAR          30       NO
'OAKLAND'                   ,  -- CITY           CHAR          20       NO
'CA'                        ,  -- STATE          CHAR          2        NO
'94618'                     )  -- ZIPCODE        CHAR          10       NO




*** END ***


1=Help      2=Run       3=End         4=Print    5=Chart     6=Draw
7=Backward  8=Forward   9=Form        10=Insert  11=Delete   12=Report
OK, 1 rows in the database were modified.
COMMAND ===> RESET QUERY                                    SCROLL ===> PAG
```

Part 6

Then, I entered a DRAW
command to direct QMF to
construct an UPDATE
statement for the
customer table.

```
SQL QUERY                                                      LINE 1








*** END ***


1=Help      2=Run       3=End         4=Print    5=Chart     6=Draw
7=Backward  8=Forward   9=Form        10=Insert  11=Delete   12=Report
OK, this is an empty SQL QUERY panel.
COMMAND ===> DRAW MMADBV.CUST (TYPE=UPDATE                  SCROLL ===> PAG
```

Figure 14-3   Using QMF to construct and issue INSERT, UPDATE, and DELETE statements (continued)

Part 7

QMF constructed an UPDATE statement with the names of all of the columns in the CUST table in a SET clause. As with INSERT, QMF included comments with information about the attributes of the columns that make up the table.

```
SQL QUERY                                           MODIFIED     LINE 1

UPDATE MMADBV.CUST SET
-- COLUMN NAME             ENTER VALUES BELOW        DATA TYPE    LENGTH    NULLS
   CUSTNO=                                           -- CHAR       6         NO
 , FNAME=                                            -- CHAR       20        NO
 , LNAME=                                            -- CHAR       30        NO
 , ADDR=                                             -- CHAR       30        NO
 , CITY=                                             -- CHAR       20        NO
 , STATE=                                            -- CHAR       2         NO
 , ZIPCODE=                                          -- CHAR       10        NO
WHERE




**** END ****


1=Help          2=Run         3=End          4=Print     5=Chart      6=Draw
7=Backward      8=Forward     9=Form         10=Insert   11=Delete    12=Report
OK, update query for table MMADBV.CUST drawn.
COMMAND ===>                                                   SCROLL ===> PAG
```

Part 8

I keyed in a new value for the ADDR column, and I completed the WHERE clause. Then, I deleted the lines that name the other columns.

```
SQL QUERY                                           MODIFIED     LINE 1

UPDATE MMADBV.CUST SET
-- COLUMN NAME             ENTER VALUES BELOW        DATA TYPE    LENGTH    NULLS
   CUSTNO=                                           -- CHAR       6         NO
 , FNAME=                                            -- CHAR       20        NO
 , LNAME=                                            -- CHAR       30        NO
 , ADDR='654 SAN PEDRO STREET'                       -- CHAR       30        NO
 , CITY=                                             -- CHAR       20        NO
 , STATE=                                            -- CHAR       2         NO
 , ZIPCODE=                                          -- CHAR       10        NO
WHERE CUSTNO = '400017'




**** END ****


1=Help          2=Run         3=End          4=Print     5=Chart      6=Draw
7=Backward      8=Forward     9=Form         10=Insert   11=Delete    12=Report
OK, update query for table MMADBV.CUST drawn.
COMMAND ===>                                                   SCROLL ===> PAG
```

Figure 14-3   Using QMF to construct and issue INSERT, UPDATE, and DELETE statements (continued)

Part 9

QMF displayed a message
to report each line I
deleted. After I had
deleted the last line I
wanted to remove from the
statement, I pressed F2 to
run the query.

```
SQL QUERY                                         MODIFIED    LINE 1

UPDATE MMADBU.CUST SET
-- COLUMN NAME          ENTER VALUES BELOW       DATA TYPE   LENGTH   NULLS
   ADDR='654 SAN PEDRO STREET'              -- CHAR          30       NO
WHERE CUSTNO = '400017'




*** END ***




1=Help      2=Run      3=End        4=Print    5=Chart      6=Draw
7=Backward  8=Forward  9=Form      10=Insert  11=Delete    12=Report
OK, DELETE performed. Please proceed.
COMMAND ===>                                        SCROLL ===> PAG
```

Part 10

After the UPDATE query
was complete, QMF
displayed a message to
report its status. Again, I
entered a RESET QUERY
command to clear the
previous query from
temporary storage so I
could enter a new one.

```
SQL QUERY                                         MODIFIED    LINE 1

UPDATE MMADBU.CUST SET
-- COLUMN NAME          ENTER VALUES BELOW       DATA TYPE   LENGTH   NULLS
   ADDR='654 SAN PEDRO STREET'              -- CHAR          30       NO
WHERE CUSTNO = '400017'




*** END ***




1=Help      2=Run      3=End        4=Print    5=Chart      6=Draw
7=Backward  8=Forward  9=Form      10=Insert  11=Delete    12=Report
OK, 1 rows in the database were modified.
COMMAND ===> RESET QUERY                             SCROLL ===> PAG
```

Figure 14-3   Using QMF to construct and issue INSERT, UPDATE, and DELETE statements (continued)

Part 11

This time, I entered a
DELETE statement to
delete the row I just added
and updated. After I
keyed in the statement, I
pressed F2.

```
SQL QUERY                                                        LINE 1

DELETE FROM MMADBV.CUST WHERE CUSTNO = '400017'














*** END ***


1=Help      2=Run       3=End       4=Print    5=Chart     6=Draw
7=Backward  8=Forward   9=Form      10=Insert  11=Delete   12=Report
OK, this is an empty SQL QUERY panel.
COMMAND ===>                                        SCROLL ===> PAG
```

Figure 14-3   Using QMF to construct and issue INSERT, UPDATE, and DELETE statements (continued)

for me to enter new values for the table's columns. It also included a starting WHERE clause that I'll complete.

For this query, I only wanted to change a single column. In part 8 of
the figure, I entered a new value for the ADDR column, and I completed the
WHERE clause to refer to the row I just added to the table. Before I ran the
query, I also had to delete the lines that refer to columns I didn't want to
update. To delete each line, I positioned the cursor on it and pressed F11. If
I hadn't deleted these lines before running the query, I would have received
a message indicating that the statement had a syntax error.

Part 9 shows how the query looked after I deleted the unnecessary
lines. From here, I pressed F2 to run the query. Again, QMF displayed the
Run Confirmation panel, and I verified that the statement should be processed. When QMF completed the processing, it redisplayed the SQL Query
panel with a message that confirmed the update. You can see this message
in part 10.

Next, I entered the RESET QUERY command again to start another
new query. This time, I wanted to issue a DELETE statement to drop the
row I just added and modified. Because DRAW doesn't include an option to
build a DELETE statement, I had to enter it myself. In part 11, you can see

the DELETE statement I entered. To run this query, I pressed F2. At that point, QMF again displayed its Run Confirmation panel. I confirmed the delete, and in a moment, the CUST table was back to the same condition it was in before I issued the INSERT statement in part 3.

Query By Example (QBE) and Prompted Queries

SQL queries are the most direct way to use QMF. However, they're not the *only* way. Two other ways to prepare a QMF query are with its *Query By Example* (*QBE*) and its *Prompted SQL* features. Since you already know SQL, you probably won't need to use these features. But if you ever do, the material in this section is enough to get you started. Before you use either of these features, though, you need to change the QMF profile to indicate the kind of query you want to use.

How to change your QMF profile to select the kind of query you want to use   QMF's default language is SQL. If you want to work with QBE or Prompted SQL, you have to change your QMF profile to request it. You can change your profile in two ways. One way is to issue a QMF SET command. The other way, and the technique I'll illustrate, is to use the Profile panel. Figure 14-4 shows the Profile panel. To access it, press F11 from the QMF Home panel.

To specify the kind of query you want to use, you change the value for the fourth item on the Profile panel, LANGUAGE. As you can see, the acceptable options are SQL, QBE, and PROMPTED. In figure 14-4, I changed SQL to QBE. After you change the LANGUAGE value, you can press Enter to use it for the current session. Or, if you want to change your profile so the new value will remain in effect for subsequent sessions, press F2 to save the profile.

After you've set the QMF language, you need to issue the command

    RESET QUERY

to remove the current query from temporary storage. If you don't issue the RESET command, the language in use for the query currently in temporary storage remains in effect. As you can see, I entered this command in the command line in figure 14-4.

How to issue QBE queries   After you've set your language preference to QBE and reset the query in temporary storage, you'll see the QBE Query panel in part 1 of figure 14-5. It looks much like the SQL Query panel. To start a QBE query, you use the DRAW command. In the command line in

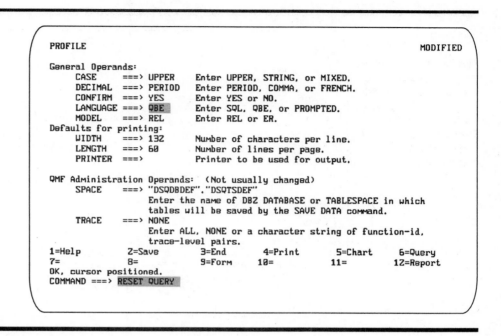

```
PROFILE                                                             MODIFIED

General Operands:
      CASE      ===> UPPER     Enter UPPER, STRING, or MIXED.
      DECIMAL   ===> PERIOD    Enter PERIOD, COMMA, or FRENCH.
      CONFIRM   ===> YES       Enter YES or NO.
      LANGUAGE  ===> QBE       Enter SQL, QBE, or PROMPTED.
      MODEL     ===> REL       Enter REL or ER.
Defaults for printing:
      WIDTH     ===> 132       Number of characters per line.
      LENGTH    ===> 60        Number of lines per page.
      PRINTER   ===>           Printer to be used for output.

QMF Administration Operands:  (Not usually changed)
      SPACE     ===> "DSQDBDEF"."DSQTSDEF"
                          Enter the name of DB2 DATABASE or TABLESPACE in which
                          tables will be saved by the SAVE DATA command.
      TRACE     ===> NONE
                          Enter ALL, NONE or a character string of function-id,
                          trace-level pairs.
1=Help           2=Save         3=End        4=Print      5=Chart     6=Query
7=               8=             9=Form       10=          11=         12=Report
OK, cursor positioned.
COMMAND ===> RESET QUERY
```

Figure 14-4   The QMF Profile panel

the screen in part 1 of figure 14-5, I entered a DRAW command for the customer table.

Part 2 of figure 14-5 shows the result of the DRAW command. As you can see, this screen looks quite different from the screen you see when you construct an SQL query. The array on this panel is called an *example* or a *framework*. It displays the name of the table you're accessing in the first column (here, MMADBV.CUST), followed by the names of all the table's columns. Notice that the CITY, STATE, and ZIPCODE columns don't fit on this screen. If you need to, you can use F10 and F11 to scroll left and right to view an entire framework.

The size of the columns that appear in a QBE framework are based on the lengths of the corresponding columns in the table. For the framework in part 2 of figure 14-5, I enlarged the CUSTNO column because I'll need more space in it for the query I'm going to construct. Here, I enlarged the column by ten spaces, the QMF default.

To enlarge a column, you position the cursor in the data area beneath the column name and press F4. Notice that QMF confirmed the operation with a message at the bottom of the screen in part 2. You can also reduce the size of a column by pressing F5. When you use F4 or F5, be sure the

Part 1

After I set my QMF profile
so it specifies QBE as the
language and after I reset
the query, QMF displayed
the QBE query panel.
Then, I entered the DRAW
command for the
customer table.

```
QBE QUERY                                                    LINE 1

***  END  ***














1=Help        2=Run        3=End        4=Enlarge    5=Reduce     6=Draw
7=Backward    8=Forward    9=Form      10=Left      11=Right     12=Report
OK, QUERY is displayed.
COMMAND ===> DRAW MMADBV.CUST                        SCROLL ===> PAG
```

Part 2

In response to the DRAW
command, QMF created a
framework for the CUST
table. Then, I used the
enlarge function (F4) to
widen the area for
CUSTNO.

```
QBE QUERY                                        MODIFIED    LINE 1

MMADBV.CUST | CUSTNO         | FNAME         | LNAME         | ADDR
------------+----------------+---------------+---------------+--------
            |                |               |               |
***  END  ***











1=Help        2=Run        3=End        4=Enlarge    5=Reduce     6=Draw
7=Backward    8=Forward    9=Form      10=Left      11=Right     12=Report
OK, the example table was enlarged.
COMMAND ===>                                         SCROLL ===> PAG
```

Figure 14-5   Using QMF to construct and issue a simple QBE query

Part 3

I entered the P. operator to
request all of the columns
in the customer table.
And, to specify a selection
condition, I entered a
comparison value for the
CUSTNO column. Then, I
pressed F2 to run the
query.

```
QBE QUERY                                            MODIFIED    LINE 1

MMADBV.CUST | CUSTNO          | FNAME         | LNAME         | ADDR
------------+-----------------+---------------+---------------+---------------
P.          | '400005'        |               |               |

**** END ****








1=Help        2=Run          3=End       4=Enlarge    5=Reduce     6=Draw
7=Backward    8=Forward      9=Form      10=Left      11=Right     12=Report
OK, the example table was enlarged.
COMMAND ===>                                              SCROLL ===> PAG
```

Part 4

QMF displayed the report
it generated.

```
REPORT                                     LINE 1     POS 1    79


    CUSTNO  FNAME                LNAME                        ADDR
    ------  -------------------- ---------------------------- ----------------
    400005  ELAINE               ROBERTS                      12914 BRACKNELL

    **** END ****








1=Help        2=            3=End       4=Print      5=Chart      6=Query
7=Backward    8=Forward     9=Form      10=Left      11=Right     12=
OK, this is the REPORT from your RUN command.
COMMAND ===>                                              SCROLL ===> PAGE
```

Figure 14-5   Using QMF to construct and issue a simple QBE query (continued)

cursor is positioned properly. These operations have different effects when the cursor is located in different positions.

To define a QBE query, you enter QBE *operators* in the data areas beneath the table and column names. The operators let you request specific columns for a report and supply selection conditions. I'll present the basic QBE operators in a moment.

The simplest way to issue a QBE query is to enter the P. operator in the first column (P. stands for "Present"), as I did in part 3 of figure 14-5. That directs QMF to present all the columns that make up the table. In effect, it's the same as entering the SQL statement

```
SELECT *       FROM MMADBV.CUST
```

So, if I simply entered the P. operator in that column and pressed F2 to run the query, QMF would return all the columns from all the rows in the table.

However, I wanted to retrieve the row for a specific customer. So, I entered the customer number as a comparison value in the data area for the CUSTNO column. This is the QMF equivalent of coding

```
WHERE CUSTNO = '400005'
```

on a SELECT statement. Note that because the customer number column's data type is CHAR, I had to enclose the comparison value in quotes. That's why it was necessary for me to enlarge the column.

To run the query in part 3, I pressed F2. The result of this query is presented in part 4. It's just what you'd expect: all the columns from the row for customer 400005.

The selection condition in this figure is a simple equality condition. When you use that kind of condition, all you need to do is enter the comparison value. If you want to specify other conditions, you can use operators like < and >, and you can combine conditions with NOT, AND, and OR. You can also use keywords you learned in standard SQL: BETWEEN, IN, LIKE, and NULL.

In fact, you can use the same range of SELECT options with QBE that you can use with standard SQL. Figure 14-6 presents the basic QBE operators. As you can see, you can specify operators that achieve the same results as SQL's DISTINCT, ORDER BY, GROUP BY, and column function features. You can even specify operators to insert, update, and delete table rows. Note that if you code multiple operators in a single column, you must separate them by one or more spaces. You'll see an example of that in a moment.

You can also do queries that involve multiple tables with QBE. Figure 14-7 shows two queries, one in standard SQL, the other in QBE, that join

P.	Present this column in the results table.
ALL.	Present all duplicate rows that are selected.
UNQ.	Present only one distinct instance of a duplicate row.
AO. or AO(n).	Sort the rows into ascending order by this column.
DO. or DO(n).	Sort the rows into descending order by this column.
SUM.	Apply the SUM function to this column.
AVG.	Apply the AVG function to this column.
MAX.	Apply the MAX function to this column.
COUNT.	Apply the COUNT function to this column.
G.	Apply the GROUP BY operation based on this column.
I.	Insert this row in the table.
U.	Update this row in the table.
D.	Delete this row from the table.

Figure 14-6   Basic QBE operators

data from the customer and invoice tables. Part 1 of the figure shows the SQL statement. Notice that the columns that will be returned in the results table are all from the customer table. However, they're selected based on the presence of related rows in the invoice table for invoices with product totals greater than $150. Also, the statement uses an ORDER BY clause to direct DB2 to sort the results table by the contents of the last name column.

The QBE equivalent of this statement is in part 2 of the figure. Notice in this example that I used two frameworks, one for each table involved in the operation. To get the second framework, I issued the DRAW command a second time, just as I did for the SQL SELECT example in figure 14-2. Then, I entered the P. operator in the columns from the customer table I wanted to retrieve (CUSTNO, FNAME, and LNAME).

For the LNAME column, I also coded the AO. operator. It directs QMF to sort the results table into ascending order based on the contents of this column. To sort a results table into descending sequence, you can specify DO. And, if you want to use two or more sort keys, you can specify the priority of each by coding a number in parentheses immediately after the AO. or DO. operator. For example, AO(1). specifies that the associated column is the primary sort column and that it should be put into ascending order.

Part 1

I entered an SQL query to
retrieve the names and
numbers of customers
who have made
purchases where the
product total was greater
than $150.

```
SQL QUERY                                          MODIFIED    LINE 1

SELECT DISTINCT CUSTNO, FNAME, LNAME
    FROM MMADBU.CUST, MMADBU.INV
        WHERE INVCUST = CUSTNO AND
              INVSUBT > 150
ORDER BY LNAME




*** END ***

1=Help        2=Run        3=End        4=Print     5=Chart       6=Draw
7=Backward    8=Forward    9=Form       10=Insert   11=Delete    12=Report
OK, QUERY is displayed.
COMMAND ===>                                            SCROLL ===> PAG
```

Part 2

I accessed the QBE Query
panel and issued the
DRAW command for the
customer and invoice
tables. Then, I entered
the specifications for the
join query. To run the
query, I pressed F2.

```
QBE QUERY                                          MODIFIED    LINE 1
MMADBU.CUST | CUSTNO | FNAME          | LNAME       | ADDR           |
------------+--------+----------------+-------------+----------------+---
            | P. _NO | P.             | P. AO.      |                |
MMADBU.INV  | INVCUST | INVNO | INVDATE | INVSUBT   |INVSHIP   | INVT
------------+--------+-------+---------+-----------+----------+-------
            | _NO    |       |         | > 150     |          |
*** END ***




1=Help        2=Run        3=End        4=Enlarge   5=Reduce      6=Draw
7=Backward    8=Forward    9=Form       10=Left     11=Right     12=Report
OK, QUERY is displayed.
COMMAND ===>                                            SCROLL ===> PAG
```

Figure 14-7   An SQL query compared to a QBE query

Part 3

QMF displayed the result of the query. This report contains the same data as the one produced as a result of the SQL query in part 1.

```
 REPORT                                           LINE 1      POS 1      79


   CUSTNO  FNAME                        LNAME
   ------  ----------------------       ----------------------------
   400002  ARREN                        ANELLI
   400014  R                            BINDER
   400004  CAROL ANN                    EVANS
   400011  WILLIAM C                    FERGUSON
   400015  VIVIAN                       GEORGE
   400012  S D                          HOEHN
   400003  SUSAN                        HOWARD
   400013  DAVID R                      KEITH
   400001  KEITH                        MCDONALD


   *** END ***


   1=Help       2=          3=End       4=Print     5=Chart      6=Query
   7=Backward   8=Forward   9=Form      10=Left     11=Right     12=
   OK, this is the REPORT from your RUN command.
   COMMAND ===>                                         SCROLL ===> PAGE
```

Figure 14-7   An SQL query compared to a QBE query (continued)

To select rows from the invoice table with product totals greater than $150, I coded

> 150

in the INVSUBT column. In this case, the comparison value is numeric. As a result, it wasn't necessary to enclose it in quotes.

The last thing I did before running the query was to specify the join condition. To do that, I assigned a QBE label to the INVCUST column:

_NO

(A QBE label starts with an underscore and can have up to 18 characters, including the underscore.) Then, I coded that label in the CUSTNO area after the P. operator. That means that QMF should present the requested data in a customer table row only when the value of CUSTNO is the same as the value of INVCUST.

Part 3 of the figure shows the result the queries in parts 1 and 2 both generate. As you can see, the three columns I requested are presented, and they're in sequence by the contents of the last name column.

If I had wanted to retrieve data from both the customer and invoice tables, this example would have been more complicated. That's because the data QMF presents in a results table can include columns from only *one* framework. So if the results table will require data from two tables, you have to add new columns to one of the frameworks and specify that their contents should be drawn from the other table. You can see examples of this technique in the QMF manuals.

How to issue Prompted SQL queries   The third way you can issue QMF queries is through its Prompted SQL feature. As far as I'm concerned, this is the least practical of the three languages you can use for QMF queries. That's because it steps you through a long series of panels to get the information necessary to construct a query. If you know how to draft your own SQL queries, there's no reason to use Prompted SQL.

Just to give you a feel for how it works, though, take a look at the two sample panels in figure 14-8. In part 1, QMF starts to construct a prompted query by asking you the names of the tables you want to access. Here, I keyed in the names of the two tables I used in the join example in figure 14-7.

Because I specified two tables, QMF assumed that I wanted to do a join operation. As a result, the next thing it did was to ask me to identify the join columns. You can see that panel in part 2 of the figure. From this point, QMF presented a number of additional prompts. First, it asked for the names of the columns I wanted to retrieve. Then, it asked for the selection conditions for the query. In all, I had to reply to 13 separate panels to build a SELECT statement equivalent to the one in part 1 of figure 14-7.

Discussion

Both QBE and Prompted SQL are designed to let users who aren't familiar with SQL create and use SQL. Although these two approaches don't require the user to enter SQL statements directly, they still demand that the user understand the stored data. Because you're already comfortable with SQL, chances are you'll find both of these alternative approaches inefficient, slow, and frustrating. I do. But, if one of these approaches *does* appeal to you, you should certainly use it.

Terms

Query By Example   example
QBE   framework
Prompted SQL   operator

Part 1

QMF's Promopted Query
panel uses a series of
dialog boxes to ask you
what values to use for a
query. Here, the dialog
box asks what table(s) the
statement I'm building will
access.

```
PROMPTED QUERY                                         LINE    1
    Tables:           +---------------------------------------------+
    > ...             |                   Tables                    |
                      |                                             |
    *** END ***       | Type one or more table names.               |
                      |                                  1_ to 7 of 15|
                      | ( MMADBU.CUST                              ) |
                      | ( MMADBU.INU                              ) |
                      | (                                         ) |
                      | (                                         ) |
                      | (                                         ) |
                      | (                                         ) |
                      | (                                         ) |
                      +---------------------------------------------+
                      | F1=Help  F4=List  F7=Backward  F8=Forward  F12=Cancel |
                      +---------------------------------------------+



    OK, this is an empty PROMPTED QUERY panel.
```

Part 2

Based on the table names
I supplied on the panel in
part 1, QMF assumed I
wanted to do a join, so it
displayed another dialog
box to determine the join
columns. The lists of
eligible columns it displays
are based on information
from the DB2 catalog.

```
PROMPTED QUERY                              MODIFIED  LINE    1
    Tables:       +-----------------------------------------------+
     MMADB        |                   Tables                      |
     MMADB  +-----------------------------------------------------+
            |               Join Columns                          |
    Join Ta |                                                     |
    > ...   | Select a column from each table.  Rows that have equal |
            | values in those columns will be joined.             |
    Columns | MMADBU.CUST                 MMADBU.INU               |
    ALL     |                                         1 to 8 of 8 |
            | _ 1. CUSTNO                 _ 1. INUCUST             |
    *** END | _ 2. FNAME                    2. INUNO               |
            |   3. LNAME                    3. INUDATE             |
            |   4. ADDR                     4. INUSUBT             |
            |   5. CITY                     5. INUSHIP             |
            |   6. STATE                    6. INUTAX              |
            |   7. ZIPCODE                  7. INUTOTAL            |
            |                               8. INUPROM             |
            +-----------------------------------------------------+
            | F1=Help  F7=Backward  F8=Forward  F12=Cancel        |
            +-----------------------------------------------------+
    OK, ENTER performed. Please proceed.
```

Figure 14-8   The first two panels from a Prompted SQL query

Objectives

1. Use the DRAW command to construct starting formats for queries that will use SELECT, INSERT, and UPDATE statements.

2. Change your QMF profile so you can use QBE or Prompted SQL queries.

3. Formulate and issue a simple QBE query.

Chapter 15

How to create reports with QMF

When I introduced QMF in chapter 13, I showed you a simple query, then I adjusted the default form QMF used to display its results. In this chapter, you'll learn more about working with forms. First, I'll expand on what I presented in chapter 13 by covering all the edit codes QMF supports. Then, I'll describe the concept of report levels and show you how to work with them in QMF.

I think you'll find numerous ways to apply QMF's reporting features as you examine tables you use during program testing. However, these features may be even more useful if you use QMF to develop applications for end users. Although you won't have the same control over report formats with QMF as you do with COBOL, the features QMF provides are sufficient for many purposes. Whether you use QMF's reporting features for program testing or for developing end-user applications, remember that you can print the reports QMF generates from the Report panel by pressing F4.

QMF edit codes

When QMF generates a default form for a query, it uses the data types and lengths of the columns in the query's results table to determine the formats of the columns in the report. Often, the options QMF selects for report columns are acceptable, especially if you're doing basic program testing and the appearance of the report isn't critical. However, you may sometimes want to adjust the options in the default form, as I did in the example in chapter 13.

The form options I think you're most likely to change all relate to columns: title, length, and edit code. The first two are easy to understand; you saw examples of adjustments to column headings and lengths in chapter 13, and I'll show you more examples in this chapter. The third option, edit code, is more complicated. That's because QMF offers a number of different values that control the way data is edited before it's presented in a report. Figure 15-1 shows the QMF edit code values for character, numeric, and date, time, and timestamp columns. To use one of these codes, you simply enter it in the EDIT column on the QMF FORM.MAIN panel (or, as you'll see in a moment, on the FORM.COLUMNS panel).

Edit codes for character data

The QMF default edit code for character data is C. C directs QMF to truncate data on the right if it's too long to fit in a report column. Remember, QMF sets starting report column widths based on the length of the data in corresponding results table columns. So, character data won't be truncated if you use the default form. However, if you reduce the width of a character column, the data it contains may be truncated in the report if you keep the C edit code. (Notice I said the data "in the report" is truncated; the data in the results table QMF uses to create the report isn't affected.)

If you don't want QMF to truncate character data, you can specify one of the three other character edit codes in the figure. They all cause QMF to wrap long character strings to following lines of the report. However, each causes QMF to split strings at different points as it wraps them from one line to the next. CW directs QMF to split a string at the end of the column, even if it's in the middle of a word. In contrast, CT directs QMF to split a string only at a space. And CD*x* lets you specify the character where QMF should split a string. For example, if a string is formatted so a slash separates data elements, you might want to specify CD/ as the edit code.

Edit codes for character data

C	Truncate on the right
CW	Wrap to the next line at the end of the column, regardless of where the text string naturally breaks
CT	Wrap to the next line with the split at the last space in the line
CDx	Wrap to the next line with the split at an occurrence of the character x

Edit codes for numeric data
(n specifies the number of decimal positions to show)

Ln	Format without leading zeros and commas, but with a negative sign (-98765.43 for L2)
Dn	Format without leading zeros, but with commas, a negative sign, and a dollar sign (-$98,765.43 for D2)
In	Format with leading zeros and a negative sign, but no commas (-00098765.43 for I2)
Kn	Format without leading zeros, but with a negative sign and commas (-98,765.43 for K2)
Jn	Format with leading zeros, but no negative sign or commas (00098765.43 for J2)
Pn	Format without leading zeros, but with commas, a negative sign, and a percent sign (-98.76% for P2)
E	Format with a negative sign in exponential notation (-9.876543E4)

Edit codes for date, time, and timestamp data
(x specifies the separation character)

TDYx	Date in the format YYYYxMMxDD
TDMx	Date in the format MMxDDxYYYY
TDDx	Date in the format DDxMMxYYYY
TDYAx	Date in the format YYxMMxDD
TDMAx	Date in the format MMxDDxYY
TDDAx	Date in the format DDxMMxYY
TDL	Date in a format defined locally
TTSx	Time in the format HHxMMxSS (24-hour clock)
TTCx	Time in the format HHxMMxSS (12-hour clock)
TTAx	Time in the format HHxMM
TTAN	Time in the format HHMM
TTUx	Time in the format HHxMM {AM|PM}
TTL	Time in a format defined locally
TSI	Timestamp in the format YYYY-MM-DD-HH.MM.SS.NNNNNN

Figure 15-1   QMF edit code options for different data types

Edit codes for numeric data

For numeric data, QMF uses L*n* as its default edit code. This code specifies that a numeric value should be displayed without leading zeros and commas, but with a minus sign if the number is negative. The *n* component of this code, and the other codes for numeric data, indicates the number of decimal positions QMF should display. The default is the number of decimal positions in the results table column. If you specify an edit code that allows fewer decimal places than the data a results table column contains, QMF rounds the number. If the edit code you specify allows more decimal places, QMF adds trailing zeros to the number.

The rest of the edit codes for numeric data provide various combinations of options. The only code you're not likely to use is E for exponential notation. In a moment, I'll show you an example of how to use the D*n* code to direct DB2 to display numeric data as financial information.

Edit codes for date, time, and timestamp data

For date, time, and timestamp data, you can use the edit codes in the bottom third of figure 15-1. These codes let you change the format of date data in two ways. First, you can change the sequence of the components that make up the date. Second, you can change the character QMF uses to separate the components. The default code is TDY-, which produces this date format: YYYY-MM-DD. You can also specify a separator character for most of the time formats. TTS. is the default code, which produces this time format: HH.MM.SS. Here, HH represents the hour on a 24-hour clock. The only edit code for timestamp data, TSI., produces this format: YYYY-MM-DD-HH.MM.SS.NNNNNN.

A sample report that illustrates different edit codes

Figure 15-2 illustrates the effects of some of the edit codes. It's a variation of the QMF session I presented in chapter 13. Parts 1, 2, and 3 of the figure show the query I issued, the report it produced, and the default form QMF based the report on.

In the example in chapter 13, you'll remember that, to make adjustments to the columns in the form, I began by entering the changes for the first five columns. Then, I scrolled to the next screen of the FORM.MAIN panel to change the last three columns. In this example, I'll show you how to display more report columns on a single screen so you don't have to scroll as often. To do that, you press PF4 from the FORM.MAIN panel to display QMF's Show Command Prompt panel. Part 4 of the figure illustrates this panel.

Part 1

I retrieved a query I
entered during a previous
session.

```
SQL QUERY          MMA002.ICJOINQ                          LINE 1

SELECT INVNO, INVDATE, INVTOTAL, CUSTNO, FNAME, LNAME, CITY, STATE
    FROM MMADBV.INV, MMADBV.CUST
        WHERE INVCUST = CUSTNO
        AND INVTOTAL > 200
ORDER BY INVNO






*** END ***


1=Help      2=Run      3=End       4=Print    5=Chart     6=Draw
7=Backward  8=Forward  9=Form      10=Insert  11=Delete   12=Report
OK, ICJOINQ is displayed.
COMMAND ===>                                      SCROLL ===> PAGE
```

Part 2

After I ran the query, QMF
displayed this report
based on the default form.

```
REPORT                                LINE 1      POS 1    79


  INVNO    INVDATE      INVTOTAL  CUSTNO  FNAME              LNAME
  -----    -------      --------  ------  -----              -----
  062308   1990-12-22     204.45  400012  S D                HOEHN
  062317   1991-03-17     298.00  400011  WILLIAM C          FERGUSON
  062320   1991-03-17    3405.00  400015  VIVIAN             GEORGE
  062321   1991-04-03     219.60  400001  KEITH              MCDONALD
  062323   1991-04-11     949.00  400011  WILLIAM C          FERGUSON
  062327   1991-04-23     221.50  400003  SUSAN              HOWARD
  062330   1991-04-30    2309.00  400011  WILLIAM C          FERGUSON

*** END ***



1=Help      2=         3=End       4=Print    5=Chart     6=Query
7=Backward  8=Forward  9=Form      10=Left    11=Right    12=
OK, this is the REPORT from your RUN command.
COMMAND ===>                                      SCROLL ===> PAGE
```

Figure 15-2   Modifying the default form for a query

Part 3

After I pressed F9 on the
Report panel in part 2,
QMF displayed the
FORM.MAIN panel.
However, I wanted to view
the form differently, so I
pressed F4.

```
FORM.MAIN

COLUMNS:                    Total Width of Report Columns: 125
   NUM COLUMN HEADING                        USAGE   INDENT WIDTH EDIT   SEQ
   ---  --------------                       ------- ------ ----- ----   ---
     1 INVNO                                            2      6   C       1
     2 INVDATE                                          2     10   TDY-    2
     3 INVTOTAL                                         2     12   L2      3
     4 CUSTNO                                           2      6   C       4
     5 FNAME                                            2     20   C       5

PAGE:      HEADING  ===>
           FOOTING  ===>
FINAL:     TEXT     ===>
BREAK1:    NEW PAGE FOR BREAK? ===> NO
           FOOTING  ===>
BREAK2:    NEW PAGE FOR BREAK? ===> NO
           FOOTING  ===>
OPTIONS: OUTLINE? ===> YES             DEFAULT BREAK TEXT? ===> YES

1=Help      2=Check   3=End       4=Show          5=Chart       6=Query
7=Backward 8=Forward  9=          10=Insert       11=Delete     12=Report
OK, FORM is displayed.
COMMAND ===>                                           SCROLL ===> PAGE
```

Part 4

After I pressed F4 on the
FORM.MAIN panel, QMF
responded by displaying
the Show Command
Prompt panel. On it, I
selected option 8 to view
the FORM.COLUMNS
panel and pressed Enter.

```
                        SHOW Command Prompt

Enter the name or number of the panel to show  ===> 8

        Panel              Description
    1.  PROFile            Current user profile
    2.  PROC               Current procedure
    3.  Query              Current query
    4.  Report             Current report
    5.  Chart              Default chart
    6.  FOrm               Current form
    7.    Form.Main        Basic report formatting
    8.    Form.COlumns     Column attributes
    9.    Form.CAlc        User-defined calculations
   10.    Form.Page        Page heading and footing text
   11.    Form.Detail      Detail text
   12.    Form.Final       Final footing text
   13.    Form.BreakN      BreakN text (where N is 1 to 6)
                             Example: FORM.BREAK2 = F.B2 = 13.2
   14.    Form.Options     Choices about a report's appearance

Please follow the directions on the command prompt panel.
ISPF Command ===>
F1=Help                              F3=End
```

Figure 15-2   Modifying the default form for a query (continued)

Part 5

The FORM.COLUMNS
panel displays all of the
columns in this form.

```
FORM.COLUMNS

                        Total Width of Report Columns: 125
    NUM COLUMN HEADING                          USAGE   INDENT WIDTH EDIT  SEQ
    --- ------------------------------------    ------- ------ ----- ----- ---
     1 INVNO                                              2      6    C     1
     2 INVDATE                                            2     10    TDY-  2
     3 INVTOTAL                                           2     12    LZ    3
     4 CUSTNO                                             2      6    C     4
     5 FNAME                                              2     20    C     5
     6 LNAME                                              2     30    C     6
     7 CITY                                               2     20    C     7
     8 STATE                                              2      5    C     8
        *** END ***



    1=Help      2=Check    3=End         4=Show       5=Chart        6=Query
    7=Backward 8=Forward  9=            10=Insert     11=Delete      12=Report
    OK, FORM.COLUMNS is shown.
    COMMAND ===>                                         SCROLL ===> PAGE
```

Part 6

I changed several of the
attributes of the current
form. Then, I pressed F12
to display the report.

```
FORM.COLUMNS

                        Total Width of Report Columns: 125
    NUM COLUMN HEADING                          USAGE   INDENT WIDTH EDIT  SEQ
    --- ------------------------------------    ------- ------ ----- ----- ---
     1 INV #                                              2      6    C     1
     2 DATE                                               2      8    TDMA- 2
     3 TOTAL                                              2     12    D2    3
     4 CUST #                                             2      6    C     4
     5                                                    2      1    C     6
     6 NAME                                               2     15    C     5
     7 CITY                                               2     10    C     7
     8                                                    2      2    C     8
        *** END ***



    1=Help      2=Check    3=End         4=Show       5=Chart        6=Query
    7=Backward 8=Forward  9=            10=Insert     11=Delete      12=Report
    OK, FORM.COLUMNS is shown.
    COMMAND ===>                                         SCROLL ===> PAGE
```

Figure 15-2   Modifying the default form for a query (continued)

Part 7

QMF responded by
displaying the Report
panel with the new version
of the report.

```
  REPORT                                    LINE 1      POS 1     79


    INV #   DATE            TOTAL  CUST #  NAME                CITY
    ------- --------    ---------- ------  ----------      -   ----------    --
    062308  12-22-90      $204.45  400012  HOEHN           S   RIDDLE        OR
    062317  03-17-91      $298.00  400011  FERGUSON        W   MIAMI         FL
    062320  03-17-91    $3,405.00  400015  GEORGE          V   PHILADELPH    PA
    062321  04-03-91      $219.60  400001  MCDONALD        K   DALLAS        TX
    062323  04-11-91      $949.00  400011  FERGUSON        W   MIAMI         FL
    062327  04-23-91      $221.50  400003  HOWARD          S   REDWOOD CI    CA
    062330  04-30-91    $2,309.00  400011  FERGUSON        W   MIAMI         FL


    ***  END  ***




    1=Help       2=          3=End        4=Print      5=Chart      6=Query
    7=Backward   8=Forward   9=Form      10=Left      11=Right     12=
    OK, REPORT is displayed.
    COMMAND ===>                                       SCROLL ===> PAGE
```

Figure 15-2   Modifying the default form for a query (continued)

The Show Command Prompt panel lists different QMF panels you can
use. As you can see, most of them are related to forms. For now, the one
I'm interested in is FORM.COLUMNS. As a result, I keyed 8 into the data
entry field at the top of the screen and pressed Enter.

Part 5 shows the FORM.COLUMNS panel. It lists all the columns in the
report with the same information as in the FORM.MAIN panel in part 3.
However, the formatting options on the bottom half of the FORM.MAIN
panel have been omitted from this panel. That lets QMF display more report
columns on the screen.

I wanted to change several of the default settings for this report. Part 6
shows the new values I supplied. As with the example in chapter 13, I
changed the headings for most of the columns, I reduced the sizes of some
of the columns, and I reversed the sequence of the first name and last name
columns.

I particularly want you to notice the codes in the EDIT column in part
6. I didn't change the edit codes for any of the character columns, even
though I reduced the widths of some of them. As a result, data may be truncated in some of these rows.

For the invoice date report column, I specified

```
TDMA-
```

as the edit code. If you look back to figure 15-1, you'll see that this code directs QMF to display the date in the format

```
MM-DD-YY
```

The edited date will use the hyphen as a separator character because I specified it as the last character of the edit code. Notice also that I reduced the width of this column; eight characters is sufficient for this format.

For the invoice total report column, I changed the edit code to

```
D2
```

I left the number of decimal places (2) unchanged. However, I specified "D" to direct QMF to present an invoice total value as a dollar amount, with a leading dollar sign and commas as separators. Although this format will require extra characters, I decided not to increase the width of this column. The column is already wide enough for my test data. (If a total value is too long to fit in a column with this edit code, QMF will display asterisks.)

Part 7 of the figure shows the report QMF produced using the form in part 6. Again, this is similar to the example you saw in chapter 13. But, notice the effects of the edit codes: QMF formatted the date and total values according to my specifications and truncated some of the city values.

Working with report levels in QMF

The report in part 7 of figure 15-2 is a simple listing. However, QMF lets you prepare more complex reports that are based on the concept of the *control break*. A control break is a change in a column value from one line of a report to the next that triggers the display of other information.

In this section, I'll describe a feature you can use to specify what happens at a control break: aggregation functions. Then, I'll describe how you can specify when control breaks occur. You accomplish both of these tasks by specifying options in the USAGE column of panels like FORM.MAIN (as in part 3 of figure 15-2) and FORM.COLUMNS (as in part 5 of figure 15-2).

AVERAGE	The average of the values in a column.
SUM	The sum of the values in a column.
MAXIMUM	The maximum value of all the values in a column.
MINIMUM	The minimum value of all the values in a column.
COUNT	The number of rows in a column.
FIRST	The value in the first row of a column.
LAST	The value in the last row of a column.
STDEV	The standard deviation of the values in a column.
PCT	The percentage that each line represents of the total for the column.

Figure 15-3   Basic QMF usage code options for aggregation functions

How to use QMF aggregation functions

Aggregation functions cause QMF to produce summary values in a report when control breaks occur. In this section, I'll present the aggregation functions I think you may want to use. Then, I'll present an example of how one of them works.

Aggregation functions you may want to use   Figure 15-3 presents the usage values you can code for the most useful aggregation functions. For example, if you specify AVERAGE usage for a column, QMF displays an average for that column each time a control break occurs. Some of these functions have parallel SQL column functions (AVERAGE, SUM, MINIMUM, MAXIMUM, and COUNT). However, some are unique to QMF (FIRST, LAST, STDEV, and PCT).

Like SQL column functions, most QMF aggregation functions ignore nulls when they compute their results. And, if all the values to be aggregated are nulls, the function returns NULL as the result. However, FIRST and LAST do *not* ignore nulls.

Most of the functions in figure 15-3 are simple aggregations. They provide some type of summary about the values in a column for a group of rows. However, PCT works differently. It actually replaces the value in each detail line of the report with a calculated percentage. So, while aggregation functions like AVERAGE and STDEV work like SQL column functions, PCT works like an SQL scalar function. QMF supports four other functions that work in this way (CPCT, CSUM, TPCT, and PCPCT). These functions are included as aggregation functions because, like the simple aggregation functions, they cause QMF to produce summary values when a control break occurs. For more information about these functions, refer to the QMF manuals.

A sample report that illustrates an aggregation function   The QMF session in figure 15-4 uses a variation of the form I presented in figure 15-2. Here, I simply added the AVERAGE aggregation function for the invoice total column, as you can see in the FORM.COLUMNS panel in part 1. Because I didn't specify any control breaks, this function will display the average invoice total at the end of the report. In effect, the report has one control break: the end.

When QMF displays the average invoice total at the end of this report, I'd like it to include a label that identifies the average. To specify that label, I pressed F4 to go to the Show Command Prompt panel, presented in part 2. Here, I selected option 12 to display a panel that lets me enter text for the end of the report. You can see that panel, FORM.FINAL, in part 3 of the figure.

In part 3, I added text for two label lines. The lines of text are short so they won't be truncated when they're presented next to the average value on the report. The scale line above the area for entering label lines helped me position the labels. I also changed the default justification for the label lines from right to left.

After I entered the specifications for the labels, I pressed F12. QMF responded by displaying the report in part 4. Notice that the report now ends with the average value the aggregation function computed and the labels I supplied on the FORM.FINAL panel. QMF computed the average based on data in the results table produced by the original query in figure 15-2. I didn't have to reissue the query.

How to produce reports with explicit control breaks

The example in figure 15-4 used an implicit control break: the end of the results table. But you can easily produce reports that use explicit control breaks as well. In this section, I'll show you how to do that.

BREAK usages   To create a report with explicit control breaks, you need to specify the columns that control the breaks. Not surprisingly, they're called *control columns*. When the value of a control column changes, a control break occurs.

To specify a column as a control column, you code the BREAK*n* option as its usage on either the FORM.MAIN or FORM.COLUMNS panel.

Part 1

I added the AVERAGE usage code to direct QMF to calculate the average invoice amount for this query. Because I wanted to add a text line to accompany the value the AVERAGE function will return, I again pressed F4 to show a different form panel.

```
FORM.COLUMNS                                          MODIFIED

                        Total Width of Report Columns: 76
   NUM COLUMN HEADING                          USAGE    INDENT WIDTH EDIT  SEQ
   --- --------------------------------------- -------  ------ ----- ----  ---
     1 INV #                                            2      6     C     1
     2 DATE                                             2      8     TDMA- 2
     3 TOTAL                                   AVERAGE  2      12    DZ    3
     4 CUST #                                           2      6     C     4
     5                                                  2      1     C     6
     6 NAME                                             2      15    C     5
     7 CITY                                             2      10    C     7
     8                                                  2      2     C     8
       *** END ***



   1=Help     2=Check    3=End      4=Show        5=Chart        6=Query
   7=Backward 8=Forward  9=         10=Insert     11=Delete      12=Report
   OK, FORM is displayed.
   COMMAND ===>                                          SCROLL ===> PAGE
```

Part 2

I selected option 12 from the Show Command Prompt panel so I could enter the text that will be printed as part of the report's final line(s).

```
                      SHOW Command Prompt

   Enter the name or number of the panel to show  ===> 12

         Panel              Description
   1.    PROFile            Current user profile
   2.    PROC               Current procedure
   3.    Query              Current query
   4.    Report             Current report
   5.    Chart              Default chart
   6.    FOrm               Current form
   7.      Form.Main        Basic report formatting
   8.      Form.COlumns     Column attributes
   9.      Form.CAlc        User-defined calculations
   10.     Form.Page        Page heading and footing text
   11.     Form.Detail      Detail text
   12.     Form.Final       Final footing text
   13.     Form.BreakN      BreakN text (where N is 1 to 6)
                              Example: FORM.BREAK2 = F.B2 = 13.2
   14.     Form.Options     Choices about a report's appearance

   Please follow the directions on the command prompt panel.
   ISPF Command ===>
   F1=Help                              F3=End
```

Figure 15-4   Using an aggregation function

Part 3

I added label text to the
final lines of the report,
and I changed their
alignment so they will be
left justified. Then, I
pressed F12 to recreate
the report from the current
query based on the new
version of the form.

```
FORM.FINAL                                        MODIFIED

New Page for Final Text?   ===> NO      Put Final Summary at Line ===> 1
Blank Lines Before Text    ===> 0
LINE  ALIGN    FINAL TEXT
----  -----    ----+----1----+----2----+----3----+----4----+----5----+
 1    LEFT     AVG. FOR INVOICES
 2    LEFT     OVER $200
 3    RIGHT
 4    RIGHT
 5    RIGHT
 6    RIGHT
 7    RIGHT
 8    RIGHT
 9    RIGHT
10    RIGHT
11    RIGHT
12    RIGHT
13    RIGHT
                 *** END ***
1=Help      2=Check   3=End        4=Show        5=Chart       6=Query
7=Backward 8=Forward 9=            10=Insert     11=Delete     12=Report
OK, cursor positioned.
COMMAND ===>                                         SCROLL ===> PAGE
```

Part 4

QMF responded by
displaying the Report
panel with the new version
of the report.

```
REPORT                                   LINE 1      POS 1      79

  INV #  DATE          TOTAL  CUST # NAME          CITY
  -----  --------   --------- ------ -----------  - ----------  --
  062308 12-22-90    $204.45  400012 HOEHN        S RIDDLE      OR
  062317 03-17-91    $298.00  400011 FERGUSON     W MIAMI       FL
  062320 03-17-91  $3,405.00  400015 GEORGE       V PHILADELPH  PA
  062321 04-03-91    $219.60  400001 MCDONALD     K DALLAS      TX
  062323 04-11-91    $949.00  400011 FERGUSON     W MIAMI       FL
  062327 04-23-91    $221.50  400003 HOWARD       S REDWOOD CI  CA
  062330 04-30-91  $2,309.00  400011 FERGUSON     W MIAMI       FL
                  ============
  AVG. FOR INVOICES  $1,086.65
  OVER $200

  *** END ***

1=Help      2=         3=End      4=Print      5=Chart      6=Query
7=Backward  8=Forward  9=Form     10=Left      11=Right     12=
OK, REPORT is displayed.
COMMAND ===>                                        SCROLL ===> PAGE
```

Figure 15-4   Using an aggregation function (continued)

Although you can specify up to six levels of control columns, in practice, you'll probably never use more than two. To specify multiple control columns, you code BREAK1 for the highest level, BREAK2 for the second level, down to BREAK6 for the sixth and lowest level.

For control breaks to be meaningful, the results table the report is based on must be sorted. That means that you need to specify the ORDER BY clause on the query that produces it. Then, the columns you name on ORDER BY correspond to those you identify with the BREAK*n* usages. The results table column with BREAK1 usage should be the first column you name on the ORDER BY clause, the one with BREAK2 usage should be second, and so on.

When you want a report to present summary data at control breaks, you code one or more of the aggregation functions I presented in figure 15-3. The values QMF uses to compute a summary are those that follow the previous control break at the same level. This will make more sense in a moment when I show you an example. You can also produce reports that contain *only* summary information. To do that, you can use two other usage options: GROUP and ACROSS. For more information about these options, refer to the QMF manuals.

A sample report that illustrates an explicit control break   Figure 15-5 shows another QMF session that uses data returned from a join of the customer and invoice tables. For this query, I want to list invoices grouped by customer. The report will contain one line for each invoice and a subtotal for all invoices associated with each customer. The report will also contain a grand total for all invoices issued.

To prepare this report, I'll specify the customer number column as a BREAK column. Then, when its value changes, QMF will produce subtotals. To prepare this report, I made two changes to the query I issued in figure 15-2. First, I removed the selection condition for invoices with totals greater than 200 so the report will be longer than a single screen. I also had to make sure the results table QMF uses is in the right sequence. Notice in part 1 of the figure that I specified

```
ORDER BY CUSTNO, INVNO
```

to direct DB2 to sort the results table into invoice number sequence within customer sequence.

Part 2 of the figure shows the form I used for the report. This form is similar to the forms I used in figures 15-2 and 15-4. However, instead of using the AVERAGE aggregation function, as I did in figure 15-4, I specified SUM for the invoice total column. I also specified BREAK1 to trigger a control break when the value of the customer number changes.

Part 1

To issue a query for a report that uses control breaks, I changed the ORDER BY clause of SELECT so it will return a results table in sequence by invoice number within customer number.

```
SQL QUERY          MMA00Z.ICJOINQ                  MODIFIED    LINE 1

SELECT INVNO, INVDATE, INVTOTAL, CUSTNO, FNAME, LNAME, CITY, STATE
     FROM MMADBV.INV, MMADBV.CUST
         WHERE INVCUST = CUSTNO
ORDER BY CUSTNO, INVNO




        ***  END  ***


1=Help        Z=Run        3=End         4=Print     5=Chart      6=Draw
7=Backward    8=Forward    9=Form        10=Insert   11=Delete    1Z=Report
OK, QUERY is displayed.
COMMAND ===>                                         SCROLL ===> PAGE
```

Part 2

I adjusted the form so the customer number is the control column for the control break. Also, I specified the SUM aggregation function for the invoice total column. Then, to add descriptive text to the subtotal lines that will print at a control break, I pressed F4 to access the Show Command Prompt panel.

```
FORM.COLUMNS       MMA00Z.ICJOINF

                    Total Width of Report Columns: 76
NUM COLUMN HEADING                            USAGE  INDENT WIDTH EDIT  SEQ
--- ------------------------------------     ------- ------ ----- ----- ---
 1  INV #                                              Z      6    C     1
 Z  DATE                                               Z      8    TDMA- Z
 3  TOTAL                                      SUM     Z     1Z    DZ    3
 4  CUST #                                     BREAK1  Z      6    C     4
 5                                                     Z      1    C     6
 6  NAME                                               Z     15    C     5
 7  CITY                                               Z     1Ø    C     7
 8                                                     Z      Z    C     8
        ***  END  ***


1=Help       Z=Check    3=End       4=Show        5=Chart      6=Query
7=Backward 8=Forward  9=          10=Insert     11=Delete    1Z=Report
OK, FORM.COLUMNS is shown.
COMMAND ===>                                     SCROLL ===> PAGE
```

Figure 15-5   Creating a QMF report that uses a control break

Part 3

From the Show Command
Prompt panel, I requested
the FORM.BREAK1 panel
by entering 13.1.

```
                            SHOW Command Prompt

        Enter the name or number of the panel to show  ===> 13.1

              Panel                  Description
        1.    PROFile                Current user profile
        2.    PROC                   Current procedure
        3.    Query                  Current query
        4.    Report                 Current report
        5.    Chart                  Default chart
        6.    FOrm                   Current form
        7.    Form.Main              Basic report formatting
        8.    Form.COlumns           Column attributes
        9.    Form.CAlc              User-defined calculations
        10.   Form.Page              Page heading and footing text
        11.   Form.Detail            Detail text
        12.   Form.Final             Final footing text
        13.   Form.BreakN            BreakN text (where N is 1 to 6)
                                       Example: FORM.BREAK2 = F.B2 = 13.2
        14.   Form.Options           Choices about a report's appearance


        Please follow the directions on the command prompt panel.
        ISPF Command ===>
        F1=Help                                      F3=End
```

Part 4

On the FORM.BREAK1
panel, I entered the
specification for the
subtotal text: "TOTAL
FOR " followed by the
current contents of
column 4.

```
    FORM.BREAK1        MMA00Z.ICJOINF                    MODIFIED

    New Page for Break?       ===> NO    Repeat Detail Heading?    ===> NO
    Blank Lines Before Heading ===> 0    Blank Lines After Heading ===> 0
    LINE  ALIGN    BREAK 1 HEADING TEXT
    ----  -----    ----+----1----+----2----+----3----+----4----+----5----+
    1     LEFT
    2     LEFT
    3     LEFT
                   *** END ***

    New Page for Footing?     ===> NO    Put Break Summary at Line ===> 1
    Blank Lines Before Footing ===> 0    Blank Lines After Footing ===> 1
    LINE  ALIGN    BREAK 1 FOOTING TEXT
    ----  -----    ----+----1----+----2----+----3----+----4----+----5----+
    1     RIGHT    TOTAL FOR &4
    2     RIGHT
    3     RIGHT
                   *** END ***

    1=Help     2=Check    3=End       4=Show       5=Chart       6=Query
    7=Backward 8=Forward  9=          10=Insert    11=Delete     12=Report
    OK, FORM.BREAK1 is shown.
    COMMAND ===>                                      SCROLL ===> PAGE
```

Figure 15-5   Creating a QMF report that uses a control break (continued)

Part 5

The first page of the report shows the subtotals and the titles I requested. To view the rest of the report, I pressed F8 several times.

```
REPORT                                          LINE 1      POS 1    79


INV #    DATE           TOTAL  CUST #  NAME            CITY
------   --------    ---------  ------  ----------------  -  ------------  --
062321   04-03-91     $219.60  400001  MCDONALD        K  DALLAS        TX

TOTAL FOR 400001      $219.60

062312   02-22-91     $173.07  400002  ANELLI          A  DENVILLE      NJ
062325   04-17-91     $147.50          ANELLI          A  DENVILLE      NJ

TOTAL FOR 400002      $320.57

062314   03-14-91     $149.80  400003  HOWARD          S  REDWOOD CI    CA
062327   04-23-91     $221.50          HOWARD          S  REDWOOD CI    CA

TOTAL FOR 400003      $371.30

1=Help          2=          3=End       4=Print     5=Chart       6=Query
7=Backward      8=Forward   9=Form      10=Left     11=Right      12=
OK, REPORT is displayed.
COMMAND ===>                                       SCROLL ===> PAGE
```

Part 6

The last page of the report shows a grand total.

```
REPORT                                          LINE 51     POS 1    79
 INV #    DATE           TOTAL  CUST #  NAME            CITY
++------++--------++  ---------++------++---------------------++--++------++--+++
 062324   04-14-91     $193.89  400014  BINDER          R  DEPEW         NY

 TOTAL FOR 400014      $403.83

 062319   03-17-91     $181.42  400015  GEORGE          V  PHILADELPH    PA
 062320   03-17-91   $3,405.00          GEORGE          V  PHILADELPH    PA
 062333   05-17-91     $178.23          GEORGE          V  PHILADELPH    PA

 TOTAL FOR 400015    $3,764.65

                     ============
                     $10,421.11

*** END ***

1=Help          2=          3=End       4=Print     5=Chart       6=Query
7=Backward      8=Forward   9=Form      10=Left     11=Right      12=
OK, FORWARD performed. Please proceed.
COMMAND ===>                                       SCROLL ===> PAGE
```

Figure 15-5   Creating a QMF report that uses a control break (continued)

When a control break occurs, I want the subtotal line QMF produces to include a label that identifies the summary information. So, I requested the Show Command Prompt panel by pressing PF4 from the panel in part 2. Then, from the panel in part 3, I requested the FORM.BREAK1 panel. You can select a specific control break by concatenating the break number, in this case, 1, with option 13 from the Show Command Prompt panel. Here, I entered 13.1.

Part 4 of figure 15-5 presents the FORM.BREAK1 panel. Here, I entered

```
TOTAL FOR &4
```

for the footer QMF will print at each control break. This directs QMF to concatenate the literal "TOTAL FOR " with the current contents of report column 4 (the customer number column). From the panel in part 4, I pressed F12 to view the report.

Part 5 shows the first page of the report. Notice the subtotal lines that appear at each control break. To review each screen of the report, I pressed F8 until I reached the end. As you can see in part 6, the SUM aggregation function automatically generated a grand total for invoices as well as customer subtotals.

Discussion

Although I haven't covered all of QMF's reporting features in this section, the simple examples I've presented should give you a good sense for what QMF can do. As I already mentioned, these features can be useful during program testing and for developing end-user applications. End users who are familiar with the underlying data can also use QMF's reporting features to develop their own applications. However, because QMF processing can be costly, many shops restrict its use.

Terms

control break
aggregation function
control column

Objectives

1. Change the edit codes used for columns in a QMF report.

2. Define and use a QMF form that includes an aggregation function.

3. Define and use a QMF form that prepares a report with control breaks.

Appendix A

SQL statements

This appendix presents the syntax for the SQL statements covered in this book and in *Part 1: An Introductory Course*. First, I'll list the SQL statements alphabetically and provide references to the text sections that cover each. Next, I'll show the column specification options that you can use in stand-alone SELECT statements and in the SELECT component of DECLARE CURSOR statements. Then, I'll show the different ways you can code selection conditions in the WHERE clauses of SELECTs and in DELETE and UPDATE statements. After that, I'll show the syntax for specifying unions. And finally, I'll list SQL's column and scalar functions.

SQL statement syntax

ALTER TABLE

```
EXEC SQL
    ALTER TABLE table-name
    (ADD column-name data-type [NOT NULL WITH DEFAULT]  )
    |ADD PRIMARY KEY (pkey-column-name[,pkey-column-name...])|
    {ADD FOREIGN KEY (fkey-column-name[,fkey-column-name...])}
    |    REFERENCES parent-table-name                       |
    |                         (RESTRICT)                    |
    (        ON DELETE {CASCADE }                           )
                       (SET NULL)
END-EXEC.
```

> For more information, refer to figure 10-11 on page 258 of this book and the associated text.

CLOSE

```
EXEC SQL
    CLOSE cursor-name
END-EXEC.
```

> For more information about CLOSE in non-dynamic SQL, refer to figure 3-15 on page 71 of *Part 1: An Introductory Course* and the associated text.
>
> For more information about CLOSE in dynamic SQL, refer to figure 3-19 on page 109 of this book and the associated text.

COMMIT

```
EXEC SQL
    COMMIT [WORK]
END-EXEC.
```

> For more information, refer to figure 4-17 on page 118 of *Part 1: An Introductory Course* and the associated text.

CREATE INDEX

```
EXEC SQL
    CREATE [UNIQUE] INDEX index-name ON table-name
        (column-name[,column name...])
END-EXEC.
```

> For more information, refer to figure 10-9 on page 257 of this book and the associated text.

SQL statement syntax (continued)

CREATE TABLE

To create a table with a structure copied from an existing table

```
EXEC SQL
    CREATE TABLE table-name
        LIKE existing-table
        IN { DATABASE database-name
             [database-name.]tablespace-name }
END-EXEC.
```

To create a table with a structure *not* copied from an existing table

```
EXEC SQL
    CREATE TABLE table-name
        (column-name data-type [{NOT NULL
                                 NOT NULL WITH DEFAULT}]
        [,column-name data-type [{NOT NULL
                                  NOT NULL WITH DEFAULT}] ...]
        [PRIMARY KEY (pkey-column-name[,pkey-column-name...])]
        [ FOREIGN KEY (fkey-column-name[,fkey-column-name...])
             REFERENCES parent-table-name
                        {RESTRICT
             ON DELETE  CASCADE }
                        {SET NULL}
        [,FOREIGN KEY (fkey-column-name[,fkey-column-name...])
             REFERENCES parent-table-name
                        {RESTRICT
             ON DELETE  CASCADE } ] ... ] )
                        {SET NULL}
        IN { DATABASE database-name
             [database-name.]tablespace-name }
END-EXEC.
```

> For more information, refer to figure 10-5 on page 252 of this book and the associated text.

CREATE VIEW

```
EXEC SQL
    CREATE VIEW view-name [column-name,[column-name...]]
        AS subselect
END-EXEC.
```

> For more information, refer to figure 10-15 on page 261 of this book and the associated text.

SQL statement syntax (continued)

DECLARE CURSOR

For use in non-dynamic SQL

```
EXEC SQL
    DECLARE cursor-name CURSOR FOR
        SELECT [DISTINCT] column-specification[,column-specification...]
                FROM   table-name[ synonym][,table-name[ synonym] ...]
                [WHERE selection-condition]
              [{FOR UPDATE OF update-column[,update-column...]    }]
               {ORDER BY sort-column[ DESC][,sort-column[ DESC]...]}
                [GROUP BY column-name[,column-name...]
                [HAVING    selection-condition]]
END-EXEC.
```

For use in dynamic SQL

```
EXEC SQL
    DECLARE cursor-name CURSOR FOR prepared-select-name
END-EXEC.
```

> For more information about DECLARE CURSOR in non-dynamic SQL, refer to figure 3-12 on page 67 of *Part 1: An Introductory Course* and the associated text.
>
> For more information about GROUP BY and HAVING, refer to figure 6-5 in *Part 1: An Introductory Course* and the associated text.
>
> For more information about *column-specification*, refer to the section on column specification options in this appendix.
>
> For more information about *selection-condition*, refer to the section on selection conditions in this appendix.
>
> For more information about unions, refer to the section on the syntax of the UNION keyword in this appendix.
>
> For more information about DECLARE CURSOR in dynamic SQL, refer to figure 3-16 on page 106 of this book and the associated text.
>
> For more information about *prepared-select-name*, refer to the entry for the PREPARE statement in this appendix.

SQL statement syntax (continued)

DELETE

```
EXEC SQL
    DELETE FROM table-name
    [WHERE {selection-condition      } ]
           {CURRENT OF cursor-name   }
END-EXEC.
```

> For more information about DELETE, refer to figure 4-3 on page 92 of *Part 1: An Introductory Course* and the associated text.
>
> For more information about *selection-condition*, refer to the section on selection conditions in this appendix.

DROP

```
EXEC SQL
         {TABLE table-name}
    DROP {INDEX index-name}
         {VIEW view-name  }
END-EXEC.
```

> For more information, refer to figure 10-18 on page 263 of this book and the associated text.

EXECUTE

```
EXEC SQL
    EXECUTE prepared-statement-name
        [USING {:host-var[,:host-var...]} ]
               {DESCRIPTOR sqlda-name    }
END-EXEC.
```

> For more information about EXECUTE, refer to figure 3-11 on page 97 of this book and the associated text.
>
> For more information about *prepared-statement-name*, refer to the entry for the PREPARE statement in this appendix.

SQL statement syntax (continued)

EXECUTE IMMEDIATE

```
EXEC SQL
    EXECUTE IMMEDIATE :host-var
END-EXEC.
```

> For more information, refer to figure 3-4 on page 86 of this book and the associated text.

FETCH

```
EXEC SQL
    FETCH cursor-name
          INTO  {:host-var[,:host-var...]}
                {:host-structure          }
          [USING DESCRIPTOR sqlda-name]
END-EXEC.
```

> For more information about FETCH in non-dynamic SQL, refer to figure 3-14 on page 70 of *Part 1: An Introductory Course* and the associated text.
>
> For more information about FETCH in dynamic SQL, refer to figure 3-18 on page 108 of this book and the associated text.

INCLUDE statement

```
EXEC SQL
    INCLUDE  {member-name}
             {SQLCA      }
END-EXEC.
```

> For more information, refer to figure 2-8 on page 41 of *Part 1: An Introductory Course* and the associated text.

SQL statement syntax (continued)

INSERT

```
EXEC SQL
    INSERT INTO table-name [(column-name[,column-name...])]
        VALUES ( {:host-var}   [,{:host-var      } ]
                 {literal  }    {literal    ...]  )
                 {NULL     }    {NULL             }
        subselect
END-EXEC.
```

> For more information about INSERT, refer to figure 4-9 on page 100 of *Part 1: An Introductory Course* and the associated text.
>
> For information about using a SELECT statement within an INSERT statement to do a mass insert, see chapter 4 and chapter 8 of *Part 1: An Introductory Course*.

LOCK TABLE

```
EXEC SQL
    LOCK TABLE table-name
        IN {SHARE    } MODE
           {EXCLUSIVE}
END-EXEC.
```

> For more information, refer to figure 5-4 on page 143 of this book and the associated text.

SQL statement syntax (continued)

OPEN

```
EXEC SQL
    OPEN cursor-name [USING {:host-var[,:host-var...]}  ]
                            {DESCRIPTOR sqlda-name    }
END-EXEC.
```

> For more information about OPEN for working with a non-dynamic SELECT, refer to figure 3-13 on page 69 of *Part 1: An Introductory Course* and the associated text.
>
> For more information about OPEN for working with a dynamic SELECT, refer to figure 3-17 on page 107 of this book and the associated text.

PREPARE

```
EXEC SQL
    PREPARE prepared-statement-name
        [INTO sqlda-name]
          FROM :host-var
END-EXEC.
```

> For more information, refer to figure 3-9 on page 95 of this book and the associated text.

ROLLBACK

```
EXEC SQL
    ROLLBACK [WORK]
END-EXEC.
```

> For more information, refer to figure 4-18 on page 119 of *Part 1: An Introductory Course* and the associated text.

SQL statement syntax (continued)

SELECT (stand-alone)

```
EXEC SQL
    SELECT          column-specification[,column-specification...]
        INTO        {:host-var[,:host-var...]}
                    {:host-structure         }
        FROM        table-name[ synonym][,table-name[ synonym] ...]
        [WHERE      selection-condition]
END-EXEC.
```

> For more information about stand-alone SELECT, refer to figure 3-1 on page 52 of *Part 1: An Introductory Course* and the associated text.
>
> For information about SELECT options you're not likely to use in stand-alone SELECTs, refer to the entry for DECLARE CURSOR (for non-dynamic SQL) in this appendix.
>
> For more information about *column-specification*, refer to the section on column specification options in this appendix.
>
> For more information about *selection-condition*, refer to the section on selection conditions in this appendix.

UPDATE

```
EXEC SQL
    UPDATE table-name

    SET     column-name={:host-var  }  [,column-name={:host-var  } ...]
                        {literal     }               {literal     }
                        {expression  }               {expression  }
                        {NULL        }               {NULL        }

    [WHERE  {selection-condition  }]
            {CURRENT OF cursor-name}
END-EXEC.
```

> For more information about UPDATE, refer to figure 4-2 on page 91 of *Part 1: An Introductory Course* and the associated text.
>
> For more information about *selection-condition*, refer to the section on selection conditions in this appendix.

SQL statement syntax (continued)

WHENEVER

```
EXEC SQL
    WHENEVER {SQLERROR  } {{GOTO } paragraph-name}
             {SQLWARNING} {{GO TO}                }
             {NOT FOUND } {{ CONTINUE            }}
END-EXEC.
```

For more information, refer to figure 2-5 on page 60 of this book and the associated text.

Column specification options

```
column-name

*

{table-name}
{synonym  }.column-name

{table-name}
{synonym  }.*

:host-var

literal

USER

expression

function
```

> For more information, refer to figure 3-3 on page 54 of *Part 1: An Introductory Course* and the associated text.

WHERE clause selection condition options

With a simple comparison

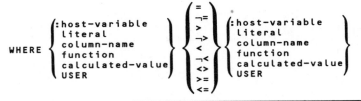

> For more information, refer to figure 3-8 on page 61 of *Part 1: An Introductory Course* and the associated text.

With IN

```
        (:host-variable)              (:host-variable)         (:host-variable)
        | literal     |               | literal     |         | literal     |
WHERE   { column-name }  [NOT] IN (   { column-name }   [,   { column-name }   ...])
        | function    |               | function    |         | function    |
        | calculated-value|           | calculated-value|     | calculated-value|
        (USER         )              (USER         )         (USER         )
```

> For more information, refer to figure 5-2 on page 134 of *Part 1: An Introductory Course* and the associated text.

With BETWEEN

```
        (:host-variable)                  (:host-variable)          (:host-variable)
        | literal     |                   | literal     |          | literal     |
WHERE   { column-name }  [NOT] BETWEEN    { column-name }   AND    { column-name }
        | function    |                   | function    |          | function    |
        | calculated-value|               | calculated-value|      | calculated-value|
        (USER         )                  (USER         )          (USER         )
```

> For more information, refer to figure 5-3 on page 135 of *Part 1: An Introductory Course* and the associated text.

With LIKE

```
                                   (literal        )
WHERE column-name [NOT] LIKE       {:host-variable }
                                   (USER           )
```

> For more information, refer to figure 5-4 on page 136 of *Part 1: An Introductory Course* and the associated text.

WHERE clause selection condition options (continued)

With AND, OR, and NOT

```
WHERE [NOT] selection-condition-1 {AND} [NOT] selection-condition-2 ...
                                   {OR }
```

> For more information, refer to figure 5-6 on page 140 of *Part 1: An Introductory Course* and the associated text.

With subqueries

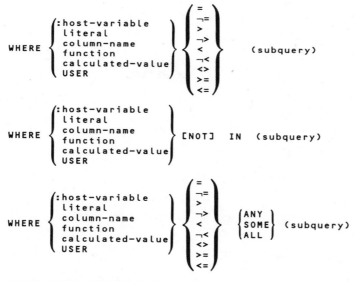

```
WHERE [NOT] EXISTS (subquery)
```

> For more information, refer to figure 8-3 on page 203 of *Part 1: An Introductory Course* and the associated text.

The syntax of the UNION keyword

```
    SELECT-statement
UNION [ALL]
    SELECT-statement

[UNION [ALL]
    SELECT-statement...]

[ORDER BY sort-column[ DESC][,sort-column[ DESC]...]]
```

> For more information, refer to figure 7-5 on page 175 of *Part 1: An Introductory Course* and the associated text.

SQL column functions

```
AVG(numeric-column-name)
SUM(numeric-column-name)
MIN(column-name)
MAX(column-name)
COUNT({*
       DISTINCT column-name})
```

For more information, refer to chapter 6 of *Part 1: An Introductory Course.*

SQL scalar functions

Scalar functions for working with string data

`SUBSTR(expression,start[,length])`

`LENGTH(expression)`

`HEX(expression)`

> For more information, refer to figure 1-6 on page 16 of this book and the associated text.

Scalar functions for working with numeric data

`INTEGER(expression)`

`DIGITS(expression)`

`FLOAT(expression)`

`DECIMAL(expression[,precision[,scale]])`

> For more information, refer to figure 1-11 on page 21 of this book and the associated text.

Scalar function for providing substitute values for nulls

`VALUE(expression,expression[,expression...])`

> For more information, refer to figure 1-14 on page 26 of this book and the associated text.

SQL scalar functions (continued)

Scalar functions for working with date, time, and timestamp data

`CHAR(expression[,format])`

> For more information, refer to figure 1-16 on page 31 of this book and the associated text.

`DAYS(expression)`

> For more information, refer to figure 1-20 on page 34 of this book and the associated text.

`YEAR(expression)`

`MONTH(expression)`

`DAY(expression)`

`HOUR(expression)`

`MINUTE(expression)`

`SECOND(expression)`

`MICROSECOND(timestamp)`

> For more information, refer to figure 1-22 on page 36 of this book and the associated text.

`DATE(expression)`

`TIME(expression)`

`TIMESTAMP(expression1[,expression2])`

> For more information, refer to figure 1-26 on page 40 of this book and the associated text.

Appendix B

SQLCODE values

This appendix lists SQLCODE values you may encounter during routine
program development work. Many other SQLCODE values can appear in
other situations. For other values, refer to the *IBM Database 2 Messages
and Codes* manual.

+100   Row not found for FETCH, UPDATE or DELETE, or the result of a query is an empty table. (Under SPUFI, a successful SELECT returns +100.)

000   Successful execution.

−117   The number of INSERT values is not the same as the number of object columns.

−118   The object table or view of the INSERT, DELETE, or UPDATE statement is also identified in a FROM clause.

−119   A column identified in a HAVING clause is not included in the GROUP BY clause.

−121   The column *name* is identified more than once in the INSERT or UPDATE statement.

−122   A SELECT statement with no GROUP BY clause contains a column name and a SQL function in the SELECT clause or a column name is contained in the SELECT clause but not in the GROUP BY clause.

−125   An integer in the ORDER BY clause does not identify a column of the result.

−126   The SELECT statement contains both an UPDATE clause and an ORDER BY clause.

−127   DISTINCT is specified more than once in a subselect.

−128   Invalid use of NULL in a predicate.

−131   Statement with LIKE predicate has incompatible data types.

−132   A LIKE predicate is invalid because the first operand is not a column or the second operand is not a string.

−133   A SQL function in a HAVING clause is invalid because it applies an arithmetic operator to a correlated reference.

−134   Improper use of long string column *column-name* or a host variable of maximum length greater than 254.

−150   The object of the INSERT, DELETE, or UPDATE statement is a view for which the requested operation is not permitted.

−161   The INSERT or UPDATE is not allowed because a resulting row does not satisfy the view definition.

-198 The operand of the PREPARE or EXECUTE IMMEDIATE statement is blank or empty.

-203 A reference to column *column-name* is ambiguous.

-204 *name* is an undefined name.

-205 *column-name* is not a column of table *table-name*.

-206 *column-name* is not a column of an inserted table, updated table, or any table defined in a FROM clause.

-207 The ORDER BY clause is invalid because it includes a column name, but it applies to the result of a union.

-208 The ORDER BY clause is invalid because column *name* is not part of the results table.

-301 The value of a host variable cannot be used as specified because of its data type.

-302 The value of an input variable is too large for the target column.

-303 A value cannot be assigned to a host variable because the data types are not comparable.

-304 A value cannot be assigned to a host variable because the value is not within the range of the data type of the host variable.

-305 The NULL value cannot be assigned to a host variable because no indicator variable is specified.

-309 A predicate is invalid because a referenced host variable has the NULL value.

-312 Undefined or unusable host variable *variable-name*.

-313 The number of host variables specified is not equal to the number of parameter markers.

-401 The operands of an arithmetic or comparison operation are not comparable.

-402 An arithmetic function or operator *arith-item* is applied to character data.

-404 The UPDATE or INSERT statement specifies a string that is too long *column-name*.

-405 The numeric literal *literal* cannot be used as specified because it is out of range.

-406   A calculated or derived numeric value is not within the range of its
        object column.

-407   An UPDATE or INSERT value, or the value in a predicate is NULL,
        but the object column *column-name* cannot contain NULL values.

-408   An UPDATE or INSERT value is not comparable with the data type
        of its object column *column-name*.

-409   Invalid operand of a COUNT function.

-412   The SELECT clause of a subquery specifies multiple columns.

-414   The numeric column *column-name* is specified in a LIKE predicate.

-415   The corresponding columns, *column-number*, of the operands of a
        UNION do not have identical column descriptions.

-421   The operands of a UNION do not have the same number of columns.

-501   The cursor identified in a FETCH or CLOSE statement is not open.

-502   The cursor identified in an OPEN statement is already open.

-503   A column cannot be updated because it is not specified in the
        UPDATE clause of the SELECT statement of the cursor.

-504   The cursor name *cursor-name* is not defined.

-507   The cursor identified in the UPDATE or DELETE statement is not
        open.

-508   The cursor identified in the UPDATE or DELETE statement is not
        positioned on a row.

-510   The table designated by the cursor of the UPDATE or DELETE
        statement cannot be modified.

-511   The FOR UPDATE clause cannot be specified because the table
        designated by the cursor cannot be modified.

-517   Cursor *cursor-name* cannot be used because its statement name
        does not identify a prepared SELECT statement.

-518   The EXECUTE statement does not identify a valid prepared
        statement.

-519   The PREPARE statement identifies the SELECT statement of the
        opened cursor *cursor-name*.

-551   *auth-id* does not have the privilege to perform the operation
        operation on object *object-name*.

−552   *auth-id* does not have the privilege to perform the operation *operation*.

−802   Arithmetic overflow or division by zero has occurred.

−803   One or more INSERT or UPDATE values are invalid because the object columns are constrained such that no rows of the table can be duplicates with respect to the values of those columns.

−805   The application program has not been bound as part of this application plan.

−811   The result of an embedded SELECT statement is a table of more than one row, or the result of the subquery of a basic predicate is more than one value.

−815   A GROUP BY or HAVING clause is implicitly or explicitly specified in an embedded SELECT statement or a subquery of a basic predicate.

−818   The precompiler-generated timestamp x in the load module is different from the bind timestamp y built from the DBRM.

−901   Unsuccessful execution caused by a system error that does not preclude the successful execution of subsequent SQL statements.

−902   Unsuccessful execution caused by a system error that precludes the successful execution of subsequent SQL statements.

−904   Unsuccessful execution caused by an unavailable resource reason *reason-code*, type of resource *resource-type*, and resource name *resource-name*.

−911   The current unit of work has been rolled back due to deadlock or timeout. Reason *reason-code*, type of resource *resource-type*, and resource name *resource-name*.

−913   Unsuccessful execution caused by deadlock or timeout. Reason *reason-code*, type of resource *resource-type*, and resource name *resource-name*.

Appendix C

DB2 data types and equivalent COBOL field definitions

This appendix presents all of DB2's data types: numeric, character (string), and date and time. The date and time data types are DB2 defaults. They may have been modified at your installation.

Numeric data types

DB2 data type	Kind of data	Description
SMALLINT	Halfword integer data	A halfword integer may contain whole-number values between -32,768 and 32,767. It is always defined in COBOL with COMP usage and PIC S9(4). A typical COBOL definition is: `10   INVCOUNT   PIC S9(4) COMP.`
INTEGER	Fullword integer data	A fullword integer may contain whole-number values between -2,147,483,648 and 2,147,483,647. It is always defined in COBOL with COMP usage and PIC S9(9). A typical COBOL definition is: `10   INVCOUNT   PIC S9(9) COMP.`
DECIMAL(p,s)	Packed decimal data	A decimal value contains an implicit decimal point. The value p (which cannot be greater than 15, or, under DB2 version 2.3, 31) specifies how many digits the number can contain, and the value s specifies how many of those digits are to the right of the implicit decimal point. The abbreviations p and s stand for precision and scale. A typical COBOL definition is: `10   INVTOTAL   PIC S9(7)V99 COMP-3.` This is an appropriate host variable definition for a column defined with DECIMAL(9,2).

FLOAT(n)	Floating point data	A floating point number, either single-precision (if n is less than 21) or double-precision (if n is between 22 and 53). COBOL definitions do not include a PIC clause and are simply a field name followed by COMP-1 (for single-precision) or COMP-2 (for double-precision). Examples are:
		
		`10   SINGLE-PRECISION-NUMBER   COMP-1.`
		
		`10   DOUBLE-PRECISION-NUMBER   COMP-2.`

String data types

DB2 data type	Kind of data	Description
CHAR	Fixed-length character (EBCDIC) data	Up to 254 bytes of alphanumeric data. Defined in COBOL as PIC X(n) where *n* is the number of characters the column contains. A typical example is:

```
01    CUSTNO              PIC X(6).
```

VARCHAR	Variable-length character (EBCDIC) data	A variable amount of alphanumeric data. The number of bytes in the data component is stored in a halfword. A typical COBOL example is:

```
01    NOTES.
      49   NOTES-LEN      PIC S9(4) COMP.
      49   NOTES-TEXT     PIC X(254).
```

The text component has a maximum length of 254 bytes in a "short" VARCHAR column. In a "long" VARCHAR column, which is subject to some processing restrictions, the text component's length can be over 32,000 bytes. The exact maximum length depends on the table's page size and the sizes of the other columns in the table.

GRAPHIC	Fixed-length DBCS data	Up to 127 characters of Double Byte Character Set (DBCS) data. Defined in COBOL with DISPLAY-1 usage and PIC G(n) where *n* is the number of characters the column contains. A typical example is:

```
01    DBCS-NAME           PIC G(20)
                          DISPLAY-1.
```

VARGRAPHIC	Variable-length DBCS data	A variable amount of DBCS data. The number of characters in the data component is stored in a halfword. A typical COBOL example is:

```
01    EXPL.
      49   EXPL-LEN       PIC S9(4) COMP.
      49   EXPL-TEXT      PIC G(127)
                          DISPLAY-1.
```

The text component has a maximum length of 127 characters in a "short" VARGRAPHIC column. As with VARCHAR, a "long" VARGRAPHIC column can be defined so it stores more characters, but it's subject to some processing restrictions. The exact maximum length depends on the table's page size and the sizes of the other columns in the table.

Date and time data type defaults

DB2 data type	Kind of data	Description
DATE	Date	A 10-byte string. A typical example is:

```
01   INVDATE            PIC X(10).
```

The internal structure of a date item is yyyy-mm-dd. To
identify the parts of a DB2 date, you can move the value to a
group item like

```
01   EDITED-DATE.
     05   ED-YEAR       PIC X(4).
     05   FILLER        PIC X.
     05   ED-MONTH      PIC XX.
     05   FILLER        PIC X.
     05   ED-DAY        PIC XX.
```

TIME	Time	An 8-byte string. A typical example is:

```
01   START-TIME         PIC X(8).
```

The internal structure of a time item is hh.mm.ss. To identify
the parts of a DB2 time, you can move the value to a group
item like

```
01   EDITED-TIME.
     05   ET-HOUR       PIC XX.
     05   FILLER        PIC X.
     05   ET-MINUTE     PIC XX.
     05   FILLER        PIC X.
     05   ET-SECOND     PIC XX.
```

TIMESTAMP	Date and time	A 26-byte string. A typical example is:

```
01 START-TIME     PIC X(26).
```

The internal structure of a timestamp item is
yyyy-mm-dd-hh.mm.ss.mmmmmm. To identify the parts of a
DB2 timestamp, you can move the value to a group item like

```
01   EDITED-TIMESTAMP.
     05   ETS-YEAR      PIC X(4).
     05   FILLER        PIC X.
     05   ETS-MONTH     PIC XX.
     05   FILLER        PIC X.
     05   ETS-DAY       PIC XX.
     05   FILLER        PIC X.
     05   ETS-HOUR      PIC XX.
     05   FILLER        PIC X.
     05   ETS-MINUTE    PIC XX.
     05   FILLER        PIC X.
     05   ETS-SECOND    PIC XX.
     05   FILLER        PIC X.
     05   ETS-MSECOND   PIC X(6).
```

Index

An introductory DB2 book from Mike Murach & Associates, Inc.

DB2 for the COBOL Programmer

Part 1: An Introductory Course   **Steve Eckols**

If you're looking for a practical DB2 book that fo-
cuses on application programming, this is the
book for you. Written from the programmer's
point of view, it will quickly teach you what you
need to know to access and process DB2 data in
your COBOL programs using embedded SQL.
You'll learn:

- what DB2 is and how it works, so you'll have
  the background you need to program more
  easily and logically

- how to design and code application programs that retrieve and update DB2 data

- how to use basic error-handling and data integrity techniques to protect DB2 data

- how to use joins and unions to combine data
  from two or more tables into a single table

- how to use DB2 column functions to extract
  summary information from a table

- how to use a subquery or subselect when
  one SQL statement depends on the results of
  another

- how to work with variable-length data and
  nulls

- how to develop DB2 programs interactively
  (using DB2I, a TSO facility) or in batch

So if you want to learn how to write DB2
application programs, get a copy of this book
today!

DB2, Part 1, 11 chapters, 371 pages, **$32.50**
ISBN 0-911625-59-3

CICS for the COBOL Programmer

Second Edition   Doug Lowe

This 2-part course is designed to help COBOL programmers become outstanding CICS programmers.

Part 1: An Introductory Course covers the basic CICS elements you'll use in just about every program you write. So you'll learn about basic mapping support (BMS), pseudo-conversational programming, basic CICS commands, sensible program design, debugging using either the Execution Diagnostics Facility (EDF) or a transaction dump, and efficiency considerations.

Part 2: An Advanced Course covers CICS features you'll use regularly, though you won't need all of them for every program. That means you'll learn about browse commands, temporary storage, transient data, data tables (including the shared data table feature of CICS 3.3), DB2 and DL/I processing considerations, distributed

processing features, interval control commands, BMS page building, and more! In addition, *Part 2* teaches you which features do similar things and when to use each one. So you won't just learn how to code new functions...you'll also learn how to choose the best CICS solution for each programming problem you face.

Both books cover OS/VS COBOL, VS COBOL II, and COBOL/370, so it doesn't matter which COBOL compiler you're using. Both of them cover all versions of CICS up through 3.3. And all the program examples in both books conform to CUA's Entry Model for screen design.

CICS, Part 1, 12 chapters, 375 pages
ISBN 0-911625-60-7; **Available July 1992**

CICS, Part 2, 13 chapters, 375 pages
ISBN 0-911625-67-4; **Available September 1992**

The CICS Programmer's Desk Reference

Doug Lowe

Ever feel buried by IBM manuals?

It seems like you need stacks of them, close at hand, if you want to be an effective CICS programmer. Because frankly, there's just too much you have to know to do your job well; you can't keep it all in your head.

That's why Doug Lowe decided to write *The CICS Programmer's Desk Reference*. In it, he's collected all the information you need to have at your fingertips, and organized it into 12 sections that make it easy for you to find what you're looking for. So there are sections on:

- BMS macro instructions—their formats (with an explanation of each parameter) and coding examples
- CICS commands—their syntax (with an explanation of each parameter), coding examples, and suggestions on how and when to use each one most effectively
- MVS and DOS/VSE JCL for CICS applications
- AMS commands for handling VSAM files

- ISPF, ICCF, and VM/CMS editor commands
- complete model programs, including specs, design, and code
- a summary of CICS program design techniques that lead to simple, maintainable, and efficient programs
- guidelines for testing and debugging CICS applications
- and more!

So clear the IBM manuals off your terminal table. Let the *Desk Reference* be your everyday guide to CICS instead.

CICS Desk Reference, 12 sections, 489 pages , **$36.50**
ISBN 0-911625-43-7

Note: This book currently covers CICS elements and programming considerations through release 1.7. A second edition is planned for the fourth quarter of 1992.

TSO books from Mike Murach & Associates, Inc.

MVS TSO

Part 1: Concepts and ISPF   Doug Lowe

See for yourself how quickly you can master ISPF/PDF (Versions 2 and 3) for everyday programming tasks in your MVS shop. This practical book will teach you how to:

- edit and browse data sets
- use the ISPF utilities to manage your data sets and libraries
- compile, link, and execute programs interactively
- use the OS COBOL or VS COBOL II interactive debugger
- process batch jobs in a background region

- manage your background jobs more easily using the Spool Display & Search Facility (SDSF)
- use member parts list to track the use of subprograms and COPY members within program libraries
- use two library management systems that support hierarchical libraries—the Library Management Facility (LMF) and the Software Configuration and Library Manager (SCLM)
- and more!

MVS TSO, Part 1, 8 chapters, 467 pages, **$31.00**
ISBN 0-911625-56-9

MVS TSO

Part 2: Commands and Procedures   Doug Lowe

If you're ready to expand your skills beyond ISPF and become a TSO user who can write complex CLIST and REXX procedures with ease, this is the book for you. It begins by teaching you how to use TSO commands for common programming tasks like managing data sets and libraries, running programs in foreground mode, and submitting jobs for background execution. Then, it shows you how

to combine those commands into CLIST or REXX procedures for the jobs you do most often...including procedures that you can use as edit macros under the ISPF editor and procedures that use ISPF dialog functions to display full-screen panels.

MVS TSO, Part 2, 10 chapters, 450 pages, **$31.00**
ISBN 0-911625-57-7

COBOL books from Mike Murach & Associates, Inc.

Structured ANS COBOL

A 2-part course in 1974 and 1985 ANS COBOL   Mike Murach and Paul Noll

This 2-part course teaches how to use 1974 and 1985 standard COBOL the way the top professionals do. The two parts are independent: You can choose either or both, depending on your current level of COBOL skill (if you're learning on your own) or on what you want your programmers to learn (if you're a trainer or manager).

Part 1: A Course for Novices teaches people with no previous programming experience how to design and code COBOL programs that prepare reports. Because report programs often call subprograms, use COPY members, handle one-level tables, and read indexed files, it covers these subjects too. But frankly, this book emphasizes the structure and logic of report programs, instead of covering as many COBOL elements as other introductory texts do. That's because we've found most beginning programmers have more trouble with structure and logic than they do with COBOL itself.

Part 2: An Advanced Course also emphasizes program structure and logic, focusing on edit, update, and maintenance programs. But beyond that, it's a complete guide to the 1974 and 1985 elements that all COBOL programmers should know

how to use (though many don't). To be specific, it teaches how to:

- handle sequential, indexed, and relative files
- use alternate indexing and dynamic processing for indexed files
- code internal sorts and merges
- create and use COPY library members
- create and call subprograms
- handle single- and multi-level tables using indexes as well as subscripts
- use INSPECT, STRING, and UNSTRING for character manipulation
- code 1974 programs that will be easy to convert when you switch to a 1985 compiler

In fact, we recommend you get a copy of *Part 2* no matter how much COBOL experience you've had because it makes such a handy reference to all the COBOL elements you'll ever want to use.

COBOL, Part 1, 13 chapters, 438 pages, **$31.00**
ISBN 0-911625-37-2

COBOL, Part 2, 12 chapters, 498 pages, **$31.00**
ISBN 0-911625-38-0

VS COBOL II: A Guide for Programmers and Managers

Second Edition   Anne Prince

If you work in an MVS COBOL shop, sooner or later you're going to convert to VS COBOL II, IBM's 1985 COBOL compiler. Whether that day has arrived yet or not, this book will quickly teach you everything you need to know about the compiler:

- how to code the new language elements... and what language elements you can't use anymore
- CICS considerations
- how to use the new debugger
- how the compiler's features can make your programs compile and run more efficiently

- guidelines for converting to VS COBOL II (that includes coverage of the conversion aids IBM supplies)

So if you're in a shop that's already converted to VS COBOL II, you'll learn how to benefit from the new language elements and features the compiler has to offer. If you aren't yet working in VS COBOL II, you'll learn how to write programs now that will be easy to convert later on. And if you're a manager, you'll get some practical ideas on when to convert and how to do it as painlessly as possible.

This second edition covers Release 3 of the compiler, as well as Releases 1 and 2.

VS COBOL II, 7 chapters, 271 pages, **$27.50**
ISBN 0-911625-54-2

Comment Form

Your opinions count

If you have any comments, criticisms, or suggestions for us, I'm eager to get them. Your opinions today will affect our products of tomorrow. And if you find any errors in this book, typographical or otherwise, please point them out so we can correct them in the next printing.

Thanks for your help.

Mike Murach

Book title: DB2 for the COBOL Programmer, Part 2: An Advanced Course

Dear Mike: _____

_____

_____

_____

_____

_____

_____

_____

_____

_____

_____

_____

_____

_____

_____

_____

_____

_____

_____

Name _____
Company (if company address)_____
Address _____
City, State, Zip _____

Fold where indicated and tape closed.

No postage necessary if mailed in the U.S.

fold

BUSINESS REPLY MAIL

FIRST-CLASS MAIL   PERMIT NO. 3063   FRESNO, CA

POSTAGE WILL BE PAID BY ADDRESSEE

Mike Murach & Associates, Inc.

4697 W JACQUELYN AVE
FRESNO CA 93722-9888

fold

fold

NO POSTAGE
NECESSARY
IF MAILED
IN THE
UNITED STATES

fold

Order Form

Our Ironclad Guarantee

To our customers who order directly from us: You must be satisfied. Our books must work for you, or you can send them back for a full refund...no questions asked.

Name & Title _____

Company (if company address) _____

Street address _____

City, State, Zip _____

Phone number (including area code)_____

Qty	Product code and title	*Price
Data Base Processing		
___ DB21	DB2 for the COBOL Programmer Part 1: An Introductory Course	$32.50
___ DB22	DB2 for the COBOL Programmer Part 2: An Advanced Course	36.50
___ IMS1	IMS for the COBOL Programmer Part 1: DL/I Data Base Processing	34.50
___ IMS2	IMS for the COBOL Programmer Part 2: Data Communications and MFS	36.50
OS/MVS Subjects		
___ MJLR	MVS JCL (Second Edition)	$39.50
___ TSO1	MVS TSO, Part 1: Concepts and ISPF	32.50
___ TSO2	MVS TSO, Part 2: Commands, CLIST, REXX	34.50
___ MBAL	MVS Assembler Language	36.50
___ OSUT	OS Utilities	17.50
DOS/VSE Subjects		
___ VJLR	DOS/VSE JCL (Second Edition)	$34.50
___ ICCF	DOS/VSE ICCF	31.00
___ VBAL	DOS/VSE Assembler Language	36.50

Qty	Product code and title	*Price
CICS		
___ CC1R	CICS for the COBOL Programmer Part 1 (Second Edition)	$35.00
___ CC2R	CICS for the COBOL Programmer Part 2 (Second Edition)	35.00
___ CRFR	The CICS Programmer's Desk Reference (Second Edition)	41.00
COBOL Language Elements		
___ VC2R	VS COBOL II (Second Edition)	$27.50
___ SC1R	Structured ANS COBOL, Part 1	31.00
___ SC2R	Structured ANS COBOL, Part 2	31.00
___ RW	Report Writer	17.50
VSAM		
___ VSMX	VSAM: Access Method Services and Application Programming	$27.50
___ VSMR	VSAM for the COBOL Programmer (Second Edition)	20.00

☐ Bill the appropriate book prices plus UPS shipping and handling (and sales tax in California) to my
    ___ VISA   ___ MasterCard:

Card Number _____

Valid thru (month/year)_____

Cardowner's signature _____

☐ Bill me.

☐ Bill my company. P.O. #_____

☐ I want to **save** UPS shipping and handling charges. Here's my check or money order for $_____. California residents, please add sales tax to your total. (Offer valid in the U.S.)

* Prices are subject to change. Please call for current prices.

To order more quickly,

Call **toll-free 1-800-221-5528**

(Weekdays, 8 to 5 Pacific Standard Time)

Fax: 1-209-275-9035

Mike Murach & Associates, Inc.

4697 West Jacquelyn Avenue
Fresno, California 93722-6427
(209) 275-3335

fold

fold

BUSINESS REPLY MAIL
FIRST-CLASS MAIL   PERMIT NO. 3063   FRESNO, CA

POSTAGE WILL BE PAID BY ADDRESSEE

Mike Murach & Associates, Inc.

4697 W JACQUELYN AVE
FRESNO CA 93722-9888

fold

fold